The Poetry
of
Christopher Smart

MOIRA DEARNLEY

LONDON
ROUTLEDGE & KEGAN PAUL

First published 1968
by Routledge & Kegan Paul Limited
Broadway House, 68–74 Carter Lane
London, E.C.4

Printed in Great Britain
by C. Tinling & Co. Ltd
Liverpool, London and Prescot

SBN 7100 6200 1

TYPOGRAPHER : Keith Kneebone

THE POETRY
OF
CHRISTOPHER SMART

CONTENTS

v

A NOTE ON EDITIONS
USED IN THIS BOOK

IN GENERAL, I have used the *Collected Poems* for quotation from Smart's work, that is, *The Collected Poems of Christopher Smart*, ed. Norman Callan, 1949, 2 vols. In quoting from *Jubilate Agno*, I have normally used the edition by W. H. Bond, 1954, but I do have occasion also to refer to *Rejoice in the Lamb | A Song from Bedlam*, ed. W. F. Stead, 1939. For quotation from the *Hymns for the Amusement of Children*, I have used the facsimile of the third edition (1775) printed for the Luttrell Society, Oxford, 1947. *The Poems of the Late Christopher Smart, M.A.*, Reading, 1791, 2 vols., is abbreviated in the footnotes to *Poems of the Late Christopher Smart*, 1791. *Poems by Christopher Smart*, ed. Robert Brittain, Princeton, 1950, is abbreviated in the footnotes to *Poems by Christopher Smart*, ed. Brittain.

Most of the other abbreviations used in this book are familiar enough—*DNB*, *Alumni Cantabrigienses*, and *Alumni Oxonienses*, for instance. Gray's *Bibliography*, however, should be explained as G. J. Gray, 'A Bibliography of the Writings of Christopher Smart', *Transactions of the Bibliographical Society*, vi, 1903, 269–303.

As far as printed books are concerned, the place of publication can be assumed to be London, unless otherwise stated.

LIST OF ILLUSTRATIONS

To my Mother
and in loving memory of my Father

ACKNOWLEDGEMENTS

I WISH TO THANK Professor Cecil Price of the University College of Swansea for all the advice and encouragement he has given me while I have been working on the poetry of Christopher Smart.

For permission to quote from manuscript material, I am obliged to the Henry W. and Albert A. Berg Collection of the New York Public Library, Astor, Lenox and Tilden Foundations, to the Bodleian Library, and to the Trustees of the British Museum. Mr. R. M. Gard, County Archivist of Northumberland, has been most helpful, and I am grateful for permission to quote from the Delaval (Waterford) MSS. belonging to the Newcastle Public Library and deposited in the Northumberland Record Office (NRO.2DE.44/1).

I am obliged to the publishers for permission to quote from the following works: Christopher Smart's *Hymns for the Amusement of Children*, published by Messrs. Basil Blackwell & Mott Ltd. for the Luttrell Society, Oxford, 1947; *Newton's Principia / Motte's Translation Revised*, edited by Florian Cajori, and published by the University of California Press, Berkeley, 1946; Frances Askham's *The Gay Delavals*, published by Messrs. Jonathan Cape Ltd., London, 1955 (Messrs. A. M. Heath & Company Ltd. have also given their permission); *The Literary Works of Matthew Prior*, edited by H. Bunker Wright and Monroe K. Spears, and published by the Clarendon Press, Oxford, 1959; *Representative Verse of Charles Wesley*, edited by Frank Baker, and published by the Epworth Press, London, 1962; Christopher Smart's *Jubilate Agno*, edited by W. H. Bond, London, 1954, and Christopher Devlin's *Poor Kit Smart*, London, 1961, both published by Messrs. Rupert Hart-Davis Ltd; Geoffrey Grigson's *Christopher Smart*, published by Messrs. Longmans, Green & Co. Ltd., for the British Council, London, 1960; *The Poems of Alexander Pope*, edited by John Butt, and published by Messrs. Methuen & Co. Ltd., London, 1965 (Yale University Press have also given their permission) ; and *Poems by Christopher Smart*, edited by Robert Brittain, and published by the University of Princeton Press, Princeton, 1950. I am indebted to the Executors of the William Force Stead Estate, and to Messrs. Jonathan Cape Ltd. for permission to quote from Christopher Smart's *Rejoice in the Lamb | A Song from Bedlam*, London, 1939.

I am also grateful for permission to quote from Moelwyn Merchant's 'Patterns of Reference in Smart's *Jubilate Agno*', *Harvard Library Bulletin*, xiv, 1960, 20–26; from Arthur Sherbo's 'The Probable Time of Composition of Christopher Smart's *Song to David, Psalms,* and *Hymns and Spiritual Songs*', *Journal of English and Germanic Philology*, lv, 1956, 41–57; from K. M. Rogers's 'The Pillars of the Lord: Some Sources of "A Song to David" ', *Philological Quarterly*, xl, 1961, 525–34; from Cecil Price's 'Six Letters by Christopher Smart', *Review of English Studies*, n.s. viii, 1957, 144–48; and from Charles Parrish's 'Christopher Smart's Knowledge of Hebrew', *Studies in Philology*, lviii, 1961, 516–32.

I should like also to add a word of thanks to my husband for sharing with me an unflagging interest in Kit Smart, and for helping me to interpret his complex personality.

M.D.

PREFACE

'THE INGENIOUS MR. SMART' was how he was described
time and time again in the eighteenth century. But despite the
fact that many people were willing to allow that he was a clever
and inventive versifier, there was some disagreement about his
stature as a serious poet. Oliver Goldsmith was more enthusiastic than most. Smart's younger daughter, Elizabeth Anne Le
Noir, tells of her chance meeting with Goldsmith at Canonbury
House, Islington, two years after her father's death: 'she recalls
it with pleasure, as likewise, his skipping across the large old-
fashioned oaken wainscotted parlour, to snatch up a book that
laid on the window seat: it was a quarto edition of her Father's
poems; opening it at the poem of the Mowers, he read aloud—

> Strong Labour got up with his pipe in his mouth,
> And stoutly strode over the dale;

adding, "There is not a man now living who could write such a
line." '[1]

The twentieth-century reader tends to find that this kind of
personification is silly and visually imprecise. Few modern
readers would exclaim with admiration on first reading the
second stanza of 'A Morning Piece Or an hymn for the hay-
makers':

> Strong Labour got up.—With his pipe in his mouth,
>   He stoutly strode over the dale,
> He lent new perfumes to the breath of the south,
>   On his back hung his wallet and flail.
> Behind him came Health from her cottage of thatch,
> Where never physician had lifted the latch.
> <div align="right">(<i>Collected Poems</i>, i. 100)</div>

It takes a considerable effort of sympathy and understanding
to read such an eighteenth-century poem with eighteenth-
century insight, but if we are willing to make the effort, we can

---

[1] *Miscellaneous Poems*, Reading, 1825, ii. 182.

sometimes enjoy an 'ingenious' poem which formerly we should have dismissed with contempt. Goldsmith was not alone in his admiration for 'A Morning Piece'. The imprecise personification obviously seemed sharply vivid to the eighteenth-century imagination, so much so, that Thomas Barker of Bath (1769–1847) was inspired to paint a picture of 'Labour and Health', complete with the thatched cottage, the peasant, Labour, striding along with his pipe in his mouth, and the girl, Health, carrying a cup and plate.[2]

But although Goldsmith enthused about Smart's poetry, Dr. Johnson found it contemptible. Asked whether Smart or Derrick were the better poet, he gave the notorious reply, 'Sir, there is no settling the point of precedency between a louse and a flea.' His ridicule of 'The Hop-Garden', which had appeared in *Poems on Several Occasions* (1752), the 'quarto edition' which Goldsmith snatched from the window seat, is rather less well-known. Dr. Johnson and Boswell were discussing Dyer's *Fleece* ('How could one write poetically of serges and druggets?') and Grainger's *Sugar Cane* ('Now, Muse, lets sing of rats'):

> He said, 'One might write *The Parsley Bed, a Poem*, or *The Cabbage Garden, a Poem*, as well as *The Fleece*. I said, 'You must then pickle your cabbage with the *sal Atticum*.' 'You know,' said he, 'there is already *The Hop-Garden, a Poem*. One could say a great deal about cabbage. The poem might begin with the advantages of civilized society over a rude state, exemplified by the Scotch, who had no cabbages till Oliver Cromwell's soldiers introduced them, and one might show how arts are introduced by conquest, as they were by the Roman arms.' He seemed diverted with the fertility of his own mind.[3]

An imaginative effort to appreciate the sort of poetry that appealed to the eighteenth-century reader may enable us to

---

[2] See Plate I. Presumably, 'Labour and Health' is identical with the picture mentioned in Sir Edward Harington's *A Schizzo on the Genius of Man*, Bath, 1793, 320: 'In one of my former sheets I mentioned the picture of the THRESHER and the GIRL, the idea taken from *Smart's* poems; this picture is just sold to Sir *Forster Cunliffe* for the sum of *three hundred guineas*! and in the estimation of many people the picture is worth more money. The Duke of Newcastle much admired the painting, but said that he could not afford to purchase it! ! !'

[3] *Boswell: The Ominous Years 1774–1776*, ed. Charles Ryskamp and Frederick A. Pottle, 1963, 285. Boswell later incorporated this material into the *Life of Johnson*.

enjoy, to a certain extent, the Miltonic sublime of Smart's Seatonian poetry. But the modern reader faces also the complementary task of trying to understand why some eighteenth-century poetry was considered badly written and absurd by contemporary readers. Our determination to enjoy the stylistic foibles of the eighteenth-century poets may encourage us to read even 'The Hop-Garden' with some amusement. But if we do so, we should remember that twentieth-century amusement often corresponds to eighteenth-century contempt. If we are tempted to laugh at a would-be serious poem, on hop-growing or on the virtues of Lady Hussey Delaval, we can be almost certain that by Dr. Johnson's standards, the poem in question would have been considered contemptible.

Until the end of the eighteenth century, much more attention was paid to Smart's secular verse and the Seatonian poetry than to his later religious work. The *Monthly Review* for August 1752 found space for a long appreciation of Smart's first major publication, the *Poems on Several Occasions*. Smart had already won the Seatonian prize for poetry in 1750 and 1751, and it was evidently felt that here was a talented young poet who was likely to become an 'ornament' of his age. The reviewer did find several faults in the work. He chided Smart for being slapdash— he was not the last to do so—'it were injustice to suppose *that* to be want of genius, which is *indolence* alone, or *inattention*.' He ridiculed the way Smart dedicated his book to the Earl of Middlesex ('tho' I have too much Diffidence to ask your Patronage as a Poet, I have Assurance enough to demand it as *a Man of Kent*'). Yet the reviewer was full of praise for the sort of poem that nowadays we normally find very tedious— 'Against Ill Nature', for instance. 'The man who could produce such lines as these, seems to hold the taste and spirit of his patron at but a low rate, when he supposes any consideration could be of superior power to recommend him to his protection.' After reading this graceful compliment, the twentieth-century reader is encouraged to go back to 'Against Ill Nature' with renewed interest. But it is very difficult to enjoy the echoes of 'Il Penseroso', the account of the genealogy of Ill Nature, the offspring of folly and pride, who was nursed up by vice, misled by pravity, and taught and bred up by pedant affectation.

Mercury ruled the poet's natal morn and Aries smiled upon the spring (Smart was born on the 11th April 1722), and therefore, 'Away, thou hideous hell-born spright'. Smart begs Ill Nature to fly away to some lonesome heath, some heaven-deserted fen, with a hideous band of minions which Smart personifies as a tribe of vices:

> Suspicion first with jealous caution stalks,
>   And ever looks around her as she walks,
> With bibulous ear imperfect sounds to catch,
>   And prompt to listen at her neighbours latch.
> Next Scandal's meagre shade,
> Foe to the virgins, and the poet's fame,
>   A wither'd, time-deflower'd old maid,
> That ne'er enjoy'd love's ever sacred flame.
> Hypocrisy succeeds with saint-like look,
>   And elevates her hands and plods upon her book.
> Next comes illiberal scrambling Avarice,
>   Then Vanity, and Affectation nice—
> See, she salutes her shadow with a bow
>   As in short Gallic trips she minces by,
> Starting antipathy in her eye,
>   And squeamishly she knits her scornful brow.
> To thee, Ill-Nature, all the numerous group
>   With lowly reverence stoop—
> They wait thy call, and mourn thy long delay,
>   Away—thou art infectious—haste away.
>   (*Collected Poems*, i. 122–23)

Try as we may, it takes a great deal of imaginative effort to share the reviewer's admiration—yet we have to realize what sort of verse appealed to the eighteenth-century public if we are going to appreciate Smart's minor poetry as it deserves.

In 1791, Smart's nephew, the Rev. Christopher Hunter, brought out *The Poems of the Late Christopher Smart, M.A.*, where the emphasis was almost entirely upon the earlier poetry. Hunter, like Dr. Johnson, was prepared to dismiss 'The Hop-Garden', because 'The Author seems to have addressed himself to the task without previous information on the art of which he treats.' But despite certain reservations about the quality of some of the early verse, Hunter's summary is very generous: 'On the whole, if we consider that every species of Poetry, not even excepting the Epic, has been attempted by our Author, and most of them with eminent success, we shall be inclined to admit that the present collection is not excelled by many in the English language; that the gay may extract amusement from it, and the grave instruction; or as all men partake at different seasons of both these humours, that no moments of leisure can occur to the admirer of poetry, in which he will not be able in these volumes to gratify his taste.'

Christopher Hunter was likely to be prejudiced in his uncle's favour, but one or two disinterested editors can be quoted to show that at one time, Smart's secular poetry was greatly admired. Alexander Chalmers, for instance, in the sixteenth volume of *The Works of the English Poets* (1810), pronounced that 'As a poet Smart exhibits indubitable proofs of genius, but few of correct taste, and appears to have seldom exercised much labour, or employed cool judgment in preparing his works for the public. Upon the whole therefore he is most successful in his lighter pieces, his odes, his songs, and fables. Of his odes, that on Ill-nature; the Morning, Noon, and Night pieces, particularly the last, if the epigrammatic turn at the conclusion does not disappoint the pensive reader, may be cited as productions of rich and original fancy, nor will it detract much from their praise that they sometimes remind us of Milton. His fables are entitled to high praise, for ease of versification and delicacy of humour; and although he may have departed from the laws which some critics have imposed on this species of composition, by giving reason to inanimate objects, it will be difficult by any laws to convince the reader that he ought not to be delighted with the Tea-pot and the Scrubbing-brush, the Bag Wig and the Tobacco-pipe, or the Brocaded Gown and Linen Rag.' The editor of the fifth volume of *The Cabinet of Poetry* (1808) was even more enthusiastic about the secular poetry. His comments on Smart's poetic talent are ecstatic, and we have to keep reminding ourselves that he is not writing about the *Song to David*, but about a handful of light lyrics and one religious poem, the *Hymn to the Supreme Being*: 'His genius has never been questioned by those who censured his carelessness, and commiserated the unhappy vacillation of his mind. He is sometimes not only greatly irregular, but irregularly great. His errors are

B

those of a bold and daring spirit, which bravely hazards what a vulgar mind could never suggest. Shakespeare and Milton are sometimes wild and irregular; and it seems as if originality alone could try the experiment. Accuracy is timid, and seeks for authority. Fowles of feeble wing seldom quit the ground, though at full liberty; while the eagle, unrestrained, soars into the unknown regions.'

During Smart's lifetime, and until the end of the eighteenth century, the poetry written before his major mental breakdown in 1756 was admired much more than the later work. His verse essays on the Attributes of the Supreme Being, composed for the Seatonian Prize awarded by the University of Cambridge, were published in 1750, 1751, 1752, 1754, and 1756 respectively. All five of the Seatonian poems went through two or more editions, and they were published in a collected edition in Dublin in 1761. A manuscript at Pembroke College, Cambridge, shows that some anonymous admirer made a partial German translation of the Seatonian poems in 1768, and the five poems were automatically included in *Musæ Seatonianiæ* (1772), a collection of all the prize poems from 1750 onward. John Abraham Fisher actually set parts of the Seatonian poems to music: in *Providence: An Oratorio* (1777), the recitatives were selected from the Cambridge prize-poems 'OF THE LATE INGENIOUS Mr. CHRISTOPHER SMART; EXCEPT WHERE THE NECESSITY OF A PROPER CONNECTION OBLIGED THE COMPILER OCCASIONALLY TO ADD A FEW LINES.'

The review of *On the Immensity of the Supreme Being* in the *Monthly Review* for May 1751 was very flattering. 'Mr. *Smart* has already gained so much reputation by several other small pieces publish'd in the *Student*, or otherwise, that it would be superfluous in us to say more of his character as a poet. . . . Mr. *Smart* has kept that most divine poet the *Psalmist* in his eye, almost through the whole of this work, and finely imitated him in several passages.' When the *Gentleman's Magazine* advertised *On the Power of the Supreme Being* in January 1754, they felt that 'we cannot deny our readers the following specimen, tho' it may encrease their desire to see the whole.' Yet there was a sharp change of attitude when Smart's fifth Seatonian poem, *On the Goodness of the Supreme Being*, was published in 1756. The *Monthly*

Review for June 1756 felt that this poem was far inferior to his former productions, that it contained irrelevancies and tautologies, and weak and bathetic descriptions. Oh for a Milton, a Cowley, or a Thomson, at whose sacred fires, if our bard had condescended to light his taper, or had taken the trouble to think a little more, he would have done more justice to his subject.

The hostility of the *Monthly Review* did not, however, destroy the reputation of Smart's Seatonian poems. Fisher wrote *Providence*, and Hunter wrote with loyal admiration that 'The five Poems on the Divine Attributes are written with the sublimest energies of religion, and the true enthusiasm of poetry; and had the pen of their author stopped with these compositions, they alone would have given him a very distinguished rank among the writers of verse.' Robert Anderson printed the Seatonian poems in the eleventh volume of *The Works of the British Poets* (1795), Thomas Park in the fifth volume of *The Supplement to the British Poets* (1809), Alexander Chalmers in the sixteenth volume of *The Works of the English Poets* (1810), and Robert Walsh in the thirtieth volume of *The Works of the British Poets* (1822). But readers were losing their taste for unwieldy imitations of Miltonic blank verse, and little attention has been paid to the Seatonian poems since the beginning of the nineteenth century. They are printed in full in Norman Callan's edition of *The Collected Poems of Christopher Smart* (1949). Percival Serle printed an extract from *On the Immensity of the Supreme Being* in his edition of *A Song to David* (Melbourne, 1923), and Robert Brittain includes *On the Immensity of the Supreme Being* and *On the Omniscience of the Supreme Being* in *Poems by Christopher Smart* (Princeton, 1950).

Jubilate Agno, the poem that Smart wrote during his mental illness, was not published until 1939, after William Force Stead discovered the manuscript in Colonel Carwardine Probert's library in Suffolk. The history of the manuscript is obscure, but it is thought that somehow or other it passed into the hands of William Hayley (1745–1820), and that Hayley left it with the Rev. Thomas Carwardine (1734–1824), at Colne Priory, when the two friends were discussing what could be done for William Cowper in one of his attacks of madness.[4] Since its first publica-

---

[4] *Rejoice in the Lamb | A Song from Bedlam*, ed. W. F. Stead, 1939, 14–15.

tion as *Rejoice in the Lamb*, the poem has attracted a good deal of attention. Ruthven Todd included extracts in his edition of *A Song to David* (1947), and so did Robert Brittain in *Poems by Christopher Smart*. Callan printed the complete text. In 1954, W. H. Bond brought out a new edition, re-named *Jubilate Agno*. At least one full-length study of the poem has been made —Thomas Foster Teevan's doctoral dissertation for the University of Washington (1957), and the strangeness of the poem has appealed to a number of artists and musicians. Benjamin Britten wrote *Rejoice in the Lamb | Festival Cantata* for the Rev. Walter Hussey and the choir of St. Matthew's Church, Northampton, on the fiftieth anniversary of the consecration of their church, on the 21st September 1943. On the 20th February 1952, Ruth Gipps's cantata, *The Cat*, was performed at the Birmingham Town Hall, and was given its first London performance at the Royal Festival Hall in February 1957— part III of the cantata is called 'My Cat Jeoffry', and the words are taken from *Rejoice in the Lamb*. *Christopher Smart's Cat Jeoffry from Rejoice in the Lamb*, with illustrations by Stanley W. Odell, was published in 1949, and Elizabeth Rivers's *Out of Bedlam*, a series of twenty-seven wood engravings with texts from *Jubilate Agno*, was published in Glenageary in 1956.

Although it is often suggested, quite wrongly, that the eighteenth century could not tolerate the pre-Romantic splendour of *A Song to David*, the poem was by no means universally damned when it was first published in 1763. The *Monthly Review* for April 1763 assessed the poem in a way that was echoed many times by nineteenth-century editors: 'From the sufferings of this ingenious Gentleman, we could not but expect the performance before us to be greatly irregular; but we shall certainly characterise it more justly, if we call it irregularly great. There is a grandeur, a majesty of thought, not without a happiness of expression in the following stanzas [X, XVII, XVIII, XXI, XL]. There is something remarkably great, and altogether original, in the last quoted stanza.' The reviewer went on to point out some of the obscurities in the *Song to David*—but his description of the grandeur, majesty, and originality of the poem was obviously written with sincere admiration for the 'ingenious' poet. In the same month, the

Critical Review suggested that the poem was 'a fine piece of ruins', but they also felt that 'great rapture and devotion is discernable in this extatic song'. But Smart was frantically angry at the insinuation in both these reviews that madness had impaired to a certain extent his skill as a poet. Certainly, the stigma of madness probably had something to do with the fact that the *Song to David* was neglected for many years after its first publication. Smart gave a second edition gratis with his *Translation of the Psalms* (1765), but this did nothing to make it more popular. The poem was something of an embarrassment to Smart's family, for Christopher Hunter dismissed it in a footnote: 'Besides the works contained in this edition, our Author wrote a Poem called *a Song to David*'. Mrs. Le Noir included a special section in her *Miscellaneous Poems* (1825), devoted to her father's religious poems, but she omitted *A Song to David*, explaining that even a daughter's partiality could not persuade her to admire the poem. She mentioned the poem in her correspondence, but it is difficult to be sure of her exact meaning—as her publishers complained, her handwriting is not the easiest to decipher. In a letter dated the 21st March 1825, she refers to the recent 'noise about the hymn to David' (the story that the *Song to David* had been composed upon the mad-house walls was still in circulation), and she seems to feel that the poem is very hard both on its author and on its subject 'poor David himself'.[5]

But while Christopher Hunter and Mrs. Le Noir were deprecating the poem, other critics and editors were beginning to admire it. Anderson echoed the *Monthly Review* and wrote of 'a grandeur, a majesty of thought', and Chalmers wrote of its 'majestic animation' and its 'grandeur and originality'—but both included only five stanzas of the poem in their respective editions. In 1819, a separate edition of the *Song to David* was published, probably edited by R. Harvey, and re-issued in 1827, and possibly in 1829 also. Robert Chambers printed the *Song to David* in his *Cyclopædia of English Literature* (Edinburgh, 1844), and stated that it 'possesses passages of considerable power and sublimity'. George Gilfillan included it in the third volume of his *Specimens with Memoirs of the Lesser-Known British*

---

[5] Ms. Montagu, d. 14, fol. 710, in the Bodleian Library.

Poets (Edinburgh and London, 1860). Some time after 1887, the *Song to David* was printed at Corvill, Worthing, for private distribution by Smart's great-great-niece, Louisa Sophia Cornish, dedicated to the memory of her brother, George Yeates Hunter,[6] Brigade Surgeon in the Bombay Medical Service. Francis Palgrave included sixteen stanzas in his *Treasury of Sacred Song* (1889), and then came a batch of new editions—one edited by F. H. D. and H. C. M. in 1895, J. R. Tutin's edition in 1898 again in 1904, C. F. Richardson's in the *Bibelot* at Portland, and Maine, in 1900, R. A. Streatfield's in 1901, and an anonymous edition from the De La More press in 1906. Percival Serle's edition came out in Melbourne in 1923, Edmund Blunden's in 1924, a facsimile of the first edition appeared in Oxford in 1926 and in Cambridge in 1927. Yet another edition appeared in Benn's Augustan Books of Poetry in 1931, and Anthony Hillyer's edition was published in Los Angeles in 1934. Ruthven Todd's edition appeared in 1947, and J. B. Broadbent's in 1960. It is printed also in Norman Callan's edition of the *Collected Poems*, in Robert Brittain's edition of *Poems by Christopher Smart*, in Donald Davie's *The Late Augustans* (1958), and with critical notes in Sophia Blaydes's *Christopher Smart as a Poet of his Time* (The Hague, 1966).

This is not meant to be an exhaustive bibliography of the *Song to David*, but I have tried to make the list of editions long enough to show how the popularity of the poem gathered momentum after Harvey's edition in 1819. It is of course characteristic of the taste of the nineteenth century, that the bizarre individuality of the *Song to David* should be preferred to the Miltonic verse-essays on the Supreme Being which had offered physico-theology spiced with Newtonian science to an eager eighteenth-century audience. The nineteenth-century admiration for *A Song to David* was almost entirely emotional. Gilfillan made the notorious statement that we have heard of

---

[6] George Yeates Hunter, M.D., F.R.C.P., J.P., was the great-grandson of Smart's sister, Margaret Hunter. The Rev. Canon F. W. Phillips, Vicar of Margate Parish Church, St. John the Baptist in Thanet, has kindly given me some information about Hunter. He was the son of Edward and Maria Hunter, and was born on the 31st January 1795. He married Mary Ann Cobb in 1827, and become the first mayor of Margate. He was buried on the 8th November 1866, and a commemoration tablet was later erected in St. John's church.

'Single-speech Hamilton', and that now we have to say something about 'Single-poem Smart'. In *English Literature* (1876), A. Stopford Brooks entirely agreed—'its power of metre and of imaginative presentation of thoughts and things, and its mingling of sweet and grand religious poetry ought to make it better known. It is unique in style and in character.' The climax of the nineteenth-century chorus of praise was reached in Robert Browning's *Parleyings with Certain People of Importance in their Day* (1887). He accepted the myth of 'Single-poem Smart', and expressed it with his own brand of jocular familiarity and ecstasy:

> Armed with this instance, have I diagnosed
> Your case, my Christopher? The man was sound
> And sane at starting: all at once the ground
> Gave way beneath his step, a certain smoke
> Curled up and caught him, or perhaps down broke
> A fireball wrapping flesh and spirit both
> In conflagration. Then—as heaven were loth
> To linger—let earth understand too well
> How heaven at need can operate—off fell
> The flame-robe, and the untransfigured man
> Resumed sobriety,—and as he began,
> So did he end nor alter pace, not he!

Palgrave quoted Lamb's description of *A Song to David* as 'a kind of medley between inspiration and possession', and added a comment of his own, that 'in its noble wildness and transition from grandeur to tenderness, from Earth to Heaven, is unique in our Poetry.' In *A History of Eighteenth-Century Literature* (1889), Edmund Gosse wrote that Smart 'unsealed the fountains of poetic language' and—inevitably—that it is 'the only real jewel in his crown'. Tutin enthused about 'this highly imaginative, passionate, and vigorous poem'. The same kind of enthusiasm lasted well into the twentieth century. R. A. Streatfield, for instance, wrote of 'that wonderful burst of devotional rapture which has no parallel between the days of Crashaw and of Blake' (Browning had placed Smart somewhere between Milton and Keats), and Edith Sitwell wrote an essay on Smart in *The Pleasures of Poetry* (1930) in which she stated that *A Song to David* has 'extraordinary beauty, a solemnity which is deeply impressive.' The editor of *A Song to David* published in Benn's Augustan Books of Poetry thought that 'Its exultation is as spontaneous and incessant as a bird's song'.

After his release from confinement for madness, Smart brought out in rapid succession the *Song to David, Poems by Mr. Smart* [1763], *Poems on Several Occasions* [1763], and *Ode to the Right Honourable the Earl of Northumberland* (1764). Smart's hostility towards the critics at this period of his life is certainly understandable in the light of the review of *Poems by Mr. Smart* that appeared in the *Monthly Review* for September 1763: 'Instead of entering on the merit of these poems, we shall transcribe a few lines from Milton's SAMSON, and leave our Readers to make the application'. The quotation was nicely calculated to wound the sensibilities of a man who had scarcely recovered from a severe mental breakdown:

> This, this is he; softly awhile,
> Let us not break in upon him;
> O change beyond report, thought, or belief!—
>
> — — — —
>
> By how much from the top of wondrous glory
> To lowest pitch of abject fortune art thou fall'n!

The quotation was spitefully apt, and in very bad taste. The *Monthly Review* tried to make amends in their notice of *Poems on Several Occasions* in November 1763: 'We are glad to find that, notwithstanding all that this ingenious bard has so long suffered, neither the glow of his imagination, nor the harmony of his numbers, are in the least impaired.' But they were piqued by Smart's justifiably angry reaction to their review of *Poems by Mr. Smart*, and they point out that although they have tried to show their sincere regard, their high veneration for the abilities which God has so bounteously bestowed upon him, Mr. Smart has chosen to misconstrue their comments and he shall therefore be troubled no further with their attentions. Despite this threat, the *Monthly Review* for September 1764 did include a review of the *Ode to the Earl of Northumberland*. They were callous enough to refer yet again to Smart's insanity: 'This Ode

is conceived in easy numbers, as every lyric performance ought
to be: but there is in the later productions of Mr. Smart, a *tour*
of expression, which we many times are at a loss to understand;
and it often seems to us, that his words, as well as his sentiments,
are rather too much under the influence of imagination.' But
perhaps they felt pity for his rage at the way the *Critical Review*
had accused him of popery in *A Song to David*, and they
qualified their criticism by suggesting that 'For this Ode, however, he merits the thanks of every true Protestant, for he fights
with a truely British spirit against the Whore of Babylon.' Then
they concluded with a little faint praise: 'The last stanza is
really very pretty. . . . The little pieces added to this Ode, are
not destitute of merit.' But the *Critical Review* made no references
to the sincere regard or high veneration they might have felt
for the ingenious but unfortunate poet. In reviewing the *Ode to
the Earl of Northumberland*, they wrote merely that 'Mr. Smart
informs us, in the advertisement prefixed to this poem, that the
excellent person to whom it is addressed was so far from
approving of the printing it, that he gave very positive injunc-
tions to the contrary. We shall add that this was a proof not
only of the noble lord's modesty, but of his taste and good sense.
Among the pieces which accompany this ode, is a song, which is
pretty and well turned.'

Despite these discouraging reviews, some of the poems in the
1763 and 1764 volumes of verse were printed again—in
Hunter's edition, in Anderson, Park, James Plumptre's *Collection of Songs* (1806), and in Chalmers and Walsh. But nothing
that Smart wrote after the *Song to David* has ever been very
popular, and there are few twentieth-century printings of the
later religious poems. Callan prints all the poems from the 1763
and 1764 volumes, Brittain prints a few, and so does Blunden
in his edition of *A Song to David*.

In April 1764, the *Monthly Review* reviewed Smart's oratorio,
Hannah, side by side with Thomas Morell's *Nabal*. Of *Nabal*, they
wrote that it is very difficult to characterize performances in
which there is so palpable a mediocrity of style and composition:
'we are sorry to find the Muses are such antique Heathens, as
to seem determined to have nothing to do with our modern
sacred Dramas.' Of *Hannah*, they wrote that 'There are in this

piece some airs superior to most we meet with in performances
of this kind. They are not of sufficient merit, however, to make
us retract the opinion we formed on reading Nabal, concerning
the heathenism of the Muses. The story of this piece is taken
from the first and second chapter of the first book of Samuel.'
Since its publication, *Hannah* has scarcely attracted any attention at all. Plumptre included two songs from it in his *Collection
of Songs*, and Brittain includes five lyrics in *Poems by Christopher
Smart*, but there is little more to be said about its reputation. As
far as I know, Smart's oratorio, *Abimelech* [1768], received no
attention when it was first published, and has received none
since, except that Brittain includes three lyrics in *Poems by
Christopher Smart*.

A *Translation of the Psalms of David* (1765) has fared little
better. It was unfortunate for Smart that James Merrick's
version of *The Psalms, Translated and Paraphrased in English Verse*
came out in the same year. The *Critical Review* for September
1765 compared the two versions, much to Merrick's advantage.
The conclusion pointedly omits any reference to Smart: 'The
reader will undoubtedly be glad to find that the Psalmist is at
last delivered from a crowd of wretched poets, who had overwhelmed his native grace and dignity under the rubbish of their
despicable rhimes: the admirers of these beautiful compositions may read them with pleasure in Mr. Merrick's translation.' The publication of the *Translation of the Psalms* was
followed up with *A Collection of Melodies for the Psalms of David,
According to the Version of Christopher Smart*, brought out in the
same year. There is some evidence that Smart's Psalms were
used occasionally in church services. They were certainly used
at a service in aid of the Blue-Coat School, Westminster, held
at the Duke Street Chapel on the 14th April 1765.[7] Smart's
Psalms were sung also at services held in aid of the Charity
Schools of St. Mary, Islington, on the 29th March 1772, and on
the 23rd April 1780.[8] But only one or two of the Psalms have
been reprinted since the eighteenth century. Psalm 148 was a

[7] See *The Rothschild Library, A Catalogue of the Collection of Eighteenth-Century Printed
Books and Manuscripts Formed by Lord Rothschild*, privately printed, Cambridge
University Press, 1954, ii. 514.

[8] See my note, 'Psalms by Christopher Smart at St. Mary Islington,' *Notes and
Queries*, n.s. vol. xv, no. vi, June 1968, 221–22.

favourite with Hunter, Anderson, Park, and Chalmers. Psalm 121 was included in *Select Psalms in Verse, with Critical Remarks, by Bishop Lowth, and Others* (1811), and Edward Blunden included portions of Psalms 104 and 147 in his edition of *A Song to David*. Brittain included seventeen Psalms, and Callan prints all of them.

A Translation of the Psalms was bound up with a second edition of *A Song to David*, and the *Hymns and Spiritual Songs for the Fasts and Festivals of the Church of England*. The *Hymns and Spiritual Songs* are superior to the *Translation of the Psalms*, yet they received no attention when they were first published. Predictably, Hunter left them out of his edition, but Mrs. Le Noir wrote from Reading on the 21st March 1825 that although the *Hymns and Spiritual Songs* are unequal and 'smothered under the preceding heep', some of them have great 'originality and fire'.[9] In her *Miscellaneous Poems*, she printed eight of her father's hymns, and introduced them by pointing out that the 'Psalms are far from being among the best of his works; and it is probable that few readers would labour through their thick shade to the flowers they precede and conceal.' She cannot admire the *Song to David*, but 'Of the Hymns here selected, she has a different opinion, conceiving that they possess so much originality, ardent piety, and true poetic fire, as cannot but render them acceptable to readers of taste and sentiment.' Smart's *Hymns and Spiritual Songs* were very occasionally reprinted elsewhere. Samuel Arnold's oratorio, *Redemption* (1786) included part of Smart's hymn for the Nativity, set to Handel's air, 'Alcina Verdi Prati'. This was included in James Plumptre's *Letters to John Aikin . . . to which are added a Collection of Songs* (Cambridge, 1811), and in the Bath Municipal Library there is a score printed in Italian ('Verdi prati e selve amene perderete la belta . . .') and in English ('Where is that stupendous stranger . . . '), as sung by Madame Mara at the Ancient Concerts *circa* 1800.

Although Gilfillan and the rest had casually decided that 'Single-poem Smart' had written nothing worth reading except the *Song to David*, Edmund Blunden at last began to ask some pertinent questions—unfortunately in Browningesque cadences:

[9] Ms. Montagu d.14, fol.710, in the Bodleian Library.

'When a man springs a surprise upon us of the degree of this
poem, it is natural to imagine that the qualities whence it was
kindled into life would reveal themselves in other of his work.
So ardent and powerful, could they be altogether hidden except
on this one occasion? Was this masterpiece sheer luck, without
any glimmerings of felicity for its prelude and its sequel?'
Blunden turned to Hunter's edition of the earlier poems, but
found nothing there to support his theory that the growth of the
Song to David must be discernible in Smart's 'previous strivings
for air'. Then Blunden turned to the poems written after
Smart's confinement for madness. He had been afraid that
A Song to David was a poetic miracle, a psychological phenomenon, that 'Smart struck the stars once only, by luck and
estrangement—an ingenious hack suddenly snatched up by the
whim of the gods'. But in Smart's later poetry Blunden discovered a commentary on the *Song to David*: 'Some of them,
without being quoted here as triumphs of his poetic spirit, are in
their minor way delicate and pleasant', and he includes, among
other pieces, extracts from nine of the *Hymns and Spiritual Songs*.
Brittain gives seventeen, Callan prints all of them, and in
1928, H. V. F. Somerset brought out a Carol or Anthem for
the Season of Easter, based on Smart's hymn, 'Now the winds
are all composure'. But by and large, the *Hymns and Spiritual
Songs* have received less attention than their quality deserves.

It is impossible to say the same for the *Parables of our Lord and
Saviour Jesus Christ* (1768). In April 1768, the *Critical Review*
wrote that 'We do not remember to have met with any poet
whose compositions are more unequal than those of Mr. Smart.
Some of his pieces are distinguished by undoubted marks of
genius, agreeable imagery, and a fine poetical enthusiasm.
Others are hardly superior to the productions of Sternhold or
Quarles. The work before us is of the lower class, containing
about seventy parables, and some other passages of the New
Testament, in plain, familiar verse, adapted to the capacities
of children; to whom it may certainly be of use, as it will serve
to give them an idea of our Saviour's discourses, and furnish
them with pious instructions; but it is not calculated to please
their imaginations, or improve their taste in poetry'. This
review is polite in comparison with the brief notice in the

Monthly Review for May 1768: 'This version of the parables is, with great propriety, dedicated to Master *Bonnel George Thornton*; a child of three years old.' They quote Parable XXI, and comment, '*Familiar* verse, indeed! as the title-page justly intimates.' Chalmers agreed: 'His last publication, in 1768, exhibited a more striking proof of want of judgement than any of his late performances. It was entitled the Parables of our Lord and Saviour Jesus Christ, done into familiar verse, with occasional applications for the use of younger minds. This was dedicated to Master Bonnel George Thornton, a child of three years old, and is written in that species of verse which would be tolerated only in a nursery.' Chalmers omitted the parables from his edition of Smart's poems, and indeed, Callan's is the only reprinting that I have come across.

Chalmers was mistaken when he said that the *Parables* was Smart's last work. The *Hymns for the Amusement of Children* was entered at the Stationers' Hall on the 24th December 1770 and listed in the *Public Advertizer* on the 27th December. The first and second editions have not come to light, but Karina Williamson has located a Dublin edition of 1772, and she has examined Mr. C. H. Wilkinson's undated edition, and has come to the tentative conclusion that it is probably earlier than the third edition (1775) in the Bodleian Library.[10] Robert Brittain has located a Philadelphia edition of 1791, and he refers to a Boston edition of 1795 listed in Evans's *American Bibliography*.[11] Hymn XXXII, 'Against Despair. Old Ralph in the Wood', appeared in a different version in the *Gentleman's Magazine* for September 1779, where it was entitled, 'Extempore, in the King's Bench, on Hearing a Raven Croak'—the title suggests that the *Hymns for the Amusement of Children* were composed during the last year of Smart's life, while he was lying in the King's Bench Prison for debt. Anderson and Park both print the *Gentleman's Magazine* version of Hymn XXXII. In 1947, the Luttrell Society brought out a facsimile of the third edition of the *Hymns for the Amusement of Children*. Brittain prints

[10] 'Another Edition of Smart's *Hymns for the Amusement of Children*', *Library*, ser. v, vol. x, 1955, 280–82.

[11] 'Christopher Smart's *Hymns for the Amusement of Children*', *Papers of the Bibliographical Society of America*, xxv, 1941, 61–65.

thirteen of the hymns, and Callan prints all of them, but with only a selection of the accompanying woodcuts. But on the whole, the *Hymns for the Amusement of Children*, which contains some of Smart's best poems, has been greatly neglected.

In this book I do not claim to cover every aspect of Smart's work—I ignore, for instance, his translations of Phædrus, and of Horace,[12] as well as most of the prose written for periodical publication. I am aware that on the other hand, I often indulge in what may seem to be myopic attention to very minor poetry. But as I have tried to demonstrate in this Preface, critics have rarely tried to appreciate Smart's work as a coherent whole: either the Seatonian verse has been enjoyed at the expense of the later religious poetry, or the *Song to David* has been praised at the expense of all else, except perhaps for a handful of the hymns. I have therefore tried to study, without prejudice, the main phases of Smart's poetic activity—the secular work, the early religious verse, the mad poetry, and the religious verse written after madness. I examine each phase of Smart's work in relation to the literary conventions of the eighteenth century, and I try to emphasize the dichotomy between the idiosyncratic aspects of his poetry, and its conventional basis in the contemporary genres of hymn, Psalm, oratorio, and the rest.

[12] See Arthur Sherbo, 'Christopher Smart's Three Translations of Horace', *Journal of English and Germanic Philology*, lxvi, 1967, 347–58.

[I]

Smart the Man

CHRISTOPHER SMART was acutely conscious of the fact that he was short and ugly. He was once described as 'a little, smart, black-eyed man'.[1] Fanny Burney was more brutal when she wrote that 'not a grace was bestowed on his person or manners; and his physiognomy was of that round and stubbed form that seemed appertaining to a common dealer behind a common counter, rather than to a votary of the Muses.'[2] His portraits bear out these descriptions. In the anonymous portrait of Smart in cap and gown, which his younger sister, Marianne, must have handed down to her descendants, the Falkiner family of Dublin, his dark eyes, double chin, and podgy fingers are plain enough. In the full-length portrait of Smart in the library at Pembroke College, Cambridge, the pot-belly under the embroidered waistcoat is unfortunately reminiscent of his own witticism on the beadles of Oxford, in 'The Temple of Dulness':

> Quàm lentè, Oxonii, solemnis pondera cænæ
> Gestant tergeminorum abdomina bedellorum.[3]

The Rev. Francis Fawkes translated the epigram as follows:

> Or, as at Oxford, on some gaudy day,
> Fat Beadles, in magnificent array,
> With big round bellies bear the pond'rous treat,
> And heavily lag on, with the vast load of meat.[4]

Smart's way of dealing with his diminutive stature and unprepossessing features was to make fun of himself. Hence the

---

[1] Quoted by Leonard Whibley in 'The Jubilee at Pembroke Hall in 1743', *Blackwood's Magazine*, January 1927, cited in *Poems by Christopher Smart*, ed. Brittain, 12.

[2] Frances D'Arblay, *Memoirs of Doctor Burney*, 1832, i.17–18.

[3] *Poems of the Late Christopher Smart*, 1791, ii.144.

[4] *Ibid.*, ii.145.

author's description of himself in Chapter I of 'A New System
of Castle-Building', which was serialized in the *Student* in 1750
and 1751. 'In the first place then, my stature is so very low, that
it has excited the jealousy of a *Dutchman* lately come over for a
show from *Holland*, and who, like some persons I don't care to
mention, expects to become a great man by no other merit than
his distinguish'd *littleness*. My eyes, which are extremely small
and hollow, may truly be styl'd of the *amorous* kind, for they are
always looking at one another. In the rest of my person there is
nothing very singular, saving that when I take the air, having
neither horse nor vehicle, I am obliged to do it upon a pair of
bandy legs.' A few months after writing this description of himself, Smart published his poem, 'The Author Apologizes to a
Lady for His being a Little Man', which is comic and pathetic
at the same time. He chides the lady, 'YES, contumelious fair,
you scorn/The amorous dwarf that courts you to his arms', and
buttonholes her, 'Say, is it carnage makes the man?', and
swaggers, 'The poets shall ensure thy name,/Who magnitude of
mind not *body* boast.' Because he was able to accept his appearance with enough aplomb to laugh about it, he was never
deterred from pursuing the 'fair'. The story goes that he was
only four years old when he fell in love with a young lady of
twelve, and this adventure was followed by the attempt at
thirteen years of age to elope with Anne Vane, granddaughter
of Lord Barnard, who was even younger than himself. He fell in
love with Fanny, and a barmaid at the Mitre Tavern in
Cambridge, and with Harriot, sister of his University friend,
Jermyn Pratt of Downham in Norfolk. Various pretty chamber-
maids, and Jenny's, and Celia's, make brief appearances in his
poetry. Then, most important of all, Anna-Maria Carnan herself appears as 'Nancy', so vividly described with her 'radiant
Locks of burnish'd Gold', that the picture of the tiny Kit
Smart shepherding 'Sweet Nancy' about London, 'At the park
in the mall, at the play in the box', is almost a ludicrous one.
He must have had charm and persuasiveness, however,
because according to the story told years later by his younger
daughter, Elizabeth Anne, 'An intimacy, which soon ripened
into affection, took place between him and Anna-Maria
Carnan . . . A clandestine marriage took place, without the

PLATE II   Frontispiece of

The Midwife, or the Old Woman's Magazine

(Reproduced by permission of the Trustees of the British Museum)

consent of Mr. Newbery [Anna-Maria's step-father, and Smart's bookseller], whose favour however was soon conciliated, and Smart was immediately established at Canonbury House, where he pursued his literary labours for several years.'[5] Mrs. Elizabeth Anne Le Noir presumably provided the relevant dates for the family tree which accompanies this account of the Smarts, according to which, the marriage took place in 1753 at St. Bride's, London, probably just in time for the birth of their first child, Marianne, on the 3rd May 1753.

The marriage was not a success. There is nothing to suggest that husband and wife ever lived together again after Smart's complete mental breakdown in 1756, when their daughters were still babies, Marianne aged three, and Elizabeth Anne aged two. Yet Anna-Maria Carnan must have realized that she was marrying a strange sort of man. It must have seemed odd that Smart, who had had a successful career at Cambridge ('Scholar of the University' in 1742, B.A. in 1744, a Fellowship in 1745, M.A. in 1747), should have suddenly given it up for a precarious existence in Grub-Street, writing poetry, and editing lightweight periodicals, and making English translations of the classics. And most strange of all, when Anna-Maria first met Smart, he was already appearing in literary and theatrical circles under the guise of Mrs. Mary Midnight, the Man-Midwife, an odd warping of the identity which will be discussed in the next chapter. There is even a hint that Anna-Maria was aware of Smart's mental instability ever before they were married, and that she nursed him through the temporary depressive illness which he recalled in his poem, 'Ode to a Virginia Nightingale':

> Me too the kind indulgent maid,
> With gen'rous care and timely aid,
> Restor'd to mirth and health;
> Then join'd to her, O may I prove
> By friendship, gratitude and love,
> The poverty of wealth.
> (*Collected Poems*, i. 130)

---

[5] Robert Surtees, *The History and Antiquities of the County Palatine of Durham*, 1840, vol. iv, part i, 143, based on information given by Mrs. Le Noir in a letter to Sir C. Sharpe.

But Anna-Maria evidently found it impossible to cope with her husband's major breakdown. At the beginning of Smart's long mental illness, his father-in-law Newbery made arrangements to look after him, but as Mrs. Le Noir put it, 'my poor Father was taken from under his protection by the mistaken kindness of ill-informed friends.' Perhaps it was these ill-informed friends who arranged for his admission to St. Luke's Hospital on the 6th May 1757—but on the 11th May 1758, he was discharged uncured.[6] Dr. Battie submitted to the weekly admission and discharge committee of governors, 'that Christopher Smart continues disordered in his Senses notwithstanding he has been admitted into this Hospital above 12 Calendar Months. And from the present Circumstances of his Case there not being sufficient reason to expect his speedy Recovery'.[7] After leaving St. Luke's, Smart may have been confined in a private madhouse until he reappeared in London society in 1763—Father Devlin suggests that he was shut up in Robert Turlington's notorious asylum in Chelsea.[8] In the meantime, Mrs. Smart went off to Mr. McMahon's shop in Caple Street, Dublin, to sell Dr. James's Fever Powder,[9] presumably in order to support her daughters while their father was incapacitated. In 1762, she went to Reading to manage the *Reading Mercury* which was owned by her family, and she seems to have lived there for the rest of her life.

According to modern medical opinion, Smart's madness can be diagnosed from *Jubilate Agno* which apparently shows all the features of maniacal excitement. 'Clearly he suffered from manic-depressive insanity or cyclothymia, a disorder characterized by recurrent attacks of depression and excitement'.[10] It is certainly possible to find various instances in Smart's behaviour which suggest that he was a very excitable man. Perhaps the earliest record of his hectic, not to say manic behaviour, is found in Thomas Gray's letter to Wharton, in

[6] *Rejoice in the Lamb*, 292.

[7] Quoted in Richard Hunter and Ida MacAlpine, *Three Hundred Years of Psychiatry*, 1963, 403.

[8] Christopher Devlin, *Poor Kit Smart*, 1961, 117.

[9] Advertisement in the *Gazeteer and London Daily Advertizer*, 3rd January 1759, cited in *Poems by Christopher Smart*, ed. Brittain, 36.

[10] Sir Russell Brain, *Some Reflections on Genius*, 1960, 117.

which he gives an account of the rehearsals at University for Smart's play, *A Trip to Cambridge* (1747): 'our Friend Lawman, the mad Attorney, is his Copyist; & truly the Author himself is to the full as mad as he. his Piece (he says) is inimitable, true Sterling Wit, & Humour by God; & he can't hear the Prologue without being ready to die with Laughter. he acts five Parts himself, & is only sorry, he can't do all the rest.'[11] The man who nearly killed himself with Laughter at his own wit, was fond of a boisterous social life. Dr. Burney told how Smart 'ruined himself by returning the tavern-treats of strangers, who had invited him as a wit, and an extraordinary personage, in order to boast of his acquaintance.'[12] This fits in with Gray's accounts of Smart's drunken and spendthrift habits at Cambridge, and with Dr. Johnson's observation that 'before his confinement, he used for exercise to walk to the alehouse; but he was *carried* back again'. Smart was insatiably sociable, and there is no doubt that the Introduction to the *Nonpareil* (1757), 'Containing Some Account of the Author', had a grain of truth in it. On or about the year 1748, 'a person who had been a great traveller came to *London*, fraught with learning and experience, and frequented the coffee-houses and other places about town, where the sage and polite resort, dressed in a high crown-hat, and otherwise accoutred like a piece of venerable antiquity. . . . From frequenting the coffee-houses late of an evening, or from some other cause unknown to us at present, she was called Mrs. *Midnight*'. We can guess that the Bedford was one of Smart's haunts, for he soon aroused the inveterate hatred of one of its habituees, the foppish, amorous, and quarrelsome John Hill. By 1752, Smart was taking part in Henry Fielding's Paper War and its aftermath, and cheerfully getting his own back on John Hill by collaborating with Arthur Murphy in writing the *Hilliad*.

Scribbling, laughing, wooing, drinking, spending, quarrelling Smart appears to have been excitable, hot-blooded, not a little absurd, and above all, sociable. Going by the evidence of his elated, jubilant state of mind in *Jubilate Agno*, written while he

---

[11] *Correspondence of Thomas Gray*, ed. Paget Toynbee and Leonard Whibley, Oxford, 1935, i. 274–75.
[12] *Monthly Review*, ser. ii, vol. vii, January 1792, 37.

was confined for madness, and in *A Song to David*, published as
soon as he was released, one would indeed expect that the manic
component of his everyday behaviour would be more obvious
than its depressive reaction. But one brief anecdote of his
behaviour, two or three years after his marriage, shows that his
hectic sociability was probably a neurotic way of covering up a
basic shyness and lack of social poise. His nephew Christopher
Hunter mentioned his uncle's shyness 'which he had in common
with literary men, but in a very remarkable degree', and went
on to tell the following incident, involving Henry Vane, father
of the Anne Vane who had 'eloped' with Smart when they
were children: 'Having undertaken to introduce his wife to my
Lord Darlington, with whom he was well-acquainted; he had
no sooner mentioned her name to his Lordship, than he
retreated suddenly, as if stricken with a panic, from the room,
and from the house, leaving her to follow overwhelmed with
confusion.'[13] Before the onset of madness, a lack of security and
self-confidence was hidden under his riotous, cheerful, apparently extraverted behaviour. Perhaps his lack of social poise
was aggravated in this case by the fact that his old friend and
patron, Henry Vane, was no less than an Earl—in his sycophantic poetry, Smart was habitually abasing himself before
his aristocratic patrons. The eighteenth-century necessity for a
poet to find a patron must be taken into account in explaining
his attitude, but Smart seems to have felt a definite sense of
social and even moral inferiority to his noblemen.

The major source of our knowledge about Smart's state of
mind during his years of insanity is *Jubilate Agno* which approxi-
mates to a kind of journal of his mad memories and meditations.
But the difficulties of understanding the language of this diary
are considerable, and will be considered in a later chapter. The
contemporary anecdotes of Smart's behaviour during the first
stages of his insanity give a clear indication of his obsessions at
that time, and suggest the way in which the subject matter of
his poetry was going to be almost completely involved with
religious feeling. The contrasting kinds of literary pursuits that
had engrossed him during the 1750s are remarkable. One
would not expect that an ugly little man, who had taken on the

[13] *Poems of the Late Christopher Smart*, 1791, I. xxviii–xxix.

literary persona of that pantomime-dame character, Mother
Midnight, was at the same time writing Miltonic verse-essays
on the Eternity, Immensity, Omniscience, Power, and Goodness of the Supreme Being—which he was. It is in keeping with
this dichotomy in literary style, that his roistering around
London should have given way to bouts of devout behaviour.
As Dr. Johnson, remarked, 'My poor friend Smart shewed the
disturbance of his mind, by falling upon his knees, and saying
his prayers in the street, or in any other unusual place', and
what was more, 'He insisted on people praying with him'.[14]
Mrs. Piozzi told a similar story—'but as soon as the Idea struck
him that every Time he thought of praying, Resistance against
y^t divine Impulse (as he conceived it) was a Crime; he knelt
down in the Streets, & Assembly rooms, and wherever he was
when the Thought cross^d his Mind—and this indecorous Conduct obliged his Friends to place him in a Confinement'.[15] She
wrote on another occasion that 'Smart's melancholy showed
itself in a preternatural excitement to prayer, which he held it
as a duty not to control or repress, taking *au pied de la lettre* our
Saviour's injunction *to pray without ceasing*, so that, beginning by
regular addresses at stated times to the Almighty, he went on to
call his friends from their dinners, or beds, or places of recrea-
tion, whenever that impetus towards prayer pressed upon his
mind.'[16] And so, in the fashionable quarter of St. James's Park
and the Mall, where the 'world' took the air, and where Smart
had escorted Anna-Maria Carnan during their courtship,
Smart knelt and prayed, 'Let Shobi rejoice with the Kastrel
blessed be the name JESUS in falconry and in the MALL. For I
blessed God in St James's Park till I routed all the company'
(*Jubilate Agno* B1.89). That was how Smart himself remembered
it after his friends had shut him up to prevent his embarrassing
'indecorous Conduct'.

It is rather sad, that after seven years of the rapturous experience of God, Smart should have emerged into society, stripped of
his eager humour and good-fellowship. When we come to study

[14] *Boswell's Life of Johnson*, ed. George Birkbeck Hill, rev. L. F. Powell, Oxford,
1934, i. 397.

[15] *Thraliana The Diary of Mrs. Hester Lynch Thrale (Later Mrs. Piozzi) 1776–1809*,
ed. Katharine C. Balderston, Oxford, 1942, ii. 728.

[16] 'Piozziana', *Gentleman's Magazine*, n.s. xxxii, 1849, 24.

his earlier poetry, we shall find that there were certain paranoid
elements in his outlook, ever before he went mad. But after his
mental breakdown, Smart's paranoia was much more obvious
as time and time again he wrote of his conviction that he was
being persecuted. Dr. John Hawkesworth visited him in
October 1764, and found him silently hostile towards his
mother, Winifred Smart, and his sister, Margaret Hunter, at
Margate. He was more obviously hostile towards his wife and
children and her step-father Newbery: 'Upon mentioning his
prose translation [of Horace], I saw his countenance kindle, and
snatching up the book, "what, says he, do you think I had
for this"? I said I could not tell. "why, says he, with great
indignation, thirteen pounds." I expressed very great astonishment, which he seemed to think he should increase by adding,
"but, Sir, I gave a receipt for a hundred"; my astonishment
however was now over, and I found that he received only
thirteen pounds because the rest had been advanced for his
family; this was a tender point, and I found means immediately
to divert him from it.'[17] Smart was bitter towards his family,
and bitter towards the critics who dared insinuate that his
Song to David had Roman Catholic tendencies (Smart was a
violent anti-papist), and who dared claim that the poem was
'a FINE PIECE OF RUINS' (Smart's capitals). In his *Poems on Several
Occasions* [1763], Smart answered them with acrimony, reviling
the '*scurrilous* Pamphlet, call'd *the Critical Review*', screaming
about this invidious cavil, this stupendous, this cruel insinuation, this scandalous fellow who had oppressed Mr. Smart
these many years, who had bribed Mr. Griffiths, editor of the
Critical Review, to defame Mr. Smart as much as he dared. Gone
were the days when Smart had enjoyed the animosity of such as
John Hill, and had defended himself against his 'Oppressors'
with the boisterous satire of the *Hilliad*. After his seven years of
insanity, Smart had lost one of the characteristic and most
endearing traits of his personality, the ability to laugh at himself and others.

In fact, in the last decade of his life, Smart presented an
altered and pathetic face to the world. The gallantry of his
youth never left him, but Fanny Burney's account of his

[17] *Poems of the Late Christopher Smart*, 1791, I. xxv.

charming compliment is a sad one. '[Poor] Mr. Smart presented me this morning with a rose, [blooming and sweet as if it were in the month of June.] "It was given me," said he, "by a fair lady—though not as fair as *you*!" I always admired *poetical* licence!' The *Critical Review*, she went on, would think that he was ready for another visit to Bedlam 'if they heard that he had descended to flatter and praise *me*! even little me, *F.B.*, or Q in a corner.'[18] The charm of manner that had attracted Harriot Pratt and Anna-Maria Carnan twenty years ago was still evident, although his appearance was more bizarre than ever: 'He is extremely grave, and has still great wildness in his manner, looks, and voice'. Fanny felt 'the utmost pity and concern for him.'[19]

Nor did Smart's generosity desert him. His nephew described him as 'friendly, affectionate, and liberal to excess; so as often to give that to others, of which he was in the utmost want himself'.[20] Even when he was ending his days as a debtor in the King's Bench Prison, he wrote to Dr. Burney 'to ask his assistance for a fellow sufferer and good offices for him in that charity over which he presides . . . he had himself assisted him *according to his willing poverty*'.[21] Fanny Burney naturally found this very touching, and we do too, although we must admit that there is just a hint of sanctimoniousness in Smart's letter. He was compelled to ask for himself as well as for others. He was well-versed in the habit of sycophancy, but there is a difference between praising a noble patron as a humble but deserving poet, and begging one's daily bread without being able to offer even a poem in return. The letters written at this time show the humiliating lengths to which he had to go in order to keep body and soul together. There is an undated letter among the Delaval manuscripts in the Northumberland County Record Office, Newcastle, addressed 'To Chr' Smart Esq'. It is presumably a rough draft of a letter written by John Delaval, and it shows that Smart had been begging for money. The deletions are as instructive as the completed letter: 'Dear Sir. I am

[18] *The Early Diary of Frances Burney 1768–1778*, ed. Annie Raine Ellis, 1907 ed., i. 66.

[19] *Ibid.*, i. 28.

[20] *Poems of the Late Christopher Smart*, 1791, I. xxviii.

[21] *Early Diary of Frances Burney*, i. 133.

really concerned ⟨for⟩ at the account of your unfortunate
situation ⟨you say that five or six guineas w⟩ which is a severe
satyr upon the age in which your merit is so much neglected
I have ⟨herein⟩ sent you a draught for six guineas ⟨of⟩ which
I desire you will accept from Durham'. In 1766 Smart was
circulating some request for patronage among his friends and
acquaintances, for he wrote to George Colman the Elder from
St. James's Park, next door to the Cockpit, on the 27th
February, 'Sir, I FIND myself reduced by the necessity of the case
to tax such of my friends as are disposed to do me the honour of
their names I am with much respect Your obliged Servant
CHRISTOPHER SMART.'[22] Smart was probably canvassing for
subscribers to yet another volume of poetry, for after telling
Paul Panton on the 22nd January 1767 that William Mason
was proposing an annual subscription of a guinea or two among
the poet's friends,[23] he wrote again from Storey's Gate Coffee
House, St. James's Park, on the 12th February, to say that
Mr. Mason was not succeeding in finding many people willing
to contribute to the scheme, and that anyway Mason's plan
was rather interfering with his own present application for
subscribers to a volume of miscellaneous poetry.[24] In the same
year, he was writing to Dr. Burney: 'This ingenious writer is
one of the most unfortunate of men—he has been twice confined in a mad-house—and but last year sent a most affecting
epistle to papa, to entreat him to lend him half-a-guinea!—
How great a pity so clever, so ingenious a man should be
reduced to such shocking circumstances.'[25] The year after that,
Smart was still humiliating himself by writing to Paul Panton
on the 4th January 1768, 'Dear Sir It is now the anniversary of
Mason's kind plan in my favour, which I humbly take the
liberty of reminding you of—You subscribed two guineas last
year & promised to continue it—If every man, that had much
more cause to use me kindly had been possessed of your
generous sentiments, I should have been well enough off with

[22] *Posthumous Letters from Various Celebrated Men; Addressed to Francis Colman,
and George Colman the Elder*, 1820, 90.
[23] Cecil Price, 'Six Letters by Christopher Smart', *Review of English Studies*,
n.s. viii, 1957, 145.
[24] *Ibid.*, 146.
[25] *Early Diary of Frances Burney*, i. 28.

regard to circumstances—I pray God bless you & many happy years attend you! Your most affectionate & most obliged friend & Servant Christopher Smart'.[26] When one realises that he had to beg in this way from a man who had been a younger contemporary at Cambridge when Smart was apparently at the beginning of a successful academic career, the pitifully degrading position to which he was reduced is even more emphasized. The following year, Panton's subscription failed to reach Smart before he wrote on the 2nd January 1769, 'I send this for the favour of your annual two guineas, which I am in want of God knows', but he managed to cheer up enough to send Paul Panton New Year greetings at the end of the letter.[27] But not a glimmer of cheerfulness is to be found in the last letter Smart is known to have written before his death in May 1771. He wrote to the Rev. Mr. Jackson, presumably from the Rules of the King's Bench Prison, 'Being upon recovery from a fit of illness, and having nothing to eat, I beg you to send me two or three shillings which (God willing) I will return, with many thanks, in two or three days.'[28] In the brief poem, 'Pray Remember the Poor', in his last volume of poetry, the *Hymns for the Amusement of Children*, illustrated with a woodcut of a small boy placing a coin in a box hung on a door with barred windows, the impoverished Smart who lived behind that door changed places with the generous child:

> I Just came by the prison-door
> I gave a penny to the poor:
> Papa did this good act approve,
>   And poor Mamma cried out for love.
>
> Whene'er the poor comes to my gate,
> Relief I will communicate;
> And tell my Sire his sons shall be
>   As charitably great as he.

[26] 'Six Letters by Christopher Smart', 147.
[27] 'Six Letters by Christopher Smart', 148.
[28] Quoted in *Poems by Christopher Smart*, ed. Brittain, 55–56.

[II]

Smart the Poet

— i —

'Me, inexpert of verse' ('The Hop-Garden')

CHRISTOPHER SMART always had a tendency to scribble verses. Just as Mrs. Lucy Porter insisted that Dr. Johnson had written his epitaph on the eleventh duckling at the youthful age of three years, despite the Doctor's vigorous protests to the contrary, so the Smart family treasured improbable tales about their infant prodigy. At four years old, 'The young rhymester was very fond of a lady about three times his own age who used to notice and caress him. A gentleman old enough to be her father to teaze the child would pretend to be in love with his favourite and threatened to take her for his wife—"You are too old," said little Smart; the rival answered, if that was an objection he would send his son; he answered in verse as follows, addressing the lady.

> Madam if you please
> To hear such things as these.
> Madam, I have a rival sad
> And if you don't take my part it will make me mad:
>
> He says he will send his son;
> But if he does I will get me a gun.
> Madam if you please to pity,
> O poor Kitty, O poor Kitty!'[1]

Having thus got off to an early start in his poetic career, Smart's next attempt in verse seems to have been 'To Ethelinda On her doing my verses the honour of wearing them in her bosom.—

---

[1] Letter from Mrs. Elizabeth Anne Le Noir to Henry Edmund Barker, *circa* 1825, in the Bodleian Library, Mss. Bodl. 1006, fol. 245.

Written at thirteen', where the boy was already calling himself
'bard' and 'poet' and referring to Ethelinda, otherwise Anne
Vane, as his 'Happy Muse'. The Muse of Smart's juvenile
poetry was almost always erotic. Having celebrated at thirteen
Ethelinda's heavenly fragrant breast, at sixteen he went on to
praise 'Fanny, Blooming Fair', her bewitching eyes, well-
turned limbs, and her waist bound with Venus's own girdle.
Smart was fortunate in being able to make his Latin studies
serve his adolescent fantasies—the Latin verses 'Arion. By a
Boy of Fourteen' were followed by 'An Epigram of Sir Thomas
More, imitated', where the mental discipline of translating 'De
Tyndaro' into English verse was compensated for by the bawdy
result.

In his undergraduate verse, written at Pembroke College,
Cambridge, Smart the poet was as usual directing 'the jingle of
the Muse' to the flattery of a young lady. But although the
description of the pretty bar-keeper of the Mitre, written when
he was seventeen years old, is more sensually vivid than ever,
Smart's sense of humour adds a charm that was necessarily
lacking in the juvenilia. With typically undergraduate humour,
he sketches the various customers at the Mitre Tavern—
Johnians with 'all the politesse of bears', 'stake-stuck CLARIANS',
'The sons of culinary KAYS', and the gloomy King's-Men—and
how these men have only one object in view:

> No handkerchief her bosom hid,
>   No tippet from our sight debars
> Her heaving breasts with moles o'erspread,
>   Markt, little hemispheres, with stars;
> While on them all our eyes we move,
> Our eyes that meant immoderate love.
>   (*Collected Poems*, i. 85)

While he was at Cambridge, Smart had the honour of being
chosen to write the Tripos verses, three years in succession.
Obviously his flair for versification was being recognised by the
University. By this time, Smart was becoming self-conscious
about his role as a poet, and his Tripos poem for 1740–41,
'Datur Mundorum Pluralitas' or 'A Voyage to the Planets',
gives an early indication of his attitude to his poetic task. He

expresses himself with the conventional modesty of a young poet who wants to try his hand at the sublime style, but who fears failure through inexperience. He is eager to be borne away by foaming Pegasus to meditate on the new worlds revolving in the sky, 'Quanquam animus secum volvens exempla priorum/Bellerophonteæ pallet dispendia famæ'.[2] Bellerophon, flushed with pride after killing the Chimera, dared to mount Pegasus to fly to heaven and see the gods face to face— and was cast down to earth for his presumption. At eighteen or nineteen years of age, Smart was terrified that his flights of imagination were going to land him in embarrassing bathos.

In his Tripos poem for 1741–42, 'Materies Gaudet Vi Inertiæ', or 'The Temple of Dulness', the young poet dealt with another enemy of his embryonic craft, the arch-enemy of eighteenth-century poetry, 'Dulness'. The Rev. Francis Fawkes translated the lines as follows:

> A river, murmuring from Lethæan source,
> Full to the fane directs its sleepy course;
> The Pow'r of Dulness, leaning on the brink,
> Here calls the multitude of fools to drink.
> Swarming they crowd to stupify the skull,
> With frequent cups contending to be dull.
> Me, let me taste the sacred stream, I cry'd,
> With out-stretch'd arm—the Muse my boon deny'd,
> And sav'd me from the sense-intoxicating tide.[3]

But if Smart felt that in 'The Temple of Dulness' he had been saved from drinking the cup of dullness, he was not so sure of himself in his next Tripos poem for 1742–43, 'Mutua Oscitationum Propagatio Solvi Potest Mechanice' or 'A Mechanical Solution of the Propagation of Yawning'. The poet obviously thinks it is his duty to vent satirical 'ire' on the dullness of bench and pulpit, the physician and the pendant. But his poem ends plaintively when he suddenly realizes that Polychasmia, goddess of dullness, has played a trick on the poet himself. While he has been condemning others for being dull, Polychasmia has been making him 'gape, unactive, and supine,/And at vast distance

---

[2] *Poems of the Late Christopher Smart*, 1791, ii. 126.
[3] *Ibid.*, ii. 149.

view the sacred Nine'. The youthful poet is denied the nectar of
the Muses, for 'These godlike Pope exhausts, and greatly
claims them all.'[4]

'The Hop-Garden' belongs with the juvenilia and the undergraduate poetry, and gives us another view of Smart's early
attitude to his poetic task. It can be dated fairly accurately,
because at the beginning of Book II, Smart states that 'At
length the muse her destin'd task resumes/With joy' after a long
period of silent grief for his friend Theophilus Wheeler, of
Christ Church, Cambridge, who died in December 1743. At
some period in 1743, then, or even earlier, Smart was setting
out to write his first 'major' work, a georgic celebrating the hop-
lands of his native Kent, planned on an epic scale, 'I teach in
verse Miltonian. Smile the muse . . .' In his poem, Smart veers
from modesty to self-confidence. In one breath he is all modesty,
sighing 'Oh! cou'd I emulate Dan Sydney's Muse', no peasants
or hops would debase his poetry:

> But I, young rustic, dare not leave my cot,
> For so enlarg'd a sphere—ah! muse beware,
> Lest the loud larums of the braying trump,
> Lest the deep drum shou'd drown thy tender reed,
> And mar its puny joints: me, lowly swain,
> Every unshaven arboret, me the lawns,
> Me the voluminous Medway's silver wave,
> Content inglorious, and the hopland shades!
> (*Collected Poems*, i. 143)

Yet in the next breath, his modesty has vanished, and he calls
upon his yeomen and countrymen to listen to his Miltonic
voice, 'The muse demands your presence, ere she tune/Her
monitory voice; observe her well,/And catch the wholesome
dictates as they fall.' The resounding polysyllables die away,
and Smart finds it necessary to add that he is quite likely to fall
into the errors of poetic inexperience, 'Thou too be here,
Experience, so shall I/My rules nor in low prose jejunely *say*/
Nor in smooth numbers musically err'. And he goes on to
invoke 'Experience' in the persons of John Milton and John
Philips:

---

[4] *Ibid.*, ii. 159.

> But vain is Fancy and Experience vain,
> If thou, O Hesiod! Virgil of our land,
> Or hear'st thou rather, Milton, bard divine,
> Whose greatness who shalt imitate, save thee?
> If thou, O Philips, fav'ring dost not hear
> Me, inexpert of verse; with gentle hand
> Uprear the unpinion'd Muse, high on the top
> Of that immeasurable mount, that far
> Exceeds thine own Plinlimmon, where thou tun'st
> With Phœbus' self thy lyre. . . .
>
> (*Collected Poems*, i. 149–50)

The passages of self-criticism in the undergraduate verse suggest, then, that Smart was basically timid about his talent for poetry; he was afraid of being bathetic, dull, and prosaic. Yet at the same time, he was envious of the godlike Pope who was drinking the nectar of the Muses at the expense of the Cambridge undergraduate; and he was ambitious, bent on modelling himself on the divine Milton and the expert Philips.

Towards the end of 1743 something happened which was to have a decisive effect on Smart's career: he was given the opportunity to contact Alexander Pope himself. Smart had made the acquaintance of William Murray who was evidently willing to recommend Smart to Pope's attention. On the 6th November 1743, Smart wrote off to Pope from Pembroke Hall, enclosing his Latin translation of the 'Ode for Musick, on St. Cecilia's Day', with the following letter: 'Sir, Mr. Murray having told me that it would, he thought, be agreeable to you to see a good Latin version of your Essay on Man, and advised me to undertake it, though I know myself vastly unfit for such a task, I will attempt to render any number of lines that you shall be pleased to select from any part of the work, and as you approve, or dislike them, will pursue or drop the undertaking. I am, Sir, with the utmost respect, yours, C. SMART.' To this characteristic mixture of eagerness and self-deprecation, Smart added a postscript, likewise forward and timid at the same time: 'I should not have presumed to have given you this trouble had not Mr. Murray assured me that I might safely venture. I have made bold likewise to send you a specimen of a translation of

your Essay on Criticism, verse the 339th.'[5] Pope replied
promptly, and although he courteously deflected Smart from
the *Essay on Man*, and suggested that he ought to try the *Essay on
Criticism* instead, his praise for Smart's translation of the 'Ode
for Musick, on St. Cecilia's Day' was unqualified: 'I ought to
take this Opportunity of acknowledging the Latin Translation
of my Ode which you sent me, & in which I c^d see little or
Nothing to alter, it is so exact.'[6] This exchange of courtesies
between the accomplished Pope and the inexperienced Smart
led to a meeting at Twickenham[7]—perhaps the famous gardens
around Pope's villa inspired the cryptic line written in madness
years later, 'For Flowers can see, and Pope's Carnations knew
him' (*Jubilate Agno* B2.568). This encounter, brief as it was, was
a source of immense pride to Smart throughout his life. In the
portrait of the poet in Pembroke College, Smart rests his hand
on Pope's letter. Then, more than twenty years after Pope had
praised Smart, the latter wrote in the Preface to his *Works of
Horace, Translated into Verse* (1767), 'I beg leave therefore to
assure the Reader, that I did not set about my work without the
consciousness of a talent, admitted of, and attested to, by the
best scholars of the times both at home and abroad. Mr. Pope
in particular, with whom I had the honour to correspond,
entertained a very high opinion of my abilities as a translator,
which one of the brightest men amongst our Nobility will be
ready (I trust) to certify, should my veracity in this matter be
called in question.' In context, this frenzied appeal to the
opinion of the long-dead Pope, and the brilliant Lord Mansfield, formerly Mr. Murray, is merely pathetic; but there can be
no doubt about it that Smart states the case accurately enough.
Although he had called himself a 'bard' at thirteen years of age,
he needed 'the consciousness of a talent' before he could set
about his poetic task in earnest, and he needed the praise and
admiration of the academic world, and the world of profes-
sional poets, before he could convince himself of his talent.

Even after Pope's encouragement, however, Smart did not
suddenly achieve entire self-confidence in his writing. In the

[5] John Holliday, *The Life of William late Earl of Mansfield*, 1797, 25.
[6] British Museum, Add. Mss. 6911. f.27.
[7] Devlin, *Poor Kit Smart*, 30.

'Secular Ode on the Jubilee at Pembroke College, Cambridge, in 1743', he was still prepared to invoke a peerless bard, Dan Spenser, begging him not to despise his inferior sons 'Chaunting her praises on this festal day'. Yet in the same month, Smart was able to write with mock pride in his own poetic powers—pride justified by the splendour of the occasion, 'On Taking a Batchelor's Degree':

> 'TIS done:—I tow'r to that degree,
>   And catch such heav'nly fire,
> That HORACE ne'er could rant like me,
>   Nor is *King's* chapel higher.
>   (*Collected Poems*, i. 88)

Eventually, there was a relative shift of emphasis between the poles of self-deprecation and self-confidence. This is shown clearly in his own 'Ode for Musick on Saint Cecilia's Day' (1746). In the Preface to this poem, Smart states that his friend, the learned and ingenious Mr. Comber of Jesus College, has suggested to him a fine subject for an Ode on St. Cecilia's Day, that is, David's playing to King Saul when he was troubled with the Evil Spirit. But, comments Smart severely, '*The chusing too high subjects has been the ruin of many a tolerable genius*', and he quotes Du Fresnoy's rule for painters in support of his own views. In 'The Hop-Garden', too, Smart had been afraid of choosing the 'high subjects' of chivalry and romance, and chose hops and peasants instead. But this feeling of in-adequacy had been flatly contradicted by the didactive assertiveness of Smart's claim, 'I teach in verse Miltonian'. In the same way, Smart dared not choose too high a subject for his 'Ode on Saint Cecilia's Day'—yet he blithely named Dryden and Pope as his poetic forbears. He admits that he has been told that writing an Ode on St. Cecilia after Dryden and Pope is a 'great presumption', but he has a string of answers to that criticism. He claims that he is not attempting to equal even the *worst* parts of Dryden and Pope. That sounds modest enough, but it is significant that he was now prepared to admit that the masters could write inferior passages at all, and he goes on to point out the various 'blemishes' in the Odes of Dryden and Pope. This confidence in his capacity to judge these poets—and

PLATE III   GUIDO RENI

'The Coronation of the Virgin'

(*Reproduced by permission of the Trustees of the National Gallery, London*)

PLATE IV   GUIDO RENI

'Liberality and Modesty'

(*Reproduced by permission of the Trustees of the British Museum*)

PLATE V   'CHRISTOPHER SMART'

From the portrait, sometimes attributed to Sir Joshua Reynolds, in
the Library of Pembroke College, Cambridge

(Reproduced by permission of the Librarian)

Smart had called Pope 'godlike' only a few years before—suggests that he was probably acquiring self-confidence in his ability to write passable poetry of his own. But it is unlikely that he ever achieved the supreme confidence of a great poet. In his undergraduate days, Smart's problem seems to have been simply that of a young, ambitious poet faced with the mature accomplishment of the poets who had gone before him; he came to terms with his immaturity, received the blessing of Alexander Pope, and went on writing. But in a sense, Smart's youthful modesty corresponded to a fundamental trait of personality that was to emerge in the distorted form of gross obsequiousness in his adult poetry, a topic which will be fully discussed later in this chapter.

In his early poetry, then, Smart's idea of himself as a poet is clear enough. He sees himself usually as a humble but talented disciple of the great poets, Sidney, Spenser, Milton, Dryden, and Pope. His persona is conventionally pastoral as 'Of Camus oft the solitary strand/Poetically pensive will I haunt' in 'To the King', and 'oft on Medway's banks/I'll muse on thee full pensive'—so he assured the late Theophilus Wheeler in 'The Hop-Garden'. But when Smart left Cambridge for London, he put away his oaten pipe and mantle blue, and put on quite another poetic disguise: that of Mrs. Mary Midnight.

— ii —

'For I is identity' (*Jubilate Agno* B2.521)

In 1751, the first volume of *The Midwife, or the Old Woman's Magazine*, a medley of essays and poems, was printed for Mrs. Mary Midnight, and sold by Thomas Carnan, soon to become Smart's brother-in-law. The frontispiece of the book (see Plate II) shows two old women sitting at a table laden with ink and paper; the old woman on the right wears spectacles, the old woman on the left smokes a pipe, and a box is prominently labelled, with anal humour, 'The Jakes of Genius'. There were evidently *two* masculine old ladies, working together on the ephemeral species of wit and humour which so charmed the public in the 1750s. In the Christmas number of the *Midwife*, there appeared a letter dated 27th November 1750 from Fleet-

Market, addressed to Mrs. Midnight and her confederate
Succubus Canidia from their deadly foe, J. Sable, who is
'determin'd to prosecute you for a Witch, together with the
other old dry'd Hurdle, whose Portraiture you exhibit in your
Frontispiece'.[8] Mr. Sable sounds suspiciously like William
Kenrick who brought out the *Old Woman's Dunciad* anonymously in 1751, and suggested that the frontispiece of the *Old
Woman's Magazine* represented Dullness and Poverty under the
characters of Mrs. Midnight and her Confederate: 'It is a
Matter of no little Dispute whether the Confederate of *Dullness*
should be called *Succubus Canidia*—the *Christian* Name, signifying
a Devil in the Shape of an Old Woman, and the Surname being
taken from that of a *Neapolitan Jezebel*, whom *Horace* calls a
Witch'.[9] There is no doubt about who was concealed behind
the witch-like face of Mrs. Midnight. Kenrick identifies her as
Christopher Smart, 'Late witty, *Smart*, he laugh'd and sung;/
E'er curst *Canidia* on him hung',[10] while several poems first
printed under the pseudonym of Mrs. Midnight were later
printed under Smart's own name.

Mrs. Midnight's other literary productions were numerous.
A second volume of the *Midwife* came out later in 1751, and a
third in 1753. This third volume was bound up with *An Index to
Mankind* by Mrs. Mary Midnight 'Which compleats her works
in English'. Other productions were *Mother Midnight's Miscellany* (1751) by Mary Midnight '*Midwife to all the Inhabitants of
this* Cosmos, *and to the Choice Spirits in the* Elysian Shades', and
Mother Midnight's Comical Pocket-Book[11] by Humphrey Humdrum
which appeared in 1753. In 1757, Thomas Carnan published
the *Nonpareil*, a selection of pieces from the *Midwife*, a gesture
probably intended to help Smart, or more likely his wife and
children, while he was insane. In 1763, the appearance of
Mrs. Midnight's Orations coincided with Smart's reappearance
in society after his confinement for madness, and the title-page
reminds us that Mrs. Midnight had always tried to dazzle
theatrical audiences as well as literary ones.

---

[8] *Midwife*, i. 98.   [9] *Old Woman's Dunciad*, 1751, 9.   [10] *Ibid.*, 14.
[11] See Arthur Sherbo, 'The Case for Internal Evidence (1) Can *Mother Midnight's
Comical Pocket-Book* be Attributed to Christopher Smart?', *Bulletin of the New York
Public Library*, lxi, 1957, 373–82.

Her theatrical career began, as far as we can tell, on the 3rd December 1751 when Christopher Smart, with Richard Rolt as a colleague and John Newbery as financier, produced the first of a series of entertainments at the Castle Tavern in Pater-Noster Row. Smart frequented this tavern as a customer as well as an entertainer, for he wrote in *The Horatian Canons of Friendship* (1750) that '*NOT many days ago, at a meeting of a club of merry fellows at the Castle, after supper was over I toasted* All our Friends round Paul's'. On the 27th December 1751, 'Mother Midnight's Entertainments or The Old Woman's Oratory' removed to the New Theatre in the Haymarket and continued there until May 1752, and included performers like the nine-year-old flautist, Benjamin Hallet, and the wooden-legged dancer, M. Timbertoe from the Opera in Paris—characters familiar enough to readers of Smart's poetry. In December 1752, the Entertainments were revived, the chief attraction being a troupe of performing animals. It is difficult to describe accurately just what went on during such ephemeral entertainments, but they seem to have contained recitations, orations, masques, dances, circus acts, and musical interludes—the kind of medley that we should now call a variety show. The entertainments were revived from time to time—in 1760, for instance, 'Mrs. Midnight's Concert and Oratory, as it was originally in the year 1754' was put on in the Haymarket for the benefit of Mrs. Midnight and Mr. Gaudry. It is also difficult to assess just what part Smart played in these performances. Probably his main function was to write the script, but it is just possible that he actually appeared on the stage, if we take into account 'An Occasional Prologue Occasion'd by [the] two Occasional Prologues To be spoken either by Mr. Garrick or Mr. Barry, or both, assisted in the delivery thereof by Mrs. Midnight, being the first time of her appearing on any Stage'. Garrick and Barry each try to blame the other for having distressed the audience, while Mrs. Midnight intervenes and sings the following simile:

> While *Garrick* smart, and blust'ring *Barry* jar,
> Like Rough and Smooth, or Oil and Vinegar,
> I, like an hard-boil'd Egg come in between,
> And mix their Matters, as I intervene;

I form (for Rhyme's sake add, with JUST INTENTION)
Betwixt their fighting Fluids a Convention;
Which being thus conjoin'd, please ev'ry Palate,
And make a pretty Figure in a Sallad.
                                        (*Collected Poems*, i. 93)

Several years later, Mrs. Midnight was confined for madness,
but *Mrs. Midnight's Orations* (1763) contains pieces that were
composed only a year or so earlier—for instance, her Loyal
Oration on the occasion of 'that late awful Solemnity, the
Coronation of our good and gracious King', commemorating
the coronation of King George III and Queen Charlotte on
22nd September 1761. Even while she was technically insane,
then, Mrs. Midnight was still writing for her Entertainments.
We do not know whether she was ever allowed to be present in
person to hear her new compositions recited.

Mrs. Mary Midnight was not Smart's only pseudonym. He
adopted her relative, 'Mrs. Midnight's Nephew' or 'Master
Christopher Midnight', as well as calling himself 'Mr. Lun' and
'Zosimus Zephyr' on various occasions. He probably assumed
the name of 'Tommy Tagg, Esq.' in *A Collection of Pretty Poems
for the Amusement of Children Three Feet High* (1756), and of
'Tommy Trapwit, Esq.' in *Be Merry and Wise* (1753).[12] One of
the most common of his pen-names was 'Ebenezer Pentweazle,
of Truro in the County of Cornwall'. Smart published the
Horatian Canons of Friendship (1750) under that name, and
contributed poems to the *Student* and the *Midwife* in the name
of Ebenezer himself, as well as in the name of his niece, 'Miss
Nelly Pentweazle, A Young Lady of 15'. In the *Horatian Canons
of Friendship*, he advertised *The History of Jack the Giant Killer*, by
Master Billy Pentweazle, a child of nine years old.

Just as Mrs. Midnight had another old hag as her accomplice,
so Ebenezer had his double—Smart was obviously collaborating
with another wit, an Oxford man, and somewhat incomprehen-
sibly, they found it a huge joke to share the same name.
William Kenrick identifies Smart and Ebenezer, how 'once
solertial *Smart*,/He laugh'd and sung', and

---

[12] See Arthur Sherbo, 'Survival in Grub-Street: Another Essay in Attribution',
Bulletin of the New York Public Library, lxiv, 1960, 147–58.

> Say, Muse, how *Ebenezer*, by her Pow'r,
> From human Frame into bubonic Form
> Fell metamorphos'd . . .[13]

But Kenrick implied also that there was another Ebenezer to be pinpricked with satire, for he went on to advertise *The Magazines Blown Up*, an account of the seizing 'of the notified *Pentweazle*, an *Oxford* scholar, in the Shape of an *Old Woman*'[14]—a pamphlet which indeed reveals that there were in fact two Pentweazles. To complicate matters further, the Midnight family interacted with the Pentweazle family. In order to satirize the Robinhood Society,[15] Bonnell Thornton printed in his *Drury-Lane Journal* (1752) several accounts of the proceedings of an imaginary society called 'The Female Disputants' which held meetings at the Silent Woman in Broad Street, St. Giles. The members of 'The Female Disputants' were supposed to be Mrs. Midnight, Lady Pentweazle, and Thornton's own literary creation, Mrs. Termagant. As well as sharing his Pentweazle family with Bonnell Thornton, Smart must have also enjoyed sharing their merits with Samuel Foote—it is notable that Samuel himself, as well as Ebenezer, came from Truro in Cornwall. The Pentweazles duly appeared in Foote's farce, *Taste* (1752), dedicated to Francis Delaval, in which Lady Pentweazle was played by a male actor, James Worsdale, showing that masculine old ladies were very much in vogue in Smart's circle. Lady Pentweazle is caricatured by Foote as an ugly old woman who has borne twenty children but who still falls hook, line, and sinker for the grossest of flattery; Alderman Pentweazle is a henpecked husband suffering from a vulgar City accent, and their son, Caleb Pentweazle, is a dim, thumb-sucking infant who comes into his own when he exposes the rogues of the piece. It seems that Kit Smart, alias Ebenezer Pentweazle, alias

[13] *Old Woman's Dunciad*, 13.

[14] *Ibid.*, 21.

[15] The Robinhood Society was founded in 1613 for the purpose of free and candid enquiry. In the middle of the eighteenth century, the society met at the Robinhood in Butcher-Row where sixpence entitled the member to his share of the drink and discourse. Members included at various times, Macklin, Foote, Derrick, Hooke, and Orator Henley. Burke, too, was probably an eloquent member at one time. Fielding's satire of the society in the *Covent-Garden Journal* (1752) implied that the discussion tended towards free-thought and deism. See the *Covent-Garden Journal*, ed. Gerard Edward Jensen, New Haven, 1915, ii. 167–70.

Mrs. Mary Midnight, sometime Fellow of Pembroke College, Cambridge, came into his own among the comedians who made their living out of coarse, slapstick versions of Ben Jonson's 'humorous' type of comedy. Smart found that there were obvious dangers in the contemporary taste for pseudonymous writing, dangers which might well have deprived him of his aristocratic patronage. For the low comedians and hacks of eighteenth-century London were frequently subsidized by rich men in search of vulgar entertainment. Like Samuel Foote, Smart had reason to be grateful to Francis Delaval, and when the Delaval family put on a private performance of *Othello* at Drury-Lane in March 1751, Smart dutifully published, in his own name, *An Occasional Prologue and Epilogue to Othello* in which the noble actors and actresses were characteristically admired and flattered. But some anonymous joker with his knife in Smart brought out another pamphlet with quite another tenor. *A Satirical Dialogue between a Sea Captain and his Friend in Town* (1751) was published under the name of Ebenezer Pentweazle, and jibed at the heedless fops and triflers who had dared to mess about with *Othello* at Drury-Lane. The fact that there were two Ebenezers was a huge joke. Presumably the appearance of a third was not so funny.

For modern readers, the eighteenth-century delight in anonymous and pseudonymous literature can be bewildering and annoying. The century took a strange pleasure in hiding the personality and disguising the person. Henry Fielding shielded himself behind the stern persona of Sir Alexander Drawcansir in order to make moral comments on his contemporaries through the medium of the Covent-Garden Journal. A more frivolous impulse to put on a disguise made the 'masque' one of the chief social pleasures of the age, so that even provincial newspapers felt honour bound to describe for the benefit of their envious readers the costumes of the great. Smart's literary disguises were symptomatic of the age in which he lived, even if he had a practical reason for his numerous pseudonyms used in the *Student*: Brittain suggests that he was willing to sign several of the poems with his own name, but lest the venture seem a closed corporation, he invented a variety of whimsical pseudonyms.[16]

[16] *Poems by Christopher Smart*, ed. Brittain, 23.

But these reasons apart, the motives for Smart's choice of 'Mrs. Mary Midnight' as a pseudonym are bound to remain problematical. Here was a man who had given up a promising academic career, who had tutored undergraduates of Pembroke College, catechized them, and read them sermons[17]—and he chose to adopt the unlikely literary image of an old woman, who as likely as not did not even have scruples about appearing on the stage like a witch in long skirts. The point has to be made that the strange female rôle that he chose to play *might* have given him some sort of transvestite pleasure, though there is nothing else in his biography or writings to suggest that he was sexually abnormal. In *Jubilate Agno* B2.578, he wrote that 'For Shaving of the face was the invention of the Sodomites to make men look like women', and 'For I prophecy that all Englishmen will wear their beards again' (C.130)—his views on the subject were mad but masculine, and no doubt influenced by the fact that Smart, like George III, must have grown a beard during the manic phases of his illness. It must be remembered also that a shiver of transvestite pleasure was commonplace in the eighteenth-century theatre—or did Mrs. Woffington and Mrs. Jordan play the dashing young hero for much the same reasons that the Principal Boys play Prince Charming in modern pantomime—to show off their legs and swagger provocatively in a way that is usually denied a woman? We may feel at first that in any age it is slightly *risqué* to portray the opposite sex on the stage, but that in the post-Freudian era a man would think twice about pretending to be Mother Midnight the Man-Midwife, while Smart and his contemporaries could cheerfully titillate the perverse fantasies of their audience in blithe ignorance of what they were in fact up to. Yet if we think again, we do wonder whether the rôle of the modern Pantomime Dame can possibly have any of these transvestite implications. It seems much more likely that from the psychological point of view, the author and actor are venting suppressed aggression against some hated old lady when they portray Widow Twanky as a fat, toothless hag in corsets and curlers. Sexual desire scarcely plays a part in the portrayal, even if the rest of the cast

---

[17] See Arthur Sherbo, 'Christopher Smart and the Problem of Ordination in the Eighteenth Century', *Church Quarterly Review*, 1966, 45–49.

do happen to be rather fond of the old girl. It would be absurd
to imply that in creating Mrs. Midnight, Smart was necessarily
venting satirical ire on some unconsciously loathed old lady.
But it is at least just as foolish to leap to conclusions and decide
once and for all that Smart was indulging in transvestism when
he put on the mask of Mary Midnight. Bonnell Thornton was a
good friend to Smart, and he too adopted a female literary
persona. Evidently it was considered normal at that time to use
the vagaries of the female sex to serve a satirical literary purpose. Thornton must have felt that in his *Drury-Lane Journal*, the
very name of that virago, Madam Roxana Termagant, would
make his literary enemies shake in their shoes. But we may
remember that Thornton's imaginary debating society, com-
prising Mrs. Midnight, Lady Pentweazle, and Mrs. Termagant,
met at the Silent Woman to hold their meetings. At first sight
the name of the tavern seems simply comic and inappropriate,
considering the voluble nature of the ladies who enjoyed
disputing there. On another level, we may reflect somewhat
uneasily that 'The Silent Woman' is the sub-title of Ben
Jonson's *Epicoene*, and that Thornton could well have been
making a smirking reference to the epicene nature of the
persons who frequented the tavern. And if Smart's pseudonym
of Mrs. Midnight *did* correspond to a sexual abnormality of the
personality, it would not be surprising to find that he enjoyed
the friendship of a man similarly orientated, calling himself
Mrs. Termagant.

And as for the fact that Smart and his friends shared their
pseudonyms, and found it hilarious that there should be *two*
old midwives, and *two* Ebenezer Pentweazles—the psychological motives for sharing a name are beyond me, but could be
weird enough, I suppose.

— iii —

'The Muse must humble e'er she rise' ('Ode to Admiral
Sir George Pocock')

There seems to be a great difference between the Cambridge
student who haunted poetically pensive the solitary strand, and
the London hack who frequented the Castle Tavern, drinking

with 'merry fellows' and entertaining them with the latest
escapades of Mother Midnight. Yet we know that the young
rustic who dared not leave his cot was nevertheless berated for
drunkenness by Thomas Gray, who thought that it was high
time Smart began to 'live in the College, soberly, & within
Bounds'.[18] It is not surprising, in view of this contradiction in
Smart's personality, that behind the facetious mask of Mrs.
Midnight was hidden the poet who still longed to write the kind
of splendid poetry that would win the admiration and respect
of his readers. Indeed, Smart craved for recognition to such an
extent that his 'consciousness of a talent, admitted of, and
attested to, by the best scholars of the times' did not entirely
solve his adolescent problems of inadequacy. While he was an
undergraduate, he felt inferior to the great poets, Sidney,
Milton, Dryden, and Pope, who had drunk the nectar of the
Muses, and left none in the cup for the aspiring young poet. But
as he grew up, his sense of inferiority changed direction, and
was focused not on the great poets, but on the great men of his
day. His attitude to royalty, to the aristocracy and to military
men, and to certain of his friends and acquaintances, became
pathetically sycophantic. In the 'Ἐπίκτητος Imitated from the
Greek', published in the *Ode to the Earl of Northumberland* in
1764, he did manage to strike a proud, independent note,
while referring perhaps to the ravages of seven years' madness
on his ugly little body:

> By birth a servant, and in body maim'd;
> By want a beggar;—worth, to beg asham'd:
> Hardships like these to certain bliss commend;
> For hence I boast immortal God my friend.
> (*Collected Poems*, i. 31)

But this is unusual, and it is much more characteristic of Smart
to make excessively humble and ingratiating gestures in his
poetry. Indeed, he was capable of subservience at its most
ludicrous, as in the Dedication of *Poems on Several Occasions*
(1752) to Lionel Cranfield Sackville (1688–1765), first Duke of
Dorset and second Earl of Middlesex, whose family seat was at
Knole:

---

[18] *Correspondence of Thomas Gray*, i. 292.

THE Critics will, undoubtedly, expect, when they see your Name
prefixed to this Volume, that I should address your Lordship,
as the Judge of Science, and the hereditary Patron of learned
Men; but I shall take the Liberty of disappointing them, having,
as I presume, a stronger and more natural Claim to your Protection from a lucky Accident, then from any real Excellence I
can pretend to, as a Writer or a Scholar.

This lucky Accident, my Lord, is the Honour (I had almost
said Merit) of being born within a few miles of your Lordship;
and tho' I have too much Diffidence to ask your Patronage as a
Poet, I have Assurance enough to demand it as *a Man of Kent*.

It is no wonder that the *Monthly Review* laughed up its sleeve
and suggested that this Dedication 'bespeaks his patronage on a
new, and what may appear to many unenlightened readers, a
very extraordinary foundation.' The reviewer pointed out that
'*Evax*, king of *Arabia*, dedicated his book, on the *nature of
precious stones*, to *Nero*, because there was an (E) in his name as
well as in the emperor's.'[19] We have already looked at the face
that the poet chose to show the world—the comic mask of Mrs.
Midnight. It is just as telling to look at the poet behind the
mask, the socially inferior Man of Kent.

Christopher Smart, knowing that he had a talent for poetry,
must have come to London with high hopes of finding noble
patronage. He had already won the admiration and friendship
of the Vanes and the Delavals, and perhaps it is to one or other
of these patrons that he addressed his paraphrase of Horace,
Book I, Ode I, 'To Mecænas':

> Thus rais'd above the vulgar Throng,
> To noble Themes I'll suit my Song,
>   And if you rank my Name;
> Among the tuneful Lyrick Train,
> My Works shall envious Time disdain;
>   Secure of deathless Fame.
>   (*Collected Poems*, i. 117–18)

But at that period of his life, he evidently suffered some
disappointment—some nobleman must have let him down, as
Chesterfield was to let Dr. Johnson down. Smart vented his
wrath in Chapter IV of his pseudonymous serial, 'A New

[19] *Monthly Review*, vii, August 1752, 133.

System of Castle-Building'. 'Moreover it is the opinion of several great men,' he spluttered, 'that the trifling requisites of meat and drink are so many spurs to make men excel; the poorer a man is kept, the more he'll endeavour to merit the publick favour; and out of necessity (if not out of *gratitude*) must do something for the common utility. Those therefore that encourage learning least are in fact the greatest MÆCENAS's, upon which principle our N – – ty are all POLLIO's and MESSALA's, LEO's and SYDNEY's, and sing *Io triumphe*, WE LIVE IN AN AUGUSTAN AGE.'[20] Smart was indulging himself in a rare outburst of bitter irony. All his poetry points to the fact that he worked best out of a sense of gratitude to those willing to encourage him, and reward his efforts—he never thrived on poverty. But he was careful to conceal his vexation under the pseudonym of 'Chimæricus Cantabrigiensis', and in the poetry published under his own name, he paid unqualified homage to the various patrons who did manage to be interested in his work. For after his student days were over, he recognized quite clearly that his poetry was dependent on no external source of inspiration like the classical Muse; Pegasus was no longer at hand to carry him away into Fontenelle's plurality of worlds. Instead, he knew that his poetic inspiration was in fact derived from an emotional force at work in his own personality; his irresistable need to kneel, even cringe, in subjection to persons greater than himself was a need inseparable from one of his most characteristic emotional responses to God and man: gratitude. Smart's insanity took the outward form of an obsessive need to kneel in prayer to the Supreme Being. One cannot help but feel that the recurring note of sycophantic adulation found in Smart's poetry is similarly obsessive. His humility before God is inseparable from his servility before sublimated human beings.

Some of these aspects of Smart's personality as a poet are revealed in a manuscript poem of uncertain date, 'On Gratitude To the Memory of Mr Seaton'. The Rev. Thomas Seaton (1684–1741) made his will on the 8th October 1738, and bequeathed his Kislingbury Estate to the University of Cambridge for ever, the rents of which were to be annually awarded

---

[20] *Student*, i, Supplement, 1750, 381.

to the Master of Arts judged to have written the best poem on one or other of the Divine Attributes.[21] Smart won the Seatonian prize five times between 1750 and 1755, for poems on the Eternity, Immensity, Omniscience, Power, and Goodness of the Supreme Being. Although there is nothing to suggest that Smart ever met Seaton, the poet considered him to be one of the most generous of patrons, as is shown in the following passage from 'On Gratitude':

> So shall we take dear *Seaton's* part
>   When paths of topmost heav'n are trod,
> And pay the talent of our heart
>   Thrown up ten thousand fold to God.
> He knew the art the World dispise
>   Might to his Merit be applied
> Who when for man he left the skies
>   By all was hated, scorn'd, denied.
> 'Then man that gives me thanks & laud
>   Does honour to my glorious name'
> Thus God did David's works applaud
>   And seal'd for everlasting fame.
> And this for SEATON shall redound
>   To praise, as long as *Camus* runs;
> Sure Gratitude by him was crown'd,
>   Who bless'd her Maker & her Sons.
> When *Spencer* virtuous *Sydney* prais'd
>   When *Prior Dorsett* haild to heav'n;
> They more by Gratitude were rais'd
>   Than all the *Nine* & all the *Sev'n*.[22]

The phrasing of this poem is obscure and clearly belongs to the body of verse written after Smart's mental breakdown in 1756. But certain points emerge distinctly enough. Smart feels that in writing his Seatonian verse, he has been a faithful steward of his God-given talent for poetry, and that by giving thanks and laud to God, he has multiplied his talent ten thousand times. But it is good for a poet to give thanks to other men as well as to God. In this poem, Smart goes on, he is

---

[21] J. W. Clark, *Endowments of the University of Cambridge*, Cambridge, 1904, 369.

[22] *Poems by Christopher Smart*, ed. Brittain, 235, printed from the manuscript in the Berg Collection in the New York Public Library.

thanking Seaton his benefactor, just as Edmund Spenser expressed gratitude to his patron, Sir Philip Sidney, in the *Ruines of Time*, in the *Shepheardes Calendar*, or in *Astrophel*, and just as Matthew Prior eulogized his patron, the Earl of Dorset (father of Smart's own patron, the first Duke of Dorset) in his *Poems on Several Occasions*. This emotion of gratitude inspires the poet—Spenser, Prior, or Smart—to produce better work than anything he could have writen under the tutelage of the classical Muses. In fact, however, Smart personifies Gratitude as the source of great poetry, and thus makes her into his private religious version of the classical Muse. Human grandeur constantly dazzled Christopher Smart, and if those brilliant creatures, the lords and ladies, the generals and admirals, condescended to be kind to him, they made him feel weak at the knees with gratitude. Gratitude clothed herself in the trappings of the Muse, and Smart was inspired to write a poem of adulation.

Much of his gratitude was justified. The Vane family, to whom Smart's father had acted as steward on their estates in Kent, had been consistently good to the Smart family. Henry Vane's sister-in-law[23] in particular was one of Christopher's earliest patrons. Henrietta Finch was a daughter of the sixth Earl of Winchelsea, and married William Fitzroy, second Duke of Cleveland. They seem to have spent much of their time at Raby Castle, County Durham, where the Duke's sister Grace Fitzroy, lived with her husband, Henry Vane, who eventually became third Baron Barnard and first Earl of Darlington. Henrietta, Duchess of Cleveland was a young woman of twenty-eight when Kit Smart, aged eleven, was sent north with his sisters after the death of their father in Kent. She never had a family of her own ('she bore her fruit *above*,/And left no issue of connubial love', wrote Smart much later), and perhaps it was thwarted maternal instinct that made her extremely fond of the puny but talented child who had just lost his father. As Christopher Hunter put it, 'he had the honour of making an acquaintance with the late Dutchess of Cleveland, who discerned and patronized his talents. She allowed him forty pounds

[23] *Not* the mother-in-law of Henry Vane, although Ainsworth and Noyes, Callan, Brittain, and Devlin all insist that she was so.

a year till her death'[24]—a grant which enabled him to go up to
Cambridge. The allowance was continued by the Duke after
the death of the Duchess at the age of thirty-seven—she died
of military fever on 14th April 1742 after less than two days'
illness. It is no wonder, then, that in the 'Epitaph on Henrietta,
Late Dutchess of Cleveland', Smart eulogized the true polite-
ness and prudence of a noble matron who had been benevolent,
patriotic, and talented, 'Such were her merits when her faith
was tried,/And to attain diviner things she died' (*Collected
Poems*, i. 35). And it is no wonder that Henrietta Finch and her
husband, William Fitzroy, appear in the garbled images of
Jubilate Agno B2.685, 'For Bullfinch is under Bull. God be
gracious to the Duke of Cleveland.'

Yet even where Smart's gratitude is justified, he often
manages to express it in rather absurd terms—or is it simply
that eighteenth-century eulogy always sounds a trifle foolish to
the twentieth century? In 'Ode to Lord Barnard On his
accession to that title', for instance, half the Vane family is
portrayed in the guise of various virtues—Hospitality, daughter
of Goodness and Honour, must have been intended for Anne
Vane, daughter of Lord and Lady Barnard, since she seems to
have been the only nymph at Raby Castle that Smart and the
gods seem to have particularly admired:

> Hark! Charity's cherubic voice
>   Calls to her numerous poor,
> And bids their languid heart rejoice,
>   And points to Raby's door;
> With open heart and open hands,
> There, Hospitality—she stands,
>   A nymph, whom men and gods admire,
> Daughter of heavenly Goodness she,
> Her sister's Generosity,
>   And Honour is her sire.
>
> (*Collected Poems*, i. 11)

After the baroque flourishes, 'Goodness' alias Lord Barnard is
seen as dignity restraining itself by condescension's silken reins;
which dignified condescension makes the poet grovel in
gratitude:

[24] *Poems of the Late Christopher Smart*, 1791, I. vii.

> While you the lowly Muse upraise;
> When such the theme, so mean the bard,
> Not to reject is to reward,
> To pardon is to praise.
>
> (*Collected Poems*, i. 12)

The Delavals, already mentioned in connection with their private performance of *Othello* in 1751, seem to have been nearly as important to Smart as the Fitzroy/Vane family. In 'Female Dignity Inscribed and Applied to Lady Hussey Delaval', Lady Susanna, like Lord Barnard, is praised for her 'Condescension, heav'nly mild', and Smart goes on to claim that Faith and Truth style her their queen. Her husband, Sir John Hussey Delaval, had been an unruly Cambridge student, in the care of an equally unruly tutor, Mr. Smart, until Delaval's undergraduate days were abbreviated when it was discovered that he had smuggled a certain Nell Burnet, disguised as Captain Hargraves, into his college rooms.[25] Sir John admired Smart's verse, and the poet therefore assures him that his name is 'HONOUR and Applause'. The rest of the Delaval family received a fair share of Smart's adulation. Sir John's elder brother, the blond and handsome Sir Francis Blake Delaval, was placed among 'The most remarkable patrons in all ages', and a third Delaval brother, Edward, was kindly noticed as deserving his medal from the Royal Society for his experiments in natural philosophy.[26] Even the nine-year-old son of Sir John and Lady Susanna was presented with a Dedication, in Smart's *Poetical Translation of the Fables of Phædrus* (1765), on account of 'THE great and frequent favours which I have received from your amiable and excellent parents'.

Other benefactors deserved Smart's gratitude, just as the Vanes and Delavals must have done. Knowing how kindly and generous Henry Fielding was, we feel sure that Smart's eulogy was entirely sincere:

> . . . the patron, and the bard were join'd;
> As free to give the plaudit, as assert,
> And faithful in the practice of desert.
>
> (*Collected Poems*, i. 35)

[25] *Correspondence of Thomas Gray*, i. 260–61.
[26] Dedication of *The Works of Horace, Translated into Verse*, 1767.

And Smart felt understandably grateful to Dr. James, for in those days the reputation of the Fever Powder was unimpaired, and no one could have forseen that Oliver Goldsmith's untimely death was going to be put down to a dose of that universal panacea of the eighteenth century. Smart's effusive letter to Dr. James in the *Hymn to the Supreme Being* (1756) is pathetically ironical in view of the fact that although Smart had got over three separate crises, he was now facing several years of severe mental breakdown: 'I think myself bound by all the ties of gratitude, to render my next acknowledgments to you, who, under God, restored me to health from as violent and dangerous a disorder, as perhaps ever man survived. And my thanks become more particularly your just tribute, since this was the third time, that your judgment and medicines rescued me from the grave, permit me to say, in a manner almost miraculous.' Smart likewise had good reason to thank John Sherratt, whose name is one of the last to be mentioned in *Jubilate Agno*, 'Let Joram, house of Joram rejoice with Meliphylla Balm Gentle God be gracious to John Sherrat' (D.235), for there seems little doubt that this merchant of St. Martin's Lane, Canon Street, was at least partly responsible for getting Smart released from confinement for madness. Hence Smart's 'An Epistle to John Sherratt, Esq.' where the merchant is assured that his achievements in the Christian cause 'Ascend to vast and sure applause', and will be immortalized 'All precious, permanent and pure' (*Collected Poems*, i. 212). The same poem praises Smart's old friends, Richard Rolt and his wife, who had also played some part in gaining Smart's release. Smart was also befriended by the Sheeles family of Queen Square, where Mrs. Sheeles ran a fashionable boarding-school for girls—Smart refers affectionately to their son in *Jubilate Agno* D.62, 'Let Flexney, house of Flexney rejoice with Triopthalmos—God be gracious to Churchill, Loyd and especially to Sheels', and when the Rev. James Sheeles died on the 29th October 1762, aged twenty-four, his father asked Smart to compose the epitaph. Smart duly wrote that 'We've learnt full well to weep and be resign'd' (*Collected Poems*, i. 36). It is generally accepted that the 'Miss A. F. S – – – – –. Of *Queen's-square*' mentioned in the 'Epistle to John Sherratt' must have been James Sheeles's sister, but it is difficult to imagine what part an eighteenth-century young lady could have played in visiting a madman, and arranging for his release—but Smart certainly suggests that she was the first person to set the machinery for his release in motion. If so, the epithets applied by the poet to the 'sublime, transcendent maid' are rather less extravagant than they appear to be on first sight.

As well as the friends and patrons already mentioned, there were a number of other people who must have shown Smart enough kindness to make him sing their praises in eulogistic verse. The Duke of Devonshire, then Lord Hartington, was appointed Lord Lieutenant of Ireland in 1754, and inspired Smart to impassioned rhetorical questions, 'Hibernia! who'll Hibernia save?', and to great relief, since ' 'Tis done, the glorious work is done,/All thanks to Heaven and Hartington, (*Collected Poems*, i. 62). Then in 1763, the Earl of Northumberland was appointed Lord Lieutenant of Ireland, and in the same year, his son and heir, Lord Warkworth, celebrated his twenty-first birthday. Smart was dazzled by two such splendid occasions in the same noble family, and knelt in poetic homage, mourning that 'In pity to our sister isle/With sighs we lend thee for a while', but brightening up to pay his gratulations to gallant Warkworth, and to hail the transcendent fair (the Duchess) who had crowned Northumberland's wishes with an heir (*Collected Poems*, i. 20).

Then there was Admiral Sir George Pocock who was in disgrace only months after distinguishing himself by taking Havanna in the Seven Years War. 'I give the glory to God, thro Chirst, for taking the Havannah. Sept.ʳ 30ᵗʰ 1762', Smart had written in *Jubilate Agno* D.112. Pocock had set out for England with five ships of the line, several prizes, and fifty transports, but the voyage home was disastrous, and a very small number of ships eventually arrived in England, and a large percentage of the crews were lost at sea, or died of fatigue, hunger, thirst, and cold. Pocock had a chilly reception at home, and the fact that Smart grieved about this ('As private as myself he walk'd along,/Unfavour'd by a friend, unfollow'd by the throng', *Collected Poems*, i. 14) is a significant one—Smart was obviously lured by the great names of his day, and no doubt

E

any Admiral would have attracted him. But Smart was loyal
to the great through thick and thin, and Pocock's failure did not
prevent him from writing that 'Grace has no worthier chief
inspir'd,/Than that sublime, insuperable man' (*Collected Poems*,
i. 14).

Brigadier General William Draper aroused similar emotions
of sounding praise and indignation. In April 1763, Lieutenant
Colonel Scott arrived in Whitehall with a letter from Draper
announcing the conquest of Manila and the port of Cavite.[27]
In May, the Spanish standards taken at Manila were carried in
procession to King's College, Cambridge, of which Draper was
a former fellow. A *Te Deum* was sung, an oration was delivered,
and the flags were placed on either side of the altar rails. Smart
wrote that Draper possessed 'the GREAT BRITISH MONARCH'S
love express', and yet, despite all this, Smart cried that Draper
was not being awarded as generously as he deserved. At one
time I suspected Smart of melodrama, and that his long-
winded denunciation of the public's neglect of General Draper
merely showed that Smart was determined to find persecuted
victims among his acquaintances in order to have emotional
companionship in his own paranoid state of mind. But on the
24th December 1767, Christopher Anstey, author of the
notorious *New Bath Guide*, wrote to Draper from Trumpington
in Cambridgeshire, enclosing a poem 'To Sir William Draper,
K.B. with a Copy of The Patriot, and a Present of Cottenham
Cheeses', and Anstey too suggests that Draper had received less
than his due, and that the poets have to make up for the
public's neglect:

> Good generals and statesmen too,
> From verse alone, must claim their due;
> And oft the friendly Muse supplies
> What an ungrateful world denies[28]

In his 'Ode to General Draper', then, Smart shows once again
that he was capable of loyalty as well as extravagant praise. He
rejoices that his Muse is somewhat stronger than she was,
despite long calamity and time; he calls on the lively spirits of

---

[27] *London Gazette*, 12–16th April 1763.

[28] *The Poetical Works of the Late Christopher Anstey, Esq. with Some Account of the Life
and Writings of the Author, by his Son, John Anstey, Esq.*, 1808, p. xxviii.

his prime to breathe their parting breath on his lyre; and pre-
suming upon his mite in this rough unbidden verse that aims to
do Draper right, Smart lauds his hero to the skies:

> A note above the Epic trumpet's reach
> Beyond the compass of the various lyre,
> The song of all thy deeds, which sires shall teach
> Their children active prowess to inspire.—
> Thou art a Master—whose exploits shall warm,
> The valiant yet to come, and future heroes form.
> *(Collected Poems,* i. 17)

I have said enough here to show that one of the main driving
forces in Smart's personality as a poet was his need to metaphor-
ically kneel before the people he admired, to thank them for
being such dazzling mortals, so sublime, so transcendent, and
so condescending as to notice his poetry, 'this rough unbidden
verse' offered them with such deference. It would not be true to
say that Smart was uniquely sycophantic in that age of sycophancy. He never anywhere attempted the pages of extravagant
flattery dedicated by Matthew Prior to the Earl of Dorset, a
generation earlier. But although Smart's sycophancy was a
characteristic attitude of the eighteenth-century poet, it can be
seen also as an individual habit of mind that developed into an
obsessional, sincere form of gratitude, an essential rather than
peripheral emotion, at the very core of Smart's poetry. 'For
there is no invention but the gift of God, and no grace like the
grace of gratitude' (*Jubilate Agno* B1.82).

— iv —

'GREAT POET of the UNIVERSE' (*On the Eternity of the
Supreme Being*)

Gradually, the picture that the poet had of himself emerges—
the young versifier aspiring to Milton's sublimity and Pope's
elegance, and dreading the enemies of youth, bathos and dullness; then the more sophisticated entertainer donning the
grotesque masks of Mrs. Midnight and Ebenezer Pentweazle,
Esq., but never entirely disguising the serious poet who recognized that his personal source of poetic inspiration was a

humble sense of gratitude to God and his patrons. It remains
for us to explore one more aspect of Smart's concept of what his
poetic task should mean—his notion of what it was to be a
'creator' of a work of art.

In the earliest of his Seatonian verse essays, *On the Eternity of
the Supreme Being* (1750), Smart's invocation is in fact a definition of God's relationship to the works of his creation:

> HAIL, wond'rous Being, who in pow'r supreme
> Exists from everlasting, whose great Name
> Deep in the human heart, and every atom
> The Air, the Earth or azure Main contains,
> In undecypher'd characters is wrote—
> INCOMPREHENSIBLE!—O what can words
> The weak interpreters of mortal thoughts,
> Or what can thoughts . . .
>   (*Collected Poems*, i. 223)

Smart expresses here the germ of an idea that he was to explore
more fully in *Jubilate Agno*—that God's name is written on the
works of creation. In *Eternity*, Smart is dazzled by the incom-
prehensible, eternal God, and he asks whether 'the youthful,
uninspired Bard' may presume to hymn the Eternal, may
presume to mix his feeble voice with the grand Chorus of
Seraphim and Cherubim. Fortunately the answer is 'yes':

> He may—if Thou, who from the witless babe
> Ordainest honor, glory, strength and praise,
> Uplift th'unpinion'd Muse, and deign t'assist,
> GREAT POET of the UNIVERSE, his song.
>   (*Collected Poems*, i. 223)

It is clear from these lines, that God does not always write his
name on the universe in simple letters. God is a Poet, and the
signature of the Lord upon his creation is written in poetry.
Smart the poet may think of himself as a mere 'witless babe'—
his terror of being bathetic was fairly realistic, one feels, as the
round little man pretends to be a stupid baby—but with God to
help him, he can be confident of writing some decent poetry,
even if the Muse has to strain her 'aching sense' to reach the
stupendous heights from which to contemplate the Attributes
of Supreme Being.

In *Jubilate Agno* B2.500, 503, 506, Smart tries to express the same kind of idea about God the Poet:

> For the flowers have their angels even the words of
> God's Creation.
> For there is a language of flowers.
> For flowers are peculiarly the poetry of Christ.

This is exquisite poetry, as Mr. Benjamin Britten recognized when he made such a beautiful setting of these words in his cantata, *Rejoice in the Lamb*. And not only is Smart writing good poetry, but he is also saying something important *about* poetry. He is making a parallel between God and his universe on the one hand, and the poet and his poetry on the other. God and the poet share the same kind of creative activity; the universe is a manuscript bearing the letters, words, language, poetry of God. According to *Jubilate Agno* B2.504–6, the divine poetry of the universe has the augustan virtues of reason and elegance:

> For there is a sound reasoning upon all flowers.
> For elegant phrases are nothing but flowers.
> For flowers are peculiarly the poetry of Christ.

The divine poetry has another attribute too, not at all augustan in character—it is subjective, intent on communicating the nature of its Author, 'For the letter ל which signifies GOD by himself is on the fibre of some leaf in every Tree' (B2.477). Smart means that the Hebrew letter Lamed is equivalent to the English letter L. He makes a pun on the sound of the English letter L, and the Hebrew name for God, '*el*, and he therefore sees God's name inscribed everywhere on the universe in the ubiquitous marking ל. Smart thought he could see God's name, the symbol ל everywhere—on the human heart and network of the skin, in the veins of stones, precious and common, upon the hair of man and beast, in the grain of wood, in the ore of metals, on the scales of fish, on the petals of flowers, on shells, in the constituent particles of air, on the mite of the earth, in the water, in the ingredients of fire, in the stars, sun, and moon, and upon the sapphire vault (*Jubilate Agno* B2.478–91). Likewise 'the Lupine professes his Saviour in Grain' since 'the whole Hebrew Alphabet may be found in a parcel of his seed'

(C.77, 79), 'For this is a stupendous evidence of the communicating of God in externals' (C.80). At first sight this seems an
engaging but unique way of seeing the impress of God upon his
works. Yet it should be noted that Smart may well have been
conscious of a philosophical basis for this view of creation. In
Berkeley's *New Theory of Vision*, one of the fundamental conceptions is that 'Vision is the language of the Author of nature',
and that the Spirit perceives and generates ideas in themselves
inactive—the one omnipresent Spirit is revealed in the persist-
ence and harmony of the universe, finite and created spirits
manifesting their own existence through their spontaneous
activity.[29] If Smart's flowers form, in the Berkeleyan phrase,
'the language of the Author of nature', they are of spiritual
origin: 'For the warp & woof of flowers are worked by per-
petual moving spirits' (*Jubilate Agno* B2.501).

God is the Poet of the Universe, and Smart the poet of
Jubilate Agno—and Smart adopts the divine subject matter and
the divine style. At one extreme, God defines himself in the
most rudimentary manner, by the simple means of inscribing
his name in Hebrew letters on the texture of his created
universe, by the letter Lamed in particular. Hence Smart's
imitation of the divine style, his simple definition of God by
English letters, 'For H is a spirit and therefore he is God' (C.1),
and so on through the letters I to Z, defining God's nature as
person ('I'), king, love, music, novelty, over, power, quick,
right, soul, truth, union, worth, and the power of three ('X'),
yea, and zeal (C.2–17). The point is clinched in C.18, 'For
Christ being *A* and *Ω* is all the intermediate letters without
doubt.' At the other extreme, God defines himself by the most
complex form of language—poetry. The universe is no longer
simply the medium upon which the letters of his name are
inscribed; the universe itself is the concrete imagery of the
divine poetry. For flowers are peculiarly the poetry of Christ. In
writing *Jubilate Agno*, therefore, Smart has only to catalogue the
wonders of God's universe in order to imitate God's poetry—

---

[29] Leslie Stephen, *History of English Thought in the Eighteenth Century*, 1962 ed.,
i. 35. For a detailed account of the influence of Berkeley on Smart's poetry, see
D. J. Greene, 'Smart, Berkeley, the Scientists and the Poets A Note on Eighteenth-
Century Newtonianism', *Journal of the History of Ideas*, xiv, 1953, 327–52.

hence the simple lists of creatures, plants and precious stones, each separate image contributing to a complex definition of God's creativity. Since the constituent letters of the divine language written on the fibre of the universe are Hebrew, one infers that the universe itself is composed in Hebrew poetry. Smart chooses to use English letters to define God, and he chooses to write *Jubilate Agno* in the English language—but it is significant that the structure of his mad verse is closely related to the principles of Hebrew poetry as they were analysed by Bishop Lowth in his *Lectures on the Sacred Poetry of the Hebrews*— a topic which will be explored more fully in a later chapter on *Jubilate Agno.*

If God the Poet writes highly subjective poetry, communicating his divine nature in the stuff of his creation, one would expect that human poetry should ideally be objective. In imitating the divine style, a man's poetic task should be, one would expect, not the revelation of his own nature, but the nature of God and his works. In human poetry, the natural phenomena of the universe are transmuted into the imagery of poetic language. David, the greatest of God's poets, 'With harp of high majestic tone', humbled himself before the Lord, 'When to his graceful harp he knelt', and imitated the supreme poetry of God's universe in the vivid poetic imagery of the Psalms. We know that Smart himself knelt to compose his religious poetry.[30] Identifying himself with David, Smart, too, tried to write the poetry of God's universe. In the breathtakingly beautiful imagery of *A Song to David*, in the polyanthus and polished porphyry, the almonds and cedars, the nectarine and quince, Smart's poetry is in fact more spectacular than anything found in David's Psalms. But Smart was not content to completely identify with King David. He was not content to play the same perfect role of selfless devotion to the Creator and his creation. By a curious twist of egocentricity, Smart praises God's poet as well as the poetry of God's universe. By applying fervently admiring epithets to David the poet—great, valiant, pious, good, clean, sublime, contemplative, serene, strong, constant, pleasant, wise—does not Smart implicitly indulge in the narcissistic pleasure of admiring Smart the poet at the same time?

[30] *Poems of the Late Christopher Smart*, 1791, I. xxviii.

In the earliest poems, Smart apologized for 'Me, inexpert of verse', but allowed the boastful tendencies of his nature to emerge obliquely in the Miltonic assertiveness of 'The Hop-Garden'. Throughout his poetic career, he knelt in subjection before God and Lord Darlington, keeping his vituperative criticism of patrons well out of sight behind the mask of Chimæricus Cantabrigiensis. He tried his best to match his lowliness of stature to a suitably modest bearing, but the effort was only partly successful. The mentally sick poet ended up by identifying himself with the all-accomplished poet of poets, King David. We may even be prepared to detect signs of a megalomania which was quite happy to form a triumvirate of great poets, Kit Smart, King David, and 'the GREAT POET of the UNIVERSE', God himself.

[III]

Theories of Poetry and Criticism

— i —

'Nature's hand by Art is check'd' ('To Miss * * * * One of the Chichester Graces')

CHRISTOPHER SMART delighted in the works of nature because they were the handiwork of God, and bore the signature of their Creator. This is évident in the passages on the wonders of creation in the Seatonian poems, in the long catalogues of creatures, plants, and precious stones in *Jubilate Agno*, and in the exquisite imagery of *A Song to David*. Agno's speech in 'The Judgment of Midas' is a fairly early statement of Smart's love of natural scenery:

> From nature's works, and nature's laws,
> We find delight, and seek applause;
> The prattling streams and zephyrs bland,
> The fragrant flow'rs by zephyrs fann'd,
> The level lawns and buxom bow'rs,
> Speak Nature and her works are ours.
> (*Collected Poems*, i. 127)

But when the whole body of Smart's poetry is studied in detail, we find that Smart's attitude to 'nature' is not always so simple as that. For his views were complicated by the eighteenth-century tendency to postulate Art and Nature as opposing forces. At his most waggish, Smart simply joked about one of the most widely discussed aesthetic principles of the age. He begs his reader to behold the great Monsieur Timbertoe, a dancer at Mrs. Midnight's Oratory, whose left leg has fallen a victim to fate, but whose right leg officiates for its absent mate. Smart comments, with macabre humour, 'Each Fair is dubious, which should win her Heart,/The Limb of Nature, or the Stump of Art' (*Collected Poems*, i. 93).

Elsewhere, however, Smart made more serious statements about the relationship of nature and art. One of his earliest expressions of this theme is found in the 'Secular Ode on the Jubilee at Pembroke College, Cambridge, in 1743', written in praise of the foundress of the college, the Countess of Pembroke. The Countess, newly married and newly widowed, is consoled by Religion and Learning, and is given the grace to pursue all that is great and good. She meditates a mansion for the muse, and founds Pembroke College, to house Edmund Spenser, and eventually Christopher Smart, who comments:

> She, by no specious flow'rs beguil'd,
> That deck *imagination's wild*,
>   And witless youth decoy,
> Chose learning's *cultivated* glades,
> And virtue's *ever-blooming* shades,
>   That give alone true joy.
>   (*Collected Poems*, i. 4)

Smart makes a distinction here between imagination on the one hand, and learning on the other, and he illustrates the distinction by the opposing images of wild flowers, and cultivated evergreen gardens. Despite his reverence for Spenser's poetic genius Smart's academic leanings were momentarily more important to him than his poetic ambitions. Here, at least, the discipline of learning and virtue is valuable, and wild imagination is quite the reverse. As a pedantic adolescent, Smart could dismiss the charms of giving free play to an exuberant imagination. Years later, being of a singularly religious turn of mind, he was still worried about the morality of indulging in unbridled fantasy. In 'Reason and Imagination', the specious flowers of imagination reappear as the ornaments of a harlot:

> In vain fair *Fancy* decks her bow'rs,
> And tempts with fruits and tempts with flow'rs;
> Her wiles in ev'ry mode express'd,
> Or leudly strip'd, or proudly dress'd
>   (*Collected Poems*, i. 78)

She tempts with all her arts, but Reason, the solid, weighty, deep, sound Attribute of Man, asserts its right and keeps its ground. Smart applies his allegory specifically to poetry in the final paragraph of 'Reason and Imagination', addressed to the same Kenrick who had once found Mrs. Midnight and Succubus Canidia so ridiculous. Kenrick is praised for achieving a compromise between Reason and Fancy. 'Thou reconcil'st with Euclid's scheme,/The tow'ring flight, the golden dream' (*Collected Poems*, i. 82). But Smart warns him that human reason and human imagination are alike inferior to the perfection of 'THE BOOK OF SEMPITERNAL BLISS'.

In these allegories of reason and imagination, Smart is trying to convey a didactic message through poetic imagery, and in the interests of morality, the wild flowers of fancy are unequivocally nasty. But the poet who wrote under the auspices of the Great Poet of the Universe found the natural landscape rather prettier when he tried moralizing on another theme. In 'The Country Squire and the Mandrake', the butt of Smart's criticism was Squire Trelooby, who preserved the game only to destroy it himself, who spent his time eating and drinking, oppressing the poor, cheating the priest, and deflowering virgins. The landscape in the early morning is beautiful, as Trelooby, the man of prey, tramps through the woods with his gun and dog:

> The dew and herbage all around,
> Like pearls and emeralds on the ground,
> The uncultur'd flowers that rudely rise,
> Where smiling freedom art defies
> (*Collected Poems*, i. 56)

Trelooby, the sensual and completely unimaginative man, is not affected by the beauty of the morning, neither does he respond to the sound of the wind, nor to the singing of the blackbird. 'For what is beauty to the blind?' 'But what **is** musick to the deaf?'

Smart appreciated the 'uncultur'd' landscape elsewhere in his secular poetry—in 'A Noon-Piece Or, The Mowers at Dinner', for instance, where he obviously enjoys the rivulets and bushes, the rushes and tangled trees, the hazels and banks of fragrant thyme. But in the same poem, he makes it quite clear that in cultivating his garden, man has in fact improved on the 'random' natural landscape:

> Or satiate with Nature's random scenes,
> Let's to the gardens regulated greens,
> Where Taste and Elegance command
> Art to lend her dædal hand,
> Where Flora's flock, by nature wild,
> To discipline are reconcil'd,
> And laws and order cultivate,
> Quite civiliz'd into a state.
>
> *(Collected Poems*, i. 102–3)

It is significant that Smart's hymn, 'Elegance', in the *Hymns for the Amusement of Children*, is about elegant clothes but is illustrated by a woodcut of a formal garden, with lawns, balustrade, steps, fountains, and trees. 'Refinement, or the perfecting of taste and choice in every particular of life, was an ideal respected by the eighteenth century, which could at least understand Christianity when it was presented as the utmost refinement of human life.'[1] The picture of Smart the dedicated gardener has been a familiar one, ever since Dr. Johnson reported on his visit to Smart while he was confined for madness, 'he has partly as much excercise as he used to have, for he digs in the garden.'[2] The evidence is supported by lines in *Jubilate Agno*, for in D.118 Smart wrote, 'Let Pink, house of Pink rejoice with Trigonum herb used in garlands—the Lord succeed my pink borders', and the lines on flowers from B2. 492–510 show that Smart was concerned about doubling flowers, naming them, and giving them spiritual significance in the scheme of the universe. It may not be going too far to say that Smart's gardening must have had a special significance for him, related to his work as a poet, for both tasks involved him in exercising control over his environment. He disciplined the natural landscape into an elegant garden in the same kind of way that he imitated the wonders of God's creation in the formal structure of human language, 'For elegant phrases are nothing but flowers' (*Jubilate Agno* B2.505).

As Smart wrote in 'The Country Squire and the Mandrake', wild flowers do defy art, however beautiful the natural landscape may be. Smart was therefore bound to see the cultivated

---

[1] W. E. M. Brown, *The Polished Shaft*, 1950, 57.
[2] *Boswell's Life of Johnson*, i. 397.

garden as a suitable environment for the poet whose task it is to
discipline language by aesthetic rules. Hence in 'The Blockhead
and the Beehive', the bard, big with the muse, measures with
poetic feet the fresh garden's still retreat. But as he walks there,
he notices that the impeccably mown lawn is 'check'd with
intermingled moss' and that by the silver serpentine, cowslips
shine like topazes:

> Rude rustics which assert the bow'rs,
> Amidst the educated flow'rs.
> The lime tree and sweet-scented bay,
> (The sole reward of many a lay)
> And all the poets of the wing,
> Who sweetly without salary sing,
> Attract at once his observation,
> Peopling thy wilds, Imagination!
> 'Sweet Nature, who this turf bedews,
> Sweet Nature, who's the thrush's Muse!
>   (*Collected Poems*, i. 70)

Although he had once rejected the wild flowers of imagination,
Smart now sees 'thy wilds, Imagination' as a subject for his art,
presided over by the muse, Nature herself. It would be foolish
to try deducing a perfectly coherent aesthetic from Smart's
random statements in his poems. But it does seem that when he
describes the rude wild flowers growing up among the educated
flowers and regulated greens of the garden, Smart intends
giving us a symbol of his aesthetic principle, that great poetry
derives from a compromise between regulation and freedom,
between reason and imagination. Smart does not invariably
make a simple dichotomy between art and nature, reason and
imagination, the garden and the countryside. But he does
admire a compromise between the two extremes. He praises
Kenrick for achieving a balance between reason and imagination, and he admires the landscape of his native Kent, 'yonder
hop-land close,/Joint-work of Art and Nature' (*Collected Poems*,
i.146). The beauty that derives from a compromise between art
and nature dominated his perception in his earlier poetry. 'To
Miss * * * * One of the Chichester Graces.—Written in Goodwood Gardens, September, 1750' gives us a rather charming
glimpse of Smart, sightseeing in Goodwood. The second Duke

of Richmond had died only a month before, but for once,
Smart was not concerned with revolutions in the aristocratic
world. He was enchanted with the Duke's property, especially
with the magnificent view from the grounds. Many years later,
Thomas Walker Horsfield wrote that 'The views from different
parts of the park are rich and extensive. The Isle of Wight
terminates the south-west prospect, and St. Roche's Hill commands it from the north. From Cairney Seat, a pleasure-house
erected with materials formerly composing the tower of Hove
church, the view is magnificent, embracing the whole tract of
plain beneath, the projections and recesses of the coast from
Brighton to the harbours of Portsmouth and Southampton, and
a considerable extent of country northward of the Downs.'[3]
Smart expressed his enthusiasm for the view by fusing an
intellectual statement about art and nature with pre-Words-
worthian vocatives of pure bliss:

> YE Hills that overlook the plains,
> Where Wealth and Gothic Greatness reigns,
> Where Nature's hand by Art is check'd,
> And Taste herself is architect;
> Ye fellows gray, ye forests brown,
> And seas that the vast prospect crown,
> Ye freight the soul with fancy's store,
> Nor can she one idea more!'
>
> (*Collected Poems*, i. 194)

(Smart was easily distracted, however, for Chloris approached,
and 'All nature vanish'd from my view!', and he revelled in
Miss — —'s lips and eyes and beauteous breasts that roused and
yet abashed desire with liquid, languid, living fire.)

It is as well to remember Smart's statements about the compromise between reason and imagination when we come to read
Jubilate Agno. As Smart's fantasies spill down the page of *Jubilate
Agno*, his imagination, like Kenrick's, indulges in a towering
flight, a golden dream, as he praises God over and over again,
calling on hundreds of creatures to rejoice in the Lamb. But
Smart praised Kenrick for reconciling the flight of imagination
with 'Euclid's scheme'. We should at least be prepared for an

---

[3] *The History, Antiquities, and Topography of the County of Sussex*, 1835, ii. 61.

attempt in *Jubilate Agno* to control fantasy with the geometric regularity of poetry written according to strict aesthetic rules.

— ii —

'When just to blame, yet fix'd to praise' ('The Snake, the Goose, and Nightingale')

We have already seen how Smart threw out random comments about his concept of his poetic task, and how he discussed sporadically the importance (and danger) of imagination, the *sine qua non* of his art. At various times during his career, Smart aired his views on critics and criticism. When we study his statements on this theme, we are in fact turning away from examining the motivation and principles of his art, in order to understand how Smart himself felt about the way his readers should judge his finished work. But as we shall see, the art/ nature conflict inevitably reappears in Smart's discussion of literary criticism.

In an age that hated critics as much as Pope did in the *Dunciad*, Matthew Prior was prepared to ignore them and speak to quite a different audience. In his poem, 'In Imitation of Anacreon', Prior therefore wrote:

> LET 'em Censure: what care I?
> The Herd of Criticks I defie.
> Let the Wretches know, I write
> Regardless of their Grace, or Spight.
> No, no: the Fair, the Gay, the Young
> Govern the Numbers of my Song.
> All that They approve is sweet:
> And All is Sense, that They repeat.[4]

Following in the footsteps of Anacreon and Prior, Smart too was prepared, at an early stage in his career, to ignore the critics—just as he was prepared to reject the rules of the classical drama 'and all the piteous prose/The pedant Frenchmen snuffle through their nose.' In writing his 'Prologue' to *A Trip to Cambridge*, that comedy which nearly made him die

[4] *The Literary Works of Matthew Prior*, ed. H. Bunker Wright and Munroe K. Spears, Oxford, 1959, i. 258.

with laughter at his own wit, Smart knew that among the audience would be his current passion, Harriot Pratt, and therefore,

> The critic's censures are beneath our care,
> We strive to please the generous and the fair;
> To their decision we submit our claim,
> We write not, speak not, breathe not, but for them.
> *(Collected Poems,* i. 91)

Similarly, in the 'Epilogue Spoken by Desdemona', Smart dismisses the critical members of the audience who are about to hurry off to Lady Bragwell's rout where Prudella, Neddy Nicely, Lady Stiffneck, and Coquetilla, are all going to condemn the play: 'In short, they all with different Cavils cram us,/ And only are unanimous to *damn us*'. Desdemona looks around her cavilling audience and finds that there are still a fair juducious few who judge unbiased and with candour view:

> Behold them here—I beaming Sense descry,
> Shot from the living Lustre of each Eye.
> Such meaning Smiles each blooming Face adorn,
> As deck the Pleasure-painted Brow of Morn;
> And shew the Person of each matchless Fair,
> Though rich to Rapture, and above compare,
> Is, ev'n with all the Skill of Heavn design'd,
> But an imperfect Image of their Mind;
> While Chastity unblemish'd and unbrib'd
> Adds a majestic Mien that scorns to be describ'd:
> Such (we will vaunt), and only such as these,
> 'Tis our Ambition, and our Fame to please.
> *(Collected Poems,* i. 96)

In his fable, 'The Snake, the Goose, and the Nightingale Humbly addressed to the hissers and cat-callers attending both Houses', Smart objects once again to theatrical critics. Smart reveres the critic's rod provided that the votary of the Delphic god is ruled by truth and nature, and is predisposed to praise rather than blame. But he rejects those critics who are 'inflam'd with spite alone', and he tells a fable to illustrate his point. A grey goose stumbles on a snake and accuses her of plagiarism. It is she, the grey goose, who first hissed at the singing nightingale and woodlark. The snake answers in rage that ever since Adam it has been her prerogative to hiss. At this point the nightingale intervenes and points out that since they are the only two creatures who hiss, they may as well become friends and brothers. After all, the snake is but a crawling goose, and the grey goose but a feathered snake. This is not one of Smart's most inspired poems, but it makes his point about critics. 'The Pig' is no more inspired, but it confirms Smart's dislike of pre-judiced and ill-natured criticism. He states that in each age and every profession, man's greatest fault is 'prepossession'. To illustrate this point, he tells how a certain nobleman built a huge stage for Foote, Massey, Shuter, Yates and Skeggs, 'all the wits and wags', to show off their talents. A 'genius' came along who claimed that he had a curious trick up his sleeve which had never been shown before. His talent was unique. He imitated a pig to the life, and the pits, galleries, and boxes duly roared and applauded 'O rare! bravo! and encore.' A certain country clown, Roger Grouse by name, heard the mimic one day, and boasted that he, Grouse, could 'out-grunt th'egregious grunter'. He too went on the stage and entertained the audience with the grunting of a pig. But he was not so fortunate and was howled down by the audience, 'Pshaw! Nonsense! blockhead! Off! Off! Off!' Grouse thereupon produced his trump card—a real live pig hidden under his jacket. With great self-satisfaction, he pointed out that the prejudiced and ill-natured audience had applauded the imitation pig, and cat-called the real one: ' "Behold, and learn from this poor creature,/How much you critics know of Nature" ' (*Collected Poems*, i. 77).

Once again in 'The Wholesale Critic and the Hop Merchant', Smart attacks the modern critics who judge with rash and partial prejudice. To make his point, Smart tells a story of two men, a wise hop merchant and a literary critic, Tom Catchup. (Perhaps Smart was thinking of a personal enemy when he named the latter, for he mentions Mr. Critic Catchup in the *Horatian Canons of Friendship* as one who felt that Smart's works were utterly worthless, and fit only to line the trunks of the Trunk-maker at the corner of St. Paul's Churchyard.) When the hops arrive from Kent, the merchant goes to the quay 'critically to explore' the quality of the goods. He thrusts his hand into the bag, examines the colour and condition of the hops, and trusting 'his touch, his smell, his eyes', approves of the goods and buys them. The merchant is observed by Catchup 'nothing, if not critical', who jeers at the merchant for buying ten tons of hops after examining only a handful. Doesn't it enter the merchant's head that some of the hops may be brown and mouldy, or half-picked or half-dried, and may not some of the sacks be filled up with leaves? The merchant retorts that he knows his 'chap' and can take his word, and that anyway his method of judging hops is not as absurd as Catchup's very similar way of judging literature:

> I here retort thy random charge,
> Who, in an hypercritic rage,
> Judgest ten volumes by a page;
> Whose wond'rous comprehensive view
> Grasps more than Solomon e'er knew;
> With every thing you claim alliance,
> Art, trade, profession, calling, science;
> You mete out all things by one rule,
> And are an universal fool.
> Though swoln with vanity and pride,
> You're but one driv'ller multiplied,
> A prig—that proves himself by starts,
> As many dolts—as there are arts.
> *(Collected Poems, i. 59)*

A crop of hops may be judged by a handful, but a work in ten volumes cannot be judged after reading only one page.

Smart despised the modern critics. But he greatly admired the ancients, and Pope and Addison among the moderns. His list of critics at the beginning of 'The Wholesale Critic and the Hop Merchant' gives us some idea of the canons of criticism that Smart himself assented to, and the standards by which he wished his own poetry to be judged by his contemporaries:

> HAIL to each ancient sacred shade
> Of those, who gave the Muses aid,
> Skill'd verse mysterious to unfold,
> And set each briliant thought in gold.
> Hail Aristotle's honour'd shrine,
> And, great Longinus, hail to thine;

> Ye too, whose judgments ne'er could fail,
> Hail Horace, and Quintilian hail;
> And, dread of every Goth and Hun,
> Hail Pope, and peerless Addison.
>
> *(Collected Poems*, i. 57)

It seems very likely that Smart hated the critics of his *Song to David* precisely because they made little attempt to 'unfold' his skilful, mysterious poem. Did he look at the reviews expecting to find each of his brilliant thoughts set in gold? His angry disappointment when he read those lukewarm comments on his poem marks the culmination of his antagonism to literary critics. The brief notice of the *Song to David* in the *Critical Review* is now notorious: 'Without venturing to criticize the propriety of a Protestant's offering up either hymns or prayers to the dead, we must be of opinion, that great rapture and devotion is discernable in this extatic song. It is a fine piece of ruins, that must at once please and affect a sensible mind.'[5] As has already been mentioned in another chapter, Smart's reply was vituperative and much longer. He had scarcely recovered from his years of confinement for madness, and he was quite incapable of dismissing the critics with the lighthearted banter that he had managed so cheerfully in the 'Prologue' to the *Trip to Cambridge*, in the 'Epilogue Spoken by Desdemona', and in the fables. In an advertisement of the *Song to David*, published in his *Poems on Several Occasions* [1763], Smart screams abuse at the *Critical Review*: 'The first Part of this invidious Cavil is stupendous impudence against the Truth of CHRIST JESUS, who has most confidently affirmed this same DAVID to be alive in his Argument for the Resurrection.—The last Assertion is an Insult by a most *cruel* insinuation upon the Majesty of the LEGISLATURE of GREAT BRITAIN.—It is a pity that Men should be permitted to set up for Critics, who make it so evident, that they have neither RELIGION nor LEARNING; since *candour* cannot subsist without the former, and there can be no Authority to pronounce *judgement* without the latter.' As if this was not enough, Smart went on to advertise his *Poems by Mr. Smart,* and added the following tirade against the *Monthly Review*: 'THE Writers of the *Monthly Review*, however, after an *invidious silence* of a considerable Time, came

[5] *Critical Review*, xv, April 1763, 324.

to the final Resolution of imposing upon such Persons as had
not seen the above Work, by a most *impudent* and *malicious*
insinuation against the Author. They are therefore summoned
to the Bar of the Publick, to answer the following *Queries*.' The
queries splutter forth. Is there anything that the *Monthly Review*
hates more than truth and merit? Have they not depended on
their malignity for the sale of their book from the beginning?
Have not the writings of Mr. Smart, his Seatonian poems
excepted, been constantly misrepresented to the public in their
despicable pamphlet? Does not the Rev. Mr. Langhorne super-
vise the poetry department in the *Monthly Review*? Did not a
scandalous fellow, who has oppressed Mr. Smart these many
years, wait upon Mr. Griffiths, the editor, and complain that
Mr. Smart had been treated too mildly in a former review? Did
not the same scandalous fellow give money to Griffiths and
others as a bribe to make them defame Mr. Smart as much as
they dared? 'Whether, if this was not the Case, they do not act
their Mischief without Motive, and serve the Devil from
affection?' In his paranoid condition, Smart's latent hostility
to the critics boiled over. He became ridiculous, and was
probably thought to deserve the cool response from the *Monthly
Review* in their notice of his *Poems on Several Occasions*: 'he may
rest assured, that he will, for the future, have very little cause to
be offended with us'. Smart had begun his career with a fashionable, lighthearted, and healthy disdain for the modern critics.
But he ended his career with an insane hatred for the critics,
inseparable from his lust for unqualified praise and admiration.

But what of the critics he did respect and admire? I do not
mean to give here a detailed analysis of Smart's debt to each of
the critics listed in 'The Wholesale Critic and the Hop Merchant'—Aristotle, Longinus, Horace, Quintilian, Pope, and
Addison. But it may be helpful to add a few notes on the two
critics who seem to have played a particularly important part in
forming Smart's critical attitudes to literature—Horace among
the ancients, and Pope among the moderns.

Smart was always enthusiastic about 'that urbane and impec-
cable pagan, Quintus Horatius Flaccus', as Robert Brittain
calls him. He did an enormous amount of work on translating
Horace's writings—the prose version appeared in 1756, and the

verse in 1767. As well as these major works, Smart did several smaller translations and versions—such as his early pieces, 'To Lyce', a version of Book III, Ode XV, the *Horatian Canons of Friendship*, a version of Book I, Satire III, and 'To Mécænas', a translation of Book I, Ode I. Robert Brittain has already given in his edition of the *Poems by Christopher Smart*, a concise and lucid exposition of Smart's views on the Horatian *curiosa felicitas*, 'the lucky risk of the Horatian boldness', 'that unrivalled peculiarity of expression'. And Brittain has also commented on Smart's celebrated theory of 'impression' in poetry, as he expressed it in the Preface to the *Works of Horace, Translated into Verse*: '*Impression*, then, is a talent or gift of Almighty God, by which a Genius is impowered to throw an emphasis upon a word or sentence in such wise, that it cannot escape any reader of sheer good sense, and true critical sagacity. This power will sometimes keep it up thro' the *medium* of a prose translation; especially in scripture, for in justice to truth and everlasting preeminence, we must confess this virtue to be far more powerful and abundant in the sacred writtings [sic].' What is relevant to the present chapter, however, is the degree to which Horace influenced Smart's views on critics and criticism.

We have already referred to 'The Wholesale Critic and the Hop Merchant', and Smart's definition of the task of the critic as basically one of understanding: the critic must 'unfold' the mysteries of the work he is reading. In his Preface to the *Works of Horace*, Smart puts forward the same view: 'It is the indispensable business of a skilful editor to discover the drift of his author's intention, when there are sufficient materials for that purpose.' In his fable, Smart has space only to theorize about the rôle of the critic. In his Preface, he has the opportunity to put his own theory into practice, and does so by interpreting the first part of Horace's *Art of Poetry* in a new way. 'I come now to a piece of classical history, which seems to have been a secret to all the commentators of *Horace* from the beginning, and yet I make no doubt, but the fact I am about to insist upon, will shortly be as evident to the Reader as it is to me.' Smart's discovery of Horace's intention is this, that Horace was setting out deliberately to ridicule Ovid's *Metamorphoses*. Ovid's work may have been 'beautiful for music and painting', but it was lacking in several major ways. When we recall how Smart's own poetry was often eulogistic and brimming over with gratitude to God and man, it comes as no surprise to find that according to Smart, Horace disapproved of Ovid because his work neither expressed gratitude, nor rewarded merit, nor promoted moral edification. And when we remember that Smart shared the conventional viewpoint of his age, that poetry should 'follow nature', it is no surprise to find that Smart and Horace censure Ovid for being decidedly unnatural: 'The *Metamorphoses* are made up of incredible prodigies, and impossible transformations, ever shocking common sense and seducing imagination into a wilderness of fruitless perplexities. Poetry and nature ought never to be set at a distance, but when a writer is summoned to such a task by real miracles and divine transcendency.' If we agree that some weight should be given to Smart's own ideas of the grounds upon which his poetry should be judged 'good' or 'bad', we are given several leads here. We must be ready to interpret Smart's more obscure intentions in his poetry. We must be prepared to praise his work when in faultlessly 'follows nature'. And if we are prepared to go all the way with Smart, we must commend his work when it expresses gratitude, rewards merit, and promotes moral edification.

In his comments on critics made during the course of his poetry, Smart constantly deplores their prejudices and ill-nature, their determination to damn a work ever before reading it. Eventually, as we have seen, Smart began to interpret the general ill-will of the critics as specifically directed at himself, and in this paranoid state of mind, he forestalls the kind of hostile comment that he feared so dreadfully: 'I must confess myself to the reader', he wrote in the Preface to the *Works of Horace*, 'that, tho' I presume upon the whole, he shall meet with entertainment and information, yet he will find but too many opportunities of exercising his candour and humanity by the faults, which shall occur. Good-nature is the grace of God in grain, and so much the characteristic of an *English-man*, that I hope every one deserving such a name will think it somewhat hard, if a gentleman derived from ancestors, who have abode on their own Lordship six hundred years in the County Palatine of *Durham*, should have been reduced in a manner by necessity to a work of this kind, which if done in a state, he had more reason to be satisfied with, had been more likely to have given satisfaction.' It is rather unfortunate that while he is appealing to the good-nature of his readers, Smart himself should obliquely indulge in rancour. While writing this pathetic plea for kindness, he was obviously thinking bitterly of his cousin, Francis Smart, and the way he had cut Christopher, his heir-at-law, out of his will in favour of other relations, Richard, Louisa, and John Smart. Smart was therefore indicating how little hope he had of ever inheriting the family estates at Snotterton on Staindrop Moor.[6] But in his Preface, Smart does give an example of a fair and unprejudiced view of another author's work. He quotes Horace's criticisms of Ovid's *Metamorphoses* with evident approval. But this does not mean that he cannot appreciate the merits of Ovid's works. 'After all we must admit that *Horace* was rather hard upon *Ovid*, who, tho his inferior with regard to some things, was altogether a better man in others, and his works, with all their defects, have justly intitled him to the *praise*, as his hardships have in a manner endeared him, to the *affection* of posterity.' As Smart wrote in 'The Snake, the Goose, and the Nightingale', he revered the critic's rod when 'just to blame, yet fix'd to praise'. As he was ready to 'blame' Ovid when it seemed just to do so, so we have the right to point out weaknesses in Smart's poetry—provided that we take into account what he intended to accomplish in his work, and provided we pay some attention to the criteria by which Smart himself wanted his work to be judged. We must at least do Smart the justice of being ready or 'fix'd' to praise his poetry.

As has already been noted, Smart was actually invited by Pope to translate the *Essay on Criticism* into Latin, and Smart's version was duly published in his *Poems on Several Occasions* (1752), side by side with Pope's English. The mental discipline involved in turning Pope's essay into Latin must have meant that Smart acquired an intimate knowledge of Pope's views on criticism, and it is possible to suggest various ways in which Smart later expressed Pope's views in his own poetry. We have

[6] See W. H. Bond, 'Christopher Smart's Last Years', *Times Literary Supplement*, 10th April 1953, 237.

already looked at 'The Wholesale Critic and the Hop Merchant', and Smart's attack on the folly of criticizing ten volumes after reading only one page. His moral is, that it is stupidly wrongheaded to try judging literature by the same techniques that a hop merchant uses for evaluating his goods. As Smart comments sarcastically, he knows many a learned brother 'Who weighs one science by another,/And makes 'mongst bards poetic schism,/Because he understands the prism' (*Collected Poems*, i. 57). Smart is making a point that Pope had made in the *Essay on Criticism* (ll. 263–66):

> Most Criticks, fond of some subservient Art,
> Still make the *Whole* depend upon a *Part*,
> They talk of *Principles*, but Notions prize,
> And All to one lov'd Folly Sacrifice.[7]

It is likely also that another of Smart's fables, 'The Blockhead and the Beehive', was sparked off by the *Essay on Criticism*. Smart's Blockhead, Squire Booby, is a busy prattling chatterer, always talking, always parading his learning: 'I am a scholar every inch,/And know each author I lay fist on,/From Archimedes down to Whiston' (*Collected Poems*, i. 71). Squire Booby's literary ancestor seems to be one of Pope's 'mad, abandon'd *Criticks*':

> The Bookful Blockhead, ignorantly read,
> With *Loads* of *Learned Lumber* in his Head,
> With his own Tongue still edifies his Ears,
> And always *List'ning to Himself* appears.
> All Books he reads, and all he reads assails,
> From *Dryden's Fables* down to *Durfey's Tales*.
>   (ll. 612–17)

And just as Smart, with heavy-handed irony, allows his Blockhead to assert that Jobson is a Machiavel and Hardwicke's judgement fails, so Pope's Blockhead is allowed to make the false claim that '*Garth* did not write his own *Dispensary*' (l. 619).

Smart also shared with Pope one of the most familiar aesthetic dicta of the age, that the poet must be judged according to how far he has 'followed nature' in depicting human emotions. 'First follow NATURE, and your Judgment frame/By her just Standard,

---

[7] All quotations from Pope's works in this book are taken from the *The Poems of Alexander Pope*, one-volume Twickenham edition, 1965.

which is still the same', wrote Pope, and he went on to point out that the ancient rules of poetry were discovered rather than devised, and that the ancient poetry was still 'nature', although nature methodized. The true poet has an instinctive 'Happiness' of style which counterpoints his careful following of the correct aesthetic rules:

> If, where the *Rules* not far enough extend,
> (Since Rules were made but to promote their End)
> Some Lucky LICENCE answers to the full
> Th'Intent propos'd, *that Licence* is a *Rule.*
> Thus *Pegasus*, a nearer way to take,
> May boldly deviate from the common Track.
> Great Wits sometimes may *gloriously offend,*
> And *rise* to *Faults* true Criticks *dare not mend;*
> From *vulgar Bounds* with *brave Disorder* part,
> And *snatch* a *Grace* beyond the Reach of Art,
> Which, without passing thro' the *Judgment*, gains
> The *Heart*, and all its End *at once* attains.
>
> (ll. 146–57)

As young Maro discovered, '*Nature* and *Homer* were, he found, the *same*' (l. 135). Smart felt the same about Shakespeare. In *An Occasional Prologue and Epilogue to Othello*, Smart thinks he sees with Fancy's magic eye the shade of Shakespeare in yon azure sky, and begs his audience to behold the bard on yon high cloud advance 'Grasping all Nature with a single Glance' (*Collected Poems*, i. 94). And in the 'Prologue' to *A Trip to Cambridge*, Smart repeats Pope's dictum that Great Wits may snatch a grace beyond the reach of art—a grace which bypasses the judgement and gains the heart:

> Fools who personate what Homer should have done,
> Like tattling watches they correct the sun.
> Critics, like posts, undoubtedly may show
> The way to Pindus, but they cannot go.
> Whene'er immortal Shakespeare's works are read,
> He wins the heart before he strikes the head.
> Swift to the soul the piercing image flies,
> Swifter than *Harriot's* wit, or *Harriot's* eyes;
> Swifter than some romantic traveller's thought;
> Swifter than British fire when *William* fought.

Fancy precedes, and conquers all the mind;
Deliberating judgment slowly comes behind;
Comes to the field with blunderbus and gun,
Like heavy *Falstaff*, when the work is done.
Fights when the battle's o'er with wondrous pain,
By Shrewsbury's clock, and nobly slays the slain.
(*Collected Poems*, i. 91)

We, as readers and critics of Smart's poetry, have here a surprising lesson in how we should best approach his work. If we are to appreciate the *Song to David* as Smart wanted us to do, we should be willing to respond with the 'heart' rather than the 'head'. One feels that Smart would have sympathized with those nineteenth-century critics who rhapsodized indiscriminately over the splendours of the *Song to David*. It is a consolation to the twentieth-century critic, however, that Smart also expected the good critic to 'set each brilliant thought in gold'—which gives us permission to try unravelling the meanings and techniques in Smart's more difficult poetry.

[IV]

The Secular Poetry

THE FIRST THREE CHAPTERS of this book have been something in the nature of an introduction to a detailed study of the poetry of Christopher Smart. We have looked at Smart's personality in some detail: if we are going to understand the changes of mood and technique in his work, we must try to understand the man who suffered a mental breakdown, but still went on writing. We have looked at some of Smart's own ideas about his rôle as a poet, in order to understand his relationship to his readers—how he entertained them as a jester, or courted them as a sycophant. Then we looked at Smart's own views on reason and imagination and literary criticism, so that if we criticize his poetry we can at least take into account the kind of standards by which Smart himself wished his work to be judged. We now move on to a more detailed study of his work.

If we ever read Smart's secular poetry for its own sake, we are likely to be amused by his sense of humour, and we may even admire his technical mastery over a variety of poetic forms and genres. But we realize also that his secular work is not particularly 'valuable' from a purely literary point of view. It is, however, invaluable in providing a background to the much greater religious poetry. For the earlier poetry, however commonplace it may be when we relate it to the literary conventions of the time, grew out of the same imagination that later fostered the more abnormal religious poetry. The earlier verse, cheerful and charming as it so often is, can be read for pleasure provided we do not take it too seriously. But read as a background to the religious poetry, the secular verse can give us a great deal of information about the literary traditions in which the poet of *Jubilate Agno* and *A Song to David* was fostered, and about the intellectual traditions in which his brilliant but unstable mind was formed.

One of Smart's tributes to the Father of English poetry was 'Chaucer's "Recantation"', first published anonymously in the *Student* on the 30th June 1750, '*As it is sung at the* SPRING GARDENS VAUX HALL *with great applause.*' Smart did not attempt to use Middle English, but simply adopted the Chaucerian themes of mutability and the inconstancy of women. He expressed himself with tongue-in-cheek humour, claiming that while the world's grown mutable and mad, women at least are miracles of steadfastness, 'And every witty pretty dame/Bears for her motto—still *the same*' (*Collected Poems*, i.107). It has not been generally recognized that Smart probably did try his hand at imitating Chaucer's wit in Middle English. The poem in question appeared in Fielding's *Covent-Garden Journal* on the 23rd June 1752, an issue which included also 'Lovely Jenny Weston', a poem usually attributed to Smart.[1] The Chaucerian poem appeared under a covering letter: '*SIR*, PErhaps your Readers will not be displeased with the Sight of the following Poem, when they are told it was written by that ancient and venerable Bard, *Dan Jeffry Chaucer*: How it came into my Hands is another Question: All I hope at present is, that the *fayre Maydens* will take fair warning from this good Counsel; or in other Words, that they will first take some Pains to read, and some more to practise.—Without further Ceremony, *I am, &c.*' The poem itself, 'A Pleasaunt Balade Or, Advice to the Fayre Maydens', went as follows:

> LIsthnith, Ladies, to youre oldè Frende:
> If yee be fayre, be fayre to sum gode Ende.
> For Gallants rath or late must loken out
> For thilk same Yoke, so ese out of Dout,
> Yclepid Marriage: Yet sootly Weman be,
> *Malum per accidens vel malum per se,*
> As lerned Clerkes saie; this Latin is,
> Ladies, tht yee al bene Mannis chefe Blis.

---

[1] See Wilbur L. Cross, *The History of Henry Fielding*, New Haven and London, 1918, ii. 381–82, and Arthur Sherbo, 'The Case for Internal Evidence (1) Can *Mother Midnight's Comical Pocket-Book* be Attributed to Christopher Smart?', 378–79.

And as a Wife is Mannis helpe and Comfort,
His Paradise, his Solace, and Disport;
So pardie, is Man Woman's chefe Stay,
Harknith then, Dames, to my moral Lay:
Ne stand ye *shill I, shall I;* 'tis childis Play:
Eke dangerous, sings the Saw, is all Delay.
Now listnith to my Similitude,
Gode is the Moral, tho' the Rime be rude.
   Where Medway's Stremes meandring, flowen wyde,
There many a Sole, and many a Made abyde:
(Tho' on the Banks, God wot, few *Mades* doe walk,
And fewer *Soles*, that think rite wel and talk.)
Now thilke same Mades, fresh broughten to the Chepe,
Are rated high; but little can they kepe:
Down fals the Price. *Ah! benedicite!*
Who bies my Mades? Ne one, ne tway, ne three;
So handled they bene, by my Father's Kin,
The *Mades* wont sell, they are not worth a Pin.[2]

Jensen suggests that Fielding himself might have done this poem in a spirit of burlesque. It is 'a very poor imitation of Middle English verse with regard to spelling and vocabulary, but a very clever reproduction of the spirited wit of Chaucer in a waggish, mock-serious mood.'[3] But it seems to me just as likely that Smart wrote the poem. It is notable that it is set 'Where Medway's Stremes meandring, flowen wyde' (the silver Medway flows through the verses on Smart's Kentish hop-garden). A more important point is that one of the footnotes to the poem explains that a 'made' is a species of fish as well as a virgin. The pun on 'made' is found also in *Jubilate Agno* B1.139, in a section devoted to fish: 'Let Mary rejoice with the Maid—blessed be the name of the immaculate CONCEPTION.' When we place the Chaucerian skit beside the mad *Jubilate Agno*, perhaps we gain some insight into the metamorphosis of Smart's sense of humour, from the light-hearted punning of secular jesting to the insane

[2] *The Covent-Garden Journal*, ed. Jensen, ii. 37–38.
[3] *Ibid.*, ii.237. Cross, *History of Henry Fielding*, ii. 282–83, points out that nowhere else does Fielding give the slightest evidence of any first-hand acquaintance with Chaucer—in the list of the world's great humourists in *Tom Jones*, the name of Chaucer is conspicuous for its absence. Cross states that the author of 'The Pleasaunt Balade' must have read Chaucer in Urry's edition.

punning of religious madness, from *risqué* jokes about virginity
to mad jokes about the Virgin Mary?

Smart's knowledge of medieval poetry seems to have been
limited, but he had more than a passing acquaintance with the
greater poets of the sixteenth century. In 'The Hop-Garden',
he mentions Sir Philip Sidney—with characteristic humility:

> Oh! cou'd I emulate Dan Sydney's Muse,
> Thy Sydney, Cantium—He, from court retir'd,
> In Penshurst's sweet Elysium sung delight,
> Sung transport to the soft-responding streams
> Of Medway, and enliven'd all her groves:
> While ever near him, goddess of the green,
> Fair Pembroke sat and smil'd immense applause.
> (*Collected Poems*, i. 142–43)

Smart's admiration for Sidney does not seem to have radically
affected his literary style. The idiom of 'The Hop-Garden' is
obviously much more indebted to Milton than to Sidney. But
the quotation is interesting from another angle, since it shows
that Smart was already using the turn of phrase that we usually
associate with the later religious poetry. When Smart was
writing this very early verse, the Countess of Pembroke already
'smil'd immense applause'—a foretaste of such lines as *Jubilate
Agno* B1.233, 'For applause or the clapping of hands is the
natural action of a man on the descent of the glory of God', or
stanza XX in the *Song to David*:

> Of man—the semblance and effect
> Of God and Love—the Saint elect
>   For infinite applause—
> To rule the land, and briny broad,
> To be laborious in his laud,
>   And heroes in his cause.

Despite his delight in the *Arcadia*, Smart felt too inexperienced
to imitate Sidney. If he had been given Sidney's poetic powers,
he too would have written on noble themes, 'The high achievements of thy warrior kings'. His enjoyment of Sidney's chivalric
tales is reiterated in 'A Noon-Piece', where Smart's sensual
delight in the coral lips and parting breasts of Harriot Pratt is
associated in his mind with a retreat to Daphne's thickest shade:

> There read Sidney's high-wrought stories
> Of ladies charms, and heroes glories;
> Thence fir'd, the sweet narration act,
> And kiss the fiction into fact.
> *(Collected Poems, i. 102)*

Smart also admired Edmund Spenser's chivalry. In the 'Secular Ode on the Jubilee at Pembroke College, Cambridge, in 1743', he showed his respect, and imitated the Spenserian diction:

> BUT chiefly thou, *Dan Spencer*, peerless bard,
> Sith in these pleasaunt groves you 'gan devise,
> Of Red-cross knight, and virtue's high reward,
> And here first plann'd thy works of vast emprize . . .
> *(Collected Poems, i. 3–4)*

Although Smart's admiration for Sidney and Spenser had only a sporadic influence on his literary style, it may well be that the *Arcadia* and *The Faerie Queen* had a lasting effect on his imagination—and that the chivalric ideals expressed in *Jubilate Agno* were in fact psychotic variations on his early enthusiasm for the sixteenth-century poets: 'For I have the blessing of God in the three POINTS of manhood, of the pen, of the sword, & of chivalry' *(Jubilate Agno* B1.129). Otherwise, Spenser's influence on Smart's poetry seems restricted to a few isolated references, such as in 'The Hop-Garden' where great Nature exerts her sway from Colin Clout to Emperors, and in 'A Noon-Piece', where the faithful dog, Tray, guards the dumplings and whey while the farm labourers, 'Collin Clout and *Yorkshire* Will/From the leathern flasket swill' *(Collected Poems,* i.102).

We have already seen, in a former chapter, that Smart was conventionally enthusiastic about Shakespeare. We may well flinch when the disreputable Mrs. Deodata Quane reappears on the stage after the tragic climax of *Othello*, and proceeds to harangue the audience with all the insensibility of an eighteenth century Desdemona, 'TRUE Woman to the last—my *peroration*/ I come to speak in spight of Suffocation' *(Collected Poems,* i. 95). But allowing for the limitations of the age in which he lived, we know that Smart sincerely admired Shakespeare. 'Grasping all Nature with a single Glance'. Shakespearian allusions and half-remembered quotations are scattered through Smart's secular

poetry. In the 'Prologue' to *A Trip to Cambridge*, Smart refers to
Henry IV, and how Falstaff comes to the battlefield 'By
Shrewsbury's clock' and how he 'nobly slays the slain.' In
'Lovely Harriote' (printed in the *Midwife* in 1751 as '*A* Crambo
SONG *by Mrs.* Midnight'*s Nephew*'), Smart compares himself with
Othello. If the adored Harriot Pratt is ever cruel enough to
admit another suitor, 'I rave like *Shakespeare's* jealous *Moor*, |And
am, as ranting *Barry* hot' (*Collected Poems*, i. 189). Having
identified himself with Othello, it is logical that Smart's
favourite enemy should be identified with Iago. In editing 'The
Wholesale Critic and the Hop Merchant', Christopher Hunter
offered an unexpected piece of pedantry when he annotated the
description of Critic Catchup ('Who like Iago, arch on all,/Is
nothing, if not critical') with a reference to *Othello* II. v, 'O,
gentle lady, do not put me to't,/For I am nothing if not
critical.' In 'To the Rev. Mr. P[owel]l' (first printed in the
third volume of the *Midwife* in 1753), Smart teases his voluble
friend who was evidently fond of long-winded grumbles about
Welsh politics and the penury of the clergy: 'A Horse!—my
Kingdom for a Horse!' (*Collected Poems*, i. 206). Several references to the Shakespearian drama are to be found in Smart's
'Epilogue' to Arthur Murphy's *The Apprentice* (1756). Smart
was well-known in theatrical circles, and familiar with plays
like Mrs. Clive's *The Rehearsal, or Bayes in Petticoats* (1753), or
William Congreve's *The Mourning Bride*, or Colley Cibber and
Sir John Vanbrugh's *The Provok'd Husband, or a Journey to
London*. But after alluding to these plays in the 'Epilogue',
Smart gave a light-hearted warning to all the milliners in the
audience who were fascinated by 'our tinsel train', and longed
to tread the boards of Drury Lane,

> And fain wou'd fill the fair *Ophelia's* place.
> And in her cock'd up hat, and gown of camblet,
> Presumes on something—*touching the lord Hamlet*.
>
>   *   *   *   *
>
> In short, we've girls enough for all the fellows,
> The ranting, whining, starting, and the jealous,
> The *Hotspurs, Romeos, Hamlets*, and *Othellos*.
>   (*Collected Poems*, i. 97)

But ye royal milliners, ye giddy things, are given the stern advice that 'A shop with virtue, is the height of bliss.'

Shakespeare had a more indirect influence on Smart's style, as can be seen in 'A Noon-Piece', where Smart invites Harriot Pratt to sit 'On a bank of fragrant thyme'. He is obviously remembering the bank whereon the wild thyme blows in *A Midsummer Night's Dream*. Titania's bank ,'Quite over-canopied with lush woodbine' appears again in Smart's 'Sweet William' (printed in the *Student* on the 30th July 1750): 'BY a prattling stream, on a midsummer's eve,/Where the woodbine and jess'-mine their boughs interweave . . .' (*Collected Poems*, i. 109). In the 'Verses written in a London Church-yard' (printed in the *Midwife* in 1751), which has been attributed to Smart,[4] there is a Shakesperian tribute to the charms of 'lovely *Jenny*', a cook in a chop-house. The poet's description of his mistress, with her hair brown as the walnut and her cheeks blooming like red cabbage, rather resembles Shakespeare's in Sonnet CXXX, 'If hairs be wires, black wires grow on her head'. The final stanza on Jenny is a deliberate parody of *Romeo and Juliet* III. ii:

> Give me my Romeo: and, when he shall die,
> Take him and cut him out in little stars,
> And he will make the face of heaven so fine
> That all the world will be in love with night,
> And pay no worship to the garish sun.

> And when at length the Beauty dies,
> Oh! cut her into little Pies!
> Like Jelly-stars she'll grace the Skies,
>   So bright is lovely *Jenny*.

In other poems, the Shakesperian echo is slight, but nevertheless loud enough to be heard in the rhythms of Smart's verse. 'Idleness', one of Smart's earliest poems (printed anonymously in the *Gentleman's Magazine* in May 1745 with music by William Boyce), is reminiscent of Hamlet's soliloquy, 'To be, or not to be':

---

[4] Cross, *History of Henry Fielding*, ii. 382. Cross compares the 'Verses written in a London Church-yard' with a similar poem, 'Lovely Jenny Weston' which appeared in the *Covent-Garden Journal*, 23rd June 1752. Sherbo, 'Can *Mother Midnight's Comical Pocket-Book* be Attributed to Christopher Smart?', 378–79, agrees with Cross's attribution of 'Lovely Jenny Weston' to Smart. Both poems are printed in full in Appendix I of this book.

> For thee, O Idleness, the woes
>   Of life we patiently endure,
> Thou art the source whence labour flows,
>   We shun thee but to make thee sure.
>
> For who'd sustain war's toil and waste,
>   Or who th'hoarse thund'ring of the sea,
> But to be idle at the last,
>   And find a pleasing end in thee.
>   (*Collected Poems*, i. 119)

The form of Smart's rhetorical question recalls Hamlet's query:
who would bear the whips and scorns of time but for the dread
of something after death? And Smart's 'hoarse thund'ring of
the sea' recalls Shakespeare's 'sea of troubles'. But where
Hamlet finds the 'end' in suicide, Smart finds the end more
facetiously in idleness and 'sweet insensibility'.

It is thus in the syntax and rhythm of Smart's early verse that
we often catch the echo of his poetic heritage. He could have
been listening to Shakespeare when he wrote his youthful poem,
'Idleness'; alternatively he could have been half-listening to
Matthew Prior, and catching his similar rhetorical note:

> WHO would, says Dryden, Drink this draught of Life
> Blended with bitter Woes and tedious Strife
> But that an Angel in Some Lucky hour
> Does healing Drops into the Goblet pour?[5]

It is not an important point, except in so far as it brings home
to us the fact that it is against a background of traditional
syntax and rhythms that we read Smart's work. In reading
Smart's earlier work, we recognize the allusions to William
Shakespeare or Matthew Prior, and accept it as the legitimate
offspring of the English poetic tradition. But in the later work,
particularly in *Jubilate Agno*, we listen in vain for such echoes.
It is a measure of its estrangement from the sane literary conventions of the eighteenth century, as it is a measure of Smart's
insanity, that the echoes of Chaucer, Shakespeare, Prior and
the rest are so few and far between in *Jubilate Agno*.

We can go further in tracing the poetic ancestors who
dominated Smart's early verse, but who suddenly lost their

[5] *Literary Works of Matthew Prior*, i. 159.

influence once he went mad. Smart would surely have experienced an ecstasy of flattered gratitude if he had sensed that Browning was going to place him on a pedestal 'for once on either hand/With Milton and with Keats'. For Milton was his idol, as indeed he was the idol of the eighteenth century. Smart set out in 'The Hop-Garden' to teach in verse Miltonian, and he went so far as to imitate the syntax of the first paragraph of *Paradise Lost* in the first paragraph of his own poem, delaying his subject and verb, 'I teach in verse Miltonian' until line 7, and thus outdoing Milton himself, who delayed 'Sing Heav'nly Muse' until line 6. Throughout his poem, Smart imitated Milton's polysyllables, substituting a Latin vision of Kent for Adam's vision of all Earth's Kingdoms and their glory, Cambalu, seat of Cathaian Can, and Samarchand by Oxus, Temir's Throne, and Paquin of Sinæan Kings, and thence to Agra and Lahor of great Mogul . . . (*Paradise Lost*, XI.381–91):

> Whether you shiver in the marshy Weald,
> Egregious shepherds of unnumber'd flocks,
> Whose fleeces, poison'd into purple, deck
> All Europe's kings: or in fair Madum's vale
> Imparadis'd, blest denizens, ye dwell;
> Or Dorovernia's awful tow'rs ye love:
> Or plough Tunbridgia's salutiferous hills
> Industrious, and with draughts chalybiate heal'd,
> Confess divine Hygeia's blissful seat
>
>   (*Collected Poems*, i. 143)

When we find such an elaborate Miltonic disguise for Maidstone, Canterbury, and Tunbridge Wells, we cannot help agreeing with T. S. Eliot's opinion, 'There is more of Milton's influence in the badness of the bad verse of the eighteenth century than of anybody's else'.[6]

Smart's admiration for Milton's work was not confined to *Paradise Lost*. In the Preface to his 'Ode for Musick on Saint Cecilia's Day', he described the 'St. Cecilia' Odes by Dryden and Pope as '*incomparably beautiful and great; neither is there to be found two more finish'd pieces of Lyric Poetry in our language,* L'allegro *and* Il penseroso *of Milton excepted, which are the finest in any.*'

---

[6] *Selected Prose*, Harmondsworth, 1958, 123.

Smart showed his admiration for 'L'Allegro' in a characteristic
way—by making a Latin translation of it, and including it in
his *Poems on Several Occasions* (1752). The rhythms of 'L'Allegro',
which Smart made no attempt to imitate in his Latin version,
emerged however in his own poetry. 'Come, and trip it as you
go', with the personifications of Care and Laughter, Liberty and
Mirth, obviously influenced the dance rhythms of Smart's 'A
Morning Piece Or an hymn for the hay-makers', printed in the
London Magazine in 1748, together with its companion pieces, 'A
Noon-Piece' and 'A Night-Piece Or, Modern Philosophy':

> Now the rural graces three
> Dance beneath yon maple tree;
> First the vestal Vitue, known
> By her adamantine zone;
> Next to her in rosy pride,
> Sweet Society the bride;
> Last Honesty, full seemly drest
> In her cleanly home-spun vest.
> (*Collected Poems*, i. 100)

'Il Penseroso' influenced Smart's conventional image of himself
as 'poetically pensive' in 'To the King', and 'full pensive' in
'The Hop-Garden'. In 'A Night-Piece', Smart made more
original use of Milton's poem. The scene in 'A Night-Piece'
(' 'TWAS when bright Cynthia with her silver car,/Soft stealing
from Endymion's bed') is similar to Milton's in 'Il Penseroso'
('While *Cynthia* checks her Dragon yoke/Gently ore th'accus-
tomed Oke'). Milton's pensive man rejects the vain deluding
joys of this world, the 'toys' that dwell in idle brains; instead, he
welcomes divinest Melancholy and walks unseen on the smooth-
shaven grass, contemplating Plato, and finally falling into 'the
dewy-feathered Sleep', waking only to hear magnificent organ
music which sends him into ecstasies. Smart's pensive man,
Sophron the wise, likewise lies down, beneath a plantain's
melancholy shade, while others toil in the town, 'Fond of
trifles, fond of toys'. Sophron, imitating Il Penseroso, welcomes
sacred Wisdom and fairest Virtue. But at this point, Smart
twists the narrative, and Sophron is revealed as a 'modern'
rather than Miltonic philosopher, a debauched version of
Milton's solemn young man:

> His speculations thus the sage begun,
>> When, lo! the neighbouring bell
> In solemn sound struck one:—
>> He starts—and recollects—he was engag'd to Nell.
> Then up he sprang nimble and light,
>> And rapp'd at fair Elenor's door;
> He laid aside Virtue that night,
>> And next morn por'd in Plato for more.
>>>> (*Collected Poems*, i. 104)

In view of the erotic pleasures described in 'A Noon-Piece' and elsewhere, it seems unlikely that Smart disapproved of Sophron. Presumably, Smart was parodying Milton in order to make fun of his high-minded pomposity—just as he parodied Shakespeare's romantic whimsy by substituting Jenny from the chophouse for Juliet.

Although Smart found 'Il Penseroso' rather pompous, it certainly influenced his religious poetry. There is a striking parallel between Milton's description of the Gothic church in 'Il Penseroso' and Smart's description of the domed cathedral in *On the Goodness of the Supreme Being*. Smart seems to have been deliberately substituting Milton's experience of Old St. Paul's[7] with his own experience of Wren's St. Paul's:[8]

[7] Kenneth Clark, *The Gothic Revival*, 3rd ed., 1962, 28–29, refers to Thomas Warton's note on 'Il Penseroso' in his edition of *Milton's Early Poems* (1785): 'Old St. Paul's Cathedral . . . appears to have been a most stately and venerable pattern of the Gothick style. Milton was educated at St. Paul's School, contiguous to the church; and thus became impressed with an early reverence for the solemnities of the ancient ecclesiastical architecture, its vaults, shrines, iles, pillars, and painted glass.'

[8] Smart refers to St. Paul's Cathedral elsewhere in his work. In the *Midwife* for September 1751 there was 'A Letter from the Whispering-Gallery in St. Paul's, to Mrs. Mary Midnight', and in the same issue there was an appeal for charity for Mrs. Sarah Rowden, Senior Organist at St. Paul's Cathedral, who is to be seen under the organ loft pressing down several pieces of timber (Mrs. Midnight imagines a contest between Goody Rowden and Handel—the musician jigging his fingers with total suspension of sound and Goody Rowden peeping out and asking 'Where are ye now?'). *Jubilate Agno* B1.136 presumably refers to St. Paul's Cathedral, 'Let Paul rejoice with the Seale, who is pleasant & faithfull, like God's good ENGLISHMAN. For I paid for my seat in St PAUL's, when I was six years old, & took possession against the evil day.' In Hymn XIII in the *Hymns and Spiritual Songs*, Smart writes that the 'Bluecap builds his stately dome', and implicitly compares the nest with the roof of St. Paul's Cathedral, 'Great to-day thy song and rapture/In the choir of Christ and WREN'. 'Taste' in the *Hymns for the Amusement of Children* is illustrated by a woodcut of St. Paul's.

But let my due feet never fail
To walk the studious Cloisters pale,
And love the high embowed Roof,
With antic Pillars massy proof,
And storied Windows richly dight,
Casting a dimm religious light;
There let the pealing Organ blow,
To the full voic't Quire below,
In Service high, and Anthems clear,
As may with sweetness, through mine ear,
Dissolve me into exstasies,
And bring all Heav'n before mine eyes.[9]

        . . . for hark the organs blow
Their swelling notes round the cathedral's dome,
And grace th'harmonious choir, celestial feast
To pious ears, and med'cine of the mind;
The thrilling trebles and the manly base
Join in accordance meet, and with one voice
All to the sacred subject suit their song.
While in each breast sweet melancholy reigns
Angelically pensive, till the joy
Improves and purifies;—the solemn scene
The Sun through storied panes surveys with awe,
And bashfully with-holds each bolder beam.
                       (*Collected Poems*, i. 242)

During the course of his poetry, Smart made occasional references to some of Milton's contemporaries. In his 'Ode for
Musick on Saint Cecilia's Day', for instance, he referred to
Edmund Waller, sick with love, striking impetuous notes from
within a hoary, moss-grown cell. In 'An Invitation to Mrs.
Tyler' (printed in the *Gentleman's Magazine* in July 1754), he
began 'HAD I the pen of sir John Suckling, |And could find out a
rhyme for duckling . . .' (*Collected Poems*, i. 208), thus making a
humorous reference to the double and trisyllable rhymes which
make his verse epistles to Mrs. Tyler, the Rev. Morgan Powell,
and Dr. Nares, so amusing—rhymes which Coleridge defined
as 'a lower species of wit and attended to exclusively for their
own sake may become a source of momentary amusement: as

---

[9] *Milton's Poems*, ed. B. A. Wright, 1959, 37.

in poor Smart's distich to the Welch 'Squire who had promised him a hare'.[10]

Smart greatly admired the work of Milton's younger contemporary, John Dryden. He praised 'Alexander's Feast' as 'incomparably beautiful and great', and it was simply a measure of his growing maturity and relative self-confidence that he was able to qualify this praise. Smart thought that the outstanding feature of the Pindaric Ode should be *'the vehemence of sudden and unlook'd-for transitions: hence chiefly it derives that enthusiastic fire and wildness, which greatly distinguish it from other species of Poesy.'* He felt that Dryden's design was too unified for a Pindaric Ode—he must have been referring to the way in which the various emotions of grief, pity, and love, are linked by a strong narrative thread, as Timotheus the musician responds to Alexander's changing moods. Smart tries to do better than Dryden in his own 'Ode on Saint Cecilia's Day', as he changes without warning from 'some sad, some plaintive ditty' to the martial pomp of kettle-drums, trumpet, and horn, in an attempt to capture the 'sudden transitions' of a 'true Pindaric Ode'. Smart criticized Dryden for other reasons too. 'Alexander's Feast' contains lines which are far removed from the majesty of an Ode, though they could well figure in a ballad:

> *Happy, happy, happy Pair!*
> *None but the Brave,*
> *None but the Brave,*
> *None but the Brave deserves the Fair.*[11]

In his own 'Ode on Saint Cecilia's Day', Smart tried to avoid 'low' expressions, and although his efforts to sustain a sublime note throughout his poem led him into the absurdities of rococo imagery, he also managed to write a few lines that hint at the power he was eventually to display in *A Song to David*. We may well ridicule the image of the patriot muse mounting Bellona's brazen car, attended by the terrific maid, Harmony, arrayed in martial pomp, and wielding sword, target, and lance. But the image of Amphitrite's Dolphin prefigures stanza XXIV in *A Song to David*:

[10] *Biographia Literaria*, ed. George Watson, 1956, 207.
[11] *Dryden's Poems*, ed. Bonamy Dobrée, 1958, 25.

> Pleas'd to obey, the beauteous monster flies,
>   And on his scales as the gilt sun-beams play,
> Ten thousand variegated dies
>   In copious streams of lustre rise,
> Rise o'er the level main and signify his way
>   (*Collected Poems*, i. 139)

> Of fishes—ev'ry size and shape,
> Which nature frames of light escape,
>   Devouring man to shun:
> The shells are in the wealthy deep,
> The shoals upon the surface leap,
>   And love the glancing sun.
>   (*Collected Poems*, i. 353–54)

The same poetic sensibility is at work in both these verses, which
illustrate the development of Smart's skill during the twenty
years that passed between the composition of the 'Ode on Saint
Cecilia's Day' and *A Song to David*. In the quotation from the
'Ode on Saint Cecilia's Day', Smart is trying to describe how
the observer can see the path of the leaping fish by the movement of light across the sea. In the second quotation, from
A Song to David, he is trying to do much the same thing, but the
development of his lyrical skill means that he is able to achieve
his aim with greater economy and vividness. In the first two
lines of stanza XXIV of the *Song to David*, Smart is stating that
nature creates the fish from escaped light—the adjective 'escape'
qualifying 'light'. The use of the word 'escape', which looks
more like a verb than an adjective, imposes an additional
emphasis on the verb 'to shun' in the next line, and increases
the sense of speed that Smart is trying to convey in this stanza.
By identifying escaped light and the escaping fish, Smart
achieves a sensuous flash of movement. Added to this, the
word-order in the second line of the stanza gives an illusion of
double-meaning—the illusion which is the basis of multiple
meanings in lyrical poetry. The verb 'frames' is equivalent to
'makes' or 'creates', but the word-pattern superimposes the
phrase 'frames of light', where 'frames' appears to be a noun,
and the skeletons of the fish are seen to be composed of light.
It is a secondary meaning, produced by the syntax, directed

towards greater visual concreteness. The technique of the 'Ode on Saint Cecilia's Day' is elementary in comparison.

Smart's final objection to Dryden's Ode was that it ended too epigrammatically. Timotheus so ravishes Alexander's senses that the monarch 'Assumes the God . . . And seems to shake the Spheres'; St. Cecilia plays the organ so ravishingly that an angel comes down from heaven to stand beside her. Hence Dryden's pithy conclusion:

> Let old *Timotheus* yield the Prize,
> Or both divide the Crown:
> He rais'd a Mortal to the Skies;
> She drew an Angel down.[12]

Smart rejected such wit in such a majestic context, and chose to end his own 'Ode on Saint Cecilia's Day' on a characteristic note of eulogy, 'Thy pow'r shall last, thy bays shall bloom,/ When tongues shall cease, and worlds consume,/And all the tuneful spheres be mute' (*Collected Poems*, i. 142).

Smart greatly admired Alexander Pope's 'Ode for Musick, on St. Cecilia's Day'. We have seen how he made a Latin translation of the poem and sent it off to Pope himself. But when Smart published a second edition of his Latin translation in 1746, together with his own original 'Ode on Saint Cecilia's Day', he had no scruples about pointing out some of the flaws in Pope's poem. Pope, like Dryden, had planned his poem with a too exact unity of design for a true Pindaric Ode. Pope, like Dryden, included lines which could have figured in a ballad, but not in a majestic Ode:

> Thus Song could prevail
> O'er Death and o'er Hell,
> A Conquest how hard and how glorious?
> Tho' Fate had fast bound her
> With *Styx* nine times round her,
> Yet Musick and Love were Victorious.[13]

And Pope, like Dryden, ends his Ode with an epigram which Smart thinks is out of place in a solemn Ode:

[12] *Dryden's Poems*, 29.
[13] *The Poems of Alexander Pope*, 141.

Of *Orpheus* now no more let Poets tell,
To bright *Cecilia* greater Pow'r is giv'n;
His Numbers rais'd a Shade from Hell,
Hers lift the Soul to Heav'n.[14]

But when Smart compares Dryden and Pope, he shows how
much he admires both poets. If Dryden is greater than Pope,
writes Smart, it is in being more sublime, more magnificent,
with more of the fire and spirit of Pindar himself. If Pope is
greater than Dryden, it is in being more elegant and correct,
with more of the terseness and purity of Horace. (As Smart
expressed it in his 'Epithalamium', if he had 'sung like Pope,
without a word in vain,/Then should I hope my numbers might
contain,/Egregious nymph, thy boundless happiness'.) Despite
his criticisms of Dryden and Pope, and despite his determination to avoid their 'blemishes', Smart learned from both poets
when he composed his own 'Ode on Saint Cecilia's Day'. This
is apparent in Smart's use of onomatopoeia. His 'Wake, wake
the kettle-drum, prolong/The swelling trumpet's silver song' is
reminiscent of Dryden's martial passage, 'And rouze him, like
a rattling Peal of Thunder./Hark, hark, the horrid Sound', and
even more reminiscent of Pope's 'Let the loud Trumpet
sound,/Till the Roofs all around/The shrill Ecchos rebound'.
Smart's attempt to slow down the speed of a line of poetry
('And her breast, the throne of love,/Can hardly, hardly,
hardly move'), imitates Dryden's technique in 'Alexander's
Feast' ('Fallen, fallen, fallen, fallen,/Fallen from his high
Estate'), and Pope's similar technique in the 'Ode for Musick'
('The Strains decay,/And melt away/In a dying, dying Fall').

Once we become aware that Smart's earlier verse derived
from conventional poetic forms and genres, we begin to see
how even the strange convolutions of *Jubilate Agno* grew out of
the same traditions. In the 'Ode on Saint Cecilia's Day', Smart
states that 'Musick's a celestial art', and then goes on to express
musical sounds by the conventional techniques of vocatives and
onomatopoeia: 'Wake, wake the kettle-drum'. In *Jubilate Agno*,
Smart was perhaps consciously refining these techniques. 'For
the spiritual musick is as follows', begins Smart in *Jubilate Agno*
B2.584, and he seems to be imagining some vast organ, 'For

---

[14] *The Poems of Alexander Pope*, 142.

there is the thunder-stop, which is the voice of God direct'
(B2.585). The divine thunder and lightning in music and poetry
is a familiar idea in Smart's work, from its early expression in
the 'Ode on Saint Cecilia's Day', where the terrific maid,
Harmony, has 'thunder in her voice and lightning in her eyes',
to *Jubilate Agno* itself, where Smart writes, 'For THUNDER is the
voice of God direct in verse and musick. For LIGHTNING is a
glance of the glory of God' (B1.271, 272). Smart then seems to
go on with his description of the great organ, 'For the rest of the
stops are by their rhimes' (B2.586). As each stop is manipulated,
we hear the trumpet, shawm [oboe], harp, cymbal, flute,
dulcimer, clarinet, bassoon and pipe. It seems as if Smart is
trying to show that the stops of an organ are equivalent to
rhymes in poetry, in that they adjust our ears to a pitch of
sound. If the poet uses rhymes like sing, ring, string, he is trying
to pitch his poem to sound like harp-music. If he uses rhymes
like bell, well, toll, soul, he is trying to make the poem sound
like cymbals—and so on. The organ-music of *Jubilate Agno* is
thus achieved by more complex, more bizarre techniques than
the conventional methods used in the 'Ode on Saint Cecilia's
Day'.

Pope's influence on Smart's work was not, of course, confined to the 'Ode on Saint Cecilia's Day'. We have seen how
Pope's *Essay on Criticism* was translated by Smart, and how he
later incorporated a number of Pope's views into his own poetry.
We may also remember that when Smart sent off his Latin
translation of Pope's 'Ode for Musick', he enclosed a specimen
of a similar translation of the *Essay on Man* for Pope's approval.
It has been suggested that Smart did in fact publish fragments
of the *Essay on Man*, since the *Reading Mercury* for the 15th July
1751 included anonymous versions of Epistle I, ll. 143 ff., and
Epistle III, ll. 105 ff.[15] Pope's *Dunciad* gave rise, of course, to
numerous eighteenth-century '-iads', and among them was
William Kenrick's *Smartiad*, and Smart's *Hilliad* (1753), a
relatively brief satire, written in heroic couplets, and accompanied by long, mocking, 'learned' footnotes, purporting to
come from a number of eminent authorities, but in fact com-

[15] E. G. Ainsworth and C. E. Noyes, *Christopher Smart A Biographical and Critical Study*, University of Missouri Studies, vol. xviii, no. iv, 1943, 19.

posed by Smart's collaborator, Arthur Murphy. The object of
Smart's satire was the learned but ridiculous John Hill who was
described by Sir John Hawkins as 'vain, conceited, and in his
writings disposed to satire and licentious scurrility, which he
indulged without any regard to truth, and thereby became
engaged in frequent disputes and quarrels that always termi-
nated in his own disgrace.'[16] Hill was Smart's dunce, the symbol
of dullness, and Smart set out in his poem to aim 'at triumph by
no common ways,/But on the stem of dulness grafts the bays.'
Murphy added a note to these lines in which the great satirist,
Pope, is praised at the expense of Hill the dullard. 'Much puzzle
hath been occasioned among the naturalists concerning the
engraftment here mentioned. Hill's Natural History of Trees
and Plants, vol. 52, page 336, saith, it has been frequently
attempted, but that the tree of dulness will not admit any such
innoculation. He adds in page 339, that he himself tried the
experiment for two years successively, but that the twig of
laurel, like a feather in the state of electricity, drooped and died
the moment he touched it. Notwithstanding this authority, it is
well known that this operation has been performed by some
choice spirits. Erasmus in his encomium on folly shows how it
may be accomplished; in our own times Pope and Garth found
means to do the same: and in the sequel of this work, we make
no doubt but the stem here-mentioned will bear some luxuriant
branches' (*Collected Poems*, i.169–70).

Often, Smart seems to have introduced into his poetry a half-
remembered quotation from Pope. For instance, a stanza from
Smart's 'Lovely Harriote' seems to be a variation on one of
Pope's juvenile poems, 'Artimesia', in which he was imitating
the Earl of Dorset's style:

> Tho' *Artimesia* talks, by Fits,
> Of Councils, Classicks, Fathers, Wits;
>   Reads *Malbranche*, *Boyle*, and *Locke*:
> Yet in some Things methinks she fails,
> 'Twere well if she would pare her Nails,
>   And wear a cleaner Smock.[17]

---

[16] *The Life of Samuel Johnson Ll.D.*, ed. Bertram H. Davis, 1962, 94.
[17] *The Poems of Alexander Pope*, 13.

Smart certainly did not intend a deliberate imitation of 'Arti-mesia' when he chose the same stanza form and similar literary references for 'Lovely Harriote'. It is unthinkable that Smart would have dared even a glancing reference to the slattern, Artimesia, 'Haughty and huge as *High-Dutch* Bride', while addressing 'dear delicious *Harriote*', but there is nevertheless a clear echo of Pope's lines in the following stanza:

> Pedants of dull phlegmatic Turns,
> Whose pulse not beats, whose Blood not burns,
>   Read *Malebranche, Boyle* and *Marriot*;
> I scorn their Philosophic Strife,
> And study Nature from the Life,
>   (Where most she shines) in *Harriote*.
>   (*Collected Poems*, i. 188–89)

As well as echoing Pope in this way, Smart seems to have incorporated something of Pope's sensibility into some of his own verse. An example of this is to be found in Smart's fable, 'The Tea Pot and Scrubbing Brush', which makes a whimsical comparison between the ornamental members of society, fair without and foul within, and the humbler people who do not shine themselves, but do help to make others shine. The descrip-tion of the ornate tea-pot is reminiscent of the pomp of Pope's tea service in *The Rape of the Lock*:

> For lo! the Board with Cups and Spoons is crown'd,
> The Berries crackle, and the Mill turns round.
> On shining Altars of *Japan* they raise
> The silver Lamp; the fiery Spirits blaze.
> From silver Spouts the grateful Liquors glide,
> While *China*'s Earth receives the smoking Tyde.[18]

> A TAWDRY *Tea-pot, A-la-mode*,
> Where Art her utmost Skill bestow'd,
> Was much esteem'd for being old,
> And on its Sides with Red and Gold
> Strange Beasts were drawn, in Taste *Chinese*,
> And frightful Fish, and hump-back Trees.
> High in an elegant Beaufet,
> This pompous Utensil was set . . .
>   (*Collected Poems*, i. 43–44)

[18] *Ibid.*, 229.

Another way in which Smart borrowed from Pope was to use
quotations from the latter's work as introductions to his own
poetry. For instance, the *Index to Mankind* (1751), by Mrs. Mary
Midnight, contains a preface 'by her good Friend, the late Mr.
POPE', which turns out to be the rather brief reflection that
'*Blessed is the Man who expects nothing, for he shall never be disap-
pointed.*' And the poem attributed to Smart, 'Lovely Jenny
Weston', is introduced with a quotation from Pope, '*I lisp'd in
Numbers, for the Numbers came*' (see Appendix I).

It is difficult to make a brief summary of Smart's debt to
Pope, who had such an all-pervading influence on his earlier
verse. It is just as difficult to sum up his debt to Matthew Prior,
who also had an important effect on his work. Smart made
several direct references to Prior in the course of his work, and
even made one of Prior's poems the starting point for one of
his own. Smart's lyric, 'On seeing the Picture of Miss R——
G——N Drawn by Mr. Varelst, of Threadneedle Street', is
based on Prior's poem, 'A Flower, Painted by Simon Varelst':

> WHEN fam'd VARELST this little Wonder drew;
> FLORA vouchsaf'd the growing Work to view:
> Finding the Painter's Science at a Stand,
> The Goddess snatch'd the Pencil from his Hand;
> And finishing the Piece, She smiling said;
> Behold One Work of Mine, that ne'er shall fade.[19]

> SHALL candid PRIOR, in immortal lays,
> Thy ancestor with generous ardour praise;
> Who, with his pencil's animating pow'r,
> In liveliest dies immortaliz'd a flow'r?
> And shall no just, impartial bard be found,
> Thy more exalted merits to resound!
> Who giv'st to beauty a perpetual bloom,
> And lively grace, which age shall not consume;
> Who maks't the speaking eyes with meaning roll,
> And paint'st at once the body, and the soul.
>   (*Collected Poems*, i. 28)

Smart obviously admired Prior's witty conceit. When we
remember that Smart felt that one of the essentials of a good

---

[19] *Literary Works of Matthew Prior*, i. 83.

poem is that it must 'reward merit', we know that Smart also admired Prior's poem because it gave generous praise to Simon Varelst, famous for his flower paintings. In his own poem, Smart imitates Prior's rhyming iambic pentameters, and likewise 'rewards merit' by praising in one breath Willem Varelst, Matthew Prior, *and* Miss R——G——N. Indeed, Smart seems to have associated Prior with his favourite theme of 'applause'. We have already seen how '*Prior Dorsett* hail'd to heav'n', and how Prior was raised higher by Gratitude than he ever could have been by the Muses alone. In 'The Hop-Garden', Smart gives fuller expression to the poet-patron relationship between Prior and the Earl of Dorset:

> Let Sevenoaks vaunt the hospitable seat
> Of Knoll most ancient: awefully, my muse,
> These social scenes of grandeur and delight,
> Of love and veneration, let me tread.
> How oft beneath yon oak has amorous Prior
> Awaken'd echo with sweet Chloe's name!
> While noble Sackville heard, hearing approv'd,
> Approving, greatly recompens'd. But he,
> Alas! is number'd with th'illustrious dead,
> And orphan merit has no guardian now!
>
> (*Collected Poems*, i. 161)

If the poet's task is to reward merit wherever it may be found, it goes without saying that his task is to adore royal merit. Smart never emulated the numerous adulatory poems that Prior lavished indiscriminately upon all royal persons, Stuart, Orange, or Hanoverian (though we may recall that Smart too tried to flatter both George II and his hated son, Frederick, Prince of Wales). But when Smart wrote 'To the King' for publication in *Gratulatio Academiæ Cantabrigiensis de Reditu Serenissimi Regis Georgii II, Post Pacem & Libertatem Europæ Feliciter Restitutam Anno M.DCC.XLVIII*, he was certainly following a tradition of literary eulogy in which Prior had been pre-eminent at the end of the seventeenth century. On reading Prior's poem, 'On the Coronation of the Most August Monarch K. James II. and Queen Mary. The 23rd. of April, 1685', we look with some scepticism at his adulation of that unfortunate monarch. Similarly, we cannot easily reconcile Lord Hervey's

account of the unattractive, red-nosed, irascible George II with
Smart's flattering account of his reign, described in 'To the
King' with images of sunlit vistas—corresponding to the
glorious eastern sun which Prior felt was a just emblem of James
II's new reign:

> See, Glorious as the *Eastern* Sun,
> Our *Monarch* from the Waters rise,
> Whilst Zealous Crowds, like *Persians* run
> To own the Blessing of their Sacrifice.
> He comes, Religious Shouts proclaim Him near,
>   JAMES and HOSANNA bless the Ear;
>   Delighted Heav'n confirms the Joys,
> And in glad sounds reflects the Image of the Voice.[20]

> As some vast vista, whose extent
> Scarce bounded by the firmament
>   From whence it's sweep begun;
>   Above, beneath, in every place,
>   Mark'd with some grand distinguish'd grace,
>   Ends with the golden sun:
>   (*Collected Poems*, i. 5)

Thus George's reign appears to the impartial view: the bright
days rise, the glorious years roll, for ever happy and for ever
new. Of all eighteenth-century poetic genres, none sounds
sillier to the democratic twentieth century than the convention
of literary eulogy. The comparison between Smart and Prior
shows that Smart's idiosyncratic view, that good poetry must
reward merit and express gratitude, was not entirely divorced
from the conventions of his age. Eulogy was not simply a means
of working through his inferiority complex and sublimating it in
the form of excessive gratitude and adulation: his personal
eccentricity derived from the literary traditions which governed
the composition of his early poetry. This point can be further
illustrated by another comparison between Smart and Prior.
Both poets wrote poems about the foundresses of their respective colleges. Smart wrote with reverent adoration of the mighty
soul of the Countess of Pembroke, and how her immortality
was expressed in the college she had founded, 'And to ensure

[20] *Literary Works of Matthew Prior*, i. 2.

that work to endless fame,/Left what can never die, her own illustrious name' (*Collected Poems*, i. 5). Prior had written 'In Praise of Lady Margaret Foundress of St. John's', and similarly revered her virtue, and described her immortality. He misquoted from Ecclesiasticus 44.8, 'There be those that leave their names behind them', and wrote:

> Margaretta's Name shal live
> And lasting Tribute of just Fame receive
> Long as the Sacred Walls she founded stand,
> The Pride, the light, the glory of our Land.[21]

Milton, Pope, and Prior, as well as Chaucer, Shakespeare and Dryden, influenced greatly the form and expression of Smart's earlier verse. There were also many minor influences at work on his poetry. At the end of the *Hilliad*, Smart felt that he had dismissed John Hill for ever, and wrote that for ever after there must be antagonism between wit and folly: 'While with joint force o'er humour's droll domain,/Cervantes, Fielding, Lucian, Swift shall reign' (*Collected Poems*, i.184). Even during his mental sickness, he remembered Jonathan Swift, John Gay, and Alexander Pope: 'Let Eliada rejoice with the Gier-eagle who is swift and of great penetration. For I bless the Lord Jesus for the memory of GAY, POPE and SWIFT' (*Jubilate Agno* B1.84). Smart must have been fond of Gay's *Beggar's Opera*, for he refers to it several times in his work. In 'An Occasional Prologue Occasion'd by [the] two Occasional Prologues', Garrick and Barry rage against one another, and then make up their quarrel:

> Ah Brother! Brother! think on *Johnny Gay*,
> Think on the Moral giv'n us in his Play;
> And let's like *Peachum*, and his Brother *Lockit*,
> Our own Affronts—with others Money, pocket.
>   (*Collected Poems*, i. 92)

In the 'Epilogue' that Smart wrote for Arthur Murphy's *The Apprentice*, one of the stage-struck, nobly-built, well-dressed, full-voiced milliners in the audience has a daughter who can sing 'O ponder well'—Smart is referring of course to Polly Peachum's song from the *Beggar's Opera*.

[21] *Ibid.*, i. 74.

H

It is more difficult to gauge whether Smart's work was influenced by contemporary poets. We do know that in 'The Brocaded Gown and Linen Rag', he included a list of contemporary poets that he currently admired:

> Th' *Athenian Akinside* may deign,
> To stamp me deathless with his pen,
> While flows approv'd by all the nine
> Th'immortal soul of every line.
> Collins, perhaps, his aid may lend,
> Melpomene's selected friend.
> Perhaps our great Augustan *Gray*
> May grace me with a *Doric* lay;
> With sweet, with manly words of woe,
> That nevously pathetic flow.
> What, *Mason*, may I owe to you?
> Learning's first pride, and Nature's too;
> On thee she cast her sweetest smile,
> And gave thee Art's correcting file;
> That file, which with assiduous pain,
> The viper *Envy* bites in vain.
>
> (*Collected Poems*, i. 50)

Although this poem was published in the *Gentleman's Magazine* as early as February 1754, two years before Smart's major mental breakdown, it is nevertheless a very strange poem. The parisian brocaded gown, made of gold tissue, insults the linen rag which is 'Vilely besmear'd' because it has been used as a 'plaister': 'Thou thing of filth, and (what is odder)/Discarded from thy owner's issue'. The rag replies that it likes a jest, and agrees with friend Horace that it is no treason to giggle and reason simultaneously. The rag goes on, somewhat inconsequentially, that the mill's refining motion and the sweetest daughter of the ocean, fair Medway, will soon restore the rag to 'virgin purity'. At this point, Smart develops the meaning of the poem, by identifying himself with the good-natured filthy rag. Just as the rag is going to have 're-inform'd existence', Smart is going to experience a 'second life divine', and in some mysterious way, it is the poets listed in the quotation above, who are going to institute this divine second life. It would seem that Smart had already experienced some form of mental sickness in which he was burdened by a sense of 'dirt' and sin. The poem is a statement of his confidence in a return to sanity and cleanliness—the kind of quasi-religious second birth described again in the *Hymn to the Supreme Being* in 1756.

Of the poets listed in 'The Brocaded Gown and Linen Rag', Mark Akenside will be mentioned again in our study of Smart's Seatonian poetry. It is difficult to know why Melpomene, of all the nine Muses, should select Collins as her friend. Perhaps Smart was thinking of the gentle melancholy of the dirges, like 'How sleep the brave', and 'To fair Fidele's grassy tomb'. Smart had known the Rev. William Mason at Cambridge, and we know from Smart's letters to Paul Panton that Mason tried to raise a subscription during the poet's impoverished last years. Perhaps Mason's influence on Smart's work was a pious one. Smart would certainly have approved of the sentiments in Mason's poem 'On the Death of a Lady', with its devout injunction:

> Yet know, vain Scepticks, know, th'Almighty mind,
>   Who breath'd on Man a portion of his fire,
> Bad his free Soul, by earth nor time confin'd,
>   To Heav'n, to Immortality aspire.[22]

The reference to Gray is an interesting one, because we know that Smart found him personally distasteful. 'Gray *walks* as if he had fouled his small-clothes, and *looks* as if he smelt it', said Smart.[23] One wonders whether Smart's 'grief-inspired Muse' led him into making a sly comment on Gray in his poem, 'On an Eagle Confin'd in a college court,' written on the 5th May 1751:

> What time by thee scholastic Pride
> Takes his precise, pedantic stride,
>   Nor on thy mis'ry casts a care,
> The stream of love ne'er from his heart
> Flows out, to act fair pity's part;
>   But stinks, and stagnates there.
>   (*Collected Poems*, i. 90)

But his dislike for the man did not prevent him reading the

---

[22] *Poems by William Mason, M.A.*, 1764, 71.
[23] Devlin, *Poor Kit Smart*, 37, quoting *Facetiæ Cantabrigienses*.

works of 'our great Augustan *Gray*' with impartiality. It is
possible that Smart had no scruples about imitating Gray's
style. It has been suggested that the elegiac poem that appeared
in the *Covent-Garden Journal* on the 7th April 1752 was Smart's
—William Mason or Henry Fielding himself have also been
suggested as possible authors.[24] The poem was signed 'Cantabrigiensis', perhaps a more sober version of the pseudonym,
'Chimæricus Cantabrigiensis' that Smart had used for 'A New
System of Castle-Building' in the *Student*. In his apology for the
delay in publishing the poem, the editor uses the adjective
'ingenious', an epithet so often applied to Smart during the
eighteenth century: 'THE following Elegy on the late Prince of
Wales, should have been published the Middle of last Month,
had it not been unfortunately mislaid. This we hope will be a
sufficient Apology to the ingenious Author; our Readers, we
doubt not, will thank us for giving it them at any Time.'[25] Like
Gray's 'Elegy', this anonymous Elegy on the Prince of Wales
is written in iambic pentameters, rhyming alternately (abab).
There are only a few indications in the poem that it could be
Smart's. He had already written *A Solemn Dirge Sacred to the
Memory of His Royal Highness Frederic Prince of Wales* which had
been performed at Vauxhall Gardens by Mr. Lowe, Miss
Burchell and Chorus soon after Frederick's death in 1751. But
there is little relationship between the anonymous Elegy and
Smart's *Solemn Dirge*. One or two phrases in the Elegy could be
Smart's. 'The village Hind' (l.33) appears in *Hannah*, Act II,
'Sweeter sleeps the Village Hind/Than the Rulers of Mankind'
—but the phrase is scarcely peculiar to Smart. We find that
William Collins uses it in his dirge, 'TO fair Fidele's grassy tomb,
/Soft maids and village hinds shall bring/Each opening sweet...'
Frederick's 'godlike Mind' (l.41) is reminiscent of George II's
'godlike soul' in Smart's 'To the King', and the poetic soul of
the Prince of Wales, seeking yon poplar shade in pensive mood
(l.42) reminds us of Smart's pensive moods in 'The Hop-
Garden' and 'To the King'. Finally, two lines in the Elegy,
'O! How we hail'd him in his mid Career!/How dawn'd his

---

[24] Cross, *History of Henry Fielding*, ii. 381, and *Covent-Garden Journal*, ed. Jensen,
ii. 211–12.
[25] *Covent-Garden Journal*, ed. Jensen, i. 298.

Morn! Meridian blaz'd how bright!', suggest a line of stanza LXXXIV in *A Song to David*: 'Glorious the sun in mid career'. But the evidence does not seem to me to be very strong, and I should not like to swear that the Elegy was written by Smart.[26]

There can be no doubt that in the body of secular poetry written before he was thirty-five years old, Smart was influenced by generations of English poets, from Chaucer to Milton, from Dryden to Gray. The mental estrangement of the poet after 1756 means that it will be more difficult to detect these cultural patterns in *Jubilate Agno* and *A Song to David*. As yet, we have not asked what happened to Smart's poetry when he returned to a precarious mental balance and began composing the huge body of verse represented by the Psalms and Hymns, the Oratorios and Parables. Were these later works written in the traditions represented by Shakespeare, Prior and Pope—or shall we find that this later verse was subjected to the influence of quite different literary conventions, the banal versions of the scriptures that proliferated in the eighteenth century? Before we go on to answer some of these questions, we have yet to study a pocket of religious verse written before Smart's major mental breakdown. The Seatonian poems, the *Hymn to the Supreme Being*, the poem 'To the Reverend and Learned Dr. Webster', and a handful of epitaphs and elegies, were being written concurrently with the secular verse. We have to ask what kind of literary traditions affected the composition of this earlier religious poetry, and what links, if any, can be established between these poems and the later religious verse.

[26] The 'Elegy on the late Prince of Wales' is printed in full in Appendix II.

[V]

The Earlier Religious Poetry

— i —

'And this for SEATON shall redound To praise, as long as
Camus runs'   ('On Gratitude)'

ON THE 8TH OCTOBER 1738, the Rev. Thomas Seaton of
Ravenstone in Buckinghamshire made his will. At one time he
had been a Fellow of Clare College, Cambridge, and he
remembered the University in the following way:

> *I Give my Kislinbury Estate to the University of Cambridge for ever: the
> Rents of which shall be disposed of yearly by the Vice-Chancellor for the
> the time being, as he the Vice-Chancellor, the Master of Clare Hall, and
> the Greek Professor for the time being, or any two of them shall agree.
> Which three persons aforesaid shall give out a Subject, which Subject shall
> for the first Year be one or other of the Perfections or Attributes of the
> Supreme Being, and so the succeeding Years, till the Subject is exhausted;
> and afterwards the Subject shall be either Death, Judgment, Heaven, Hell,
> Purity of heart, &c. or whatever else may be judged by the Vice-Chancellor,
> Master of Clare Hall, and Greek Professor to be most conducive to the
> honour of the Supreme Being and recommendation of Virtue. And they shall
> yearly dispose of the Rent of the above Estate to that Master of Arts, whose
> Poem on the Subject given shall be best approved by them. Which Poem I
> ordain to be always in English, and to be printed; the expence of which
> shall be deducted out of the product of the Estate, and the residue given
> as a reward for the Composer of the Poem, or Ode, or Copy of Verses.[1]*

Thomas Seaton died on the 18th August 1741, but because the
will was disputed by his executors, nine years passed before the
first competition took place, and the first successful candidate
collected the prize, which amounted to about thirty pounds.[2]
Christopher Smart was awarded the prize on the 25th March

---

[1] As printed in *On the Eternity of the Supreme Being*, 1750.
[2] *Monthly Review*, iv, May 1751, 508.

1750 for his poem *On the Eternity of the Supreme Being*, which was duly published later in the year. He went on to win the prize another four times. On the 20th April 1751, he was awarded the prize for *On the Immensity of the Supreme Being*, which was published the same year. On the 2nd November 1752 he received the prize for *On the Omniscience of the Supreme Being*, published the same year, and dedicated to Thomas Herring, Archbishop of Canterbury, 'with all humility Inscribed, By His GRACE'S *most dutiful most obliged and most obedient humble Servant* C. SMART.' On the 5th December 1753, Smart received the prize for *On the Power of the Supreme Being*, which was published the following year. In 1754, the prize was awarded to George Bally for his poem *On the Justice of the Supreme Being*—we do not know whether Smart failed to enter a poem for the competition, or failed to please the judges. But on the 28th October 1755, Smart won the prize for the fifth time for his poem *On the Goodness of the Supreme Being*, which was published in 1756, and dedicated to his faithful patron, Henry Vane, Earl of Darlington, 'By His LORDSHIP'S *most obliged and obedient Servant* C. SMART.'

It is a strange contrast, the jester who presented his light poetry under the guise of Mrs. Midnight, and the sometime Fellow of Pembroke College who composed these solemn verse essays in Miltonic blank verse. Yet an anecdote told by Christopher Hunter fits in with what we already know about Smart's feckless nature: 'One of these Essays, that on the Divine Goodness, which was written in London, he so long delayed to undertake, that there was barely opportunity to write it upon paper, and to send it to Cambridge by the most expeditious conveyance, within the time limited for receiving the Compositions. That he waited for the moments propitious to invention, I will not plead as his apology'.[3]

We usually associate Smart's outbursts of devout praise in *Jubilate Agno* and *A Song to David* with the manic phase of an obsessively religious form of mental sickness. But ever before his major mental breakdown, Smart was meditating upon the universal adoration offered the Creator by his creatures, and composing jubilant poetry of his own. The following lines from

---

[3] *Poems of the Late Christopher Smart*, 1791, I. xvi.

On the Immensity of the Supreme Being express the same theme as
Jubilate Agno A.3, 'Let man and beast appear before him, and
magnify his name together':

> List ye! how Nature with ten thousand tongues
> Begins the grand thanksgiving, Hail, all hail,
> Ye tenants of the forest and the field!
> My fellow subjects of th'eternal King,
> I gladly join your Mattins, and with you
> Confess his presence, and report his praise.
>
> (*Collected Poems*, i. 227)

It was a view of the creation that the physico-theological
scientists of the seventeenth century had expressed in their
writings. As John Ray had written in the Preface to *The Wisdom
of God Manifested in the Works of Creation* (1691), the Works of
Creation '*serve to Stir up and Increase in us the Affections and Habits
of Admiration, Humility and Gratitude.*' It was a view ultimately
derived from the Psalmist, and Ray goes on to quote from Psalm
8, 'When I consider thy heavens, the work of thy fingers, the
moon and the stars, which thou hast ordained; What is man,
that thou art mindful of him? and the son of man, that thou
visitest him?' Ray is explicit on this point: '*the Holy Psalmist is
very frequent in the Enumeration and Consideration of these Works,
which may warrant me doing the like, and justifie the denominating such
a Discourse as this, rather Theological than Philosophical.*' The
reviewer of *On the Immensity of the Supreme Being* felt that Smart's
poem, too, derived from the Psalms. 'Mr. *Smart* has kept the
most divine poet the *Psalmist* in his eye, almost through the
whole of this work, and finely imitated him in several passages.
Take the following lines from the exordium, or beginning of the
poem, for a specimen. . . .'[4] The reviewer went on to quote the
first five lines of the poem, and a further forty lines beginning
'Now from the plains . . .', in which Smart was elaborating on
Psalm 139. Although the themes of the Seatonian poems
obviously derive from the Psalms, we have to ask whether
Smart was fashioning his verse with only the Bible or the Book
of Common Prayer to help him. Or was he sharing a convention of other eighteenth-century poets and elaborating his

---

[4] *Monthly Review*, iv, May 1751, 508–9.

Seatonian poems according to the accepted physico-theological literary traditions of the age?

Smart's theme of the creatures rejoicing in their Creator can certainly be traced in other eighteenth-century poetry. In *Horæ Lyricæ* (1706), for instance, Isaac Watts shows that it is the duty of the creatures to praise the Creator. In 'The Universal Hallelujah', a paraphrase of Psalm 148, the birds and beasts are meaner creatures than man, yet they honour God with their song:

> Let the shrill birds his honour raise,
> And climb the morning-sky:
> While grovelling beasts attempt his praise
> In hoarser harmony.[5]

In *On the Goodness of the Supreme Being*, Smart too writes of the touching 'hoarser harmony' of the creatures:

> And though their throats coarse ruttling hurt the ear,
> They mean it all for music, thanks and praise
> They mean, and leave ingratitude to man
>   (*Collected Poems*, i. 242)

(It would nevertheless be misguided to make too close a parallel between Watts and Smart. In 'The Universal Hallelujah', Watts showed how the creatures expressed their gratitude to God. But he wrote also 'The Creator and the Creatures' where the creation is bound to its Maker only by a bond of terrified submission, and in 'The Hazard of Loving the Creatures', Watts complains, 'Lord, how they twine about our heart,/And draw it off from thee!' It is certain that Smart, the loving owner of Jeoffry, could never have understood Watts's otherworldliness.)

Smart's theme can be traced also in the poetry of James Thomson, especially in the 'Hymn on the Seasons', which is, in effect, a religious apology for the essentially secular nature of *The Seasons*:

> Nature, attend! join, every living soul
> Beneath the spacious temple of the sky,
> In adoration join; and ardent raise
> One general song![6]

[5] In Chalmers's *English Poets*, 1810, xiii. 27.
[6] *The Complete Poetical Works of James Thomson*, ed. J. Logie Robertson, 1961, 246.

Thomson's eighteenth-century editor, Percival Stockdale, tried
to extract as much religious feeling as possible from *The
Seasons*. He quoted from 'Spring' (ll. 169–71):

> > > 'man superiour walks,
> > 'Amid the glad creation; musing praise;
> > 'And looking lively gratitude.'

and commented, 'This charming, moral, and pious picture, is a
just and severe reproof to those unfeeling souls who pay not a
tribute of ardent gratitude, and praise, to the goodness, and
greatness of their Creator.'[7] Stockdale also commented on a
similarity of theme in Thomson's 'Hymn' and Pope's 'Universal
Prayer':

> To Thee, whose Temple is all Space,
> > Whose Altar, Earth, Sea, Skies;
> One Chorus let all Being raise!
> All Nature's Incence rise![8]

Samuel Boyse's *Deity* (1741) must also be mentioned in this
context, although it will be discussed more fully below. The
whole poem, but especially the final section on 'Glory', strikes a
note of jubilation as Boyse invokes the planets, oceans, trees,
birds, and beasts, to praise God. Finally, he summons man himself to sing an ecstatic hymn of praise to the 'Great Lord of Life':

> Nor thou, vain lord of Earth, with careless ear
> The universal hymn of worship hear!
> But ardent in the sacred chorus join,
> Thy soul transported with the task divine!
> While by his works th'Almighty is confess'd,
> Supremely glorious, and supremely bless'd![9]

We know that Smart too was worried about the vain and care-
less lord of earth who persists in ingratitude while the birds and
beasts try to praise God with their 'coarse' music.

We could multiply examples of eighteenth-century poets who
took as their theme the universal adoration of the Creator. So
long as Smart expressed himself in Miltonic blank verse, his
jubilant religious feeling was entirely conventional. Likewise,

[7] *The Seasons*, ed. Percival Stockdale, 1793, 218.
[8] *The Poems of Alexander Pope*, 248.
[9] In Chalmers's *English Poets*, xiv.

the subject-matter of the Seatonian poems, 'the Perfections or Attributes of the Supreme Being' was a commonplace topic in eighteenth-century literature. When we ask what was the nature of the eighteenth-century writings on the Attributes of the Deity, and how was Smart affected by these works, we are forced to distinguish between the metaphysical and physico-theological literature of the age, and its influence on the poetic sensibility of the eighteenth century, and on Smart's in particular.

We know from the Library Register (1746–66) at Pembroke College, Cambridge, that Smart once borrowed the second volume of Samuel Clarke's *Works*—a volume which contains two series of sermons, and the *Discourse Concerning the Being and Attributes of God* which had been originally published in 1705. Clarke declared in his Preface that '*I have also confined my self to One only Method or continued Thread of Arguing; which I have endeavoured should be as near to Mathematical, as the Nature of such a Discourse would allow*'. He goes on, therefore, to offer twelve propositions about the nature of God, according to the *a priori* method of reasoning. Smart was familiar with both methods of philosophical reasoning: 'For the Argument A PRIORI is GOD in every man's CONSCIENCE. For the Argument A POSTERIORI is God before every man's eyes' (*Jubilate Agno* B2.359, 360). To compare Clarke's discussion of the Attributes of God, and Smart's expression of the same subject in his Seatonian poems, is to compare an 'abstract' and a 'concrete' presentation of the divine nature—or in other words, to compare a metaphysician with a physico-theological poet. It is only to be expected that a true poet should adopt an *a posteriori* argument for the existence of God. By arguing from the fact of the universe to the existence of God, the poet works with the concrete imagery of nature, the raw material of his craft, and has only to imply the abstraction, God. The two methods of discussing the nature of God can be illustrated by comparing Clarke's proposition of the Eternity of God, and Smart's treatment of the same theme in *On the Eternity of the Supreme Being*. Clarke's proposition is as follows:

That Being therefore, which has no other Cause of its Existence, but the absolute Necessity of its own Nature; must of necessity have existed from everlasting, without Beginning; and must of necessity exist to everlasting without End.[10]

In the first paragraph of *On the Eternity of the Supreme Being*, Smart hails the wondrous Being who, like Clarke's God, abstractly 'Exists from everlasting'. But Smart, as a poet, wants his reader to be able to visualize God's Eternity, and does so by giving us concrete images of the Creation, as a measure of the unimaginable Eternity implied in the adverb, 'Before':

> Before this earthly Planet wound her course
> Round Light's perennial fountain, before Light
> Herself 'gan shine, and at th'inspiring word
> Shot to existence in a blaze of day,
> Before 'the Morning-Stars together sang'
> And hail'd Thee Architect of countless worlds—
> Thou art—all glorious, all-beneficent,
> All Wisdom and Omnipotence thou art.
>
> (*Collected Poems*, i. 223)

Smart thus gives a pictorial rendering, with images of the birth of the sun and morning stars, of Clarke's succinct definition of the Being 'without Beginning'. Likewise, while accepting the metaphysical statement that the Supreme Being is 'without End', Smart gives the abstract notion a concrete poetic form, by measuring Eternity against a vision of the end of the world—to complement the lines on the creation of the world earlier in the poem:

> But tho' the earth shall to the center perish,
> Nor leave behind ev'n Chaos; tho' the air
> With all the elements must pass away,
> Vain as an ideot's dream; tho' the huge rocks,
> That brandish the tall cedars on their tops,
> With humbler vales must to perdition yield;
> Tho' the gilt Sun, and silver-tressed Moon
> With all her bright retinue, must be lost;
> Yet thou, Great Father of the world, surviv'st
> Eternal, as thou wert: Yet still survives
> The soul of man immortal, perfect now,
> And candidate for unexpiring joys.
>
> (*Collected Poems*, i. 225–26)

[10] *The Works of Samuel Clarke, D.D.*, 1738, ii. 539.

The metaphysical Clarke was nevertheless prepared to admit that when it comes to defining the divine Attribute of Intelligence, we are hindered by 'the Imperfection of our Faculties', and the concept of a Self-existent Being as an understanding and really active Being 'does not indeed so *obviously* and directly appear *to Us* by Considerations *a priori*'. Clarke concedes that there is another way of understanding the Intelligence of God: '*a posteriori*, almost everything in the World, demonstrates to us this great Truth; and affords undeniable Arguments, to prove that the World, and all Things therein, are the Effects of an *Intelligent* and *Knowing* Cause.'[11] Clarke lists the writers who have already dealt with this argument for the existence of God, and names the physico-theologians, Boyle, Ray, and Derham. He goes on to give an example of the *a posteriori* argument which moves from the fact of the cosmos to the Wisdom of God:

> The *Exquisite Regularity* of all the Planets Motions, without Epicycles, Stations, Retrogradations, or any other Deviation or Confusion whatsoever . . . The *inexpressible Nicety* of the Adjustment of the Primary Velocity and Original Direction of the *Annual* Motion of the Planets, with their distance from the Central Body and their force of Gravitation towards it . . . The wonderful Motions of the *Comets*, which are Now known to be as exact, regular, and periodical, as the Motions of Other Planets . . . Lastly, the Preservation of the *several Systems*, and of the *several Planets* and *Comets* in the *same System*, from *falling upon* each other . . .[12]

Smart is arguing in the same physico-theological way when he describes the cosmos and infers the Immensity of God—an example, by the way, of his method of elaborating his Biblical text, Psalm 139.8, 'If I ascend up into heaven, thou art there', almost beyond recognition:

> Whether the mind along the spangled sky
> Measures her pathless walk, studious to view
> Thy works of vaster fabric, where the Planets
> Weave their harmonious rounds, their march directing
> Still faithful, still inconstant to the Sun;

[11] Clarke, *Works*, ii. 543.
[12] *Ibid.*, ii. 570–71.

Or where the Comet thro' space infinite
(Tho' whirling worlds oppose, and globes of fire)
Darts, like a javelin, to his destin'd goal.
Or where in Heav'n above the Heav'n of Heav'ns
Burn brighter suns, and goodlier planets roll
With Satellits more glorious—Thou art there.

(*Collected Poems*, i. 228)

For Clarke, it was a sign of 'the Imperfection of our Faculties' that we are driven to understanding certain Attributes of God through our senses rather than through our intellects. Fénelon would have agreed with him, for in the *Traité de l'Existence et des Attributs de Dieu* (1713), he too asserted that the manifestation of God in nature is a concession to those inferior intellects that are incapable of perceiving God by pure ratiocination: 'il y a une autre voie moins parfaite, et qui est proportionnée aux hommes les plus médiocres. Les hommes les moins exercés au raisonnement, et les plus attachés aux préjugés sensibles, peuvent, d'un seul regard, découvrir celui qui se peint dans tous ses ouvrages.'[13] Fénelon's contemptuous phrase for those inferior mortals who have to understand God through their senses rather than through their intellects, 'des hommes qui dépendent de leur imagination', tells us how the physico-theological argument for the existence of God had a special importance for the religious poets of the age. Among the men who depended on imagination for understanding God, were the poets who depended on imagination for describing God in terms of concrete imagery. This was so in the case of Joseph Addison, for instance, who was perfectly aware of the imaginative value of the new theology. He expressed his views in a series of essays on 'The Pleasures of the Imagination', that appeared in the *Spectator* between the 21st June and the 3rd July 1712. On the 20th September 1712, he returned to the same subject: 'I must confess, it is impossible for me to survey this World of fluid Matter, without thinking on the Hand that first poured it out, and made a proper Channel for its Reception. Such an Object naturally raises in my Thoughts the Idea of an Almighty Being, and convinces me of his Existence as much as a metaphysical Demonstration. The Imagination prompts the Understanding, and by the Greatness

[13] François de Salignac de la Mothe-Fénelon, *Oeuvres*, Paris, 1835 ed., i.1.

of the sensible Object, produces in it the Idea of a Being who is neither circumscribed by Time nor Space.'[14] Addison expressed his theology in his paraphrase of Psalm 19, which was printed in the *Spectator* on the 23rd August 1712:

> *The Spacious Firmament on high,*
> *With all the blue Etherial Sky,*
> *And spangled Heav'ns, a Shining Frame,*
> *Their great Original proclaim:*
> *Th'unwearied Sun, from Day to Day,*
> *Does his Creator's Pow'r display,*
> *And publishes to every Land*
> *The Work of an Almighty Hand.*[15]

Many of the illustrations in physico-theological poetry were derived from the scientific writings of Isaac Newton. Newton's influence on the Seatonian poetry is most evident in Smart's images of the 'harmonious rounds' of the planets, but there are one or two further points that we should discuss in this connection. In *On the Omniscience of the Supreme Being*, Smart is pointing out the inferiority of man's scientific knowledge and craftsmanship as compared with the instinctive wisdom and skills of the lower creation: the bee-hive is a sweet society, and 'There Machiavel in the reflecting glass/May read himself a fool.' And when Philomela migrates in winter, she reveals Isaac Newton's intellectual limitations:

> Who points her passage thro' the pathless void
> To realms from us remote, to us unknown?
> Her science is the science of her God.
> Not the magnetic index to the North
> E'er ascertains her course, nor buoy, nor beacon,
> She Heav'n-taught voyager, that sails in air,
> Courts nor coy West nor East, but instant knows
> What Newton, or not sought, or sought in vain.
>
> (*Collected Poems*, i. 233)

Yet the next verse-paragraph qualifies this derogatory reference to Newton. Smart uses a Biblical image from Isaiah 40.12, 'Who hath measured the waters in the hollow of his hand, and

---

[14] *The Spectator*, ed. Henry Morley, 1896, 699.
[15] *Ibid.*, 666.

meted out heaven with the span, and comprehended the dust
of the earth in a measure, and weighed the mountains in scales,
and the hills in a balance?' Smart addresses Newton, and skil-
fully identifies the Biblical image of God with the image of a
physicist working with balances:

> Illustrious name, irrefragable proof
> Of man's vast genius, and the soaring soul!
> Yet what wert thou to him, who knew his works,
> Before creation form'd them, long before
> He measur'd in the hollow of his hand
> Th'exulting ocean, and the highest heav'ns
> He comprehended with a span, and weigh'd
> The mighty mountains in his golden Scales;
> Who shone supreme, who was himself the light,
> E'er yet Refraction learn'd her skill to paint,
> And bend athwart the clouds her beauteous bow.
> *(Collected Poems*, i. 233–34)

By juxtaposing God and Newton, Smart pays tribute to the huge
potentiality of the human brain, yet by his sentence-structure,
'Yet what wert thou to him . . .', he subordinates Newton's
great mind to the omniscience of God. Smart is in fact sharing
the conventional attitude of eighteenth-century poets, who
'treated the idea of the limitation of science as a part of the
larger effort to make man see that nature reveals the wisdom of
God. Seldom were they hostile to science but only aware of its
shortcomings.' Smart considered Newton's science to be inferior to brute instinct or divine omniscience, but he was not
prepared to 'reject the glory that Newton and other scientists
had brought to man's imaginative concept of a vast and
orderly universe.'[16]

Smart's image of the cosmos, like the cosmic imagery of a
large body of eighteenth-century verse, was based on Newton's
'imaginative concept of a vast and orderly universe'. Newton
expressed his religious view of the orderly universe in the
'General Scholium' to the second edition of the *Principia* (1713):
'This most beautiful system of the sun, planets, and comets,
could only proceed from the counsel and dominion of an

---

[16] William Powell Jones, 'The Idea of the Limitations of Science from Prior to
Blake', *Studies in English Literature*, i, 1961, 107–8.

intelligent and powerful Being.'[17] Smart might have wished to
deny the supremacy of human intellect, and Newton's in particular, but he could not escape the effect of Newtonian physics
upon the imagery of his poetry. In *On the Goodness of the Supreme
Being*, for instance, he makes a sophisticated rendering of
St. Matthew 6.28–29, 'Consider the lilies of the field, how they
grow; they toil not, neither do they spin: And yet I say unto
you, That even Solomon in all his glory was not arrayed like
one of these.' Smart is describing the interdependence of beauty
and light, the prime production of God:

> O thrice-illustrious! were it not for thee
> Those pansies, that reclining from the bank,
> View through th'immaculate, pellucid stream
> Their portraiture in the inverted heaven,
> Might as well change their triple boast, the white,
> The purple, and the gold, that far outvie
> The Eastern monarch's garb, ev'n with the dock,
> Ev'n with the baneful hemlock's irksome green.
>
> (Collected Poems, i. 241)

Smart was probably influenced here by Newton's *Opticks* (1704).
Marjorie Hope Nicolson has commented on the fusion of
Miltonic and Newtonian elements in *On the Goodness of the
Supreme Being*: 'Newton might say that, thanks to his prism, the
"Science of Colours" had become a truly mathematical speculation, but the interest of the descriptive poets in the *Opticks* had
nothing to do with mathematics. It is no exaggeration to say
that Newton gave color back to poetry from which it had
almost fled during the period of Cartesianism.'[18] Smart's
delicate perception of the pansies through the eyes of Newtonian
science seems to me preferable to Mark Akenside's *discussion* of
his scientific appreciation of the rainbow:

> Or shall I mention, where cœlestial truth
> Her awful light discloses, to effulge
> A more majestic pomp on beauty's frame?
> For man loves knowledge, and the beams of truth
> More welcome touch his understanding eye,

---

[17] *Newton's Principia Motte's Translation Revised*, ed. Florian Cajori, Berkeley,
1946 ed., 544.
[18] *Newton Demands the Muse*, Princeton, 1946, 22.

I

Than all the blandishments of sound, his ear,
Than all of taste his tongue. Nor ever yet
The melting rainbow's vernal-tinctur'd hues
To me have shone so pleasing, as when first
The hand of science pointed out the path
In which the sun-beams gleaming from the west
Fall on the watry cloud, whose darksome veil
Involves the orient . . .[19]

Yet the hostile reviewer of *On the Goodness of the Supreme Being* suggested that 'There are at least as many lines on the pansy as it deserves; which, however, blows more beautifully in the poet's bank than it does in the bed of nature.'[20] We may remember, however, that Smart felt that the true poet, walking over the immaculate turf of a formal garden, should be aware of the wild cowslips that grow like topazes by the side of the stream: his imagination should be stimulated by the humbler wild flowers as well as by the 'educated' flowers of the garden. Smart therefore observed the cowslips and pansies, with a sensitivity to colour inspired directly or indirectly by the *Opticks*. The ornate, pompous description of the pansies in *On the Goodness of the Supreme Being* became transmuted into the miniature but brilliant images of fruit and flowers in *A Song to David*—the peaches and pomegranates among the wild carnations, the burnished crocus on the snow-clad earth, the rain in clasping boughs enclosed, and vines and oranges disposed. We should remember, however, that the sensibility revealed in the Seatonian poems and *A Song to David* was not peculiar to Smart. His pansies, lilies, tulips, and 'auricula's spotted pride' were no more daring than Thomson's flowers in *The Seasons*—'auriculas, enriched/With shining meal o'er all their velvet leaves', 'The yellow wall-flower, stained with iron brown', 'hyacinths, of purest virgin white,/Low bent, and blushing inward'.

While we are discussing Smart's sensibility, we may notice here that just as the sensitivity to colour in the floral imagery of *On the Goodness of the Supreme Being* is developed into the miniatures of *A Song to David*, so do the jewel images of *On the Immensity of the Supreme Being* reappear in the *Song to David*:

[19] *The Pleasures of Imagination a Poem*, 1744, Book II, ll. 97–109.
[20] *Monthly Review*, xiv, June 1756, 555.

> Hence thro' the genial bowels of the earth
> Easy may fancy pass; till at thy mines,
> *Gani*, or *Raolconda*, she arrive,
> And from the adamant's imperial blaze
> Form weak ideas of her maker's glory.
> Next to *Pegu* or *Ceylon* let me rove,
> Where the rich ruby (deem'd by sages old
> Of sovereign virtue) sparkles ev'n like Sirius
> And blushes into flames. Thence will I go
> To undermine the treasure-fertile womb
> Of the huge *Pyrenean*, to detect
> The Agat and the deep-intrenched gem
> Of kindred Jasper—Nature in them both
> Delights to play the Mimic on herself;
> And in their veins she oft pourtrays the forms
> Of leaning hills, of trees erect, and streams
> Now stealing softly on, now thund'ring down
> In desperate cascade, with flow'rs and beasts
> And all the living landskip of the vale.
>> (*Collected Poems*, i. 228–29)

> Of gems—their virtue and their price,
> Which hid in earth from man's device,
>> Their darts of lustre sheathe;
> The jasper of the master's stamp,
> The topaz blazing like the lamp
>> Among the mines beneath.
>> (*Collected Poems*, i. 354)

> Precious the bounteous widow's mite;
> And precious, for extream delight,
>> The largess from the churl:
> Precious the ruby's blushing blaze,
> And alba's blest imperial rays,
>> And pure cerulean pearl.
>> (*Collected Poems*, i. 366)

These examples show how the brilliant catalogues of the *Song to David* grew out of a conventional descriptive method. The passage from *On the Immensity of the Supreme Being* is reminiscent of the physico-theology of *The Wisdom of God Manifested in the Works of Creation*, where Ray describes the various gems, the lively, sparkling, beautiful colour of the carbuncle or ruby shining with red, the blue sapphire, the green emerald, the yellow or gold topaz or chrysolite, the amethyst 'as it were tinctured with Wine', and 'the *Opal* varying its colours like changeable Taffaty, as it is diversly exposed to the Light.'[21] Just as Smart shows that Nature portrays hills and trees, streams and cascades, flowers and beasts, in the veins of precious stones, Ray wrote, in a later edition of the *Wisdom of God*, 'My honoured Friend Dr. *Tancred Robinson*, in his Manuscript *Itinerary of Italy*, relates the many various Figures he observ'd naturally delineated and drawn on several Sorts of Stones digged up in the Quarries, Caverns and Rocks, about *Florence*, and other Parts of *Italy*, not only representing Cities, Mountains, Ruins, Clouds, Oriental Characters, Rivers, Woods, Animals, but also some Plants . . . so exactly design'd and impress'd upon several Kinds of Stones, as though some skilful Painters or Sculpters had been working upon them'.[22] The catalogue of gems was a familiar item in physico-theological poetry in the eighteenth century—as in *The Seasons* ('Summer', ll. 140–59):

> The unfruitful rock itself, impregned by thee,
> In dark retirement forms the lucid stone.
> The lively diamond drinks thy purest rays,
> Collected light compact; that, polished bright,
> And all its native lustre let abroad,
> Dares, as it sparkles on the fair one's breast,
> With vain ambition emulate her eyes.
> At thee the ruby lights its deepening glow,
> And with a waving radiance inward flames.
> From thee the sapphire, solid ether, takes
> Its hue cerulean; and, of evening tinct,
> The purple-streaming amethyst is thine
> With thy own smile the yellow topaz burns;
> Nor deeper verdure dyes the robe of Spring,
> When first she gives it to the southern gale,
> Than the green emerald shows. But all combined,
> Thick through the whitening opal play thy beams;
> Or, flying several from its surface, form
> A trembling variance of revolving hues
> As the site varies in the gazer's hand.[23]

[21] *The Wisdom of God Manifested in the Works of Creation*, 1691, 107–8.
[22] *Ibid.*, 1717 ed., 93–94.   [23] *Complete Poetical Works of James Thomson*, 58–59.

Another example can be given from Henry Brooke's *Universal Beauty A Poem* (1735), Part III, ll. 47–54:

> Thro' sparkling gems the *plastick Artists play*,
> And *petrify* the Light's embodied Ray;
> Now *kindle* the Carbuncle's ruddy Flame;
> Now *gild* the Chrysolite's transparent Beam;
> *Infuse* the Saphire's subterraneous Sky,
> And *tinge* the Topaz with a Saffron Dye;
> With Virgin Blush within the Ruby *glow*,
> And o'er the Jasper *paint* the showry Bow.

Examples could be multiplied, but we have wandered from our original intention, to compare Smart's Seatonian verse with other eighteenth-century literature written specifically on the Attributes of the Supreme Being. We have mentioned Clarke's *Discourse Concerning the Being and Attributes of God*, and Fénelon's *Traité de l'Existence et des Attributs de Dieu*, theological works written in prose. Various poems written on the Attributes of the Supreme Being can also be related to Smart's Seatonian verse. One or two can be dismissed in a sentence or two, for they have little apparent influence on his work. John Pomfret (1667–1702) wrote 'Upon the Divine Attributes', which deals with the Unity, Eternity, Power, Wisdom, Providence, Omnipresence, Immutability, Justice, and Goodness of God. Pomfret attacks various erroneous theories of the Creation, and unlike Smart, he tries to explain God's nature in metaphysical terms:

> As the supreme, omniscient mind,
> Is by no boundaries confin'd;
> So Reason must acknowledge him to be
> From possible mutation free:[24]

Pomfret feels that if any of the Divine Attributes outshines the rest, it is Goodness. The celestial spirits pay incessant praise to the good God, and every rational creature on this earth 'Whose breast one spark of gratitude contains' should do likewise. Just as Smart complains that the birds, beasts, and flowers 'leave ingratitude to man', so Pomfret writes that the inanimate creation gives prompt obedience and instinctive honour to their Lord, 'And shame the thinking world, who in rebellion live.'

[24] In Chalmers's *English Poets*, 1810, viii. 326.

Pomfret bids his soul unite with heaven and earth to adore and bless God, just as Smart tries 'to praise . . . God on earth, as he is prais'd in heaven.' Pomfret was writing before Newtonian science had activated the imagery of religious poetry. Elizabeth Rowe (1674–1737) was writing at about the same time, and her poem 'On the Divine Attributes' is similarly untouched by images of the Newtonian cosmos. The poem expresses her own brand of religious mysticism that is quite different from the rapture in the created universe as expressed in Smart's Seatonian poems:

> Be thou my life,
> Its spring, its motion, constant as my breath;
> Dwell on my tongue, and givern all my soul,
> Till faith and love be swallow'd up of thee.[25]

In the 1730s, the *Gentleman's Magazine* sponsored a literary competition for poems written on the Attributes of the Supreme Being. It is thought that the competition might well have influenced the form of Thomas Seaton's bequest to the University of Cambridge.[26] The poems, which all appeared anonymously,[27] are theologically distinct from one another. No. I argues about scientific speculation on the nature of the universe. No. II is more mystical, and claims that God's judgements are 'an abyss'; no wit can trace, no reason can fathom, no words can express, the Attributes of God, which are too great for thought and overwhelm the human mind. No. III blends a physico-theological approach with references to 'revelation'—this is unusual in the sense that New Testament theology is generally absent from eighteenth-century arguments about the nature of God. No. IV derives from the metaphysical theologians—from Samuel Clarke, or even Matthew Tindal perhaps—giving a definition of God in terms of essence and accident and 'th'unalterable relations' of things. The theology of these poems bears little relation to Smart's Seatonian poems, but it is inevitable that somewhere in these four poems the divine cosmos

---

[25] *Miscellaneous Works in Prose and Verse*, 1739, i. 164.

[26] Aleyn Lyell Reade, 'The Seatonian Prize at Cambridge', *Notes and Queries*, cxc, 23rd February, 1946, 68–69.

[27] The first poem appeared in two parts, in April and May 1737; the second appeared in June 1737; the third in May 1738, and the fourth in June 1738.

of Isaac Newton should be described in terms similar to those used in *On the Immensity of the Supreme Being*. No. I includes images that remind us of Smart's harmonious, whirling planets 'Still faithful, still inconstant to the Sun':

> Shew from what source the wand'ring planets stray,
> Pleas'd to revere the potentate of day;
> In ambient gyres they tread th'expansive round,
> And distant regions hear the heav'nly sound:

Like so many other contemporary poets, this anonymous writer derives his world view from the Psalmist—he annotates this passage with a reference to Psalm 19, 'Their sound is gone out into all lands'—but he also pays homage to the scientists. When he writes of the atoms that 'in curves harmonious dance', he refers his reader to Newton and to Whiston, '*It is demonstrated that the orbits of the planets are ellipses, and that the comets move in ellipses very eccentric, approaching nearly to* Parabolas.'

When we turn to Samuel Boyse's *Deity* (1741),[28] we discover a poem that has many affinities with Smart's Seatonian poems. For Boyse's religious thought, like Smart's, was essentially physico-theological. In fact, he later made a translation of Fénelon's *Demonstration of the Existence of God*, and published it in 1749. We fully expect then that Boyse will illustrate the Divine Wisdom by an orthodox image of the harmonious planetary motions:

> See how, associate, round their central sun
> Their faithful rings the circling planets run;
> Still equi-distant, never yet too near,
> Exactly tracing their appointed sphere

It is a line of theological thought that can be traced directly to John Ray who had written, 'For the Celestial of Heavenly Bodies, the Equability and Constancy of their Motions, the Certainty of their Periods and Revolutions, the Conveniency of their Order and Situations, argue them to be ordain'd and govern'd by Wisdom and Understanding; yea, so much Wisdom as Man cannot easily fathom or comprehend'.[29]

I think it is fair to argue that a comparison of Boyse's *Deity*

[28] In Chalmers's *English Poets*, 1810, xiv. 545–52.
[29] *The Wisdom of God Manifested in the Works of Creation*, 1717, 45.

and Smart's Seatonian poems shows that although they had much in common, Smart had generally a better intellectual grasp of his subject. In discussing the nature of Eternity, for instance, both poets express the abstract concept by measuring Eternity against 'time' as it began when God created the universe. We have already looked at Smart's account of creation, in relation to the abstract metaphysics of Samuel Clarke, and we find that it is more vivid than Boyse's similar discussion of the Eternity of God,

> Whose Word from nothing call'd this beauteous whole,
> This wide expanded all from pole to pole!
> Who shall prescribe the boundary to thee,
> Or fix the era of eternity?

We do not find in Boyse's account anything so energetic as Smart's 'th'inspiring word/Shot to existence in a blaze of day'— a foretaste of the imagination at work in *Jubilate Agno* B1.272, 'For LIGHTNING is a glance of the glory of God.' Apart from this, it is notable that Smart's concept of Eternity spans the two poles of Christian time, the Last Judgement as well as the Creation. Boyse does paraphrase Revelation 1.8, 'I am Alpha and Omega . . . which is, and which was, and which is to come, the Almighty':

> That what for ever was—must surely be
> Beyond commencement, and from period free

—but he made no attempt to translate 'Omega' into concrete poetic terms. There is nothing in Boyse's 'Eternity' comparable with Smart's account of the final destruction of the earth a concept which owes little to the orthodox sorting of the sheep and the goats, but much to the conventional eighteenth-century 'sublime', as he uses thundering rhetoric, repeated invocations to ye rocks and ye mountains, and a violent descent to plaintive elegy,

> Yet I must weep for you, ye rival fair,
> Arno and Andalusia; but for thee
> More largely and with filial tears must weep,
> O Albion, O my country; thou must join,
> In vain dissever'd from the rest, must join
> The terrors of th'inevitable ruin.
>
> (*Collected Poems*, i. 225)

The same point can be made by comparing Boyse's 'Omnipotence' and Smart's *On the Power of the Supreme Being*. Boyse does refer briefly to the destructive power of God, 'Nor only does thy pow'r in forming shine,/But to annihilate, dread King! is thine', and he goes on to mention the decay of the vegetable kingdom. But he makes no attempt to translate 'annihilate' into poetic imagery. Smart does just this, and his passage on earthquakes must be quoted in full, since it suggests another 'source' of his theology:

> But not alone in the aërial vault
> Does he the dread theocracy maintain;
> For oft, enrag'd with his intestine thunders,
> He harrows up the bowels of the earth,
> And shocks the central magnet—Cities then
> Totter on their foundations, stately columns,
> Magnific walls, and heav'n-assaulting spires.
> What tho' in haughty eminence erect
> Stands the strong citadel, and frowns defiance
> On adverse hosts, though many a bastion jut
> Forth from the ramparts elevated mound,
> Vain the poor providence of human art,
> And mortal strength how vain! while underneath
> Triumphs his mining vengeance in th'uproar
> Of shatter'd towers, riven rocks, and mountains,
> With clamour inconceivable uptorn,
> And hurl'd adown th'abyss. Sulphureous pyrites
> Bursting abrupt from darkness into day,
> With din outrageous and destructive ire
> Augment the hideous tumult, while it wounds
> Th'afflicted ear, and terrifies the eye
> And rends the heart in twain. Twice have we felt,
> Within Augusta's walls, twice have we felt
> Thy threaten'd indignation, but ev'n Thou,
> Incens'd Omnipotent, art gracious ever,
> Thy goodness infinite but midly warn'd us
> With mercy-blended wrath: O spare us still,
> Nor send more dire conviction: we confess
> That thou art He, th'Almighty: we believe:
> For at thy righteous power whole systems quake,
> For at thy nod tremble ten thousand worlds.
>   (*Collected Poems*, i. 237–38)

The last ten lines of this passage refer to the earthquake that occurred in London in 1750. It seems more than likely that Smart was consciously paraphrasing the Pastoral Letter written by Thomas Sherlock, Bishop of London, after the earthquakes. Various words and phrases in Smart's lines—'warn'd', 'mercy-blended wrath', 'Thou . . . art gracious ever'—echo phrases used by Sherlock:

> IT is every Man's Duty, and it is mine to call upon you, to give Attention to all the Warnings which God in his Mercy affords to a sinful People: Such Warning we have had, by two great Shocks of an Earthquake; a Warning, which seems to have been immediately and especially directed to these great Cities, and the Neighbourhood of them; where the Violence of the Earthquake was so sensible, tho' in distant Parts hardly felt, that it will be Blindness wilful and inexcusable not to apply to ourselves this strong Summons, from God, to Repentance.[30]

Sherlock goes on to stress the evils of contemporary society, he condemns blasphemy, lewdness, debauchery, sodomy, dancing and play-acting during Lent, the increase of Popery, and then comforts his sinful flock:

> BUT let us not despair; there is still one Remedy left, and whatever Reason we have to condemn ourselves, yet of this we may be sure, that God has not *forgotten to be gracious*. To him then let us turn, with hearty Repentance for our Sins; and with a Resolution to do, each of us in his proper Station, what lies in our Power to stem the Torrent of Iniquity which threatens our Ruin.[31]

Smart was writing *On the Power of the Supreme Being* in 1753, three years after the earthquakes. Perhaps he was paying a compliment to Thomas Sherlock who had subscribed to Smart's *Poems on Several Occasions* in 1752. Certainly, he remembered him with affection, even during his mental breakdown, for in *Jubilate Agno* B2.606, he wrote, 'For Levi is Pious. God be gracious to the Bishop of London.'[32]

[30] *A Letter from the Lord Bishop of London, to the Clergy and People of London*, 1750, 4.
[31] *Ibid.*, 12.
[32] According to Arthur Sherbo's method in 'The Dating and Order of the Fragments of Christopher Smart's *Jubilate Agno*', *Harvard Library Bulletin*, x, 1956, 201–7, this line would have been written at the beginning of July 1760, that is, a year before Sherlock's death in 1761.

But to return to our comparison between Smart and Boyse, and to give one or two further examples of the way in which Smart was eager to seize any opportunity to make his poetry more concrete, more vivid. Boyse in 'Omnipresence' and Smart in *On the Immensity of the Supreme Being* both take Psalm 139 as their theme. The difference in the way they interpret the 'darkness' in verse 11, 'If I say, Surely the darkness shall cover me: even the night shall be light about me', makes the point. For Boyse, it is the darkness of death, 'the black mansions of the silent grave', which stand revealed to the piercing sight of the omnipresent God. But for Smart, it is the darkness of the bowels of the earth—which gives him opportunity for a sensuous recognition of God's presence in the blazing gems of 'the treasure-fertile womb/Of the huge *Pyrenean*'. A similar thing happens in their respective treatment of verse 9, 'If I take the wings of the morning, and dwell in the uttermost parts of the sea'; Boyse ignores the second part of the line, while Smart seizes the chance to describe the beauties of the deep—and prepares himself for *A Song to David*:

> Behold! behold! th'unplanted garden round
> Of vegetable coral, sea-flow'rs gay,
> And shrubs of amber from the pearl-pav'd bottom
> Rise richly varied . . .
>
> *(Collected Poems,* i. 228)

Only occasionally does Boyse outshine Smart in this respect, but this is so when they both point out that God's Power can manifest itself in small as in great bodies. Smart is content to observe that 'your Maker,/Who yet in works of a minuter mould/Is not less manifest, is not less mighty.' But Boyse illustrates the point more vividly, by comparing the elephant with the ant, the whale with the insect in the grass, 'Ev'n the blue down the purple plum surrounds,/A living world, thy failing sight confounds'.

Because Smart's Seatonian verse is usually more intelligent and sensuous than Boyse's *Deity*, it does not necessarily follow that the Seatonian poems are particularly important. When we read these verse-essays, we find that Smart was certainly developing his imagination and acquiring the skills needed for

composing *Jubilate Agno* and *A Song to David*. He was therefore
already composing lines that are sensuously appealing. But it
should have become clear that a large proportion of Smart's
Seatonian verse is theologically and poetically conventional.
Literary convention as such may be acceptable—but the slavish
following of a convention, with little individual variation or
adornment, can only result in tedious and banal poetry. It is
not therefore complimentary to Smart to go on comparing his
work with more and more eighteenth-century verse written in
the same genre: his poetry merely seems more and more conventional with every fresh comparison. The reviewer of *Jerusalem Destroyed* (1782), a Seatonian prize poem by William
Gibson, made some perceptive comments: 'whether it be, that
poets naturally abhor confinement, and seldom succeed where
the subject is not chosen by themselves, or that the banks of
Cam are too remote from the regions of Paranassus, certain
it is, that, since the publication of Mr. Seaton's will to this day,
not above five or six of the prize-poems have reflected any
honour on the victors in this annual race, the rest being con-
signed, like birth-day odes, to eternal oblivion.'[33] We do not
know whether he included Smart's poems among the honourable five or six, but Christopher Hunter naturally did so. He too
complained that it is useless to expect genius to appear simply
by offering a poetry prize, but he admitted that 'To the foundation of Seaton, however, we are indebted for the poems of a
Smart, a *Glynn*, and a *Porteus*'.[34] But when we turn to the
Seatonian poems of Robert Glynn, and Beilby Porteus—who
eventually became Bishop of London—we do not find that
Smart is in particularly impressive company. John Nichols
went into ecstasies about Glynn's *The Day of Judgment* (1757),
'which is one of the most excellent compositions produced by
that institution, and ranks with the sublime and beautiful
productions of Christopher Smart on the same occasion.'[35] Yet

[33] *Critical Review*, liii, 1782, 69.
[34] *Poems of the Late Christopher Smart*, 1791, I. xxxiv.
[35] *Literary Anecdotes of the Eighteenth Century*, 1812–15, viii. 216. In a later volume,
Nichols added the expostulations of F. Wrangham, 'Surely you could have found
in Porteus' "Death," and in Smedley's "Saul and Jonathan" (the laurel'd Poem
of 1813) better companions, than in Smart's Seaton Compositions, for Glynn's
"Day of Judgment" ' (*ibid.*, ix. 688).

we find that the poem contains a tedious account of how pale Virtue sits in pain, while pampered Vice sits in splendour, and how they will be separated on the right hand and left hand of God. (We find among the virtuous, Thomas Seaton himself, whose well-judged benevolence fosters fair genius.) There are one or two similarities to the less attractive aspects of Smart's Seatonian poems. Glynn, like Smart, favours Miltonic invocation, and begins 'THY Justice, heav'nly King! and that great Day . . . I sing advent'rous', and he too includes the inevitable cosmic image:

> Whether (so
> Some think) the Comet, as through fields of air
> Lawless he wanders, shall rush headlong on,
> Thwarting th'Eliptic where th'unconscious Earth
> Rolls in her wonted course; whether the Sun
> With force centripetal into his orb
> Attract her long reluctant . . .[36]

In *Death* (1759), Beilby Porteus gives an uninspired account of the Fall. He does not entirely avoid Miltonic echoes, and he attempts the conventionally sublime roar of destruction, like the rumblings of the London earthquakes in *On the Power of the Supreme Being*:

> But ah! what means this ruinous roar? Why fail
> These tottring feet?—Earth to its centre feels
> The Godhead's power, and trembling at his touch
> Through all its pillars, and in every pore,
> Hurls to the ground with one convulsive heave
> Precipitating domes, and towns, and towers,
> The work of ages.[37]

While we are on the subject of other Seatonian prize poems, we should just glance at George Bally's *On the Justice of the Supreme Being* which won the prize in 1754 after Smart had taken first place on four consecutive occasions between 1750 and 1753. Smart would have deplored Bally's theme. Bally states that Mercy is superior to Justice; but there can be no doubt that he nevertheless enjoyed the 'hideous yell' of the damned, for God's Justice means 'His Equal Ways illustriously reveal'd/In Vice's

[36] In *Musæ Seatonianæ*, 1772, 100.   [37] *Ibid.*, 136.

torments, and in Virtue's bliss'. But, inevitably, there is common ground between Smart and Bally in their use of Newtonian imagery:

> Orb within orb involv'd, Thy mystic Wheels,
> On which this politic machine is whirl'd
> Incessant, with no giddy devious flight
> Precipitate their course: with eyes they glow
> Distinct, and in a measur'd orbit move.[38]

As a footnote to this study of Smart's Seatonian poems, it is notable that in 1771, William Hayward Roberts brought out his *Poetical Essay on the Existence of God*. The second of its three parts was entitled *A Poetical Essay on the Attributes of God*, and resembles Smart's Seatonian poems in theme, theology, and range of imagery. This can be shown by comparing, for instance the way in which they deal with the theme of God's Goodness. Smart shows how the flowers and birds gratefully declare the Goodness of God:

> To him who feeds, who clothes and who adorns,
> Who made and who preserves, whatever dwells
> In air, in steadfast earth, or fickle sea.
> O he is good, he is immensely good!
> Who all things form'd, and form'd them all for man
> *(Collected Poems*, i. 242)

Smart then ranges over the four corners of the earth and its products, showing how all peoples bow down to God, but—as befitted God's good Englishman of the mad verse—'chiefly thou, Europa, seat of grace' must join in the general chorus. William Hayward Roberts likewise writes of the creatures declaring the Goodness of God:

> Beasts wild, or tame, that o'er the forest range,
> Or crop the flowery mead; the finny race,
> And that Leviathan, who wont to sport
> In oceans of thick ice; the birds, that sail
> O'er the clear azure on expanded wing,
> All, all declare thy GOODNESS.[39]

He goes on to write of the different products of different

---

[38] *Ibid.*, 50.   [39] *A Poetical Essay on the Attributes of God*, 2nd ed., 1771, 18.

countries, which leads him to the idea of commerce, and the supply of quinine from Peru to the distant sons of Britain, Queen of waters. Another example of parallels in Smart's Seatonian poems, and William Hayward Roberts' *Poetical Essay on the Attributes of God* is the fact that they choose the same Biblical story to illustrate the Power of God. Smart asks:

> Need I sing
> The fate of Pharaoh and his numerous band
> Lost in the reflux of the watry walls,
> That melted to their fluid state again?
> *(Collected Poems*, i. 239)

—and Roberts commands:

> Stop, Pharaoh, stop. Behold the waves return:
> Hark, how the mighty waters round thee roar!
> While yon vile slaves, safe landed on the beach,
> Defy those idle threats: the Arabian gulf
> Shuts close, and swallows thee with all thine host.[40]

Once again, we could multiply the parallels, and make a detailed comparison between the two poets to show how they shared a similar physico-theological viewpoint, and had similar ideas about a sublime literary style. But this would be superfluous, since it is clear that both poets were using eighteenth-century clichés—the parallels in their work certainly do not imply that William Hayward Roberts was necessarily using Smart's Seatonian poems as a model when he wrote his *Poetical Essay on the Attributes of God*. This point is brought home to us by the fact that when he wrote his *Poetical Epistle, to Christopher Anstey, Esq; on the English Poets, Chiefly those who have Written in Blank Verse* (1773), William Hayward Roberts praised Philips, Thomson, Armstrong, Somerville, Akenside, Mason, Gray, Pope, Gay, Butler, Swift, Prior, and Anstey himself—but not Christopher Smart.

There is, however, something to be gained from reading and studying Smart's Seatonian poetry. Geoffrey Grigson gives a good summary of the importance of the Seatonian poems: 'images and glittering objects in array are one thing, poetry is another. For the most part these Seatonian poems by Smart

[40] *Ibid.*, 11.

indicate, but do not involve, do not create and proffer. . . .
These Seatonian exercises declare his bent, in the intervals
between the writing of facetiae and empty lyrics, or in the
intervals of being carried home dead drunk from the London
beer-houses. They exhibit a ranging, but not yet a compelled
constructive sensuality, a quadripartite openness to sight,
sound, touch, scent:

> . . . sweeter than the breath of May
> Caught from the nectarine's blossom

—yet not much more than the spectator, facing the wonders of
creation, reciting his own Benedicite.'[41]

— ii —

'He drove out Satan from the tortur'd soul' (*Hymn to the
Supreme Being*)

Our interest in the *Hymn to the Supreme Being On recovery from a
dangerous fit of illness* (1756) is bound to be much more biographical than literary, yet the poem does give us some valuable
insight into the psychological changes that were taking place
between the composition of *On the Goodness of the Supreme Being*
and *Jubilate Agno*. The poem was published with an introductory letter addressed to Dr. Robert James, the famous physician,
now remembered for his invention of the Fever Powder.
Smart's father-in-law, Newbery, had half shares in the Fever
Powder, but it seems that Dr. James himself was called upon to
administer the dose to Smart during his illness. Several interesting points emerge from the letter to Dr. James. Firstly, Smart
considered that his recovery was an instance of Divine Providence, 'HAVING made an humble offering to HIM, without whose
blessing your skill, admirable as it is, would have been to no
purpose, I think myself bound by all the ties of gratitude, to
render my next acknowledgments to you, who, under God,
restored me to health from as violent and dangerous a disorder,
as perhaps ever man survived.' We do not know just when
Smart's obsessively religious behaviour began, but it seems
logical to suppose that it stemmed from the enormous gratitude

[41] *Christopher Smart*, 1961, 13–14.

he felt on recovering from this illness. Perhaps his excessive public prayer was a form of gratitude to God for restoring him to sanity—an ironical sign of the impending major breakdown threatening him in 1756.

We also notice that the strange contrasts in Smart's behaviour before his major breakdown—drinking himself into stupors, playing at being Mother Midnight, writing verse-essays on the Attributes of the Supreme Being—are probably partly explained by the fact that he was experiencing even in these early years in London, a series of mental illnesses. For he writes to Dr. James, 'my thanks become more particularly your just tribute, since this was the third time, that your judgment and medicines rescued me from the grave, permit me to say, in a manner almost miraculous.'

Another point to notice is the fact that Smart was already becoming paranoid. It is a strange fact about him, that not only did he feel persecuted himself, but he became extremely indignant about the way his acquaintances were being persecuted. Dr. James aroused Smart's sympathies in the way that Admiral Sir George Pocock and General Sir William Draper were to do, several years later. Smart therefore begs Dr. James to arm himself 'against the impotent attacks of those whose interest interferes with that of Mankind; and let it not displease you to have those for your particular enemies, who are foes to the Public in general.' It is no wonder, Smart continues, that retailers should oppose someone who is likely to endanger their trade. But it is amazing that there should be mean and mercenary physicians ready to patronize such retailers, and 'by the strongest efforts to prejudice the inventor of the Fever Powder at the expence of honour, dignity, and conscience.' Smart assures Dr. James, however, that most of the physicians in Britain who were born gentlemen and whose fortunes place them above sordid dependence on the retailers of medicine, think, and speak of him as does '*Your most obliged, And most humble Servant*, c. smart.'

In the first three stanzas of the *Hymn to the Supreme Being*, Smart describes the sickness and recovery of King Hezekiah whose story is to be found, as it was pointed out in the first edition of the poem, in Isaiah 38. King Hezekiah lay in anguish and perturbation, crying and sighing, unable to sleep and tor-

K

mented by horror and dismay. The King begged God to
remember that like his forefather King David, he had lived a
sinless life, 'The sovereign of myself and servant of the Lord!'
God heard his prayer, restored him to health, and to confirm
the miraculous recovery, made the sun retreat ten degrees. We
notice Smart's eulogistic references to King David who had
already appeared in his poetry a year before in *On the Goodness
of the Supreme Being* ('ORPHEUS, for so the Gentiles call'd thy
name,/Israel's sweet psalmist')—for Smart's admiration was
eventually going to spill over into *A Song to David*. But in the
Hymn to the Supreme Being, Smart's hero is King Hezekiah, for he
feels that he has suffered the same kind of terrible illness, and
like Hezekiah, he has come to the gates of the grave, 'I said,
I shall not see the LORD, even the LORD, in the land of the living:
I shall behold man no more with the inhabitants of the world'
(Isaiah 38.11). But there is a great difference between Hezekiah
and Smart. The King had served God in faith and truth. In
infancy, youth and manhood, no foul crime had dyed his snow-
white conscience. But Smart is conscious only of how much he
has sinned, and he addresses Hezekiah and David:

> But, O immortals! What had I to plead
>   When death stood o'er me with his threat'ning lance,
> When reason left me in the time of need,
>   And sense was lost in terror or in trance,
> My sick'ning soul was with my blood inflam'd,
>   And the celestial image sunk defac'd and maim'd.
>   (*Collected Poems*, i. 245)

He sends back his memory to search the records of preceding
years, and like the raven returning to the ark, she croaks bad
tidings to his trembling ears: 'O Sun, again that thy retreat was
made,/And threw my follies back into the friendly shade!' Most
of Smart's religious poetry is joyful, and although we know from
Jubilate Agno B1.132 that 'I have a greater compass both of
mirth and melancholy than another', we usually find that he
wrote poetry in the manic or mirthful phases of his illness. The
Hymn to the Supreme Being, frankly autobiographical, gives us
some idea of what he suffered during the melancholic fits, 'My
sick'ning soul was with my blood inflam'd, |And the celestial

image sunk, defac'd and maim'd'—surely a hint of violent and bestial behaviour?

If we were aware only of the 'manic' poetry, the jubilant celebration of God and the wonders of his Creation, we should probably think of Smart as a typically 'once-born' personality— optimistic, cheerful, sociable, outward-looking, and quite without consciousness of personal sin. But we know from the *Hymn to the Supreme Being* that Smart was in fact among the 'twice-born', overwhelmed with the burden of his own guilt and needing to shed the load or place it on the shoulders of someone else. The story of his recovery from sickness is therefore told in terms of a religious conversion, as Redemption and Forgiveness bid his affliction cease, 'Behold the balm that heals the gaping wounds':

> My feeble feet refus'd my body's weight,
>   Nor wou'd my eyes admit the glorious light,
> My nerves convuls'd shook fearful of their fate,
>   My mind lay open to the powers of night.
> He pitying did a second birth bestow
> A birth of joy—not like the first of tears and woe.
>   (*Collected Poems*, i. 246–47)

Very diffidently, he hopes that Christ is caring for him, now that the all-sufficient Lamb has exercised his power over death. Smart describes how his health has gradually returned, how he grows physically well, and how 'exil'd reason takes her seat again'. Anna-Maria and the children, Marianne and Elizabeth Anne, put in a rare appearance in Smart's poetry:

> The virtuous partner of my nuptial bands,
>   Appear'd a widow to my frantic sight;
> My little prattlers lifting up their hands,
>   Beckon me back to them, to life, and light;
> I come, ye spotless sweets! I come again,
> Nor have your tears been shed, nor have ye knelt in vain.
>   (*Collected Poems*, i. 246)

Then, to celebrate his recovery, Smart glorifies God in terms that allude to the subject matter of the Seatonian poems, just as the title, *Hymn to the Supreme Being*, is obviously intended to link the two sets of verse: 'All glory to th'ETERNAL, to th'IMMENSE,/

All glory to th'OMNISCIENT and GOOD,/Whose powr's uncircum-
scrib'd, whose love's intense,/But yet whose justice ne'er could
be withstood.' The poem ends with a series of images that also
recall the Seatonian poems. He is writing of Charity which is
supreme in heaven, while faith, hope, and devotion take a lower
place. To illustrate this point, he shows that gold is supreme
among metals, the 'brilliant' among gems, the rose among
flowers, the eagle among birds, the lion among animals, and the
Leviathan among the fishes. Yet superior to all these is man,
'For all was made for him—to serve and to obey.' This recalls
On the Goodness of the Supreme Being, 'Who all things form'd, and
form'd them all for man'. In the final stanza, Smart prays that
the supreme virtue, Charity, may grow in his heart so that the
future may attone for the past, 'That I may live for THEE and
THEE alone', in order to justify those sweetest words from
Heaven, 'THAT HE SHALL LOVE THEE MOST TO WHOM THOU'ST
MOST FORGIVEN.' Smart added a footnote to this line, a reference
to St. Luke 7.41–43. The man who had barely escaped arrest
for debt while he was still in Cambridge, and who eventually
died in a Debtors' Prison referred with some self-knowledge to
the story of the two debtors, one of whom owed five hundred
pence, and the other fifty. The creditor forgave both, but which
of them was likely to love him most? 'Simon answered and said,
I suppose that he, to whom he forgave most. And he said unto
him, Thou hast rightly judged.'

— iii —

'Guide our disgusted thoughts to things above' ('To the
Reverend and Learned Dr. Webster')

Before we move from the precarious mental stability of the
Hymn to the Supreme Being to the insanity of *Jubilate Agno*, we still
have to look at one or two pieces of minor religious poetry
written before Smart's major mental breakdown. The first of
these pieces is 'To the Reverend and Learned Dr. Webster
Occasioned by his Dialogues on Anger and Forgiveness', which
was first printed in the second volume of the *Student*.

During 1750, the *Student* made several appeals in aid of a
scheme to help the widows and children of the inferior clergy.

As we have seen, Smart was glad of any opportunity to win the patronage of the Archbishop of Canterbury or the Bishop of London, but in the September issue of the *Student* he used 'A New System of Castle-Building' to air his opinions on the corruptions in the Church: 'let the *well-fed pluralists,* that batten in the sunshine of prosperity, and indulge in the luxury of Cathedral magnificence, on some fast-day or other reflect on the miseries and hardships of the inferiour Clergy, on their sons who are reduced to beggary to avoid theft, and on their daughters who must submit to prostitution to keep them from starving'. In Book II, Chapter II of 'Castle-Building', Smart wrote a chapter on the expediency of bowing, and how certain individuals 'by *scraping* acquaintance with the ministry have *bowed* themselves into bishopricks.' Full of indignation, Smart goes on, 'I know one of the most eminent divines in *England,* who is starving upon a paltry vicarage, merely because he cannot make a bow; and who, upon making application to a certain great man, received for answer, "That it was impossible a fellow with such a damn'd hobble in his gait shou'd ever rise in the church."' There can be little doubt that he was referring to Dr. William Webster, and that as early as 1751, Smart's latent paranoia was sympathetically seeking out poor victims of persecution.

Dr. Webster brought out *A Casuistical Essay on Anger and Forgiveness . . . In Three Dialogues between a Gentleman and a Clergyman,* in 1750. The dialogues between Generosus and Clericus are written in a racy, colloquial prose style, and they talk about the ordinary man's conflicting passions of anger and forgiveness, the treatment of children, servants, and criminals, and, most important of all, they condemn the practice of duelling. In the poem that was 'occasioned' by these Dialogues, Smart takes very little notice of all this. Instead of dealing with anger and forgiveness as everyday human passions, Smart makes a brief but grandiloquent comparison of Old Testament anger as personified in Moses, and New Testament forgiveness as personified in Christ. He then goes on to address Webster himself: 'Well hast thou, WEBSTER, pictur'd Christian love,/And copied our great master's fair design'. We cannot agree very heartily, for Webster's notions of Christian love and forgiveness

are severe, to say the least. Erring children, such as those who
make runaway marriages, must be forgiven: 'I am willing to
restore her to the Affection of a *Parent* for a *Child*; but I must
give a *greater Share* of my Affection to those who have been
always dutiful, and encourage her only so far as shall be consistent with *Justice* and *Prudence*.' Forgiveness, says Webster, does
not oblige us to restore the offender to the same degree of our
favour which he enjoyed before. The Prodigal Son was
accepted, but his father told the elder son that all he had was
his.[42] Webster's attitude to criminals was barbarous for he
suggests that because it is wrong to punish simple robbery and
murder with the same death penalty, the murderer's death
must be made more painful. This is the opinion of Clericus, the
plain country clergyman. Since Webster himself was a vicar,
one only hopes that Clericus is meant to be speaking here with
heavy-handed irony. Smart would never have agreed with such
a barbarous attitude to criminals, for in *Jubilate Agno* B2.476, he
wrote that 'For, when the nation is at war, it is better to abstain
from the punishment of criminals especially, every act of human
vengeance being a check to the grace of God.' In C.65, he
wrote, 'For I prophecy that there will be more mercy for
criminals.' But Smart would have agreed wholeheartedly with
Webster's condemnation of duelling—one has only to turn to
his fable, 'The Duellists', to be sure of that.

What really interested Smart was not Webster's discussion of
anger and forgiveness, but his portrayal of Clericus, the country
clergyman. In the first Dialogue, Clericus complains of the way
gentlemen of fashion and fortune treat honest vicars, and how a
clergyman is obliged to live in a state of vassalage because of the
evils of patronage. Later in the book, Generosus, the country
squire, describes a visit to a poverty-stricken clergyman:
'Through the defect of the Timbers, the Rain had made many
Gutters down the dirty Walls; the Furniture was, a Couple of
old Maps, the *Bottom* of an old *Windsor* Chair, and a *Rush* one,
quite whole, a large brown Table, a great *Bin* for *Corn*, with a
rusty Lock to it, but quite empty, and a monstrous Chimney
without a Grate.'[43] Generosus is tactfully describing a visit to
Clericus himself, who retorts, 'You was afraid of affronting me,

---

[42] *A Casuistical Essay on Anger and Forgiveness*, 94–95.   [43] *Ibid.*, 85.

if you had directly told me that my House and Furniture want repairing.' Dr. Webster must have wanted his readers to realize that when he described the plight of Clericus, he was in fact describing his own poverty. Smart's indignation boiled over at the idea:

> Behold where poor unmansion'd Merit stands,
>   All cold, and crampt with penury and pain;
> Speechless thro' want, she rears th'imploring hands,
>   And begs a little bread, but begs in vain
>
> (*Collected Poems*, i. 222)

In his Dialogues, Webster stated that anger is a concession to our human frailities, and that as Dr. Clagget once observed in his sermon on the passions, anger makes us watchful against injuries and gives us resolution to do ourselves justice—and this is an even stronger truth when applied to the injuries done to others. Smart felt that New Testament forgiveness was superior to Old Testament anger, but he felt also that there is such a thing as righteous indignation, 'Oh Indignation, wherefore wert thou given,/If drowsy Patience deaden all thy rage?' But after venting his wrath against Webster's persecutors, he says that 'we must *bear*', and thus guide our disgusted thoughts to things above.

Smart's championship of Dr. Webster suggests that he knew him personally, and certain lines in the poem indicate that Smart certainly knew Webster's life history. Smart felt very strongly that Webster had been passed over, and that promotion had been given to less able men than he, Webster has 'no modern arts to please', and he has only an empty claim to preferment—that he deserves it:

> Else thou'dst been plac'd, by learning, and by wit,
> There, where thy dignify'd inferiours sit—
>   Oh *they* are in their generation wise,
> Each path of interest *they* have sagely trod,—
>   To live—to thrive—to rise—and still to rise—
> Better to bow to men, than kneel to God.
>
> (*Collected Poems*, i. 222)

Bribery and Dulness pass by impoverished Merit, and barbarously tell her to starve and die:

'Away' (they cry) 'we never saw thy name
Or in Preferment's list, or that of Fame;
Away—nor here the fate thou earn'st bewail,
Who canst not buy a vote, nor hast a soul for sale.'
(*Collected Poems*, i. 222)

Father Devlin suggests that Smart was supporting Webster
against William Warburton, but he does not take the point any
further.[44] Certainly, Webster's periodical, the *Weekly Miscellany*,
published between 1732 and 1741, is notable for the attacks it
made on Warburton's *Divine Legation of Moses* (1737–41), and
Webster later published his criticisms in book form, as *Remarks
on the Divine Legation* [1739]. But I wonder whether Smart was
in fact defending Dr. Webster against none other than Thomas
Sherlock, Bishop of London. Smart later found the Bishop
pleasant enough (for reasons of his own, no doubt), but in his
poem 'To the Reverend and Learned Dr. Webster', it seems
probable that he was attacking the Bishop.

   Dr. Webster had indeed been frustrated in his career, and
Thomas Sherlock had been at least partly responsible. Using
Webster's own account of his career, Nichols records two
occasions when Sherlock might have used his influence on
Webster's behalf. As curate of St. Dunstan's, Webster had had
the honour of intimacy with Dr. Sherlock, and when the latter
was made Bishop of Bangor [in February 1727/28], he made
Webster great professions of friendship which no occasion
offered of putting into practice. When Sherlock was translated
to the see of Salisbury, Dr. Webster flattered himself with the
hopes of obtaining a prebend in that church, which happened
to be vacant, but was mortified with a positive denial. When
Sherlock was translated to London [in 1748], Webster applied
to him at Fulham for charity, but received 'a reprimand for
going about the country in that manner, without being asked
to *drink*, though he had walked all the way from London.'[45]
This sounds very much like Smart's comment in the *Student*,
that when the eminent divine applied to a certain great man,
he received the reply that it was impossible a fellow with such a
damned hobble in his gait should ever rise in the church.

[44] *Poor Kit Smart*, 106.
[45] *Literary Anecdotes of the Eighteenth Century*, v. 162.

Webster does make one or two references to Sherlock in the Dialogues. He suggests that Dr. Middleton will fare most sumptuously upon the eminent writings and eminent character of Bishop Sherlock, the pamphleteers will subsist upon Dr. Middleton, while the printers will live upon both.[46] Then he goes on to say that an able clergy in London are of infinite consequence, and that he is satisfied that a learned, prudent, and able person has been chosen to succeed Dr. Berriman, which calls for another compliment to Sherlock, 'For the sake of *Christianity*, the *Establish'd Church*, and the *Publick*, may God Almighty long preserve his Lordship, that he may live to send a great many more such Labourers into this *great Vineyard* . . .'[47] Unless Webster was being extremely sarcastic, he was evidently trying to be magnanimous to the man who had treated him so badly. Such heroism appealed to Smart, and making a holy martyr of Webster, he bids him preach seraphic love and turn our thoughts to heaven. Dr. William Webster thus joins the ranks of the heroes of Smart's altruistic paranoia—Dr. James, Pocock, and Draper.

— iv —

'He spurns all empires and asserts the skies' ('Epitaph on the Rev. Mr. Reynolds')

In 1762, Smart's father-in-law, John Newbery, brought out *The Art of Poetry on a New Plan*, which included an essay 'Of the Epitaph', and gives us some idea of what was expected of a writer of epitaphs in the eighteenth century. The essay distinguishes between three types of epitaph. The first kind 'generally contain some Elogium of the virtues and good qualities of the deceased, and have a turn of seriousness and gravity adapted to the nature of the subject.' But although the true characteristic of the epitaph is seriousness and gravity, there is a second type which is 'jocose and ludicrous'. The third type is 'between prose and verse, without any certain measure, tho' the words are truly poetical'.

We have no direct evidence that Smart actually wrote 'jocose and ludicrous' epitaphs, which would have been quite in keep-

[46] *A Casuistical Essay on Anger and Forgiveness*, 115.
[47] *Ibid.*, 126.

ing with Mother Midnight's buffoonery, but quite anathema to the pious writer of verse essays on the Attributes of the Supreme Being. Yet if Smart did edit the *Nut-Cracker* (1751), written by 'Ferdinando Foot' and published by Newbery—and it is generally assumed that he did—it seems that he appreciated a number of jocose and ludicrous epitaphs. In the *Art of Poetry on a New Plan*, the 'Epitaph on a Miser' is given as an example of 'a punning and ludicrous' kind of epitaph:

> Beneath this verdant Hillock lies
> *Demer*, the wealthy and the wise.
> His *Heirs*, that he may safely rest,
> Have put his *Carcass* in a *Chest*;
> This very *Chest*, in which, they say,
> His *other Self*, his *Money*, lay.
> And if his heirs continue kind,
> To that dear *Self* he left behind,
> I dare believe that four in five
> Will think his *better Half* alive.

This had already appeared in the *Nut-Cracker*, and a much more ludicrous example could have been chosen from the following gems. 'On Richard Button, Esq.':

> Oh Sun! Moon! Stars! and ye celestial Poles!
> Are *Graves* then dwindled into *Button-holes*?

Or 'An Epitaph on Mr. Foot':

> Here lies one *Foot*, whose Death may Thousands save;
> For Death has now *one Foot* within the Grave!

Or 'On Mr. John Day', the most dazzling of them all:

> Here lies the Body of *John Day*;
> What *young John*? no, no. *Old John*? Aye.

The editor of the *Nut-Cracker* obviously had a macabre sense of humour.

But the epitaphs known to be by Smart are all of the first type, eulogizing the merits of the deceased and having 'a turn of seriousness and gravity'. Of the earliest epitaphs, the one written on the second Duke of Argyle (1678–1743) is almost too brief for comment. It was first printed in the *Ode to the Earl of*

Northumberland, but there is also a manuscript copy in the Library at Pembroke College:

> To Death's grim shades let meaner spirits fly,
> Here rests JOHN CAMPBELL who shall never die.
>
> *(Collected Poems,* i. 37)

Smart's epitaph does not, of course, appear on Argyle's tomb, designed by Roubiliac, in Westminster Abbey—but it does seem that while the monument was being built (and finally erected in May 1749), a number of versifiers were writing epitaphs for the Duke of Argyle.[48] Presumably they were contending for the honour of supplying the epitaph for the tomb itself, and perhaps Smart was among them. But there is no evidence as yet that there was any connection between Smart and the Duke.

The 'Epitaph on Henrietta, Late Dutchess of Cleveland' was not printed until the *Poems on Several Occasions* came out in 1763, but it was presumably written after her death in 1742. Her important rôle as one of Smart's earliest patrons has already been mentioned, so we need only make a literary comment on the poem, the obvious point that Smart was following a strong literary convention when he praised the domestic virtues of the Duchess of Cleveland in hyperbolic terms:

> Yet was the noble matron well sustain'd,
> And true politeness serv'd, where prudence reign'd.
> She check'd all thoughts wherein the temper [sic] lurks,
> By keeping Fancy busied on her works.—
> A taste for hist'ry with gen'rous aim,
> And strict attention to her country's fame.—
> A skill in picture, genius in design,
> 'Twas nature copy'd nature line for line.
> Such were her merits when her faith was tried,
> And to attain diviner things she died.—
> Amen,—The paths of life so justly trod,
> Bespeak the welcome due, thro' CHRIST, from GOD.
>
> *(Collected Poems,* i. 35)

[48] The *Scots Magazine,* xi, February 1749, 87, prints 'An inscription designed for the monument of the late Duke of Argyll, erected in Westminster-abbey by Mr. Roubillac', and the April issue (p. 164) contained 'An attempt towards an Epitaph on the late Duke of Argyll and Greenwich'. In the May issue there was a full description of the tomb, and the epitaph that had actually been chosen.

This celebration of a noble matron, who cherished with a mother's care, and filled the orphan's mouth with praise and prayer, is similar to Dryden's eulogy of Lady Whitmore, which was also included in the *Nut-Cracker*:

> Fair, kind, and true, a Treasure each alone;
> A Wife, a Mistress, and a Friend in one;
> Rest in this Tomb, rais'd at thy Husband's Cost,
> Here sadly, suming what he had, and lost.

> Come, Virgins, ere in equal Bands you join,
> Come first and offer at her sacred Shrine;
> Pray but for half the Virtues of this Wife,
> Compound for all the rest with longer Life,
> And wish your Vows like her's may be return'd,
> So lov'd when living, and when dead so mourn'd.

Smart uses the same tranquil poetic measure for his epitaph 'On the Death of Master [Newbery]', published in the third volume of the *Midwife* (1753), in the *Christian's Magazine* in March 1762—and notably in the *Art of Poetry on a New Plan* where it is given as an example of the 'serious' type of epitaph. Anna-Maria Carnan's half-brother, John, was later described in the autobiography of his younger brother, Francis Newbery, as 'a boy of singular acuteness and sense, but he had the misfortune so to injure his spine by a fall down some stone steps when a child, that he died after a lingering illness, aged eleven years.' Francis added that Christopher Smart, the poet, celebrated the boy's memory in a 'very nervous and appropriate epitaph', and went on to quote the poem in full.[49] Smart gives the bereaved parents calm, solemn consolation, in the heroic measure that was considered as appropriate for children as for adults:

> HENCEFORTH be every tender Tear supprest,
> Or let us weep for Joy, that he is blest;
> From Grief to Bliss, from Earth to Heav'n remov'd,
> His Mem'ry honour'd, as his Life belov'd.

> *(Collected Poems*, i. 32)

This passage can be compared with the conventional, measured gravity in the 'Epitaph on a Young Lady in Devonshire',

49 Charles Welsh, *A Bookseller of the Last Century*, 1885, 7.

printed anonymously in the *Christian's Magazine* for May 1763, where the poet consoles the parents of a ten-year old child:

> Fond parents cease, the falling tears restrain,
> Cease to lament her fate, cease to complain:
> Among the glorious saints in Heav'n she's blest
> With endless joy, and everlasting rest.

It is true that the poet of the 'Epitaph on an Infant in Wisbech Church-yard', which appeared in the *Nonpareil* (1757) and therefore could be Smart's, abandoned the heroic couplet for a much lighter measure:

> BENEATH a sleeping infant lies,
>   To earth her body's lent;
> More glorious she'll hereafter rise,
>   Tho' not more innocent.
>
> And when the archangel's trump shall blow,
>   And souls with bodies join,
> Millions shall wish their life below
>   Had been as short as thine.

Yet even this does not approach the tenderness and charm of the seventeenth-century epitaphs for children—Herrick's 'Upon a child that dyed', for instance:

> Here she lies, a pretty bud,
> Lately made of flesh and blood:
> Who, as soone, fell fast asleep,
> As her little eyes did peep.
> Give her strewings; but not stir
> The earth, that lightly covers her.[50]

One of the most important models for the dignified, 'heroic' epitaphs of the eighteenth century must have been Pope's epitaph on John Gay. It was printed both in the *Nut-Cracker* and in the *Art of Poetry on a New Plan*, where it was highly praised, 'Mr. *Pope* has drawn the character of Mr. *Gay*, in an Epitaph now to be seen on his monument in *Westminster-Abbey*, which he has closed with such a beautiful turn, that I cannot help looking upon it as a master-piece in its kind'. The epitaph is as follows:

[50] *Robert Herrick*, Penguin ed., 1961, 104.

Of Manners gentle, of Affections mild;
In Wit, a Man; Simplicity, a Child;
With native Humour temp'ring virtuous Rage,
Form'd to delight at once and lash the age;
Above Temptation, in a low Estate,
And uncorrupted, ev'n among the Great;
A safe Companion, and an easy Friend,
Unblam'd thro' Life, lamented in thy End.
These are Thy Honours! not that here thy Bust
Is mix'd with Heroes, or with Kings thy dust;
But that the Worthy and the Good shall say,
Striking their pensive bosoms—*Here* lies GAY.[51]

Smart seems to have followed Pope's poem very closely when he came to write his epitaph on Henry Fielding, who died at Lisbon on the 8th October 1754. Pope's panegyric on Gay's character is paralleled by Smart's eulogy of Fielding's merits as a patron and justice of the peace, and just as Gay delighted and lashed the age, Fielding was 'The lively scorner of a venal age, /Who made the publick laugh, at publick vice'. Since we are dealing here specifically with religious poems written before Smart's major breakdown in 1756, it should be mentioned that this epitaph was not necessarily written immediately after Fielding's death in 1754, but may have been written after the publication of Arthur Murphy's edition of Fielding's *Works* in 1762. There are certainly several parallels between Smart's epitaph and the 'Essay on the Life and Genius of Henry Fielding, Esq.' which Murphy wrote as a Preface to the *Works*. Smart's first line, describing Fielding as 'THE Master of the GREEK and ROMAN page' may be compared with Murphy's account of Fielding's education at Eton, 'and when he left the place, he was said to be uncommonly versed in the Greek authors, and an early master of the Latin classics; for both which he retained a strong admiration in all the subsequent passages of his life.' Smart described Fielding as a 'Student of nature, reader of mankind', while Murphy described Fielding's 'study of man', and called him 'an observer of mankind, yet a scholar of enlarged reading'. Smart wrote of Fielding as 'The lively scorner of a venal age', while Murphy wrote of his lively

[51] *The Poems of Alexander Pope*, 818.

understanding and described him as 'a satirist of vice and evil manners'. Smart was anxious to compliment Fielding's generosity as a patron—he was 'As free to give the plaudit, as assert,/ And faithful in the practice of desert'. Murphy also described this aspect of Fielding's personality: he was 'overflowing with gratitude at every instance of friendship or generosity'. Smart felt that Fielding's death was a release 'From toils like these, too much for age to bear,/From pain, from sickness, and a world of care', and Murphy felt much the same: 'THUS was closed a course of disappointment, distress, vexation, infirmity, and study'. The parallels do not prove without a shadow of doubt that Smart was consciously picking up ideas and phrases from Murphy's 'Life' when he wrote his epitaph, but there are enough similarities to make it a possibility.

Another epitaph which was probably written before 1756 was the 'Epitaph on the Rev. Mr. Reynolds at St. Peter's in the Isle of Thanet'. The earliest printing that I know of is found in the *Christian's Magazine* for August 1761, but there are several reasons for thinking that it was written as early as 1754. In *Alumni Oxonienses*, there is a Thomas Reynolds who was the son of William Reynolds of Canterbury, and matriculated at University College in 1740 and graduated B.A. in 1744. A Rev. Mr. Reynolds, presumably the same man, was buried in St. Peter-in-Thanet in 1754. I am grateful to the Rev. P. J. Gausden for locating Reynolds's monument, and for transcribing the inscription, which is as follows: 'Near this place lie the remains of the Revd Tho. Reynolds, who whilst he liv'd was greatly belov'd by all who knew him, and as much lamented when he died, the 14th of October, 1754. And also Susanna, his wife who died on the 13th of May 1780, aged 46 years. She was the daughter of Thos. and Susanna Gray, of this parish.'[52] The monument does not bear Smart's epitaph, but since new pew flooring was put down a century ago, the grave of Thomas Reynolds—and with it, Smart's epitaph, perhaps—is probably

[52] I first found the inscription in Edward Hasted's *History and Topographical Survey of Kent*, 1778–99, iv.366, where the date of Susanna Reynolds's death is given as 1783. Hasted shows that John Deane was presented to the living of St. Peter-in-Thanet in 1715, and Cornelius Willes in 1757, after Deane's death. The Rev. Thomas Reynolds did not therefore hold the living of the church in which he was buried.

obscured. Reynolds might have been acquainted with Smart
through the Newbery family, for in 1752, Francis Newbery was
sent to a school kept by the Rev. Mr. Reynolds at Ramsgate.[53]
It is surely not mere coincidence that in 1754, Francis was
removed to Mr. Bennet's school at Hoddesdon—the year in
which the Rev. Mr. Thomas Reynolds was buried in St.
Peter-in-Thanet. Smart's epitaph on Reynolds is not one of his
better efforts. Instead of adopting the calm, measured eulogy
found in the epitaph on Henry Fielding, he made grand
gestures—if rhetoric hung on the lips of sorrow, if affliction
could lend the heart a tongue, Smart's soul, in noble anguish
free, would do glorious justice to Reynolds and herself. Smart's
sorrow was shallow enough for some rhetoric to escape his lips,
'Blush, power! he had no interest here below;/Blush, malice!
that he dy'd without a foe' (*Collected Poems*, i. 37). This engaging
universal friend ('whilst he liv'd was greatly belov'd by all who
knew him' says the monument in St. Peter-in-Thanet) was far
too precious for this world and age, and kind Heaven called him
to eternal youth.

Yet perhaps it is unfair to suggest that Smart's feeling was
shallow. We know that he was extremely fond of the Duchess of
Cleveland, yet she too is remembered in ponderous heroic
couplets. It is as if the eighteenth century had outgrown the
Jacobean horror of death and its *memento mori* symbols of ghastly
corruption, and took instead the calm view that death is simply
a translation to heavenly bliss; 'He spurns all empires and
asserts the skies' wrote Smart of the Rev. Mr. Reynolds. Even
Dr. Johnson, for all his profound horror of death and the
terrors of Hell and Damnation, could bid Claudius Phillips,
'Sleep undisturb'd within this peaceful shrine,/Till Angels wake
thee with a note like thine.' Personal terror of death was not
permissible in eighteenth-century epitaph writing, yet the
fanatical fringe cannot be entirely ignored. R. D. wrote a letter
to the *Christian's Magazine*'s 1764 Supplement, more or less
shouting that 'Methinks, an *epitaph*, if tolerably well wrote, and
seriously perused, may tend to the advantage of the well-
disposed reader; especially, if, instead of those extravagant
encomiums too commonly made use of in subjects of this kind,

[53] Welsh, *A Bookseller of the Last Century*, 119.

some concise and pathetic hints are faithfully exhibited to the view of the public. Such awful monitory *mementos*, and alarming addresses, must greatly edify, no doubt, all good people in general; as well as help (one would hope) to *waken* and *reclaim* the vicious, and *rouse* them from that *carnal security*, or *spiritual slumber*, into which the far greater part of mankind seems to be so deplorably fallen.' R. D. then contributes a poem bidding his brethren who pass by to remember that they may lie in the grave much sooner than expected; if they spend their little span of life wisely and well, they can hope for unbounded heavenly bliss, but if otherwise, they will suffer 'Fierce, everlasting flames in hell.' But despite R. D. and his brethren, there can be no doubt that the literary tradition of epitaph writing, exemplified by Dryden and Pope, favoured a calm, optimistic, and eulogistic form of remembering the deceased, and Smart characteristically followed in their footsteps.

If Smart's personal grief is heard at all, it is in his elegies. The lines on Theophilus Wheeler in 'The Hop-Garden', written when Smart was about twenty-one years old, after Wheeler's death at the age of eighteen, recall with obvious affection the 'much-loving, much-lov'd youth', the 'dear departed soul' who had encouraged the young poet:

> What flattering tales thou told'st me? How thou'dst hail
> My muse, and took'st imaginary walks
> All in my hopland groves.
>
> (*Collected Poems*, i. 155)

Yet it is doubtful whether even this elegy is quite so spontaneous as it seems at first sight. In 'The Hop-Garden', Smart admitted his debt to John Philips ('thou tun'st/With Phoebus' self thy lyre'). It is notable that the second book of Philips's *Cyder. A Poem* (1708) also begins with a lament for a young man, Simon Harcourt:

> O *Harcourt*, Whom th'ingenuous Love of Arts
> Has carry'd from Thy native Soil, beyond
> Th'eternal *Alpine* Snows, and now detains
> In *Italy*'s waste Realms, how long must we
> Lament Thy Absence? Whilst in sweet Sojourn
> Thou view'st the Reliques of old *Rome* . . .

L

Philips implores the 'Dear Youth' to return at length to grace Britain's Isle with Latian Knowledge. Smart was possibly trying to improve upon Philips's lament for the absent Harcourt, by substituting the more melodramatic elegy for the dead Wheeler. In expressing his grief for Wheeler, Smart's conceits are certainly conventional enough:

> In vain forlorn
> I call the Phoenix, fair Sincerity;
> Alas!—extinguish'd to the skies she fled,
> And left no heir behind her. Where is now
> The eternal smile of goodness? Where is now
> The all-extensive charity of soul,
> So rich in sweetness . . .
>
> *(Collected Poems*, i. 154)

The sentiment is similar to Pope's in the 'Elegy to the Memory of an Unfortunate Lady':

> Fate snatch'd her early to the pitying sky.
> As into air the purer spirits flow,
> And sep'rate from their kindred dregs below;
> So flew the soul to its congenial place,
> Nor left one virtue to redeem her Race.[54]

In the elegy 'On the Sudden Death of a Clergyman', published in the *Student* in 1751, Smart again sounds as if he may be expressing genuine sorrow, for he writes of his 'arbitrary grief':

> 'Tis impotence of frantic love,
> Th'enthusiastic flight of wild despair,
> To hope the Thracian's magic power to prove
>
> *(Collected Poems*, i. 33)

His feeling was certainly strong enough to override the contemporary theory of what a correct elegy should look like. The essay 'Of the Elegy' in the *Art of Poetry on a New Plan* specified that 'the numbers should be *smooth* and *flowing*, and captivate the ear with their uniform sweetness and delicacy.' It was a rule strictly observed in the elegy by Pope quoted above, or in Gray's 'Elegy Written in a Country Churchyard', both of which are

---

[54] *The Poems of Alexander Pope*, 262.

quoted in the *Art of Poetry on a New Plan* as fine examples of the elegy. Smart's feeling was strong enough to break the rules of elegy, but not strong enough to avoid conventional imagery:

> And you, his kindred throng, forbear
> Marble memorials to prepare,
> And sculptur'd in your breasts his busto wear
> *(Collected Poems*, i. 34)

The conceit is to be found also in the epitaph on Richardson, printed in the *Christian's Magazine* for December 1763, 'Ah no! expect not from the chissel'd stone/The praises graven on our hearts alone,/*There* shall his fame a lasting shrine acquire'—a conceit which is also implicit in Pope's epitaph on Gay quoted above. Even when he failed to observe the strict rules of his art, Smart could not at this stage of his career avoid the influence of his literary forbears.

[VI]

Jubilate Agno

— i —

'a methodical, rational, and entertaining Common-Place-Book (*An Index to Mankind*)

WHEN WE PICK UP *Jubilate Agno* for the first time, its appearance strikes us as being very strange. In Bond's edition, the extant fragments of the manuscript are set out in five sections, Fragments A, B1, B2, C, and D. Except for the first two lines, all 113 lines of Fragment A begin with the hortatory 'Let'. The long series of commands—'Let Huz bless with the Polypus—lively subtlety is acceptable to the Lord. Let Buz bless with the Jackall—but the Lord is the Lion's provider' (A.84, 85), and so on—is strange enough. But in Fragment B1, we have the unusual task of reading across the verso and recto pages, following a 'Let' verse on the left-hand page with a qualifying 'For' line on the right-hand page. 'Let Anath rejoice with Rauca who inhabiteth the root of the oak. For I bless God for my Newcastle friends the voice of the raven and heart of the oak. Let Cherub rejoice with the Cherub who is a bird and a blessed Angel. For I bless God for every feather from the wren in the sedge to the CHERUBS & their MATES' (B1.121, 122) and so on, through 295 'Let' verses and 295 'For' verses. Fragment B2 consists of another 475 'For' verses; Fragment C consists of 162 'Let' verses and 162 matching 'For' verses; Fragment D consists of 237 'Let' verses.

After reading Smart's secular poetry and his earlier religious poetry, we see at a glance that Smart has suddenly rejected the literary forms used by Milton, Dryden and Pope, and for the first time in his career, he has evolved his own individual poetic form. We realize immediately that structurally, *Jubilate Agno* is unique—and we shall find that it is unique in thought, style, and expression, as well as in structure. It would therefore be foolish to make over-ingenious parallels with other eighteenth-century poems. Yet it is possible to suggest that *Jubilate Agno* was nevertheless influenced, though by no means dominated, by several contemporary literary fashions.

Firstly, we find that *Jubilate Agno* has something in common with the commonplace books, the anthologies of epigrams and maxims that were so popular at the time. This is especially important when we remember that several collections of maxims have been attributed to Smart himself. The *Student's Companion* was first published in 1748 and was subsequently appended to the Dublin edition of *An Index to Mankind* in 1754. (Although it is now listed with Smart's works in the General Catalogue of the British Museum, it is not mentioned in Gray's *Bibliography*.) Under the heading 'Writing', the *Student's Companion* recommends the kind of sententious style that we find in *Jubilate Agno*: 'Many Words are seldom us'd, but to magnify great Actions, alleviate ill ones, or deceive the Ear with false Argument. Truth is plain, and may be revealed in very short Sentences.' Smart himself made the point more forcefully in his poem 'On the Merit of Brevity', first published in the second volume of the *Midwife*:

> If you think that my Works are too puft up with Levity,
> Yet at least approbation is due to my Brevity,
> The Praises of which shou'd be now more egregious,
> As our Bards at this Time are confoundedly tedious.
>
> (*Collected Poems*, i. 28)

The Preface to the *Student's Companion* points out that students usually attend to superficialities of style rather than to beauties of sentiment, and that they are quite distracted by the multiplicity of voluminous treatises. The *Student's Companion* intends therefore to sum up important passages of history, and the sentiments of the great men of antiquity. The extracts are collected under general headings, arranged alphabetically, beginning with Age and Abstinence, and ending with Yielding and Zeal. ('For Z is zeal', wrote Smart in *Jubilate Agno* B2.536, and 'For Z is zeal and therefore he is God, whom I pray to be gracious to the Widow Davis and Davis the Bookseller', he wrote in C.17—both being final lines in Smart's mad, poetic

versions of the alphabet.) Both the *Student's Companion* and
Jubilate Agno offer pearls of wisdom 'in very short sentences'.
As will be seen from the following quotation from Plutarch's
Life, under the heading 'Images', the *Student's Companion* was
more lucid but less pithy than *Jubilate Agno*:

> *Numa* forbad the *Roman* People from worshipping God under any
> known Form. All Images therefore, or Pictures of him were, at
> that Time, entirely abolished in *Rome*: He beautify'd and adorn'd
> the Temples, but without any Figure; saying, it was Sacrilege to
> endeavour to represent cælestial Objects by terrestrial; and that
> it was impossible to have any Knowledge of the Divinity, but by
> the Eyes of the Soul.

> For Painting is a species of idolatry, tho' not so gross as statuary.
> (*Jubilate Agno* B2.673)

If indeed Smart edited the *Student's Companion*, he showed an
early taste for the kind of Biblical, proverbial wisdom found in
Jubilate Agno. 'The royal Prophet, speaking of Man, says, his
Days are as a Flower in the Fields, beauteous, but tender, and
liable every Instant to Destruction', wrote the editor of the
Student's Companion. *Jubilate Agno* A.69 is a more pious version
of the same sentiment, 'Let Nebuchadnezzar bless with the
Grashopper—the pomp and vanities of the world are as the herb
of the field, but the glory of the Lord increaseth for ever.'

A similar taste for 'maxims' can be found in *An Index to Mankind*, first published in 1751, issued with the third volume of the
Midwife in 1753, published in Dublin in 1754, and issued with
the *Nonpareil* in 1757. Gray feels that it is an open question
whether it was in fact edited by Smart; Goldsmith, and even
Newbery himself, have also been suggested as possible editors.[1]
There are many similarities between the sentiments of the *Index
to Mankind* and those of *Jubilate Agno*. The Introduction to the
Index to Mankind therefore gives some warrant for our tentative
classification of *Jubilate Agno* as a type of commonplace book:
'the following Sheets are presented to the Public, as a methodical, rational, and entertaining Common-Place-Book.' The
editor means to strike a happy medium between recent

---

[1] See *Notes and Queries*, ser. iii, vol. iv, 19th September 1863, 229; 26th September
1863, 254.

commonplace books—of which there are too many on the market—because some are ill-connected, while others are so formally disposed 'that they have the Pedantic Regularity of a Dictionary'. This looks suspiciously like an ironically malevolent reference to the formal, alphabetical arrangement of the *Student's Companion*. Certainly, the aims of the editor of the *Index to Mankind* are similar to those of the editor of the *Student's Companion*, for he too intends to offer his readers what he himself has digested of the knowledge of mankind, and the wisdom of the ancients. In 1753, another commonplace book, *Be Merry and Wise*, was published, including 211 maxims from *An Index to Mankind* as well as numerous jests from another anonymous publication attributed to Smart, the *Nut-Cracker* (1751). The close relationship between *An Index to Mankind*, *Be Merry and Wise*, and *Jubilate Agno*, has been demonstrated by Dr. Sherbo. He quotes, for instance, a maxim from *An Index to Mankind*, 'It is impossible that an ill-natured man can have public Spirit, for how should he love ten thousand Men who never loved one?', and points out that this maxim appears in *Jubilate Agno* B2.496. 'For a man cannot have publick spirit, who is void of private benevolence', and is repeated in *Jubilate Agno* B2.564.[2]

It is not really relevant at this point to discuss whether in fact Smart edited the *Student's Companion*, the *Index to Mankind*, or *Be Merry and Wise*. What is important, is that they throw some light on the 'genre' to which *Jubilate Agno* seems to belong. It can be seen as a collection of wise and pithy sayings, not scattered at random down the sheets of manuscript, but collected in a 'methodical, rational, and entertaining' anthology. We shall see that *Jubilate Agno* has some kind of methodical not to say rational organization, and it is always entertaining. It is even possible that the *Student's Companion* sheds some light on the genesis of *Jubilate Agno*. For the definition of 'Memory' taken from Plutarch, 'Memory is the Mother of the Muses', is curiously illustrated by the fact that '*Seneca* repeated two thousand Names, having heard them but once, beginning at the last, and calling them in order till he ended with the first.' Perhaps Smart took literally the commonplace idea that poetry

[2] 'Survival in Grub-Street: Another Essay in Attribution', *Bulletin of the New York Public Library*, lxiv, 1960, 147–58.

derived from memory, and perhaps the long lists of names from
Pliny and the Bible are intended to demonstrate that the poet
of *Jubilate Agno*, like Seneca, has a brilliantly poetic memory.

— ii —

'[*De Sacra Poesi Hebræorum*] one of the best performances that
has been published for a century' (*The Universal Visiter*)

Having looked at one genre that probably affected the shape
and style of *Jubilate Agno*, we now turn to a literary manifesto
that might have influenced the structure and expression of
Smart's mad poem. Ever before W. H. Bond discovered that
Jubilate Agno was based on the antiphonal structure of Hebrew
poetry, W. F. Stead felt sure that the poem was influenced by
Robert Lowth's *De Sacra Poesi Hebræorum*, a course of lectures
delivered before the University of Oxford and published in
Latin in 1753. Smart had read and appreciated the book, for
he had brought it to the attention of his readers in successive
issues of his periodical, *The Universal Visiter*, in January and
February 1756: 'This work, which for its elegance, novelty,
variety, spirit, and (I had almost said) divinity, is one of the
best performances that has been published for a century.'[3]
Stead made one or two comparisons between Lowth's discussion of parallelism in Hebrew poetry, and Smart's technique
in *Jubilate Agno*, but it was not until Bond made his discovery
that the full extent of Lowth's probable influence on *Jubilate
Agno* was revealed.

   In his *Lectures*, Dr. Lowth referred a number of times to the
responsive nature of Hebrew ritual. What was said of the
Heathen Muses may still more strictly be applied to those of
the Hebrews, they love alternate song. The word 'gnanah',
Lowth continued, means 'to answer', but is used to denote any
song or poem, and we can infer from that, that the word passed
from particular to general use, and that among the Hebrews
almost every poem possesses some sort of responsive form.[4] In
Lecture XXVII, Lowth referred again to the responsive form
of Hebrew poetry, but this time in the context of a jubilant

³ *Rejoice in the Lamb*, 297.
⁴ *Lectures on the Sacred Poetry of the Hebrews*, trans. G. Gregory, 1787, ii. 32–33.

gathering before the Lord. 'The induction of the ark of God to mount Sion by David, gave occasion to the twenty-fourth Psalm. The removal of the ark was celebrated in a great assembly of people, and with suitable splendour during every part of the ceremony. The Levites led the procession, accompanied by a great variety of vocal and instrumental music; and this Ode appears to have been sung to the people when they arrived at the summit of the mountain. The exordium is expressive of the supreme and infinite dominion of God, arising from the right of creation'.[5] When the ark was brought in, the Levites divided into two choirs and sang alternately the final part of the Psalm. At the beginning of *Jubilate Agno*, Smart's use of the responsive form (always assuming that he wrote a 'For' section to match the 'Let' lines of Fragment A) might well have been chosen to express the kind of jubilant assembly described in Psalm 24. It is important that it was King David himself who took the ark of God to Mount Sion—Smart's identification with David became stronger and stronger, as will be seen in our discussion of *A Song to David*. In A.16, 'Let the Levites of the Lord take the Beavers of yᵉ brook alive into the Ark of the Testimony', and it does seem that the long lists of persons and creatures in Fragment A are intended to rejoice in the Lord as the Ark of the Testimony is carried to Sion, with Smart in charge. But it is entirely characteristic that Smart should have cheerfully complicated this theme with a pun on 'ark'. In A.4, he wrote, 'Let Noah and his company approach the throne of Grace, and do homage to the Ark of their Salvation.' Smart seems to have used the idea of pairs of creatures entering the ark, their salvation from the flood—not pairs of the same species, as in the Bible, but pairs made up of one human being and one animal.

It is coincidental that when Smart's version of Psalm 121 was included in *Select Psalms in Verse* (1811), it was illustrated by a paragraph from Lowth's *Lectures*: 'THE hundred-and-twenty-first psalm is of the same kind with the twenty-fourth already noticed, that is, of the genuine dramatic, or dialogue form; and as it is both concise and elegant, I shall quote it at large. The king, apparently going forth to battle, first approaches the ark

[5] *Ibid.*, ii. 238.

of God upon Mount Sion, and humbly implores the Divine
assistance, on which alone he professes to rest his confidence.
. . . The high-priest answers him from the Tabernacle'. It seems
a remarkable coincidence that Smart's Psalms should be discussed in relation to the very principles upon which *Jubilate
Agno*, a psychotic and presumably absolutely private work, was
based. One is bound to ask whether *Jubilate Agno* was entirely
private, and whether the editor of *Select Psalms* knew something
about it. We do not know whether Lowth himself had any
suspicion of the way his *Lectures* were apparently affecting the
work of the mad poet, but he was certainly in touch with Smart
after his release from confinement. Dr. Hawkesworth's letter to
Smart's sister, written in 1764, mentions the fact that Smart
'had lately received a very genteel letter from Dr. Lowth'.

Yet, after saying this, we are bound to realize that far from
using Lowth's aesthetic principles, Smart might simply have
been obsessed with the rhythms and structure of the Psalms.

> Let them praise his Name in the dance: let them sing praises
> unto him with tabret and harp.
> For the Lord hath pleasure in his people: and helpeth the meek-
> hearted. (Psalm 149. 3, 4)

Except that these lines from the Book of Common Prayer lack
the mad convolutions of allusion and pun, they could well be
taken from Smart's poem, where line after line begins with
'Let', and line after line answers, 'For'. And, 'Let Jakim with
the Satyr bless God in the dance', wrote Smart in *Jubilate Agno*
A.67.

Much the same can be said about Smart's use of parallelism in
Jubilate Agno. It was very likely influenced by the principles that
were so lucidly set out in Lowth's *Lectures*—but Smart could
have imitated the Biblical style without reference to Lowth at all.
In Lecture XIX, Lowth described parallelism as follows: 'The
poetical conformation of the sentences, which has been so often
alluded to as characteristic of the Hebrew poetry, consists
chiefly in a certain equality, resemblance, or parallelism
between the members of each period; so that in two lines (or
members of the same period) things for the most part shall
answer to things, and words to words as if fitted to each other

by a kind of rule or measure.'[6] Lowth distinguishes three species of parallelism, the synonymous, the antithetic, and the synthetic.

Synonymous parallelism occurs where 'the same sentiment is repeated in different, but equivalent terms.' Lowth illustrates his point with numerous examples. A pair of lines from Psalm 114 is sufficient here:

> The mountains leaped like rams;
> The hills like the sons of the flock.

In *Jubilate Agno* A.68, 69, Smart complicates this simple figure in order to emphasize the transience of this world and the eternity of the next:

> Let Iddo praise the Lord with the Moth—the writings of man perish as the garment, but the Book of God endureth for ever.
> Let Nebuchadnezzar bless with the Grashopper—the pomp and vanities of the world are as the herb of the field, but the glory of the Lord increaseth for ever.

The sentiment of these lines is parallel, although it is worked out in different images: the Eternity of the Lord is contrasted with the transience of man. It should be noted that while the antiphonal structure of *Jubilate Agno* links 'Let' verse to 'For' verse—that is, in a horizontal pattern—the parallelism links 'Let' verse to 'Let' verse—that is, in a vertical pattern. There seems no doubt that Smart had planned a rigid structure, when he began writing *Jubilate Agno*.

Antithetic parallelism occurs where 'a thing is illustrated by its contrary being opposed to it.' One of the examples given by Lowth is taken from Proverbs 27.6:

> The blows of a friend are faithful;
> But the kisses of an enemy are treacherous.

This is one type of parallelism that Stead discovered in *Rejoice in the Lamb*. For in *Jubilate Agno* B1.287, 288, Smart wrote,

> For Solomon said vanity of vanities vanity of vanities all is vanity.
> For Jesus says verity of verities verity of verities all is verity.

---

[6] *Lectures on the Sacred Poetry of the Hebrews*, ii. 34.

But there are other examples of the same technique to be found in *Jubilate Agno*, for instance, B2.369, 370,

> For a DREAM is a good thing from GOD.
> For there is a dream from the adversary which is terror.

We feel that here, at least, the technique of parallelism is directly related to a dualism in Smart's experience, the terrifying opposition between his consciousness of God and his consciousness of the Devil, the opposition between the manic and depressive phases of his illness.

The third type of parallelism is synthetic or constructive, 'in which the sentences answer to each other, not by the iteration of the same image or sentiment, or the opposition of their contraries, but merely by the form of construction.' Lowth illustrates this point from Psalm 19:

> The law of JEHOVA is perfect, restoring the soul;
> the testimony of JEHOVA is sure, making wise the simple:
> The precepts of JEHOVA are right, rejoicing the heart;

A notable example of Smart's use of this device is in *Jubilate Agno* B1.46–48:

> For I this day made over my inheritance to my mother in consideration of her infirmities.
> For I this day made over my inheritance to my mother in consideration of her age.
> For I this day made over my inheritance to my mother in consideration of her poverty.

Lowth's *Lectures* certainly help us to recognize and describe the techniques used in *Jubilate Agno*, provided that we always bear in mind that since Smart's intimate knowledge of the Bible is manifest throughout the religious poetry, his style might well have been influenced directly by the parallelism of the Biblical text, without reference to the principles of parallelism as explained by Dr. Lowth.

It is nevertheless possible that Lowth's remarks about the characteristic brevity of the Hebrew style might have affected Smart's elliptical expression in *Jubilate Agno*. We have already seen that Smart's taste for maxims might have derived from the

contemporary fashion in commonplace books. An additional
influence might have been exercised by Lowth's account of the
sententious style of the Hebrews, 'This being always accounted
the highest commendation of science and erudition; "To understand a proverb and the interpretation; the words of the wise
and their dark sayings . . ." Brevity or conciseness was a
characteristic of each of these forms of composition, and a
degree of obscurity was not unfrequently attendant upon this
studied brevity.'[7] Smart certainly enjoyed 'dark sayings' in
Jubilate Agno, despite the fact that perspicuity was a *sine qua non*
of contemporary poetry. Professor Merchant has demonstrated
how Smart's concentrated form of symbolical utterance allows
him to speak volumes in a very few lines of poetry. A studied
brevity and a degree of obscurity are marked in *Jubilate Agno*
B1.43, for instance:

> Let Jubal rejoice with Cæcilia, the woman and the slow-worm
> praise the name of the Lord.
> For I pray the Lord Jesus to translate my MAGNIFICAT into verse
> and represent it.

The 'conciseness' of these lines becomes apparent if their full
significance is unravelled. Merchant interprets as follows:
'Here the names and the doctrines are interwoven into two
word complexes. Jubal as the inventor of music and the pun on
Cæcilia as both lizard and Saint Cecilia, patroness of music,
have been noted by Stead (cited by Bond); the verbal patterns,
with overt and latent suggestions, then take on these forms:
Jubal—Cecilia—Praise—Magnificat and Caecilia—Lizard—
Slowworm—[Serpent]—[Eve]—Woman—[Mary]—Magnifi-
cat, a very great deal of significance to pack into two antiphonal statements, with the implications of the Fall and
Redemption'.[8]

There is yet another aspect of Lowth's *Lectures* that may be
relevant to the structure of *Jubilate Agno*. Several times, Lowth
refers to the alphabetic poems of the Hebrews: 'There existed
a certain kind of poetry among the Hebrews, principally

---

[7] *Lectures on the Sacred Poetry of the Hebrews*, i. 97–98.
[8] W. Moelwyn Merchant, 'Patterns of Reference in Smart's *Jubilate Agno*',
Harvard Library Bulletin, xiv, 1960, 23.

intended, it should seem, for the assistance of the memory: in
which, when there was little connexion between the sentiments,
a sort of order or method was preserved, by the initial letters of
each line or stanza following the order of the alphabet.'[9] Perhaps Smart's exercise on the alphabet in B2.513–536, B2.538–
561, and C.1–17, are attempts to transpose the alphabetic
structure of Hebrew verse into English poetry. Lowth discusses
the alphabetic poems as being opposed to the inspired composition of prophetic poetry: 'such an artificial arrangement would
be utterly repugnant to the nature of prophecy; it is plainly the
effect of study and diligence, not of imagination and enthusiasm; a contrivance to assist the memory, not to affect the
passions.'[10] Smart certainly indulged in 'prophecy' in *Jubilate
Agno* C.57 to the end of Fragment C. Yet perhaps Smart was
painfully aware of his madness, and consciously exploited the
'artificial arrangement' of alphabetical lines in order to regulate
his over-exuberant 'imagination and enthusiasm'. It is, perhaps,
a regulating device similar to beginning a series of 'Let' verses
with the names of the Disciples, or describing Jeoffry's move-
ments in a series of ten degrees, a device to give shape to an
unruly mass of images and ideas. Indeed, Dr. Sherbo has indi-
cated that Smart might have been advised to compose *Jubilate
Agno* as a distraction from madness. He refers to the long lists of
names, still largely unidentified, in Fragment D, 'a practice that
Styan Thirlby, an abortive editor of Shakespeare, is reported to
have followed in an effort to distract his mind. "Such employment," says Dr. Johnson, authority for the anecdote, "as Dr.
Battie has observed, is necessary for madmen." '[9] Dr. Battie was,
of course, the mad-doctor of St. Luke's Hospital, where Smart
was confined for a year. Once again, we have to remember that
Smart's alphabetical verses might have been directly influenced
by the Biblical text—he had only to go as far as Psalm 119,
with its paragraph headings, Aleph, Beth, Gimel, and so on
through the Hebrew alphabet. Bond suggests that Smart was

[9] *Lectures on the Sacred Poetry of the Hebrews*, i. 57.

[10] *Ibid.*, ii.10–11.

[9] 'The Probable Time of Composition of Christopher Smart's *Song to David*,
Psalms, and *Hymns and Spiritual Songs*', *Journal of English and Germanic Philology*, lv,
1956, 54.

familiar with the profound meanings attached to the Hebrew characters by occult writers, and that he was obviously trying to establish the significance of his native alphabet.[10] I remain sceptical about Smart's debt to 'occult' literature, but we shall deal with this point more fully when we come to discuss the 'content' of *Jubilate Agno*.

If we are willing to allow that Smart was influenced by Lowth's *Lectures*—and I have tried to show that this was not necessarily so—we may feel that the following passage could well have encouraged Smart to write an autobiographical outpouring of the soul in *Jubilate Agno*—his memories, meditations, terrors, and pleasures:

> Frequently, instead of disguising the secret feelings of the author, it lays them quite open to public view; and the veil being as it were suddenly removed, all the affections and emotions of the soul, its sudden impulses, its hasty sallies and irregularities, are conspicuously displayed.[11]

In writing *Jubilate Agno*, Smart possibly felt that he was purging the 'affections and emotions' of his soul—but only as a true poet should, by expressing himself in a controlled, traditional poetic form. He did not choose the traditional forms acceptable to Pope, Dryden, or Prior—they had not suffered his insane affections and emotions—but he chose instead, consciously or unconsciously we do not know, the Psalms of David as his model, with their jubilant praise of the Lord, the imagery of the procession of the Ark of the Testimony to Mount Sion, the technique of parallelism and alphabetical arrangement. Smart's identification with David, the poet, was beginning to develop.

—iii—

'I shall take the liberty of contradicting him, before he arrives at existence' ('A New System of Castle-Building')

In the first part of this chapter we have suggested several conventions which probably influenced the structure and expression of *Jubilate Agno*. But when we come to try understanding

---

[10] *Jubilate Agno*, p. 106.
[11] *Lectures on the Sacred Poetry of the Hebrews*, i 312

what Smart was actually saying and meaning in *Jubilate Agno*, we have a rather more difficult task. We can easily recognize some of the poetic principles that controlled the composition of *Jubilate Agno*. But what about the content and the meaning of the words that Smart marshalled and organized according to fairly straightforward aesthetic laws?

There has been some disagreement about the intellectual foundations of *Jubilate Agno*. W. F. Stead suggests that Smart was familiar with the occult philosophers: 'As he unveiled his hidden life during these years of silence and confinement, there came up out of the deep places a mystical or occult philosophy derived from such writers as Pythagoras, Hermes, the Cabalists, Cornelius Agrippa, Eugenius Philalethes, and Henry More the Cambridge Platonist.' Stead points out that this literature is extensive and that we must be careful not to attribute an image or idea to one specific writer as though he were the only possible source. He has illustrated Smart's mystical interpretation of Jacob's Ladder by a passage from Eugenius Philalethes, the occult significance of numbers by a passage from Cornelius Agrippa, and his use of the word 'centre' by a passage from Henry More. But the mystical interpretation of Jacob's Ladder was used by medieval theologians as well as by the Renaissance occultists; the mystical meaning of numbers was the common property of the Pythagoreans as well as of the Cabalists, and the special meaning of 'centre' is found also in the school of nature mystics to which Henry Vaughan belonged. Stead's illustrations are therefore intended to show only the community of thought between Smart and the authors of these various kinds of esoteric philosophy. 'That he was acquainted with some of their writings, and found them congenial, is, I think, beyond question. One might describe him as the last of the Cambridge Platonists. He was not at home either in the orthodoxy or scepticism of his age; in the Cambridge of Henry More he might have been a different man.'[12]

Dorothy Griffiths adopted Stead's ideas about the intellectual content of *Jubilate Agno*, and over and over again, she discusses Smart's imagery in terms of the occult writers listed by Stead. For instance, in discussing Smart's statement that the universe

[12] *Rejoice in the Lamb*, 37–38.

is sustained by spirit, she refers to Henry More's belief in a universe where souls were never sundered from matter, a universe in which even the most aetherial and refined activities of the soul could take place only in the expressive form of some matter: she cites More's *Immortality of the Soul* (1659), and then goes on to refer to Ralph Cudworth's *The True Intellectual System of the Universe* (2nd edition, 1743) where he suggests that it is reasonable to suppose that angels have bodies as well as souls.[13]

Thomas Foster Teevan discusses the occult background to *Jubilate Agno* in terms of Jacob Boehme and his eighteenth-century disciple, William Law. He quotes, for instance, a long passage from *Signatura Rerum* and intersperses parallel passages from *Jubilate Agno*. 'If Boehme was Smart's source for such verses as I have selected—verses dealing with movement, contrariety, pressures, tensions, dualities, the resolving fire—we can see how Smart adapted the source to his own use. He seems first of all to be calling the references up from his reservoir of memory rather than using an opened text. The prolixity of Boehme has been condensed into gnomic statement, oracular in tone, and allied to others not through argumentative, rhetorical form, but by embodying a mystical feeling, its "mystical essence" as the Boehme chapter title just quoted suggested.'[14]

Sherbo has attacked this thesis, that Smart was well-read in occult literature: 'when Stead insists, as he does, on Smart's knowledge of occult literature other than that of Freemasonry, his belief becomes suspect when particular lines, explained by him in terms of occultism, are equally understandable against a Masonic frame of reference.'[15] Sherbo makes his point by referring to *Jubilate Agno* B2.317–319, 'For the SUN is an intelligence and an angel of the human form. For the MOON is an intelligence and an angel in shape like a woman. For they are together in the spirit every night like man and wife.' Stead interprets these lines by referring to *Anthroposophia Theomagica* by Eugenius Philalethes, 'The Sun and Moon, are two Magicall

[13] *The Poetry of Christopher Smart*, Ph.D. thesis, University of Leeds, April, 1951, 126.

[14] *A Study of Christopher Smart's 'Jubilate Agno'*, Ph.D. thesis, University of Washington, 1957, 58.

[15] 'Christopher Smart, Free and Accepted Mason', *Journal of English and Germanic Philology*, liv, 1955, 664.

M

principles, the One active, the other passive, this *Masculine*, that
Fæminine.'[16] Sherbo points out that the sun and moon are also
Masonic symbols, masculine and feminine respectively, and
that anyway, Smart's image of the female sun could have been
taken from Psalm 19.4–5. Sherbo returned to the attack in an
article, ironically entitled 'Christopher Smart's Knowledge of
Occult Literature': 'What I wish to suggest, then, is that where
Stead quotes or cites a mystical or occult writer as a possible
source for an image or idea in the poem there is a possible
source much readier at hand in Masonry, the Bible, or elsewhere.' Sherbo devotes the rest of his article to showing that for
every occult reference cited by Stead, a Masonic one can be
put in its place. It is as well that Dr. Sherbo qualifies with the
following sensible statement, 'It does not seem to me un-
necessarily impertinent and repetitious to state again that a
great deal of what Stead looks upon as stemming from mystical
and occult literature is merely the product of Smart's imagination. Need a poet . . . be held to a source for every line he
writes? A study of the sources for *Jubilate Agno* is still a desidera-
tum, yet the interest of such a study would almost certainly
center in the transformation of the source materials in Smart's
hands.'[17]

I have already said that I too am sceptical about Smart's debt
to the occult literary tradition. We do know that Smart borrowed
Iamblichus's *Life of Pythagoras* from the Pembroke College
Library at some time between 1743 and 1745, and although it is
therefore perfectly justified to trace Iamblichus's influence on
Smart's poetry, it is not logical to infer that the huge body of
occult writing necessarily affected his work. *The Life of Pythagoras* is mainly concerned with the ascetic way of life of
Pythagoras and his disciples. The references to Pythagorean
philosophy are few and far between, but they do throw some
light on certain lines of *Jubilate Agno*. Iamblichus states that the
Pythagorean philosophy 'was symbolic, and resembled enigmas
and riddles, consisting of apothegms',[18] which could describe in
broad terms Smart's style in *Jubilate Agno*. Iamblichus writes

[16] *Rejoice in the Lamb*, 212.
[17] *Journal of the History of Ideas*, xviii, 1957, 241.
[18] *Iamblichus' Life of Pythagoras*, trans. Thomas Taylor, 1818, 175.

that in order to understand the derivation of Pythagorean philosophy, 'a perspicuous paradigm of the Pythagoric theology according to numbers, is in a certain respect to be found in the writings of Orpheus. Nor is it to be doubted, that Pythagoras receiving auxiliaries from Orpheus, composed his Treatise Concerning the Gods, which on this account also he inscribed the Sacred Discourse, because it contains the most sacred flower of the most mystical place in Orpheus'.[19] Iamblichus goes on to quote from the *Sacred Discourse*: '*Orpheus the son of Calliope, having learnt wisdom from his mother in the mountain Pangæus, said, that the eternal essence of number is the most providential principle of the universe, of heaven and earth, and the intermediate nature; and further still, that it is the root of the permanency of divine natures, of Gods and dæmons.*' Iamblichus comments, 'From these things, therefore, it is evident that he learnt from the Orphic writers that the essence of God is defined by number, *Through the same numbers also, he produced an admirable fore-knowledge and worship of the Gods, both which are especially most allied to numbers.*'[20] That the essence of God can be defined by number brings to mind *Jubilate Agno* C.18, 19, 'For Christ being A and Ω is all the intermediate letters without doubt. For there is a mystery in numbers.' Iamblichus gives a moral definition of numbers, and so does Smart in *Jubilate Agno*, but it is doubtful whether Smart was being deliberately Pythagorean. Iamblichus states that according to Pythagoras, the universal unity is the most honourable of all things, and that the number two is the most honourable in a house, city, camp, and in all such systems. Smart would have agreed that unity is 'honourable', for he wrote in *Jubilate Agno* C.20, 'For One is perfect and good being at unity in himself.' But he thought that the number two is 'dishonourable', for he wrote in *Jubilate Agno* C.21, 23, 'For Two is the most imperfect of all numbers. . . . For the Devil is two being without God.' Iamblichus and Smart agree that three and six are good numbers. Iamblichus wrote of the Pythagorean dictum that men should make libations thrice, that Apollo delivered oracles from a tripod because the triad is the first number, that sacrifices to Venus should be made on the sixth day because six is the first that partakes of every number, and when divided in

[19] *Ibid.*, 105.   [20] *Ibid.*, 105–7.

every possible way, recives the power of the numbers sub-
tracted and of those that remain. Smart wrote in *Jubilate Agno*
C.22, 26, 'For every thing infinitely perfect is Three. . . . For
three is the simplest and best of all numbers.' In C.30, he wrote,
'For Six is very good consisting of twice three.' But Smart was
obviously thinking of the Christian Trinity rather than of the
Pythagorean symbol, for in *Jubilate Agno* C.15, he substituted
'X' for 'Christ', and wrote, 'For X has the pow'r of three and
therefore he is God.'[21]

It is certainly possible that Iamblichus's *Life of Pythagoras* had
some effect on the symbolism of *Jubilate Agno*. But perhaps
Smart himself should have the last word on what he felt about
occult literature in general. He wrote in the 'Introduction to
the Second Book of Castle-Building',

> Some antiquarian therefore will arise, who shall take it into his
> head, to give certain satisfactory and cogent reasons, why the
> first book of CASTLE-BUILDING consists of ten chapters precisely.
> He will urge perhaps, that I had a particular attachment to the
> number ten, as some of the ancient philosophers had to the
> number seven; or that the aforesaid number is lucky; or that it is
> an ecclesiastical number, and has a connection with the tythe. But
> in order to be beforehand with a vengeance, I shall take the
> liberty of contradicting him, before he arrives at existence. I
> protest then, that it is not *because* I have any particular liking to
> the number ten, or because the number is either philosophical,
> ecclesiastical, or civil. In short, the word *because* is impertinent
> and entirely out of the question, *because* it is merely from the
> prerogative of an author, and no other reason, that I have
> ordain'd, and by these presents do ordain, that every book of
> CASTLE-BUILDING shall consist of ten chapters, neither more nor
> less . . .[22]

This should deter us from reading too many elaborate occult
significance into *Jubilate Agno*.

[21] Stead interprets this line as follows, 'the letter X is pronounced EKS and thus
has the value of three letters; also it contains a V, and an inverted V, as well as its
own significance as X; the *power of three* is a reference to the Trinity' (*Rejoice in the
Lamb*, 252). A crux in *Jubilate Agno* B2.534, 'For X is hope—consisting of two check
G' is the subject of a correspondence between Reginald Horrox and W. H. Bond
in the *Times Literary Supplement*, 12th May 1961, 293; 21st July 1961, 449; 10th
November 1961, 805.

[22] *Student*, ii. 245–46.

While we argue about the 'ideas' expressed in *Jubilate Agno*, we are in fact begging several questions about its meaning. It may seem more or less certain that Smart was using Newton's *Principia*, or some scientific work derived from the *Principia*, when he wrote certain passages in *Jubilate Agno*. Compare, for example, *Jubilate Agno* B1.161, 'For MOTION is as the quantity of life direct, & that which hath not motion, is resistance', with Newton's definition, '*The quantity of motion is the measure of the same . . . The* vis insita, *or innate force of matter, is a power of resisting, by which every body, as much as in it lies, continues in its present state, whether it be of rest, or of moving uniformly forwards in a right line.*'[23] Or compare *Jubilate Agno* B1.180 with Newton's definition:

> Let Addi rejoice with the Dace—It is good to angle with meditation.
> For the power of the WEDGE is direct as it's altitude by communication of Almighty God.
>
> The forces by which the wedge presses or drives the two parts of the wood it cleaves are to the force of the mallet upon the wedge as the progress of the wedge in the direction of the force impressed upon it by the mallet is to the velocity with which the parts of the wood yield to the wedge, in the direction of lines perpendicular to the sides of the wedge.[24]

Smart's debt to Newtonian physics is obvious here. Yet we are not at all sure what he actually means by his compressed, garbled scientific statements. He is not simply weaving Newtonian physics into the texture of his poetry as he did when he used the *Opticks* as a basis for the light imagery in *On the Goodness of the Supreme Being*. Instead, he is adopting and altering Newton's definitions to suit his own fanatically religious, pseudo-scientific view of reality. '*A centripetal force is that by which bodies are drawn or impelled, or any way tend, towards a point as to a centre*',[25] wrote Newton. 'For the Centripetal and Centrifugal forces are GOD SUSTAINING and DIRECTING', wrote Smart in *Jubilate Agno* B1.163. Admittedly, William Derham was also

[23] *Newton's Principia Motte's Translation Revised*, ed. Florian Cajori, Berkeley 1946, 1–2.
[24] *Newton's Principia*, 27.
[25] *Ibid.*, 2.

prepared to suggest a religious interpretation of Newtonian physical law. Derham made straightforward statements like the following: 'But by reason the *Gravitating Power* exceeds the *Centrifugal* as 2174 exceeds 7,54054 . . . therefore all parts lye quiet and secure in their respective places, and enjoy all the benefits, which I shewed do accompany this Motion without any disturbance from it. THUS is our own Globe guarded by its *Gravity* against the *Centrifugal Force* of its Rotation.'[26] Derham also made a religious statement about the law of gravity: 'AND now from the consideration of what I have shewn in this sixth Book, to be either highly probable, or very certain, concerning *Gravity*, we have another manifest demonstration of the infinite CREATOR's Wisdom and Care, and another cogent argument to excite the highest Veneration and Praise in his Creatures.'[27] But to say that the force of gravity illustrates the Wisdom and Care of God is very different from Smart's dynamic statement that God *is* Force. Derham allows that God controls physical law. Smart implies that God is physical law, a more immediate vision of God.

We can suggest a large number of intellectual 'sources' for *Jubilate Agno*. I have referred only to a handful. But even if we know that Smart is referring to the *Principia* or to *Astro-Theology*, we are not sure whether he is in fact talking *about* Newtonian physics. Rather, Smart uses the Newtonian definitions as metaphors, in order to express poetically his concept of the universe as activated by the presence of a dynamic God. Smarts garbled expression of Newton's laws (together with characteristic puns, like the double-meaning in *Jubilate Agno* B1.180 on the geometric angle and angling for fish—dace in particular) suggests that his religious vision of the physical universe was a mad one. We have reached an important new position: if anything in the design of *Jubilate Agno* points to the insanity of its author, it is the way in which Smart arranges his ideas in to bizarre word-patterns. We shall find that it is a difficult task, trying to discuss this aspect of Smart's poetic technique—for how can we begin to understand language that is mad?

[26] *Astro-Theology Or a Demonstration of the Being and Attributes of God, from a Survey of the Heavens*, 1721 ed., 148–49.
[27] *Ibid.*, 164–65.

— iv —

'the grappling of the words upon one another in all the modes
of versification' (*Jubilate Agno* B2.632)

In discussing contemporary reactions to the poetry of William
Blake, Dr. Bronowski has pointed out how difficult it is to
understand and criticize poetry which appears to be mad: 'they
did not doubt that Blake spoke what he thought. But they
doubted whether his language, however like theirs, was the
same as theirs. And unless Blake spoke their langauge, could he
speak to them? unless he hit the pitch of ther ears, could he be
said even to be thinking aloud? Were Blake's writings less aim-
less than those vast harangues, ten, twelve, sixteen hours
together, in which George III foamed into madness in 1788?'[28]
Indeed, if we were to decide finally that a mad poet speaks a
completely private language, we should have to put down
Jubilate Agno or *The Marriage of Heaven and Hell*, and admit
once and for all that the writings of insanity are beyond our
comprehension. But before we take such a drastic step, we
should pause to ask an important question: how far is it true to
say that a madman *can* speak his own language? To those who
are acquainted, say, with the linguistic philosophy of Ludwig
Wittgenstein, it is obvious that a single use of language does not
stand alone, but is intelligible only within the general context in
which language is used. It is possible within a human society
as we know it for an individual to follow a private rule of conduct,
just as it is possible for a madman to follow a private set of
linguistic rules. But it must be in principle possible for other
people to grasp that rule and to judge when it is being correctly followed. It makes no sense to suppose anyone capable of
establishing a purely personal standard of conduct, or a purely
personal language, if he had never had any experience of
human society with its socially established rules and its socially
established language.[29] It follows, then, that the special use of
language in *Jubilate Agno* can be understood within the context
of eighteenth-century literary English. Also, that we should be

[28] *A Man Without a Mask*, 1944, 14.
[29] I have adapted Peter Winch's exposition of Wittgenstein in *The Idea of a Social Science*, 1960, 32–33, 39.

able to grasp Smart's linguistic 'rules' and to judge when he is following them correctly. The only way, therefore, in which we can understand *Jubilate Agno* is by using normal language as a measuring-rod for the abnormality of Smart's language. Only against the established rules of language do the deviations of *Jubilate Agno* become apparent.

In practical criticism, however, it is difficult to decide how far Smart's language deviates from the norm. Take *Jubilate Agno* B1.272, for example, 'For LIGHTNING is a glance of the glory of God.' This line can be analysed in at least three different ways. At one level, it displays the logic of any poetic metaphor, and the parts of the metaphor can be separated to make a rational simile. To see God's glory is like seeing lightning, the common factor in the two experiences being the dazzling, blinding quality of glory and lightning. On another level, the line can be interpreted according to the logic of eighteenth-century physico-theology: if all natural phenomena show forth the Attributes of their Creator, as John Ray or William Derham would have argued, Smart can say logically if elliptically that lightning displays the glory of God. On yet another level, this line from *Jubilate Agno* can be understood as a mad account of reality. As 'T. I.' wrote in a letter to Dr. Battie, the mad-doctor of St. Luke's Hospital, where Smart had spent a year's confinement:

> Suppose a man, through a disorder in the optic organs, perceiveth that phænomenon which is called Lightening [sic]; this man, if he considers the species as connected with a distemper in the eye, is not thought mad; but if he takes it to be a sign of thunder, rain, &c. we do not hesitate to pronounce him fit for Bedlam.
>
> From hence it is evident, that a man is not mad for perceiving this or that species, but for making a wrong judgment concerning it, or, in other words, for being deceived by it.[30]

Suppose a man, Smart, perceiveth that phenomenon which is called lightning; this man, if he takes it to be a sign of the glory of God, do we hesitate to pronounce him fit for St. Luke's?

I have taken a relatively simple line in *Jubilate Agno* to show that the 'insanity' of Smart's language is often difficult to

[30] *Gentleman's Magazine*, xxxiii, January 1763, 21.

recognize. It would be impossible to decide which of the three interpretations is correct—whether the line should be understood as a poetic metaphor, as a physico-theological statement, or as an insane statement about the nature of reality. The problem can be illustrated by another example. Dr. Sherbo was once cautioned by a neurologist of his acquaintance, who happened to be a learned student of the history of the treatment of the insane in the eighteenth century, that he was not to give any credence to what Smart was writing in *Jubilate Agno* while confined for insanity. Dr. Sherbo was reluctant to take this advice to its logical extreme: 'I must say, as one example, that the well-known passage on Smart's cat Jeoffrey in the *Jubilate* is, of course, drawn from the life. He had a cat, a real one, not the product of his diseased imagination, and he described his cat in words that show his powers of observation and description.'[31] But having accepted the 'fact' of Smart's cat in this way, it is still possible to claim that his description of Jeoffry is mad, the product of a diseased imagination. W. F. Stead has contrasted the exquisitely controlled description of Selina in Thomas Gray's 'On a Favourite Cat'—'a brilliant sanity combined with infinite grace and sprightliness'—with Smart's reckless statements about Jeoffry in *Jubilate Agno*. Stead quotes 'For in his morning orisons he loves the sun and the sun loves him' (*Jubilate Agno* B2.723), and points out that though it is reasonable to say that the cat loves the sun, what rational man would say that the sun loves the cat? And similarly, what sense is there in speaking of the Cherub Cat as a member of the angel tribe of Tiger: 'Blake, to be sure, had a somewhat similar notion, but Blake also was regarded as insane.'[32]

This, then, is the position at the moment. We realize that it is sometimes difficult, even impossible, to distinguish between sane metaphor and insane vision in *Jubilate Agno*. Yet the imaginative fantasies and strange grammatical forms suggest that the poem is the reckless product of a deranged imagination. In either case, whether we choose to read *Jubilate Agno* as conscious metaphor or as unconscious fantasy, we have to accept with Sherbo the

[margin annotation: Selima]

[margin annotation: if one apprehends sun = cat as a relationship – if its mad its also child-like animism]

[31] '*Jubilate Agno*: the Mind of Christopher Smart', *Papers of the Michigan Academy of Science, Arts, and Letters*, xlv, 1960, 422.
[32] 'Christopher Smart's Cat', *Criterion*, xvii, 1938, 684–85.

'fact' of Smart's cat or the 'fact' of his lightning. I myself prefer
to discuss *Jubilate Agno* as fantasy, and in doing so I have to
take a certain amount of sense for granted. Something like an
act of faith is necessary if we are going to take lightning as that
flash of light that we all understand by common sense in our
common language—and a similar act of faith is necessary if we
are going to take Jeoffry as a cat, though a particular cat, such
as we understand by common sense. If Smart means something
completely different by 'lightning' or 'Jeoffry', we shall have
to deny any possible communication between writer and reader.
This denial is certainly a valid approach: scepticism about the
possibility of communication between the mad poet and his
readers could annul anything attempted below by way of a
rational discussion of the way in which Smart chooses his words
and arranges them into a mad but aesthetically logical pattern
in *Jubilate Agno*.

The complex interdependence of words is fundamental to
Smart's theory of poetry in *Jubilate Agno*. Smart makes this
clear in B2.600–602:

> For the relations of words are in pairs first.
> For the relations of words are sometimes in oppositions.
> For the relations of words are according to their distances from
> the pair.

It seems certain that Smart is writing here about poetic
language, not about language in general, because these lines
occur in a passage which relates poetic rhyme and word-
structure to the aural qualities of musical instruments. The
principles which Smart states here can indeed be illustrated
from other parts of *Jubilate Agno*—if we are courageous or rash
enough to try interpreting Smart's rules and applying them to
Jubilate Agno. The simplest illustration of his first principle
could be the Biblical association of man and beast—'the
relations of words are in pairs first' could apply to Balaam and
the Ass in A.11, Daniel and the Lion in A.13, David and the
Bear in A.41, and so on. His second principle, 'the relations of
words are sometimes in oppositions' could be illustrated by the
antithesis in A.90, 'Let A Little Child with a Serpent bless Him,

who ordaineth strength in babes to the confusion of the Adversary.' The Child and the Serpent are the opposed powers of good and evil, for in Psalm 8.2, 'Out of the mouth of very babes and sucklings hast thou ordained strength, because of thine enemies: that thou mightest still the enemy, and the avenger' (Book of Common Prayer). In his own version of the Psalms, Smart transcribed 'enemy and avenger' as 'fiend', and in this line of *Jubilate Agno*, he is obviously trying to reconcile the innocent child with the devil—or trying, perhaps, to reconcile life and death, for Teevan gives persuasive reasons for thinking that one of the major themes of *Jubilate Agno* is the conflict of life, and death symbolized by the 'Adversary'.[33]

Smart's third and most complex principle is that 'the relations of words are according to their distances from the pair.' He seems to mean here that the pair of words that begin a line forge a relating link between the disparate elements of the rest of the line. For instance, take *Jubilate Agno* A.68:

Let Iddo praise the Lord with the Moth—the writings of man perish as the garment, but the Book of God endureth for ever.

This line can be seen as a pair of words—Iddo and the Moth—linked to two disparate statements, 'the writings of man perish as the garment', and 'but the Book of God endureth for ever.' As it happens, these two statements are logically linked by the conjunction, 'but'. Yet the two statements are also linked by reference back to the pair of names at the beginning of the line. The Book of God refers back to Iddo, the writer of genealogies, 'Now the acts of Rehoboam, first and last, are they not written in the book of Shemaiah the prophet, and of Iddo the seer concerning genealogies?' (II Chronicles 12.15). Smart seems to connect the Book of God with the early genealogical books of the Bible, a connection which is balanced against 'the writings of man'. The perishing garment refers back to the Moth, and is related to the words 'endureth for ever' in the antithetical clause, by the following verse in Isaiah 51.8, 'For the moth shall eat them up like a garment, and the worm shall eat them like wool: but my righteousness shall be for ever, and my salvation from generation to generation.'

[33] *A Study of Christopher Smart's 'Jubilate Agno'*, 186–96.

Another example is to be found in *Jubilate Agno* A.58, 'Let Benaiah praise with the Asp—to conquer malice is nobler, than to slay the lion.' Once again, the clauses that make up the 'maxim' are related to each other by means of their connection with the pair of names at the beginning of the line, Benaiah and the Asp. The connection between Benaiah and the slain lion is clear enough, for in II Samuel 23.20, 'Benaiah the son of Jehoiada . . . slew two lionlike men of Moab: he went down also and slew a lion in the midst of a pit in time of snow'. The connection between the Asp and the conquest of malice is not quite so straightforward. In the Bible, the Asp and the Adder seem to be identified, and both are symbolical of malicious speech. One of the Biblical asps appears in Romans 3.13, 'with their tongues they have used deceit; the poison of asps is under their lips', and the targum refers to Psalm 140.3. This appears in the Book of Common Prayer as 'They have sharpened their tongues like a serpent: adder's poison is under their lips'. In his version of the Psalms, Smart associated this adder (or asp) with malice:

> Their tongue, by malice sharpen'd, works
>   With anger and untruth;
> The venom of the viper lurks
>   Beneath their lip and tooth.
> > (*Collected Poems*, ii. 762)

It seems, then, that Smart took his cue from the Bible, and associated in his mind the four words, viper-asp-adder-malice, and therefore forged a logical association between the Asp and the conquest of malice in *Jubilate Agno* A.58.

Another example is to be found in A.91, 'Let Huldah bless with the Silkworm—the ornaments of the Proud are from the bowells of their Betters.' Once again, Smart relates his maxims to the pair of names at the beginning of the line by a complicated system of cross-reference. Huldah had a direct interest in the ornaments of the proud, for in II Kings 22.14, there is a reference to 'Huldah the prophetess, the wife of Shallum the son of Tikvah, the son of Harhas, keeper of the wardrobe; (now she dwelt in the college)'—'keeper of the wardrobe' being, of course, the operative words for our analysis of *Jubilate Agno*

A.91. The relationship between the Silkworm and the bowels of their betters is an obvious reference to the way silkworms spin silk—for Huldah's wardrobe—out of their own bodies.

Yet another example of Smart's third principle can be given from A.92, 'Let Susanna bless with the Butterfly—beauty hath wings, but chastity is the Cherub.' The interaction of the two clauses of the maxim are here quite obviously dependent on reference back to the pair of names at the beginning of the line. Susanna's great virtue was chastity, for she withstood the lascivious Elders. The Butterfly is a beautiful, winged creature. By cross-reference, Smart shows that Susanna was not only chaste, but beautiful and angelic as well. The image is reminiscent of some lines in *Susannah. An Oratorio. With Alterations and Additions. As it is Perform'd at the Theatre-Royal in Covent-Garden. Set to Musick by George Frederick Handel, Esq.* (1759):

> Chastity, thou Cherub bright,
> Gentle as the Dawn of Light,
> Soft as Musick's dying Strain:
> Teach the Fair how vain is Beauty,
> When she breaks the Bounds of Duty,
> Vain are Charms, and Graces vain.

The comparison is particularly interesting because this oratorio was published in 1759, the year in which Fragment A was probably begun.[34] Once again we see that the madness of *Jubilate Agno* often lies in its complex, unique word-patterns rather than in the actual images or ideas used.

When we interpret *Jubilate Agno* according to Smart's own principles of versification, we begin to understand the logic of the poem. Based on a coherent theory of the interdependence of clause and phrase within a single line of poetry, the logic here is essentially the logic of poetic metaphor rather than the insane connection of disparate words—or is it? Iddo and the Moth, apparently discrete, are poetically linked when the underlying aesthetic principle is grasped and applied to the whole line. We may therefore be willing to concede that Smart does not fling

[34] Arthur Sherbo, 'The Dating and Order of the Fragments of Christopher Smart's *Jubilate Agno*', *Harvard Library Bulletin*, x, 1956, 205, suggests March 1759 as a possible *terminus a quo* for the beginning of *Jubilate Agno*.

words together with the abandon of a maniac throwing furniture round a room. Yet we do not feel sure that Smart's metaphorical method, however logical, is entirely sane. The means by which he felt constrained to express his moral vision of the world seem disturbingly erudite and complex. Fragment A of *Jubilate Agno* reads as if it were written by a highly intelligent man whose too-active brain created for him tortuous poetry composed of complicated, interrelating Biblical allusions, in order to express fairly simple concepts. For the 'meaning' of the lines discussed above seems straightforward. Iddo and the Moth are paired to show that man is transient but that God is eternal. The link between Benaiah and the Asp shows that moral victory (over malice) is greater than physical victory (over the lion). Huldah and the Silkworm are paired to show that man's pride is dependent on the work of the lower creation. Susanna and the Butterfly are paired to show that chastity has aesthetic beauty as well as divine virtue.

How Smart's restless and over-active brain composed ever more complicated poetic forms in *Jubilate Agno* will be more fully explored below. But—and there is always a 'but' when one tries to understand *Jubilate Agno*—it must be remembered that the poetic principles used above to help us understand Fragment A were themselves derived from Fragment B2. In fact, we were rationalizing twice over. In the first place, we were trying to make sense of Smart's aesthetic rules. In the second place we were trying to make sense of the principles in relation to Fragment A. Were we not in danger of analyzing at two removes from the essential madness of *Jubilate Agno*? It depends on our point of view, how to answer this question. If we are determined to be sceptical, and state that we cannot hope to be *sure* of understanding either Smart's poetic theory, or its application, since both are couched in insane language, then we have to put the poem away and forget about it. On the other hand, if we feel that Smart's language, however mad, cannot be entirely divorced from the eighteenth-century English that we read and understand so easily, then we can be prepared to go forward, trying again to 'understand'.

As Professor Merchant wrote of *Jubilate Agno*, 'no ingenuity will ever make of this shattered ruin of a poem a symmetrical and well-ordered whole, but it now seems possible to recognize indications of a coherence and insight in Christopher Smart that drew together a remarkable body of heterogeneous learning.' Some of the methods by which Smart achieved 'coherence' have already been discussed—his unique way of relating word to word by cross-reference and Biblical allusion. Merchant has emphasized another method by which Smart made his poem coherent and therefore comprehensible—his trick of multilingual punning. I mean to show first of all just what has been discovered about Smart's puns in *Jubilate Agno*. As will be seen, this mechanical analysis of his punning will eventually enable us to make assumptions about Smart's particular, mad viewpoint—what I think of as his 'philological vision of reality'.

Two examples from Merchant's article show what an important breakthrough he achieved in understanding Smart's language in *Jubilate Agno*. We have already looked at his interpretation of B1.43, and how the meaning is dependent on the English-Latin pun on 'Cæcilia' as meaning both St. Cecilia and a lizard. Merchant shows that *Jubilate Agno* B1.5 contains an English-Greek-Hebrew system of punning, 'Let Raguel rejoice with the Cock of Portugal—God send good Angels to the allies of England! For I have abstained from the blood of the grape and that even at the Lord's table.' Merchant interprets, 'Here Raguel is related to ῥάϵ, a grape, maintaining the reference to Portugal in the *Let* verse and the "blood of the grape" in the *For* verse, while Raguel in its Hebrew sense, "friend of God," is related to "good *Angels*" and "the *allies* of England."'[35]

Merchant admitted that his examples are 'fragmentary and suggestive only', and his suggestion that there is Hebrew punning in *Jubilate Agno* was taken up by Charles Parish, who attempted a thorough analysis of the Hebraic aspects of *Jubilate Agno*.[36] Some examples of Parish's method can be given as follows. In connection with *Jubilate Agno* B1.76, for instance, 'Let Elishua rejoice with Cantharis God send bread and milk to

[35] 'Patterns of Reference in Smart's *Jubilate Agno*', 22.
[36] 'Christopher Smart's Knowledge of Hebrew', *Studies in Philology*, lviii, 1961, 516–32.

the children. For I pray God to give them the food which I cannot earn for them any otherwise than by prayer', Parish gives 'Elishua' in its Hebrew form, 'eliyshuw'a' meaning 'God of (or *is*) riches'. 'Shuw'a' means 'riches', or alternatively 'a liberal, opulent person'. An identically-spelt homophone means 'a cry for help', and 'yishuw'a', from the same root, means 'help' or 'deliverance'. Parish interprets, therefore, 'Smart supplicates God, the liberal and opulent, for financial help.' This example belongs to Parish's first group of correspondences —those which seem to him definite proof of Smart's knowledge of Hebrew. An example from his second group, those which indicate a good deal of probability, shows that a method may lead the analyst to over-ingenious interpretation, though it is Parish's saving grace that he admits it. 'Let Achsah rejoice with the Pigeon who is an antidote to malignity and will carry a letter. For I bless God for the Postmaster general & all conveyancers of letters under his care especially Allen and Shelvock', wrote Smart in *Jubilate Agno* B1.22, referring to Ralph Allen of Bath, who instituted a system of cross-country posts, and to George Shelvocke, Secretary to the Postmaster General. Parish gives the Hebrew form of 'Achsah' as ' 'akhsa', meaning 'anklet' or 'fetter', and thus suggesting the means by which a pigeon carries a letter. Parish refers to Bond's note on the 'antidote to malignity', that a fresh-killed pigeon was split and placed on a festering wound to draw out the poison. He feels that the word ' 'akhsa' therefore points to an 'irresistible but farfetched allusion'. It is possible to trace the word for 'adder' to the same root, and one concordance actually translates 'Achsah' as 'snake charmer'. In view of the total context of Smart's line, the idea, says Parish, is delightful.

When Parish introduces his third group of correspondences, he is still afraid of being farfetched. 'In defense of the correspondences which I offer in this group I have only this to say: while the linkage may appear to be occasionally tenuous— indeed, hairbrained—the particulars in Groups I and II make one receptive even to vague connections. My fundamental premise is that once we concede to Smart some knowledge of Hebrew, we must also allow that that knowledge may function periphally as well as centrally.' Parish places *Jubilate Agno*

B1.45 in his third group, 'Let Areli rejoice with the Criel, who is a dwarf that towereth above others. For I am a little fellow, which is intitled to the great mess by the benevolence of God my father.' Parish gives the Hebrew form of 'Areli' as ' 'ar'eli' meaning 'heroic'. He suggests that Smart is trying to say that everything is relative—the lesser white heron is a dwarf compared with men, but towers above other birds. Perhaps Smart himself considers that he is ' 'er'el', a strong and mighty man, although he is a little fellow. A Talmudic use of the word introduces another twist of meaning—' 'er'eliym' came to mean 'angels', and Parish feels that this reminds us of an important motif in *A Song to David*, the hierarchy of God, angel, and man. Parish's scholarship and ingenuity are admirable, but he ends his article with the comment that 'the ability to see the wit is dependent on the wit of the searcher, and, after all, it is only when the wind is southerly that one can tell a hawk from a handsaw.'

We have now discussed Smart's puns at some length, and we now need to ask whether the discussion of word-patterns in *Jubilate Agno* gives us any insight into what belongs to Smart's 'realm of reality'. I have already suggested that Fragment A can be interpreted as conventional religious thought expressed through images interrelated by a logical poetic theory and that his theme seems to be the nature of God and the significance of moral behaviour. But after examining the theories of Moelwyn Merchant and Charles Parish, I am inclined to think that instead of pointing to a coherent body of religious thought and sentiment, Smart's multilingual punning points to a mad, philological vision of reality. It is as if Smart's obsession with the sound, texture, and meaning of words in various languages has transformed the concrete reality of sanity into the philological reality of madness.

We can begin to illustrate this rather obscure point by looking at *Jubilate Agno* B2.632, where Smart makes a vigorous statement of his theory, that the complex interdependence of words is fundamental to poetic language: 'For Clapperclaw is in the grappling of the words upon one another in all the modes of versification.' 'Clapperclaw' is an archaic verb, meaning to scratch and claw, to attack with tooth and nail. Smart seems to

N

be implying that the words in a poem should be associated as violently and powerfully as cats in a fight claw and bite one another. The metaphor, implicitly comparing words with cats, is complicated by a pun in *Jubilate Agno* B2.628, 'the power and spirit of a CAT is in the Greek'—he means that the common Greek preposition κατ' (B2.629) is identical in sound to the English noun, 'cat', and that therefore 'the pleasantry of a cat at pranks is in the language ten thousand times over' (B2.630). The Greek preposition so obsesses Smart's imagination, that eventually the English cat becomes inseparable from the Greek language, 'For the Greek is thrown from heaven and falls upon its feet' (B2.634). For all its oddity, the metaphorical and punning image of the cat is obviously meant to express the protean quality of the Greek language, for Smart goes on to say that 'For the Greek when distracted from the line is sooner restored to rank & rallied into some form than any other' (B2.635). We now begin to see what it means for a series of multilingual puns to point to a mad vision of reality. Smart's grotesque, undeniably insane vision, means in fact that the Greek language takes on the concrete form of an animal, expressed by means of a pun on κατ' and cat.

Smart does not limit this sort of pun to the Greek language. He sees the Latin language as a mouse, a quasi-logical connection with the Greek cat. He takes the Latin 'mus' as a verb-ending in *Jubilate Agno* B2.639, 'For Edi-mus, bibi-mus, vivi-mus—ore-mus.' But in B2.638, he takes 'mus' as a noun meaning 'mouse', 'For the Mouse (Mus) prevails in the Latin.' As Charles Parish puts it, 'Smart takes part of the word and finds in it a sense that it was never intended to have; he takes the bound morpheme '-mus'—the first-person plural marker—and equates it with the word (i.e., the free morpheme) "mus." The question of his seriousness or levity is irrelevant.'[37] Smart's fantastic metaphorical girth thus encompasses the abstract qualities of bravery and hospitality as they are manifest in the Latin language and Roman character (let us eat and drink, live and pray, 'For bravery & hospitality were said & done by the Romans rather than others'—B2.644), and as they are manifest in the English creature, 'For the Mouse is a creature

[37] 'Christopher Smart's Knowledge of Hebrew', 519.

of great personal valour. . . . For the Mouse is of an hospitable disposition'—B2.640, 643.

Smart discusses the English language in the same grotesque animal terms. His initial statement in *Jubilate Agno* B2.645, 'For two creatures the Bull & the Dog prevail in the English', refers of course to the bulldog as a type of the Englishman. In his fable, 'The English Bull Dog, Dutch Mastiff, and Quail', Smart had written,

> Well, of all dogs it stands confess'd,
> Your English bull dogs are the best;
> I say it, and will set my hand to 't,
> Cambden records it, and I'll stand to 't.
> (*Collected Poems*, i. 60)

In *Jubilate Agno*, Smart takes the word 'bulldog', and identifies the sound 'bull' with the sound 'ble', and proceeds to a characteristic punning metaphor whereby the animal, the bull, permeates the English language just as the cat permeated the Greek, 'For all the words ending in ble are in the creature. Invisi-ble, Incomprehensi-ble, ineffa-ble, A-ble' (B2.646). I am at a loss to know why the bull should have rampaged through the English language in the words specifically used to define the nature of the Supreme Being. (Smart returned to the same subject in *Jubilate Agno* B2.676 when he wrote 'For BULL in the first place is the word of Almighty God', and went on to say that the bull is a creature of infinite magnitude in the height, and that there are many words under Bull—the month (was Smart thinking of the astrological sign of Taurus?), the sea, the brook, the rock, the bullfinch (he is punning on bull and bullfinch), the bluecap, humming-bird, beetle, toad, frog, pheasant-eyed pink, bugloss, bugle, oxeye (did bull remind him of the ox?), and fire.) Certainly, Smart's grotesque animal-languages are devout ones, 'For the Greek & Latin are not dead languages, but taken up & accepted for the sake of him that spake them' (B2.647), where Smart is referring perhaps to the Latin Vulgate Bible and the Septuagint. Having dealt with the Bull, Smart proceeds to the Dog. He switches with characteristic fluency to its Latin form, 'canis', and splits it down the middle into two English words, 'can' and 'is'. The dog then prevails in the English language, 'For can is (canis) is cause & effect a dog' (B2.648). Smart ends his account of the animal English language by writing, 'For the English is concise & strong. Dog & Bull again' (B2.649). Language and bulls are strong perhaps. Language and dogs are concise only by means of an atrocious pun on concise/canis.

This is not the logic of the relation of one thing to another as in the concrete reality we express through our common language. Nor is it the relation of one thing to another as in simple metaphor, the language of poetry. It appears to be the eccentric logic of a multilingual, mercurial shift from one word to another according to their identity of sound. If it is at all possible to 'understand' the aspect of reality expressed in the language of *Jubilate Agno* in the passages examined above, we understand a reality given significant pattern only by the philological, as opposed to syntactical, associations between word and word. The curiosity of these fantastic associations is the curiosity of Smart's psychotic vision, and by trying to understand his mad language, we are enabled to enter his insane world and its obsession with the sound of words. As Wittgenstein stated in the *Tractatus Logico-Philosophicus*, 'That the world is *my* world shows itself in the fact that the limits of my language (of the only language that I can understand) means the limits of *my* world.' When we study the language of *Jubilate Agno*, we are in fact trying to define the limits of Smart's world.

[VII]

A Song to David

'The man of God's own choice' (*A Song to David*)

ANYONE WHO HAS HEARD of Christopher Smart usually knows that the *Song to David* was written on the walls of the madhouse. The *Monthly Review* for April 1763 first printed the story: 'It would be cruel, however, to insist on the slight defects and singularities of this piece, for many reasons; and more specially, if it be true, as we are informed, that it was written when the Author was denied the use of pen, ink, and paper, and was obliged to indent his lines, with the end of a key, upon the wainscot.' This story was repeated many times, but by January 1817 the details had changed. In an article on the 'Rise and Progress of Popular Disaffection', the *Quarterly Review* pronounced that 'there are worse evils than neglect, poverty, imprisonment, and death . . . Boyse in his blanket, Savage in a prison, and Smart scrawling his most impassioned verses with charcoal upon the walls of a madhouse, are not the most mournful examples which might be held up as a warning to kindred spirits.' The legend is repeated again and again in nineteenth-century editions and criticisms of *A Song to David*— Smart scratches with his key or scrawls with his charcoal, or even does both, indenting his verses with a key and afterwards shading them off with a rough piece of charcoal.[1] We do not know how the *Monthly Review* got hold of the original story but the later 'charcoal' theory is based perhaps on a confusion between the Smart legend proper, a couplet by Pope, and an anecdote about Goldsmith. Dorothy Griffiths has pointed out the relevant lines in the *Epistle to Dr. Arbuthnot*:

> Is there, who lock'd from Ink and Paper, scrawls
> With desp'rate Charcoal round his darken'd walls?[2]

---

[1] *Notes and Queries*, ser. iii, vol. ii, 1862, 139.
[2] *The Poems of Alexander Pope*, 598.

The anecdote about Goldsmith would be even more significant if the legend had grown around the composition of *Jubilate Agno* rather than *A Song to David*: 'The following Monday, May 4 [1772], Boswell and his friend William Julius Mickle borrowed General Oglethorpe's coach and drove out to the Selbys' farm house to call on Goldsmith. He was not at home, but they browsed about his room looking at his volumes of natural history and chuckling at his unorthodox method of taking notes: by scratching on the wall with a lead pencil descriptions of the grampus, the louse, the serpent, and other animals.'[3] The reader has to make up his own mind whether the original story about the key on the wainscot may or may not contain a grain of truth.

During the nineteenth century, *A Song to David* gradually came to be recognized as Smart's greatest poem, and in our own time, this is still the accepted view. In this chapter, we shall be examining certain aspects of the structure and expression of Smart's most admired poem. But before we do so, we need to give some attention to the subject matter of the poem, which poses an interesting literary and psychological question: *why* did Smart choose to address King David as his ideal man?

In his earliest work, Smart had been frightened of the subject. His learned and ingenious friend, Mr. Comber, had suggested that a poem about David's playing to Saul when he was troubled by the evil spirit might be suitable for an Ode on St. Cecilia's Day, but Smart had felt that the choosing too high subjects had been the ruin of many a tolerable genius. Then, in *On the Goodness of the Supreme Being*, Smart had invoked Orpheus, Israel's sweet Psalmist, who gave motion to the hills, rocks, and floods, and 'Drove trembling Satan from the heart of Saul,/ And quell'd the evil Angel'. Smart had begged Orpheus-David to breathe some portion of genuine spirit into his breast:

> . . . so shall the muse
> Above the stars aspire, and aim to praise
> Her God on earth, as he is prais'd in heaven.
> (*Collected Poems*, i. 241)

Then, in the *Hymn to the Supreme Being*, Smart had identified

---

[3] Ralph M. Wardle, *Oliver Goldsmith*, Lawrence, Kansas, and London, 1957, 227, citing the *Boswell Papers*, ix. 262, and the *Life of Johnson*, ii.182.

himself with King Hezekiah; he had described the virtuous king as having a snow-white conscience which no foul crime has dyed 'Like *David*, who have still rever'd thy word/The sovereign of myself and servant of the Lord!' (*Collected Poems*, i. 245). In *Jubilate Agno* A.41, Smart had referred directly to King David, 'Let David bless with the Bear—The beginning of victory to the Lord—to the Lord the perfection of excellence—Hallelujah from the heart of God, and from the hand of the artist inimitable, and from the echo of the heavenly harp in sweetness magnifical and mighty', and as we have seen, Smart used many techniques in *Jubilate Agno* that had originated in the poetry of King David. Yet there is nothing in these earlier poems to suggest how far Smart was going to develop his idealization in *A Song to David*. I wonder, therefore, whether some of the impetus for describing David in unqualified, idealistic terms came from the contemporary controversy concerning the character of David.

The man who set the controversy in motion was, not sur-surprisingly, Pierre Bayle. We know that Smart once borrowed the *Dictionary* from the Pembroke College Library, and this gives us an additional motive for quoting Bayle's opinions on the character of King David—opinions that aroused the righteous indignation of every pious clergyman in the eighteenth century: 'DAVID, King of the *Jews*, was one of the greatest Men in the World, even tho' we should not consider him as a Royal Prophet, who was after God's own Heart.'[4] Bayle pretends to preserve a due balance between admiration and criticism. David's piety is so shining in his Psalms and in many of his actions that it cannot be sufficiently admired. He is the sun of holiness in the Church over which he spread a wonderful light of consolation and piety by his works. But—we are ready for Bayle's malicious smile—David had his faults. This is a characteristic understatement, for Bayle goes on to catalogue David's crimes—the numbering of the people, the murder of Uriah, the adultery with Uriah's wife. Yet Bayle concludes, piously, that David expiated these 'very heinous Crimes' by such admirable repentance that his life is a fine model for the edification of faithful souls, teaching us the frailty of the saints and how we must be vigilant and bewail

---

[4] *An Historical and Critical Dictionary*, 1710, ii. 1059.

our sins. Smart ignores David's sins of murder and adultery and includes even purity in his catalogue of David's twelve virtues. Smart was at least not alone in this absurd falsification of David's character.

In 1740, Patrick Delany brought out his *Historical Account of the Life and Reign of David*. His aim was to remove the greater objections to the character of David, and in the course of his book, he attacks Bayle by calling him 'a great broahcer[*sic*] of paradoxes, an industrious dissenter from men of learning, and a known patron of all the errors that ever obtained in the world from its foundation; a defender even of contrary and contradictory errors.'[5] Delany 'cannot but reflect with astonishment, upon the applause which Mr. *Bayle* hath gained; and with horror, upon the evil errors he hath spread by his casuistry!'[6] I prefer Bayle's casuistry to Delany's, but there is no denying which author Smart would have supported. Where Bayle writes of David that 'we should not consider him as a Royal Prophet, who was after God's own Heart', Smart refers to David as 'The man of God's own choice' (stanza V) and writes of 'that diviner part/Of David, even the Lord's own heart' (stanza LXXXIII).

Smart knew and admired Delany's book. He probably read it while he was still at Cambridge, for there is a mutilated entry in the Library Register under his name: ' <. . .> of K. David'. The *Catalogus Bibliothecæ Pembrokianæ* (1704–40) includes a *Life of King David* (London 1740). Smart had certainly read the book by 1755 when he wrote the first paragraph of *On the Goodness of the Supreme Being*, identifying Orpheus and David, and added the footnote, 'See this conjecture strongly supported by *Delany*, in his *Life of David*.' 'What if *Orpheus* in *Thrace* was no other than *David* in *Paran*?'[7] Dr. Delany had written, making his point with a long, specious argument that had evidently appealed to Smart. Robert Brittain feels that it was fortunate that Smart did not repeat the identification of David and Orpheus in *A Song to David*. But he finds several passages in the poem that suggest that Smart had not forgotten Delany's work. Brittain quotes three lines from stanza LXVI:

[5] *An Historical Account of the Life and Reign of David*, 1740–42, i. 241.
[6] *Ibid.*, iii. 156.   [7] *Ibid.*, i. 195.

> For ADORATION, in the skies,
> The Lord's philosopher espies
> The Dog, the Ram, and Rose
> *(Collected Poems, i. 363)*

and comments that the phrase 'the Lord's philosopher' seems
somewhat obscure and strained until we find Delany's note that
the Greek word 'sophos', which was originally the title of
astronomers, might have been derived from the Hebrew word
'Zoph' which signified a prophet. 'Smart's phrase then becomes
a happy epithet for David, and his use of it serves artfully to
reintroduce the symbol around which his main theme is
woven.'[8] Brittain suggests another link with Delany when
Smart writes 'in gladsome Israel's feast of bow'rs' in stanza
LXXXII. Delany's description of the Feast of the Tabernacles
repeatedly refers to the 'bowers', a word which does not occur in
the Authorized Version. Brittain then quotes from stanza XVI,
'Wise are his precepts, prayer and praise,/And counsel to his
child', and quotes Delany's opinion that the first nine chapters
of Proverbs were David's instructions to his son, Solomon.

In his edition of *Poems by Christopher Smart*, Brittain makes
further comparisons between Smart and Delany. It would be
superfluous here to look at each one of his points, but one is
important, stemming from stanza VII of the *Song to David*:

> Pious—magnificent and grand;
> 'Twas he the famous temple plan'd,
> (The seraph in his soul:)
> Foremost to give the Lord his dues,
> Foremost to bless the welcome news,
> And foremost to condole.
> *(Collected Poems, i. 350)*

Brittain suggests that these lines refer to David's actions when
he was informed by Nathan that God would not permit him to
build the temple, but that it would be built by his son. He
points out that Delany discusses this episode at some length,
devoting most of his space to David's prayer of thanksgiving
and praise for God's promise. 'David's *gratitude* is the point

---

[8] 'Christopher Smart and Dr. Delany', *Times Literary Supplement*, 7 March 1936,
204.

stressed by Delany.'[9] The importance of gratitude as a central
theme in Smart's religious poetry has been emphasized in
Chapter II of the present study, and it seems worth extending
Brittain's point, in order to suggest other passages in Delany's
book which might have influenced the *Song to David*, and
possibly the excessive sense of gratitude expressed elsewhere in
Smart's verse. It should be remembered at this point that
Smart himself saw the *Song to David* as essentially an exercise in
gratitude, for he advertised the poem as one 'composed in a
Spirit of Affection and thankfulness to the great Author of the
Book of Gratitude, which is the *Psalms* of DAVID the King.'[10]
We notice with interest, therefore, Delany's comment on the
Psalm in I Chronicles 16, 'IN this Psalm, after *David* hath exhorted the people to praise and to give thanks to GOD, for his
peculiar mercies to them there recited, he then breaks out into
a rapture of gratitude, in contemplation of the infinite bounty
and benignity of the Creator, and calls upon the whole creation,
to fill up the chorus of his praise'.[11] Later, Delany makes even
more explicit comment on the theme of gratitude in David's
Psalms: 'ALTHOUGH *David*'s main purpose in publishing these
divine hymns, setting them to suited music, and singing them
in the public worship of GOD, was, to publish to the whole
world, his endless gratitude, for the various and wonderful
mercies of GOD, bestowed upon him; yet had he a further, and,
if possible, a nobler purpose, in this conduct; I mean, to dis-
perse true religion throughout every part of his dominions; to
inspire the hearts of his people with a true and lively sense of
gratitude to GOD, their Benefactor, Protector, and Saviour, as
well as his. *David* well knew, that true gratitude to GOD is the
surest source of true religion, and every duty injoined by it.
And when it is poured out for public blessings, in which all
partake, naturally mixes with every social affection, and blends
them, as it were, into its own being; and by this means, becomes
the very best bond of society.'[12] Already, Smart's cast of mind,
as it is expressed in *A Song to David*, does not seem so strangely

[9] *Poems by Christopher Smart*, 299.

[10] *Proposals for Printing, by Subscription, a New Translation of the Psalms of David . . . .
By Christopher Smart*, 8 September 1763.

[11] *An Historical Account of ihe Life and Reign of David*, ii. 135–36.

[12] *Ibid.*, iii. 235.

unique, once his poem is compared with other contemporary writings on the character of King David.

It does seem quite likely that Delany's book had some influence on the thought and style of *A Song to David*. But if we are going to argue that Smart wrote his poem in response to the contemporary controversy about David's character, we have to look at the next phase of the row, which flared up again in the 1760s. In 1760, Samuel Chandler brought out his sermon on the death of George II, *The Character of a Great and Good King Full of Days*. Chandler makes a detailed and rather astonishing comparison between King David and King George, and the eulogistic, enthusiastic tone of the sermon is very similar to Smart's in the *Song to David*. According to Chandler—who was not being strictly honest, despite his clerical calling—David and George were pious, graceful of person, modest, prudent, courageous, honest, constant, faithful, patient, charitable, compassionate, moderate, just, equitable, tender, and affectionate. Smart's catalogue of David's twelve Cardinal Virtues—identical with those listed in *Jubilate Agno* B2.604–15, except that in the *Song to David*, Smart substitutes 'serene' for 'happy'—reads something like Chandler's:

> Great, valiant, pious, good, and clean,
> Sublime, contemplative, serene,
> Strong, constant, pleasant, wise!
> (*Collected Poems*, i. 349)

In 1761, an anonymous wit, thought to be John Noorthouk, brought out the disreputable *History of the Man after God's own Heart*. He suggests in the Preface that some reverend panegyrists on our late King have, a little unfortunately, been fond of comparing him with a monarch in no respect resembling him. Chandler is not spared, and neither is Dr. Delany, 'whose gross palliations, puerile conjectures, and mean shifts to which he has been driven, prove the difficulty of the task; while they are too frivolous to bias any, but the most *Catholic believers.*' The author's racy detachment, humorous cynicism, and total disregard for learned references, conceal a serious purpose. Writing of David's delight in bloodshed, he comments, 'It argues nothing to plead the different manners of mankind, in those early and less civilized ages of the world: for, if he was *then* the man after God's own heart; *God is unalterable*; and always required that we should do justly, love mercy, and walk humbly with him.'[13] It is a paradox that while the *Song to David* was strange and unconventional by the literary standards of the age, it was at least theologically orthodox, and we wonder whether Smart's poem was a deliberate attempt to defend Delany and Chandler against the author of the *History of the Man after God's own Heart*. Unfortunately, it is not much to Smart's credit that he supported Delany and Chandler. In comparison with their facetious opponent, the author of the *History of the Man after God's own Heart*, the reverend panegyrists are wilfully blind and deluded about the nastier aspects of David's character, and wilfully sycophantic in their allegiance to the impossible idealization of their hero.

Smart turned a blind eye to David's uxoriousness and the murder of Uriah, and he insisted in the *Song to David* that he *was* the man after God's own heart. It was not until he wrote his version of the *Psalms* that Smart revealed how disturbed he was by David's belligerent nature. We shall see in the next chapter that when Smart refused to accept the violent parts of the *Psalms*, he was in fact working in a definite literary tradition. But perhaps we should notice here that Smart's distaste for David's violence was shared wholeheartedly by the anonymous author of the *History of the Man after God's Own Heart*. David is called a holy psalmist only on account of the psalms that exemplify repentance for his frailty, writes the author, 'Yet, even in his psalms, he frequently breathes nothing but blood, and the most rancorous resentment against his enemies.'[14] Among the examples given to prove his point, he quotes Psalm 69. 24, 'Let their eyes be blinded, that they see not: and ever bow down their backs' (Book of Common Prayer). It is notable that Smart translated this verse as:

> Ope thou their eyes, that they may see
> Thy glory's heav'nly tracks,
> And lay, while they submit their knee,
> Thy burden on their backs.
>   (*Collected Poems*, ii. 548)

---

[13] *The History of the Man after God's own Heart*, 15.   [14] *Ibid.*, 83.

The *Song to David* could have been written as a lyrical criticism of the *History of the Man after God's own Heart*—but if that was so, Smart perhaps learned something from that irreverent work and incorporated the lesson into his version of the *Psalms*. Smart must have parted company with Chandler when the latter replied to the *History of the Man after God's own Heart* with vicious and jovial irony, 'Does our author wish the *British* arms success over the enemies of his country? He so far wishes then the destruction of his enemies; and if he rejoiceth to hear of a compleat victory over them, bloody minded man as he is, he rejoiceth to hear of their destruction; and when God makes them in battle to flee before us, and gives them up to the sword, the necessary effect is the shedding their blood, so that the conquerors may tread in it, and the dogs lap it up.'[15] Chandler was supported by Thomas Patten's *King David Vindicated from a late Misrepresentation of his Character* (Oxford, 1762), which indulged in uncritical transports of enthusiasm comparable with the emotional tone of the *Song to David*, 'So exalted conceptions of GOD's majesty, such a love of him, such a zeal for his honour, such a self-resignation to his will, so steady a confidence in his truth and goodness, so lively a faith in his promises of redemption, such earnestness of prayer, such humility of penitence, so exquisite sentiment of the riches of GOD's bounty, such transports of gratitude to him, so pathetic declarations of the Redeemer to come, such rejoicing in his salvation, and so zealous denunciations of the wrath against his despisers; these noble traits which adorn that exquisite picture of David, sufficiently unfold the meaning of the title which heaven conferred upon him, "The man after GOD's own heart".'[16] There were other supporters too—Beilby Porteus's *The Character of David King of Israel, Impartially Stated* (Cambridge 1761), and William Cleaver's *An Inquiry into the True Character of David King of Israel* [1762]. The battle raged on as Chandler, Patten, Porteus, and Cleaver were ridiculed in *A Letter to the Rev. Dr. Samuel Chandler: From the Writer of the History of the Man after God's own Heart* (1762), and as Chandler 'like the frog in the fable, after much puffing and straining', brought out a two-

[15] *A Review of the History of the Man after God's own Heart*, 1762, 249.
[16] *King David Vindicated from a Late Misrepresentation of his Character*, 122.

volume work, very much longer than the original sermon on George and David, *A Critical History of the Life of David* (1766), two years after John Francis had entered the war with his *Reflections on the Moral and Religious Character of David, King of Israel and Judah*.

It seems more than pure coincidence that the *Song to David* should have been published in the middle of this controversy. At the very least, the works of Chandler and the rest show us that Smart's devotion to King David was not a strange, emotional orgy of private admiration. His enthusiasm for David almost certainly fulfilled a psychological necessity to identify with a divine poet who possessed all twelve of Smart's Cardinal Virtues. But Smart's enthusiasm probably had a literary bias as well—the contemporary vindication of the character of King David. The *Song to David* has to be seen as controversial and didactic, as well as lyrical and jubilant.

King David was for Christopher Smart a personification of the religious poet, singing Hallelujahs to the Lord, the perfection of excellence, 'from the hand of the artist inimitable, and from the echo of the heavenly harp in sweetness magnifical and mighty' (*Jubilate Agno* A.41). The first three stanzas or 'Invocation' to the *Song to David* express the same theme, for Smart places David upon a throne, praising the King of Kings with harp and voice—we recall *Jubilate Agno* B2.589, 'For the harp rhimes are sing, ring, string & the like.' But King David is not simply a poet, he is also a monarch and Smart expresses this new idea by a kind of pun in stanza II: 'To *keep* the days on Zion's Mount,/And send the year to his account,/With dances and with songs'. The word 'keep' was italicized in the first edition of the *Song to David* (1763) but not in the second (1765). But at least we can be sure that Smart wanted to draw attention to the use of the word. 'To keep' means 'to celebrate a feast or a ceremony', and Smart connects this meaning with the dances and songs in the third line of the quotation. But it means also 'to maintain a diary, account, or books, by making requisite entries', and Smart connects this meaning with 'account' in the second line of the quotation. Perhaps this idea of keeping an account of the year is taken up again in the account of the changing seasons in the 'Adoration' stanzas of the *Song to David*. The second meaning certainly links up with the imagery of stanza III: 'O Servant of God's holiest charge,/ The minister of praise at large, /Which thou mayst now receive'. In 'Munificence and Modesty', printed in *Poems on Several Occasions* [1763], the Archangel Liberality is described as 'the Almoner of God' and his 'commission's to dispense/The meed of God's munificence'. Smart seems to be saying the same sort of thing about King David—that as God's minister, it is his duty to dispense the praise of God, 'at large', with its implications of largesse, generosity. But, says Smart, it is now David's turn to receive praise, and he is summoned from his blest mansion and topmost eminence 'To this the wreath I weave.'

In the next group of thirteen stanzas (IV–XVI), Smart shows that David is worthy to wear the wreath by virtue of 'The excellence and lustre of David's character in twelve points of view'. *A propos* these stanzas, Frank Baker makes a useful comparison between Charles Wesley's 'homiletic' style, and Smart's technique in *A Song to David*. Baker analyses Wesley's hymn, 'What shall I do my God to love', where the text of the sermon is based on Ephesians 3.18–19, 'To apprehend . . . the breadth and length and height and depth, and know the love of Christ which passeth knowledge':

> What shall I do my God to love,
>   My loving God to praise!
> The Length, and Breadth, and Height to prove,
>   And Depth of Sovereign Grace!

Having given the text, Wesley goes on to preach the sermon. 'The following stanza is his "firstly"—the *length* of God's love, which "to all extends". Next comes his "secondly", its *breadth*—"Throughout the world its breadth is known, Wide as infinity." Then his "thirdly", the *height*, both of his own sin, "grown up to heaven", but even higher still—"far above the skies"—the soaring mercies of God in Christ. And "fourthly", "The *depth* of all-redeeming love", in two verses, the second of which (usually omitted from our hymn-books) underlines the idea of depth—"Deeper than hell . . . Deeper than inbred sin". Having made his points, like any good preacher Charles

Wesley applies them in a prayer of supplication, and for a final knock-down blow . . . he works his spatial relationships into a paradox parallel to . . . St. Paul's paradox about knowing the love which passes knowledge: And *sink* me to Perfection's Height,/The *Depth* of Humble Love.'[17] Baker suggests that Smart too uses a kind of homiletic structure, but he feels that in comparison with Wesley's artistry, Smart's is blatantly inferior: 'Wesley is not alone in this kind of structure, of course. There are even more notable examples in Christopher Smart's *A Song to David*. Indeed, they are perhaps *too* notable—the machinery tends to creak. The opening lines of stanza 4 furnish us with a catalogue of David's virtues . . . The following 12 stanzas each deal (in the same order) with one of these virtues, and to ensure that the reader does not miss the point, each epithet opens its respective stanza, followed by a dash. Charles Wesley is never as obvious as that, and is a far greater artist as a result.'[18] We may well protest that self-effacement is not necessarily the hallmark of a great artist, but at least Baker's comparison does throw some light on one aspect of the structure of *A Song to David*. It suggests that the technique of Smart's poem was not as unconventional as is generally supposed.

In these thirteen stanzas, Smart was trying to express the almost inexpressible grandeur of David's character. In *Jubilate Agno*, the twelve Cardinal Virtues, 'the gifts of the twelve sons of Jacob' (B2.603), are shared among twenty-four different people: Reuben and Hugh Boscawen, second Viscount Falmouth, are Great; Simeon and Edward, ninth Duke of Somerset, are Valiant; Levi and Thomas Sherlock, Bishop of London, are Pious; Judah and John, first Earl Granville, are Good; Dan and Brigadier-General William Draper are Clean; Naphtali and Philip Stanhope, fourth Earl of Chesterfield, are sublime; Gad and Charles Compton, seventh Earl of Northampton, are Contemplative; Ashur and George Bowes are Happy; Issachar and Lionel Cranfield Sackville, first Duke of Dorset, are strong; Zabulon and William Pulteney, tenth Earl of Bath, are Constant; Joseph and Frederick St. John, second Viscount Bolingbroke, are Pleasant; Benjamin and Honeywood

---

[17] *Representative Verse of Charles Wesley*, 1962, p. xli.
[18] *Ibid.*, p. xlii.

(was Smart referring to Sir John Honywood of Kent, or to one of his three surviving sons, William, Filmer, or John?), are Wise (B2.604–15). King David has all the virtues of the twelve sons of Jacob and all the virtues of twelve illustrious eighteenth-century gentlemen—Smart could scarcely be more eulogistic.

Smart then shows how this brilliant man, King David, 'consecrates his genius for consolation and edification.' The 'consolation' is expressed through the image of 'balm for all the thorns that pierce,/For all the pangs that rage' (stanza XVII), and perhaps Smart is alluding to the way in which David soothed Saul's mental sickness. The 'edification' of David's poetry is expressed in the image of 'Blest light, still gaining on the gloom' and refers probably to the kind of statement that David makes in Psalm 49.4, 'I will incline my ear to the parable: and shew my dark speech upon the harp.'

The next nine stanzas (XVIII–XXVI) deal with 'The subjects he made choice of—the Supreme Being—angels; man of renown; the works of nature in all directions, either particularly or collectively considered'. When Smart describes the Supreme Being as 'the stupendous force/On which all strength depends', we know from our study of *Jubilate Agno* that this definition has a precise, Newtonian significance: 'For the Centripetal and Centrifugal forces are GOD SUSTAINING and DIRECTING' (B1.163). It is characteristic of Smart that he should refer to 'men of renown' as one of the subjects of David's divine poetry. 'Let us now praise famous Men, and our Fathers that begat us,—such as found out Musical Tunes, and recited Verses in writing', quoted Smart from Ecclesiasticus in the advertisement for the *Song to David* in *Proposals for Printing, by Subscription, a New Translation of the Psalms of David* (8th September 1763). And we know from our study of Smart's ruling passion, gratitude, that he himself wrote many ardently grateful poems to 'men of renown'. The subject matter of David's poetry is similar to Smart's in other ways. David sang of plants, birds, fishes, beasts, and gems, just as Smart had catalogued these various works of creation in *Jubilate Agno*. But instead of the exhaustive lists of, say, strange birds in Fragment B1 of *Jubilate Agno*, we find in the *Song to David* a brief but vivid account of the 'fowls'. David sang:

o

> Of fowl—e'en ev'ry beak and wing
> Which chear the winter, hail the spring,
>   That live in peace or prey;
> They that make music, or that mock,
> The quail, the brave domestic cock,
>   The raven, swan, and jay.
>
>   (*Collected Poems*, i. 353)

It is the brief, evocative pictures like 'the sleek tigers roll and bask' or 'The jasper of the master's stamp' that have done much to make the *Song to David* the most admired of Smart's poems.

In stanzas XXVII and XVIII, Smart restates the theme of how David consecrated his genius for 'consolation', and describes how David knelt tenderly to his graceful harp, 'When satan with his hand he quell'd,/And in serene suspence he held/ The frantic throes of Saul.' Stanza XXIX describes how David 'wins the heart of Michal'. When Smart paraphrases her naive admiration for her lover, she sounds rather silly: ' "so brave,/ And plays his hymns so good." ' The stanza is not quite so irrelevant as it may seem at first glance, for in stanza XVII Smart had compared the blest light of edification, rather surprisingly, with David's wives, 'The more than Michal of his bloom,/The Abishag of his age.' Just as in stanza XXVII and XVIII Smart returns to the theme of consolation, so in stanza XXIX Smart implicitly refers to the theme of edification by mentioning Michal's name again. The reference to Michal therefore leads logically to the seven pillars of knowledge, 'the monuments of God's works in the first week' (stanzas XXX–XXXVII).

The technique used in these eight stanzas is once again homiletic. In stanza XXX, Smart gives his text, 'The pillars of the Lord are seven,/Which stand from earth to topmost heav'n'. Each of the next seven stanzas deals with one of the pillars, and each pillar is given a Greek initial—Alpha, Gamma, Eta, Theta, Iota, Sigma, or Omega, and each pillar represents one phase of the creation—God's creation of the light, the firmament of heaven, the plant life, the fishes and fowls, the beasts and man, and God's sanctification of the seventh day as a day of rest. The imagery suggests that Smart saw the universe as a great temple supported by seven pillars, that reached from

earth to heaven. Each pillar is elaborately carved with emblems
of the creation:

> Eta with living sculpture breathes,
> With verdant carvings, flow'ry wreaths,
>   Of never-wasting bloom;
> In strong relief his goodly base
> All instruments of labour grace,
>   The trowel, spade, and loom.
>   (*Collected Poems*, i. 355–56)

But what of the Greek letters? Even the *Monthly Review* for
April 1763 attempted to get some sense out of the seven pillars:
'We meet with some passages . . . in this performance that are
almost, if not altogether, unintelligible. Few Readers probably
will see into the Author's reason for distinguishing his seven
pillars or monuments of the six days of creation, by the seven
Greek letters he hath selected. These, we conjecture, are made
choice of, as consecrated for the following reasons. *Alpha* and
Omega, from a well-known text in the Revelation. *Iota, Eta* and
Sigma, because they are used to signify our Saviour, on altars
and pulpits. *Theta*, as being the initials of θεος, God; and *Gamma*
as denoting the number *three*, held sacred by some Christians.'
But in our own day, such a simple interpretation as this is
considered unsophisticated. Katherine M. Rogers, for instance,
has attempted an erudite analysis of the meaning of the Greek
pillars of knowledge in the *Song to David*.[19]

She alludes to stanza XXI of *A Song to David* in which
David sings of 'The multitudinous abyss,/Where secrecy
remains in bliss,/And wisdom hides her skill,' and also to
Smart's note in the 'Contents' to the poem, that 'the pillars of
knowledge are the monuments of God's works in the first week'.
She suggests that this is a cryptic reference to Proverbs 9.1,
'WISDOM hath builded her house, she hath hewn out her seven
pillars'. Smart's allusion to Proverbs can be paralleled with
similar ideas expressed in the Cabala. Katherine Rogers
quotes from Schachter and Freedman's translation of *The
Babylonian Talmud: Seder Nezikin: Sanhedrin* (1935): '*Wisdom
hath builded her house,*—this is the attribute of the Holy One . . .

---

[19] 'The Pillars of the Lord: Some Sources of "A Song to David"', *Philiological
Quarterly*, xl, 1961, 525–34.

who created the world by wisdom. *She hath hewn out her seven pillars*,—these are the seven days of creation.' Cabalistic writers, she says, followed this interpretation and frequently alluded to the seven pillars on which the universe was established. She alludes to stanza XXX of the *Song to David*, and Smart's conception of God's creating the world through wisdom and then through his word: 'His wisdom drew the plan;/His WORD accomplished the design'. She suggests that Smart might have been thinking here of Cabalistic speculation, and seriously considers that Smart could have been alluding to the idea that God created the world through ten emanations called *Sefirot*. The first three *Sefirot*—the Crown, Wisdom, and Understanding—produced seven other *Sefirot*, which created the material world and were sometimes compared with the seven days of creation. Smart's account is Christian, but Katherine Rogers points out that according to a Cabalistic work like *The Zohar*, the first three *Sefirot* were the only ones of a truly divine nature: Rosenroth's Latin translation of 1677 attempted to Christianize the Cabala, and seized on the three divine *Sefirot* as a version of the Trinity.

Having suggested a general frame of ideas which might have influenced the thought and imagery of the *Song to David*, Katherine Rogers makes a precise analysis of the seven pillars, and states categorically that Smart 'certainly got from Jewish mysticism the idea of using letters in connection with the Creation.' She suggests that Smart could have read in the Latin translation of the *Sefer Yezirah* (Postell's in 1552 or Rittangel's in 1642) that God used the twenty-two letters of the Hebrew alphabet to create the world, which he did by the power of his Name—the creative power of the name of God being fundamental to Jewish mysticism and magic. 'As Smart may have known, most of the Hebrew letters are supposed to represent a name of God. Probably this was the principle he used for selecting his own letters, although of course the actual significations attributed by Jewish scholars would be far too recondite for English readers.' Rogers's interpretation of Smart's seven letters is based on two assumptions—that Cabalistic lore filtered through Masonic symbolism during the eighteenth century, and that while Smart was aware of the Cabalistic significance of the Hebrew alphabet, he transposed it into Greek. 'The reason for transliterating is obvious: combining letters from various alphabets would be confusing and untidy, and the Greek letters provide a golden mean between the prosaic familiarity of the English alphabet and the esoteric strangeness of the Hebrew.'

As Katherine Rogers interprets each of the letters on Smart's seven pillars as a name of God, and that she traces a Hebrew-Greek-English meaning for each of these letters, we can summarize her analysis as follows. She deals briefly with Alpha and Omega, noting that according to *The Zohar*, the first of the seven lower *Sefirot* was sometimes symbolized by the letter *aleph*, and the last by *zayin*. Smart transliterated the first as the Greek *alpha*, but rejected *zeta*, the Greek equivalent of *zayin*, in order to allude to the Revelation texts in which Alpha and Omega are names for God.

She then points out that although the *Sefer Yezirah* associates the different Hebrew letters with particular phases of the creation, only one of them actually occurs in the *Song to David—gimel* which Smart transliterates as *gamma*. The most important letter in Freemasonry is G which is placed aloft in the East in every Lodge. It is the symbol of God, and possibly the Masonic G was originally represented as *gamma* which has the form of a basic Masonic symbol, the artisan's square. The third pillar is problematical, because *eta* does not figure in Freemasonry. Katherine Rogers suggests, however, that Smart could have taken his interpretation from Cornelius Agrippa's *Occult Philosophy* where H is said to represent the spirit of the world. Or perhaps *eta* represents a Greek transliteration of the Hebrew *heh*: the Tetragrammaton, YHWH, the name of God, was considered too sacred to be written, and was commonly replaced by *heh*, from which custom *heh* acquired the magical significance of a name of God. *Theta*, the letter on the fourth pillar is also difficult for the same reason, that it does not figure in Freemasonry, but it is the initial letter of θεός which can be taken as a symbol of God. But Katherine Rogers thinks that this is a weak interpretation and points out that an Egyptian symbol for the cosmos, a circle representing the world with a stroke in the middle representing the good spirit holding it

together, resembles *theta* and was therefore thought worthy
of inclusion in the *Song to David*. She points out that the
Tetragrammaton was often expressed by its initial letter *yod*
which was often depicted like the Masonic G, within a triangle.
The Freemasons adopted this representation of God, but the
significance of *yod* (I, Y, or J, *iota*) was soon lost among those
who did not know the Cabala and was replaced by the more
obvious G. Smart's *sigma* is a transliteration of *shin*, she says,
and was one of the four symbols used by Jews for the Tetragrammaton, being the initial letter of *Shaddai*, the Almighty.
The three bars of *shin* are said to symbolize the three highest
Sefirot and are therefore identified with the Trinity by Christian
Cabalists. Masonic writers, bent on Christianizing the Cabala,
point out that when *shin* is inserted into the middle of the
Tetragrammaton, the word becomes Yeheshuhe, Jesue or Jesus.

Despite the fact that these suggestions are tentative and the
fact that there are obvious lapses in meaningful evidence
(there is no Masonic significance for *eta* and *theta* for instance),
Katherine Rogers feels justified in her 'interpretation of the
group—that he [Smart] coupled each phase of the Creation
with a mystical name for the God Who brought it about,
Whose very name, in Cabalistic belief, had creative power.'
Perhaps my philistine stubbornness makes me wonder, especially
when one is offered Egyptian as well as Hebrew, Greek, and
English characters, whether Katherine Rogers is not displaying
her own great learning rather than Smart's.

Father Devlin has also attempted a detailed, but in many
ways simpler, analysis of the seven pillars in the *Song to David*.[20]
He takes quite a different course, because being a Roman
Catholic, he is of course very anxious to prove that none of the
sources of the *Song to David* are to be found in Masonic symbolism. 'The suggestion that the letters are Masonic symbols
should be set aside. There is no evidence for it; rather the
reverse. A writer in *Miscellanea Latomorum* (October 1924)
states: "I am unable to offer any suggestion as to the reason for
selecting these particular letters of the Greek alphabet." The

[20] Devlin's analysis was first printed as 'Christopher Smart and the Seven
Pillars', *Month*, n.s.xxiv, 1960, 86–98. My notes on his method of analysis are based
on Devlin's account of the seven pillars in *Poor Kit Smart*, 140–49.

Curator of the Grand Lodge Library, London, through whose courtesy I was shown this article, adds: "I, too, am defeated in spite of my familiarity with the ritual of numerous masonic degrees." 'Smart *was* a Freemason, but we are inclined to agree with Devlin that any interpretation of the *Song to David* that relies solely on Masonic symbolism is in danger of being far-fetched. Devlin feels that in spite of the cryptogrammatic appearance of the seven letters, they can in fact be explained in terms of Christian orthodoxy: 'the seven stanzas describe seven aspects or appearances of Christ, the Word made Flesh.' Each pillar, he goes on, represents not only a stage in the creation, but an aspect of God becoming man—which means that the incarnation of God and the creation of the universe are seen as being part of the same plan.

According to Devlin, therefore, Alpha symbolizes the original creation of the light of the world and the Son coming forth from the Father, according to the Christian parallel between the opening of Genesis and the opening of St. John's Gospel. Gamma expresses Christ as an Angel and High-Priest of Creation. Devlin derives this interpretation from the image of the angelic legions marching across the 'glorious arch' of the sky, and also from the significance of Gamma as the third letter of the alphabet: the number three denotes spiritual perfection and is used here of Christ the Holy One, the apex and spear-point of creation. Devlin's interpretation of the Eta stanza is even more ingenious. Smart associates Eta with the creation of verdure and flowers. Devlin deduces: 'The picture of Christ which unifies the stanza is that created form, whatever it was, which the Son of God took when he walked with Adam "in the garden in the cool of the day" (*Genesis*, iii. 8). You could call it "the Paradisal Christ", or "Christ in Nature"—or even, remembering Piero della Francesca, "Christ the Gardener." ' (When we turn to stanza XXXIII we find no references to Christ, Genesis, Paradise, or Nature, and what relevance has Piero della Francesca?) Smart's Theta stanza, with its imagery of the sun and moon in marriage garments of silver and saffron presents Christ the Bridegroom, whose bride is Israel. Devlin supports this interpretation by means of a reference to Ephesians 5.22–23 where St. Paul states the relation of marriage to the 'great mystery' of Christ and his church. Devlin's analysis of stanza XXXV is intricately clever. From a stanza about the creation of the birds and fishes, he extracts a symbolical account of the descent of Christ into Mary's womb at the Annunciation. He argues this point by suggesting that Iota, the ninth letter of the Greek alphabet, symbolizes harmony: 'For Nine is a number very good and harmonious', Smart had written in *Jubilate Agno* C.33. The implicit idea of harmony in stanza XXXV links up with the imagery of the choral hymns of birds. The image of birds leads Devlin directly to the idea of angels and thence to the Angel Gabriel and the Annunciation. Devlin supports his theory by referring to *Jubilate Agno* B1.122, 'Let Cherub rejoice with the Cherub who is a bird and a blessed Angel. For I bless God for every feather from the wren in the sedge to the CHERUBS and their MATES.' Devlin works from the Annunciation to the Conception via Smart's image of fish and a quotation from *Jubilate Agno* B1.139, with its pun on 'maid' as a virgin and a fish. Smart associates the Sigma stanza with the creation of beasts and man. Devlin feels that by implicitly associating Christ with the beasts, Smart is presenting the idea of the Nativity or the Temptation in the Wilderness when he retreated into the wilderness 'and was with the beasts'. The description of man in this stanza could denote Adam, but, says Devlin, this man induces 'occular belief', and therefore he must be Christ himself. According to Devlin, Omega is a sign for what the Greek fathers call the 'apokatasisis', the restoration of all things. Devlin links this idea with *Jubilate Agno* and the description of the twenty-four elders of Revelation, for Omega is the twenty-fourth letter of the Greek alphabet. Hence the Omega stanza symbolizes the redeeming Christ: 'Thus *Omega* returns to *Alpha* in a circle. The sequence "From Christ enthroned to man" goes back to Christ enthroned, but this time bearing with him human nature made immortal. *Omega* is Christ the "Pantokrator" of Greek theology.' Personally, I do not think there is much to choose between Rogers's Freemasonry and Devlin's Roman Catholicism, but at least these conflicting accounts of Smart's seven pillars demonstrate that these eight stanzas are the most obscure in the whole poem, and that they have not yet been satisfactorily interpreted.

Since, in Smart's words, these are the 'pillars of knowledge', it is logical that in stanza XXXVIII David should be acclaimed as the 'scholar of the Lord!' But there is a sudden shift of meaning in the next stanza, which is a statement of the unity of God who sent his semblance from himself, 'Grand object of his own content,/And saw the God in CHRIST.' There is yet another shift of meaning in stanza XL, for Smart suddenly and irrelevantly begins to describe God's commandments to Moses in 'An exercise on the decalogue'.

The first commandment, 'I am the LORD thy God . . . Thou shalt have no other gods before me' (Exodus 20.2) is faithfully reproduced in the *Song to David*, 'Tell them, I am, JEHOVA said/ To MOSES'. But Smart is writing an 'exercise' on the decalogue, which allows him to make all sorts of variations on his theme. Smart's commandments have a definite New Testament bias— a man must not call his brother fool, he must be merciful to his domestic animals, and polite to the elderly. He must follow the pattern of Christ who prayed 'Not as I will, but as Thou wilt', and he must use all his passions—love, joy, and jealousy—for thrift will counterbalance the passion for idleness, and fear will counterbalance the lust of the body. Man must always act simply, always avoiding 'commixtures foul and fond': till not with ass and bull. Man must give generously, spurning slander, and honouring all who are wiser, happier, and wealthier than himself. Smart's version of the decalogue is summed up in stanza XLVII, 'Turn from Old Adam to the New;/By hope futurity pursue;/Look upwards to the past.' Smart's tendency to interpret the Old Testament in the light of the New was fundamental to his religious outlook in his later poetry. As we shall see, the tendency reached its most extreme point in the *Translation of the Psalms*.

Smart's exercise on the decalogue could almost be placed in parentheses, but in stanza XLIX, he returns to his central theme, 'o DAVID, highest in the list/Of worthies'. David, like Moses, must repeat the genuine word of God, because the documents of man are vain and conceited. We recall *Jubilate Agno* A.68, 'the writings of man perish as the garment, but the Book of God endureth for ever.' Smart obviously feels that David's rôle is not to transcribe the commandments of God,

but to set down in poetry the praise of the Lord. In stanzas
L and LI, therefore, Smart introduces 'The transcendent virtue
of praise and adoration'. The stanza on 'PRAISE' is linked with
Smart's version of the decalogue, for just as a man must spurn
'The slander and its bearer', so must the generous soul be ready
to give praise for 'peevish obloquy degrades'. The introductory
stanza on 'ADORATION' describes how all the ranks of angels,
with David in their midst, give thanks to God. This verse,
where Smart the grateful poet so transparently identifies himself with King David the grateful poet, introduces the most
beautiful part of *A Song to David*, the 'Adoration' stanzas, which
Smart describes as 'An exercise upon the seasons, and the
right use of them'.

The technique of this group of stanzas is based on the
rhetorical repetition of the word 'ADORATION'. In stanza LII,
'ADORATION' appears in the first line, in stanza LIII it appears
in the second line, in stanza LIV it appears in the third line, in
stanza LV it appears in the fourth line, in stanza LVI it
appears in the fifth line, and in stanza LVII it appears in the
sixth line. Then the whole process begins again as 'ADORATION'
appears in the first line of stanza LVIII and so on until it
appears in the sixth line of stanza LXIII. But in the next eight
stanzas, Smart places 'ADORATION' in the first line of each
verse. The change of technique corresponds to a change of
subject matter, for in stanza LXIV the exercise on the seasons
gives way to 'An exercise upon the senses and how to subdue
them'. In his edition of *A Song to David* (1960), J. B. Broadbent
argues that 'Schematic rhetoric so overt as the anaphora of the
"Amplification in five degrees" (72 ff.) and the cadencing of
ADORATION down the stanzas, was extraordinary for his time,
when rhetoric was small-scale and syntactical and often satirical
in function; it is a conscious reversion to the mode of Herbert's
"Easter-Wings" and Milton's paraphrase of the *Benedicite* in
Paradise Lost.' I do not think it is really necessary to trace the
ancestry of the *Song to David* back to the poetry of George
Herbert. Admittedly, Smart never quite shook off Milton's
influence. Even the *Song to David* has Miltonic echoes, for the
lines in stanza XIX, 'Angels—their ministry and meed,/Which
to and fro with blessings speed,/Or with their citterns wait', are

obviously reminiscent of the concluding lines of Milton's sonnet 'On his Blindness': 'Thousands at his bidding speed/And post oer Land and Ocean without rest:/They also serve who only stand and waite.'[21] But I do not think that Milton's influence is particularly relevant to the 'Adoration' stanzas. It seems to me much more sensible to compare Smart's rhetorical flourishes with contemporary poetic conventions. Without supposing a direct relationship between the poetry of Christopher Smart and the hymns of Charles Wesley, I think it is fair enough to suggest that a common intellectual background is probably responsible for some of the similarities in their poetic technique. Writing of Wesley's rhetorical devices, Frank Baker says that 'it is no perversity of the enthusiastic researcher who is imagining minutiae which do not really exist . . . It was all there in his classical training, a training so thorough that the vocabulary, the style, and the structure of his verse was markedly affected by it.'[22] Not only did Smart have the conventional grammar-school/University education, but in 1746 he was actually appointed Praelector of Rhetoric at Pembroke College. In discussing Wesley's hymn, 'The Communion of Saints', Baker admires Wesley's disciplined use of rhetorical repetition, constantly varied before it is becoming too obvious and 'appreciated all the more when turning from Christopher Smart. Stanzas 51–71 in Smart's *A Song to David* overdo the word "ADORATION" (always printed in capitals) and the following stanzas dwell at length on the adjective "sweet" (72–4), "strong" (75–7), "beauteous" (78–80), "precious" (81–3), "glorious" (84–6), and their comparatives. It is all a little too obvious as if he were saying: "See how clever I am!" Wesley is much more subtle and self-effacing.'[23] Once again, the comparison between Smart and Wesley throws some light on the technique used in the *Song to David*, but once again we cannot agree with Baker that subtlety and self-effacement are not necessarily the hallmarks of great artistry.

In our study of the subject matter of King David's poetry, we found that Smart chose a small number of creatures and plants,

---

[21] *Milton's Poems*, 84.
[22] *Representative Verse of Charles Wesley*, pp. xiii–xiv.
[23] *Ibid.*, p. xliii.

and described them briefly but evocatively. We contrasted this technique with the long lists of creatures in *Jubilate Agno*, and we find the same contrast between *Jubilate Agno* and the "Adoration" stanzas of *A Song to David*. The exquisite imagery is patterned by a seasonal cycle as well as by the Romance stanza form and the rhetorical play with the word 'ADORATION'. The formal beauty of these stanzas is accepted as Smart's greatest poetic achievement. He begins with three stanzas on spring, with rich almonds colouring to the prime, the fruit-trees pledging their gems, the humming-bird with her gorgeous vest, the bell-flowers bending their stems, the vinous syrup spouting from the cedars, pure honey gushing from the rocks, and—surprisingly—the scaled infant clinging to the mermaid's breast. The Biblical imagery of almonds, cedars, and honey, is placed side by side with imagery drawn from landscapes which Smart had observed for himself. Geoffrey Grigson has pointed out that in stanza LII of the *Song to David*—

> The grass the polyanthus cheques;
> And polish'd porphyry reflects,
>   By the descending rill
>   (*Collected Poems*, i. 360)

—the polished porphyry is the polished limestone of County Durham, and the polyanthus chequering the grass are the thousands of lilac umbels of the Birdseye Primrose found among the rocks there.[24] As for the mermaid, she is more than an eccentric symbol of spring, a strange maternal image suckling a strange infant. Father Devlin suggests that Smart was remembering Durham Cathedral where part of the stonework is carved with the figure of a mermaid.[25]

In the stanzas on summer, the lynx and her cubs run among the flowering shrubs, the 'large quadruped that preys upon fish, and provides himself with a piece of timber for that purpose, with which he is very handy'[26] embarks upon a calm sea, the peaceful nation of Israel sits under the fig trees, the 'wean'd

---

[24] 'Three lines in "A Song to David"', *Times Literary Supplement*, 14 April 1961, 233, and *Christopher Smart*, 27–28.

[25] *Poor Kit Smart*, 149.

[26] Smart's note in the second edition of the *Song to David*, in *A Translation of the Psalms of David* (1765).

advent'rer' (presumably the mermaid's offspring) sports among coral and amber, the palm cleaves the jasmine, and

> Increasing days their reign exalt,
> Nor in the pink and mottled vault
>   The opposing spirits tilt;
> And, by the coasting reader spied,
> The silverlings and crusions glide
>   For ADORATION gilt.
>   (*Collected Poems*, i. 361)

Here too Smart places the Biblical imagery of figs and palms beside his own minute observation of living creatures. Grigson points out that 'Silverlings are presumably roach, the crusion (properly Crucian or Crusian) is a fish of the carp family, yellow (i.e. gilt), introduced from Asia to continental Europe, and thence to England, where it was often put into ponds in the eighteenth century. *Jubilate Agno* shows that, in autumn 1759, in his madhouse, Smart had been recalling the fishponds and the fish of that Fairlawn [in Shipbourne, Kent] where he had spent his childhood'.[27] He quotes *Jubilate Agno* B1.168, 'Let Mary rejoice with the Carp—the ponds of Fairlawn and the garden bless for the master.'

In the three stanzas on autumn, the sugar canes ripen, the cocoa's purest milk detains the western pilgrim's staff, clasping boughs enclose the rain and intertwined vines and oranges, the rice crop whitens among spice groves, 'marshall'd in the fenced land,/The peaches and pomegranates stand,/Where wild carnations blow', and

> Now labour his reward receives,
> For ADORATION counts his sheaves,
>   To peace, her bounteous prince;
> The nectarines his strong tint imbibes,
> And apples of ten thousand tribes,
>   And quick peculiar quince.
>   (*Collected Poems*, i. 361)

These lines make it necessary for us to discuss an aspect of the technique of the *Song to David* which we have not yet touched upon. In *Poems by Christopher Smart*, Robert Brittain discusses the

---

[27] *Christopher Smart*, 26.

influence of Horace's *Art of Poetry* on the *Song to David*—how the Horatian 'curiosa felicitas' probably affected Smart's use of archaic words, the coinage of new ones, the use of unusual words, or of usual words in an unusual way.[28] Brittain suggests also that one of the rules laid down in the *Art of Poetry* is particularly important for understanding the *Song of David*:

> In verbis etiam tenuis, cautusque serendis.
> Dixeris egregie, notum si callida verbum
> Reddiderit junctura novum

—which Smart translated as 'In the interspersing of his words too he must be nice and wary. You will express yourself well, if a clever connection should impress an air of novelty to a common word.' Brittain comments, 'A distinct feature of Smart's best work is the artful grouping of words within the phrase, the use of unfamiliar grammatical constructions, the alteration of normal arrangement—in short—the use of various technical devices all designed to "throw an emphasis upon a word or sentence."'[29] He goes on to give several examples, and among them he includes the last three lines of stanza LIX quoted above. He does not explain why these lines on the nectarine, apples, and quince demonstrate how Smart was able to throw an emphasis, or make an 'impression', upon a word or sentence. But we can try to explain it for ourselves. The rhetorical 'anastrophe' or powerful wrenching of the correct grammatical order of the words means that the emphasis falls upon the verb 'imbibes'. Normally the line would be written as 'The nectarine imbibes his strong tint', (admittedly only Smart could have made such an odd statement). The following lines appear to have no verbs, and indeed the images of the apples and quince are vivid enough to stand alone. But in fact, these two lines are the subjects of the verb 'imbibes', which Smart has expressly stressed, and their object is 'strong tint'. The meaning is not absolutely clear. By a curious reflexive action, the fruits drink in their own bright colours; Smart's compact syntax is

---

[28] Smart's choice of words has been discussed also by Susie Tucker in 'Christopher Smart and the English Language', *Notes and Queries*, cciii, 1958 468–69.

[29] See *Poems by Christopher Smart*, 68–72.

aimed at giving us an immediate sensation of the colour and juiciness of the fruit. By making the verb 'imbibes' the focal point of the three lines, Smart is directing the movement of the stanza into its centre, he is coiling the movement like a knot, and tying the words into an odd but tight pattern. The elliptic grammar is not conventional in the way that the homiletic structures are conventional, but both techniques fulfil the same purpose of framing the exquisite, sensuous beauty of the *Song to David* within a strong, taut structure.

In the three stanzas on winter, Smart describes how the laurels strive with winter, 'The crocus burnishes alive/Upon the snow-clad earth', the myrtles keep the garden from dismay and bless the sight from dearth, the pheasant, ermine, and sable are observed, the cheerful holly, pensive yew and holy thorn renew their trim, the squirrel hoards his nuts and all the creatures live on their stores as careful nature shuts all her doors 'For ADORATION'.

At this point, Smart turns from his demonstration of David's talent for praise and adoration as it is expressed in an exercise on the seasons. Instead, he shows how David could be didactic as well as lyrical. He begins therefore 'An exercise upon the senses, and now to subdue them'. In stanza LXIV David's Psalms lift up the heart to deeds of alms, and he who kneels and chants overcomes his passions. As we have seen in the first part of this chapter, this view of David's character is completely deluded, and we suspect Smart of indulging in propaganda in support of Samuel Chandler and the rest. But at this stage we are not particularly concerned with Smart's theological errors. We are much more concerned with his vision of David and the way he expresses it. It is difficult to understand Smart's views on the 'senses'. It is clear enough that in stanza LXVIII Smart is writing about the sense of smell, that incense comes from bezoar, Arabian gums and the civet's fur, but 'Far better is the breath of saints/Than galbanum or myrrh.' In stanza LXIX he is writing about the sense of taste: God sends the damsons and pineapples to tempt the taste, but the desire for the luscious zest of the fruit is commanded to be chaste. But I am not certain about the correct interpretation of the other stanzas in this group. In stanza LXV, Smart is perhaps illustrating the correct use of the sense of touch when he compares the bull-finch's attempts 'to catch/The soft flute's iv'ry touch' with 'The damsel's greedy clutch' as she tries to grab the daring redbreast who sits on the hazel bough. I cannot make any sense out of stanza LXVI, unless the image of the Lord's philosopher espying the various planets, the Dog, the Ram, and the Rose, is meant to illustrate the correct use of the sense of sight. Stanza LXVII is similarly obscure. Smart is evidently writing about the sense of hearing, but since the sound imagery is God's still small voice making the cataracts to fall and the sea be smooth, it is strange that this sense should be 'subdued'. Stanza LXX is evidently meant to sum up the previous five stanzas on the five senses of the body, for Smart claims that for ADORATION all the paths of grace are open and all the baths of purity refresh, and that all the rays of glory deck the man of God's esteem (David presumably) who triumphs over the flesh (which David most surely did not). The final stanza of the 'Adoration' group implies that the chaste man is also a humble man, and Smart sees David as another St. Francis of Assisi:

> For ADORATION, in the dome
> Of CHRIST, the sparrow's find an home;
>   And on his olives perch:
> The swallow also dwells with thee,
> O man of God's humility,
>   Within his Saviour CHURCH.
>   (*Collected Poems*, i. 364)

The imagery is so quaint that it comes as something of a surprise that in Psalm 84, David cries out that 'Yea, the sparrow hath found her an house, and the swallow a nest where she may lay her young: even thy altars, O Lord of hosts, my King and my God.' There seems to be only a tenuous link between Smart's stanza on the sparrows and the swallows, and his previous stanza on the paths of grace and baths of purity. Yet the association of ideas probably derived from Psalm 84, for in verse 6, David writes, 'Who going through the vale of misery use it for a well: and the pools are filled with water'. Smart interpreted this verse as a symbol of cleansing grace, as is shown by his version in the *Translation of the Psalms*:

> As thro' this vale of tears he goes,
> He purifies his flesh,
> And washes, while the fountain flows,
> Which rain and dews refresh.
> > (*Collected Poems*, ii. 591)

We may recall also that in *Jubilate Agno* B2.384, Smart had written, 'For to worship in the Rain is the bravest thing for the refreshing & purifying the body', and that in C.113 he had written, 'For it is good to let the rain come upon the naked body unto purity and refreshment.'

In the final stanzas of the poem, Smart turns back to the theme with which he began—the eulogy of King David. At the climax of the poem, where David is praised with due pomp and circumstance, Smart takes five adjectives—sweet, strong, beauteous, precious, and glorious—and devotes three stanzas to each word, making fifteen stanzas in all. In the group of stanzas which deals with the adjective 'sweet', for example, Smart makes a series of simple statements:

> Sweet is the dew that falls betimes,
> And drops upon the leafy limes;
> > Sweet, Hermon's fragrant air:
> Sweet is the lilly's silver bell,
> And sweet the wakeful tapers smell
> > That watch for early pray'r.
> > (*Collected Poems*, i. 364)

He continues to make similar statements in stanza LXXIII: sweet is the young nurse who smiles with love intense over sleeping innocence, and sweet is the musician's ardour while his wandering mind quests for the sweetest flowers of his art. In the third stanza of this group, Smart changes to the comparative, 'sweeter', and thus praises David above the sweetness of the dew and the lily, the young mother and the musician:

> Sweeter, in all the strains of love,
> The language of thy turtle dove,
> > Pair'd to thy swelling chord;
> Sweeter, with every grace endu'd,
> The glory of thy gratitude,
> > Respir'd unto the Lord.
> > (*Collected Poems*, i. 365)

P

Smart repeats this technique four times. The horse and the lion, the gier-eagle and the whale are strong, 'But stronger still, in earth and air,/And in the sea, the man of pray'r' (stanza LXXVII). The fleet and the army, the garden and the full moon, the virgin and the temple are all beauteous, but 'Beauteous, yea more beauteous than these,/The shepherd king upon his knees' (stanza LXXX). The widow's mite and the churl's generosity, the ruby and pearl, the penitential tear and the flowers decorating the Feast of Bowers, are all precious, but 'More precious that diviner part/Of David, even the Lord's own heart' (stanza LXXXIII). The sun and the comet, the trumpet and alarms, the northern lights and thunder, the catholic amen and martyr's gore, are all glorious, but,

> Glorious,—more glorious, is the crown
> Of Him that brought salvation down,
> By meekness, called thy Son:
> Thou at stupendous truth believ'd;—
> And now the matchless deed's atchiev'd,
> DETERMINED, DARED, and DONE.
> *(Collected Poems*, i. 367)

Smart pays King David the supreme compliment of comparing him with the Son of God himself.

This part of the poem is rich in rhetorical flourishes. Anaphora, the repetition of the same word at the beginning of consecutive phrases or sentences, is used frequently in *A Song to David*. Just as Charles Wesley used the device in many of his hymns—for instance, in 'Desiring to Love',

> Thou know'st, for all to Thee is known,
> Thou know'st, O LORD, and Thou alone,
> Thou know'st, that Thee I love

—so does Smart write in stanza VII of the *Song to David*, 'Foremost to give the Lord his dues,/Foremost to bless the welcome news,/And foremost to condole.' At its most subtle, anaphora can be used as in stanza XXIV of the *Song to David*, where the assonance of 'shells' and 'shoals' merely hints at a 'fine turn': 'The shells are in the wealthy deep,/The shoals upon the surface leap,/And love the glancing sun.' At the climax of the poem, the device is used in its most extreme form, as six lines of a single stanza are connected by the same word:

> Glorious the northern lights a-stream;
> Glorious the song, when God's the theme;
> Glorious the thunder's roar:
> Glorious hosannah from the den;
> Glorious the catholic amen;
> Glorious the martyr's gore:
> *(Collected Poems*, i. 367)

In this stanza Smart makes use of another rhetorical device— ecphonesis. Frank Baker writes of Wesley's hymns that 'It was impossible to confine the rapture of the Christian experience of God to a mere statement of fact, and sometimes it could only be expressed (and quite imperfectly at that) in a series of exclamatory phrases, which had ceased to be a part of a normal sentence.'[30] Baker illustrates his point with four lines from Wesley's hymn, 'The Invitation':

> Th' o'erwhelming Pow'r of saving Grace,
> The Sight that veils the Seraph's Face,
> The speechless Awe that dares not move,
> And all the silent Heaven of Love!

As Smart gets more and more excited as he approaches the climax of his poem, the exclamatory technique becomes more and more appropriate, and in stanza LXXXV quoted above he manages a total omission of main and subordinate verbs. This omission of verbs is related to the ellipsis which is common throughout the *Song to David*. The Horatian canon that 'Whatever precepts you give, be concise', was always a favourite maxim of Smart's. The elliptical haste with which he wrote stanza LXXXV can be compared with that of stanza LXXVII where an abbreviation of the syntax is substituted for the exclamatory technique:

> But stronger still, in earth and air,
> And in the sea, the man of pray'r,
> And far beneath the tide;

[30] *Representative Verse of Charles Wesley*, p. xxviii.

> And in the seat to faith assign'd,
> Where ask is have, where seek is find,
> Where knock is open wide.
>
> (*Collected Poems*, i.365)

The elliptical expression of this stanza is even more obvious when it is compared with the fuller expression of the same theme in Smart's version of Psalm 118.19:

> As in the faith of God I knock,
> The gates of righteousness unlock,
> That I may enter first;
> And there the fragrant odours burn,
> And there demonstrate and return
> The thanks with which I burst!
>
> (*Collected Poems*, ii. 694)

Both stanzas vary considerably on their source, 'Ask, and it shall be given you; seek, and ye shall find; knock, and it shall be opened unto you' (St. Matthew 7.7). But the point to be made is the grammatical differences between the two versions. The elliptical omission of part of the infinitive verbs in the *Song to David* stanza ('Where ask is have') is in marked contrast to the normal grammar of the verse from Psalm 118 where the first and third lines are subordinate adverbial clauses modifying the verb 'unlock' in the second line.

When we return to the climax of *A Song to David* we see that Smart implies that the most glorious thing that can be said of King David is the statement in St. Matthew 1.1: 'THE book of the generation of Jesus Christ, the son of David, the son of Abraham.' Smart describes the climax of his poem as 'an amplification in five degrees, which is wrought up to this conclusion, That the best poet who ever lived was thought worthy of the highest honour which possibly can be conceived, *as the Saviour of the world was ascribed to his house, and called his son in the body*.' The whole bent of Smart's thought in his later religious poetry was the transposition of the Old Testament into the ethical framework of the New. 'Turn from Old Adam to the New', Smart wrote in stanza XLVII of *A Song to David*. It is entirely characteristic that he should have omitted the violence and uxoriousness of David's character, the tyrannical attributes of an Old Testament patriarch. It is also characteristic that having devoted a whole poem to the praise of King David, he should finish with the Incarnation of Christ, that stupendous truth and matchless deed that Smart states with a thunder of alliteration and capital letters: 'DETERMINED, DARED and DONE.'

The Minor Poetry of 1763 and 1764

A SONG TO DAVID was published in 1763, and during the same year Smart brought out two small volumes of poetry. *Poems by Mr. Smart* included 'Reason and Imagination', the Odes to Admiral Sir George Pocock and General Draper, and 'An Epistle to John Sherratt, Esq.' *Poems on Several Occasions* contained 'Munificence and Modesty', 'Female Dignity. To Lady Hussey Delaval', 'Verses from Catullus, after Dining with Mr. Murray', the epitaphs on the Duchess of Cleveland, Henry Fielding and the Rev. James Sheeles and the 'Epitaph from Demosthenes'. In the following year, Smart brought out the *Ode to the Right Honourable Earl of Northumberland* which included, besides the title poem, 'To the Honourable Mrs. Draper', 'On being asked by Colonel Hall to make Verses upon Kingsley at Minden', 'On a Bed of Guernsey Lilies', the epitaph on the Duke of Argyle, 'ΞΠΙΚΤΗΤΟΣ ... Imitated', 'Epigramma Sannazarii . . . Translated', a 'Song' ('Where shall Cælia fly for shelter'), and 'The Sweets of Evening'. Not all these poems were recent productions. 'Mr. Murray', who had recommended Smart to Pope's attention many years ago, had become Lord Chief Justice and Lord Mansfield in 1756, seven years before the 'Verses from Catullus' appeared in *Poems on Several Occasions*. Some of the epitaphs must have been written many years ago, for the Duchess of Cleveland had died in 1742, the Duke of Argyle in 1743, and Henry Fielding in 1754. When we come across music settings of 'Where shall Cælia fly for shelter', we suspect that it was written for performance at the Vauxhall Gardens during Smart's early years in London.

We have already studied in Chapter II most of the eulogistic poems printed in these three volumes of verse: the poems on Pocock, Draper, Sherratt, Lady Hussey Delaval, and the Earl

of Northumberland. In this chapter, therefore, we need only to
look at the remaining eulogies, those on Mr. Murray, Mrs.
Draper, and Major-General Kingsley. We have already looked
at the epitaphs on the Duchess of Cleveland, the Duke of
Argyle, Henry Fielding, and the Rev. James Sheeles, and as for
the two allegorical poems printed in the 1763 volumes of verse,
we have already mentioned 'Reason and Imagination' in
relation to Smart's theory of poetry. In the present chapter, we
are left with 'Munificence and Modesty', which should be
studied in some detail, and we need to discuss also two of
Smart's lyrics, 'On a Bed of Guernsey Lilies', and 'The Sweets
of Evening'.

Time and again in this book, we have noticed Smart's need to
humble himself before God, and before the great men and
women of eighteenth-century society. The 'Verses from
Catullus' are not so charming as the bread-and-butter poem
written to Mrs. Tyler, but it is typical of Smart's self-deprecat-
ing enthusiasm for the great. Indeed, the second line of the
poem makes Murray into a minor god, complete with the
attributes of Alpha and Omega (the italics are Smart's):

> O THOU, of British orators the chief
> That *were*, or *are* in *being*, or belief;
> All eminence and goodness as thou art,
> Accept the gratitude of Poet Smart,—
> The meanest of the tuneful train as far
> As thou transcend'st the brightest at the bar.
> (*Collected Poems*, i. 32)

As yet, we have no idea how intimate Smart was with Murray.
But we do know that his admiration overflowed into another
poem, 'The Brocaded Gown and Linen Rag', where Murray
takes his place beside Athenian Akenside and Augustan Gray:

> O *Murray*, let me then dispense,
> Some portion of thy eloquence;
> For *Greek* and *Roman* rhetoric shine,
> United and improved in thine.
> The spirit-stirring sage alarms,
> And *Ciceronian* sweetness charms.
> (*Collected Poems*, i. 50

The Honourable Mrs. Caroline Draper, second daughter of Lord William Beauclerk, and granddaughter of the first Duke of St. Albans, was the wife of Brigadier-General William Draper. The paranoid aspects of Smart's 'Ode to General Draper' are absent from the poem written to his wife, but there are definitely some odd quirks of sentiment in the poem. In 'To the Honourable Mrs. Draper', Draper is seen as a military hero, and his wife as a kind of Volumnia figure:

> Take the laurel for thy frontlet,
> On thy breast the myrtles place,
> For young DRAPER wears the gauntlet
> Of all chivalry and grace.
> *(Collected Poems*, i. 21)

Smart was presumably referring to Draper's heroism at Manila, but if this was the case, Smart was praising a man of forty-one, a year older than himself. The Hon. Mrs. Draper is seen as 'NOBLE, lovely, and judicious', and she is zealous, of course, for her country's cause. Smart's admiration for this formidable matron was no doubt encouraged by the fact that she was willing to employ her 'exquisite discernment' in listening to Smart's poetry: 'Hear the verse the muse officious/Now presents thee to revise.' But Smart always knew when he was in the presence of his superiors:

> Thus I greet thee at a distance,
> Checking love by learning awe;
> Grandeur gives the muse assistance,
> And the lighter thoughts withdraw.
> *(Collected Poems*, i. 21)

The withdrawal of lighter thoughts means that the Hon. Mrs. Draper must be depicted as being entirely sexless. All things are untainted when we think of heavenly things, says Smart, and that is why cherubs are painted without sex, composed only of heads and wings. We are led to think about cherubs because we are thinking about Mrs. Draper: 'Looks and life thou art a lecture/On th'angelical degree.' We can only speculate on Smart's psychological motives for painting Caroline Draper without sex—we wonder whether he was uncomfortably attracted to her, despite his efforts at 'Checking love by learning awe'.

In his poem, 'On being asked by Colonel Hall to make Verses upon Kingsley at Minden', Smart devotes the first part to praising Hall, and the second part to praising Kingsley. Smart cannot understand why Colonel Hall should have give him this task. 'THIS task of me why does thou crave?/Thyself ingenious, learn'd, and brave,/And equal to th'immortal theme!' But if the learned and ingenious Colonel Hall really feels unequal to his subject, then he must join forces with Smart, although he too feels unfit to do full justice to Major-General William Kingsley, the hero of the Battle of Minden (1759): 'Then let us both at once confess/Our meanness, and the man address/Who soars above our song.' So they sing together a hymn of praise, and thus fight 'The grudging silence of mankind'. Smart was evidently suffering from his usual delusion that the heroes of mankind are universally neglected or persecuted. According to Smart, the artists who try to represent the glories of Kingsley's deeds are bound to fail in their task, and it is only God who can finally praise him as he deserves:

> 'Say leader of the glorious few,
> What can impoverish'd fancy do
>   On paper, canvas, or on stone?
> Thy work so great, thy name so bright,
> That God himself, with all his might
>   Must give th'applause alone.'
>   (*Collected Poems*, i. 22)

'Munificence and Modesty' deals with Smart's obsessional humility in an allegorical form. Smart's excessive self-deprecation did not prevent an overweening pride in his poetic genius, and this paradox is implicit in the opening paragraph of 'Munificence and Modesty', where the 'spirits still demanding less' are just those meritorious souls who are entitled to 'approbation':

> O VOICE OF APPROBATION, bless
> The spirits still demanding less,
> The more their natures have to need,
> The more their services can plead;
> The more their mighty merits claim—
> The voice of Approbation came.
>   (*Collected Poems*, i. 213)

Nowadays, such self-effacing mortals seem intolerably saccharine, but Smart felt quite differently about them. He personifies Modesty as a fair, divinely sweet young girl, with 'garb prepared, and lamp replete'. With cheeks that reflect the blushing evening sky, she prostrates herself on the glossy turf, conscious of the fact that she has received much but done nothing, her abstinence is insincere, her studies are not severe enough, her thoughts are at fault, her words are weak and inadequate, her actions are wretched, her passions are not properly reined. She seems to us to be going through a characteristic phase of adolescence, especially when her self-deprecation is associated with the worship of nature: she enthuses about the landscape around her—the flowers and the grass, the stately pine trees and the bulrushes, the brooks and the swans, and the reflection of the whole scene in the shaded lake. But in Smart's eyes Modesty is saintly, and she prays to the 'FATHER of SIMPLICITY':

> 'Consider for the poor infirm,
> The harmless sheep, th'obnoxious worm,
> The stooping yoke that turn the soil,
> And all the children of thy toil.
> In fine, of all the num'rous race,
> Of all that crowd and ought to grace
> Thy vast immeasurable board,
> To me the lowest lot afford.'
>   (*Collected Poems*, i. 214)

At such an exemplary prayer, the immense applause of thunder is heard in the heights, all the host of heaven appears in a great and glorious throng and among these seraphim, ten thousand strong, descends 'Th'archangel LIBERALITY':

> A crown of Beryls graced his head,
> His wings were closed, his hands were spread;
> His stature nobler than the rest,
> A sun and belt adorn'd his breast;
> His voice was rapture to the ears,
> His look like GRANBY in his geers
>   (*Collected Poems*, i. 215)

Smart is referring to John Manners, Marquis of Granby, who had fought at Minden in 1759, and had been appointed commander-in-chief of the British contingent in Germany later that year. He was given a tremendously enthusiastic welcome when he returned to England in 1763, and it seems likely that Smart was writing his poem about that time and making a topical comparison between the warlike Archangel and the popular soldier. But in 'Munificence and Modesty', the relationship between Modesty and the Archangel is similar to the relationship between Smart and his patrons—that is, Modesty cringes and the Archangel supplies the 'voice of Approbation'. At one time, therefore, I wondered whether the identification of Liberality and the Marquis of Granby meant that Smart was looking for yet another military patron, but I have found no evidence that this was so.

The Archangel personifies Liberality or Munificence, and is therefore seen as the Almoner of God who has been sent to reward Modesty for asking for 'the lowest lot'. The Archangel bids Modesty survey the earth from east to west, the olives and forests, rocks and elm trees, golden meadows and silver streams, corn and larks, bees and canals, grottoes and precious stones, and begs her to take it as a gift:

> 'I, whose commission's to dispense
> The meed of God's munificence,
> To thy undoubted worth resign,
> These joys of thought and sense, as thine.'
> *(Collected Poems, i. 215)*

Modesty, very naturally, does not wish to accept all this wealth, but she would certainly be glad to accept a little cottage just big enough for herself, with room enough to pray in. The Archangel, just as naturally, will not take no for an answer:

> 'Then take a view of yonder tow'rs,
> Where Fortune deals her gift in flow'rs;
> Where that vast bulwark's proud disdain
> Runs a long terras on the main;
> Whose strong foundation Ocean laves,
> And bustles with officious waves,
> To bring with many a thousand sail,
> Whate'er refinement can regale;
> Rich fruits of oriental zest,
> Perfumes of ARABY the blest,

> With precious ornaments to wear,
> Upon thy hands, thy neck, thy hair:
> O Queen of the transcendent few,
> All decoration is thy due.'
>
> (*Collected Poems*, i. 216)

In this great house, remote from the noise of cities, she will enjoy serenity and will be clothed in innocence. And if her elevated mind is willing to choose the pleasures designed for her sex, Liberality will provide her with a blooming youth to make her a transported bride. But Modesty, true to her name, cannot bear the idea. 'Let other nymphs their swains endear,/For my affections are not here./The refusal to part with her virginity is evidently her crowning glory, for Modesty is now all set for 'vast and popular acclaim'. Poor Modesty objects yet again:

> O rather may I still refrain,
> Nor run the risk of being vain;
> To peace and silence let me cleave,
> And *give* the glory—not receive.
>
> (*Collected Poems*, i. 217)

Once again she is persuaded to accept a gift of love, a royal sceptre and a dove, which will entitle her to command all things on earth. But Modesty looks at the floor and begs that Liberality will not talk about crowns. She is finally overruled as a vast cherubic flight hands down from the zenith a chariot emblazoned with an emerald crown and drawn by peacocks:

> Lo! this is SHE,
> Which has achieved the first degree;
> And scorning MAMMON and his leav'n,
> Has one Eternity and Heav'n.'
>
> (*Collected Poems*, i. 217)

Personally I find that the sentiment of this poem reflects one of the more distasteful aspects of Smart's personality and religious outlook. But I am nevertheless intrigued by the sub-title of the poem. Smart called his poem 'Munificence and Modesty A Poem; The Hint from a Painting of Guido'. Father Devlin had no doubts about which of Guido's pictures Smart was referring to: 'He had become aware that his doctrines laid him open to suspicions of "popery," and he was beginning to make efforts to dispel such suspicions. An example of this was the title-piece "Munificence and Modesty"; the inspiration for it came from "a painting by Guido"—obviously "The Coronation of the Virgin" by Guido Reni, in which Mary is depicted as a peasant girl being crowned by a multitude of angels. But in the poem there is no mention of Mary, and all is treated as fable.'[1] I feel sure that the idea that Smart was fascinated by the Blessed Virgin Mary but dared not speak about her openly, was just wishful thinking on Father Devlin's part. He did stop to ask how Smart could have seen 'The Coronation of the Virgin' before composing his poem: 'This picture, originally in Madrid, now in the National Gallery, probably did not come to England before the Napoleonic Wars. It is not known where Smart could have seen a copy; perhaps his wife had one; perhaps in the trip abroad, of unknown date, mentioned in *Jubilate Agno*, D.42.'[2] It is true that the encounter between Modesty and Liberality in Smart's poem is reminiscent of the encounter between Mary and the Archangel Gabriel, and Smart does emphasize Modesty's virginity and eventual apotheosis. I suppose that Guido Reni's 'Coronation of the Virgin' (see Plate III) could have influenced the imagery of the final lines of Smart's poem, though there is no phoenix-drawn chariot in the painting. A more important point is that the central theme of 'Munificence and Modesty', the confrontation between the young virgin and the Archangel, is entirely absent from Guido Reni's picture. With uplifted eyes, the Virgin Mary is accompanied to heaven by hosts of angels, but the Archangel Gabriel is lost in the crowd.

In the Print Room of the British Museum, I searched in vain for a picture by Guido Reni that reflected more accurately the theme and imagery of 'Munificence and Modesty'. What I did find, was a remarkable print, 'Liberality and Modesty From the Original painting of Guido Rheni in the Collection of Henry Furnese Esq.' Sold by Rob.' Strange Engraver, at the Golden Head, in Henrietta Street, Covent Garden, London.

---

[1] *Poor Kit Smart*, 157.

[2] *Poor Kit Smart*, 157. I examine *Jubilate Agno* D. 42 and the date of Smart's trip abroad in Appendix III.

Publish'd according to Act of Parliament. 1755' (see Plate **IV**).[3]
The imagery of the picture has little in common with Smart's
images in 'Munificence and Modesty'. The naked figures of
Liberality and Modesty in Guido's picture are quite different
from Smart's Liberality, clothed like Granby in his geers, and
Modesty, with garb complete and lamp replete. If we want to
stretch a point, we can suggest that when the Archangel
offers Modesty 'a long terras on the main;/When strong
foundation Ocean laves', Smart is describing the paved terrace
and the sea in the background of Guido's picture. Similarly, the
'precious ornaments to wear,/Upon thy hands, thy neck, thy
hair', refer perhaps to the jewels that Liberality offers Modesty
in Guido's picture. But it seems to me more likely that Smart
was not so much attracted to the imagery of Guido's picture as
to its central theme, the conflict between Liberality and
Modesty—and that he developed the theme along the lines of
his own individual poetic imagination.

In the *Ode to the Earl of Northumberland*, Smart printed two
brief but poignant lyrics, 'The Sweets of Evening', and 'On a
Bed of Guernsey Lilies'. The former poem expresses his joy in
freedom, and a serenity which he had tried to find while he was
confined for madness: when God plays upon the harp of
stupendous magnitude and melody, malignity ceases and the
devils themselves are at peace, 'For this time is perceptible to
man by a remarkable stillness and serenity of soul' (*Jubilate*

---

[3] As yet, I know nothing of Henry Furnese, and I have no idea therefore whether
Smart could have based his poem on the original picture rather than on Strange's
engraving. I do not know what happened to the original. After reading M. F.
Sweetser's *Guido Reni*, Boston, 1878, 158, I assumed that the original was to be
found in Cobham Hall, Kent. But Mr. Felix Hull has kindly given me information
about the catalogue of pictures at Cobham Hall made by Douglas Guest in 1833.
Item no. 30 was Guido's 'Liberality and Modesty', engraved by Strange ('what
Liberality presents with an open hand Modesty only touches with her finger')
with figures larger than life, and valued at £1,500. Item no. 69 was a smaller
engraving, probably a model for the larger 'Liberality and Modesty' in the
Gallery of Cobham Hall, valued at £150. One of these engravings, valued at £500,
was included in an inventory of oil paintings and statuary at Cobham Hall,
made about 1913. It is not known who bought the engravings at Cobham Hall, nor
what date they arrived there. There is no evidence in Esmé Wingfield-Stratford's
The Lords of Cobham Hall, 1959, that Smart was acquainted with the Earls of
Darnley. My thanks to Mr. Ralph Arnold for his help in tracking down the
history of 'Liberality and Modesty'.

Agno B1.249). During the daytime, writes Smart in 'The Sweets of Evening', the mind sickens in the sultry atmosphere. But in the evening, the body is confined no longer, he can take exercise in freedom, and the all-serene summer moon shines through the trees and the nightingale sings:

> A nosegay, every thing that grows,
>   And music, every sound
> To lull the Sun to his repose;
> The skies are coloured like the rose
>   With lively streaks around.
>   (*Collected Poems*, i. 134)

Church bells are heard as the poet imagines that he is communing with superior beings—men or angels we cannot tell:

> Of all the changes rung by time
>   None half so sweet appear,
> As those when thoughts themselves sublime,
> And with superior natures chime
>   In fancy's highest sphere.
>   (*Collected Poems*, i. 134)

After a hectic social life in London, Smart had obviously been lonely during his confinement for madness. 'Let Bold, house of Bold rejoice with the Hop-Hornbeam. God send me a neighbour this September', he had written in *Jubilate Agno* D.97, while his imagination invented hundreds of names with which to people the emptiness. After his release from confinement, Smart was still lonely, and he still needed to imagine that he was conversing with 'superior natures'.

'On a Bed of Guernsey Lilies Written in September 1763' is another expression of Smart's loneliness. The poem was written just a year after Smart had prayed to God to send him a neighbour, and during that year, John Sherratt, Miss Sheeles, and Mr. and Mrs. Rolt had helped to bring about Smart's release from confinement. Smart was now free, but still longing for friends and neighbours, as is shown in this poem on the guernsey lily, in which he takes a pathetic delight in some unexpected visitors. The guernsey lilies bring sweetness to bless the latter spring after all the other flowers have died off:

How kind the visit that ye pay,
Like strangers on a rainy day,
When heartiness despair'd of guests
(*Collected Poems*, i. 134)

Smart was still all sociability, all 'heartiness', but only a few months ago he had been officially a madman, and when he was finally released, people no longer flocked to see him—or so these poems imply, despite Hawkesworth's assurance that Smart 'is by no means considered in any light that makes his company as a gentleman, a scholar, and a genius less desirable.'[4] But Smart refused to despair. Gay nature grieves as the autumn winds prevail over the falling leaves, but the guernsey lilies bloom as symbols of hope: 'We never are deserted quite'.

Smart's poem is a transparently personal one, a lyrical expression of his attempt to adjust himself to the loneliness of freedom after the loneliness of madness. It comes as something of a surprise, therefore, that we find that both theme and imagery were by no means original. In the Supplement to the *Christian's Magazine* in 1760 there is an essay by 'Juvenis', entitled 'Some Account of the Guernsey Lilly, with Animadversions thereon'. The essay has remarkable affinities with *On the Goodness of the Supreme Being*, as well as with 'On a Bed of Guernsey Lilies'. The image cluster in *On the Goodness of the Supreme Being*, where the Trinity is symbolized by the threefold colours of the pansies and where Smart describes the dependence of the colour upon the 'vivifying beams' of 'yonder golden globe', is found also in Juvenis's essay. He writes of the guernsey lily, that 'This flower, when exposed in the sun-beams, seems to be cloathed in nature's most gorgeous attire'. He compares it with the peacock, the pheasant, and polished gold, 'yet cannot the most beautiful of them all excel it.' The guernsey lily gently divides itself into three small particles surrounded by little stems which 'seem to bow their powder'd crests in a profound adoration. Doth not this afford us a lively emblem of the glorious Trinity?' There are also some notable verbal parallels between Juvenis's essay and Smart's 'On a Bed of Guernsey Lilies'. Juvenis begins, 'SO great and infinite are the beauties

---

[4] *Poems of the Late Christopher Smart*, 1791, I. xxv.

display'd by the Almighty in the vegetable creation, that one can hardly imagine any man so void of thought, as not sometimes to meditate upon them'. Smart begins, 'YE beauties! O how great the sum/Of sweetness that ye bring'. Juvenis writes that useless weeds may have no beauty and no scent, 'yet will the contemplative mind, like the busy bee, suck some sweet from the most nauseous herb'. Smart writes that although nature is brief and frail, 'Yet still the philosophic mind/ Consolatory food can find'. Juvenis's closing exhortation states the central theme of Smart's poem:

> Be not disheartened at your lot, O Christian, when God seems to have withdrawn his holy assistance from you; contemplate on the various changes which this flower undergoes; submit and support yourself with Christian fortitude and resignation; and rely on this, that God will not utterly forsake you, but that the sun of righteousness shall rise on you again, shall enable you to conquer that three headed monster, sin, death, and hell; and shall raise you to the greatest splendor in heaven, there to dwell when time shall be no more.

This reassurance from Juvenis, that 'God will not utterly forsake you' is identical with the lesson that Smart learns from the guernsey lilies:

> We never are deserted quite;
> 'Tis by succession of delight
> That love supports his reign.
> (*Collected Poems*, i. 135)

Smart had to keep reminding himself to be resigned to the will of God. Hannah sings an air where resignation is emphasized by capital letters:

> *IF RESIGNATION be*
> *The Name that's giv'n to Thee,*
> *O lend thy passive Smile;*
> *Thy meek unstudied Style,*
> *That exampled in thy Ways*
> *Grief may learn to bless and praise.*

In the last days of his life, Smart was still fighting against despair. 'EXTEMPORE *By the late* C. SMART, *in the* King's-Bench,

Q

on hearing a Raven croak' was printed in the *Gentleman's Magazine* for September 1779:

> YON Raven once an acorn took
>   From Romney's stoutest, tallest tree;
> He hid it by a limpid brook,
>   And liv'd another oak to see.
>
> Thus Melancholy buries Hope,
>   Which Providence keeps still alive;
> Bids us with affliction cope,
>   And all anxiety survive.

It had already appeared in the *Hymns for the Amusement of Children*, where it had been given another title: 'Against DESPAIR. OLD RALPH in the WOOD'.

[IX]

The Oratorios

'Let Japhia rejoice with Buteo who hath three testicles.
For I bless God in the strength of my loins and for the voice
which he hath made sonorous' (*Jubilate Agno*, B1.80)

IN ORDER TO KEEP body and soul together, the eighteenth-
century poet was practically forced to produce a heap of second-
rate anonymous literature to subsidize the more important
works that he chose to publish under his own name. Dr. Sherbo
therefore chooses the title 'Survival in Grub Street' for his
article that attributes to Smart the anonymous or pseudonymous
works, *The Muses Banquet* (1752), *A Collection of Pretty Poems for
the Amusement of Children Three Feet High* [1756], *A Collection of
Pretty Poems for the Amusement of Children Six Foot High* [1756], and
Be Merry and Wise [1753].[1] I wonder whether Smart undertook
oratorio libretti, at a later period of his life, for similar economic
reasons. He certainly could not have expected to enhance his
literary reputation by doing so, for in his *Dissertation on the Rise,
Union, and Power, the Progressions, Separations, and Corruptions, of
Poetry and Music*, John Brown wrote, 'the *musician's* character
hath here, in many instances, assumed the *precedence*; and the
poet become *subservient* to him, as his *director*. How this came to
pass, may be easily explained. This kind of poem being unknown in England when Handel arrived; and that great
musician being the first who introduced the *oratorio*; it became
a matter of necessity, that he should *employ* some writer in his
service. Now this being a degradation, to which men of genius
would not easily submit, he was forced to apply to *versifiers*
instead of *poets*. Thus the poem was the effect either of hire or

[1] 'Survival in Grub Street: Another Essay in Attribution', *Bulletin of the New
York Public Library*, lxiv, 1960, 147–58.

favour, when it ought to have been the voluntary emanation of genius. Hence, most of the poems composed to, are such, as would have sunk and disgraced any other music than his own.'[2] Brown must have forgotten that the words of Handel's first oratorio are generally attributed to Pope and Arbuthnot, after Racine. But there can be no question of the poor reputation of the librettist in the 1760s. We are not very confident therefore that we are going to discover great literary merit in Smart's oratorios, but it is worth reading them over once or twice if only because they illustrate one of the more banal but popular aspects of literary production in the eighteenth century.

On the 17th April 1712, the 'Articles for regulating Opera and Comedy' forbade stage performances on Wednesdays and Fridays during Lent. Inevitably a convenient loop-hole was found in the law by stressing the sacred nature of oratorios, in order to set them apart from other theatrical performances. The oratorios escaped the ban, but historians of music point out that despite their sacred subject matter, the oratorios were nevertheless theatrical entertainments. Handel was writing for the theatre not for the church, and his oratorios display a variety of theatrical devices—the imposing choruses of *Solomon* and *Israel in Egypt*, the judicious blend of Biblical history and decorous 'love-interest' in *Joseph* and *Jephtha*, the vivid drama in *Saul* and *Belshazzar*. The Handelian oratorio is 'of the earth, earthy', and the atmosphere of the theatres in which these works were produced hangs around them.[3]

It comes as no surprise, therefore, that in Smart's oratorios, 'earthy' human experience like sexual jealousy is harnessed to devout sentiment. The association is not a particularly happy one for the sanctification of the mundane in the eighteenth century rarely resulted in a healthy identification of the spiritual and the corporeal. It much more often resulted in blasphemy, as in Pamela's version of Psalm 137 ('BY the waters of Babylon') in which she expresses her hypocritical sorrow at being imprisoned by the lascivious Mr. B. In *Hannah* (1764), which was set to music by John Worgan, Peninnah's fertility makes her gloat over her rival, Hannah, who has borne Elkanah

---

[2] Printed in the *Critical Review*, xv, April 1763, 254.

[3] See *Grove's Dictionary of Music and Musicians*, under 'Oratorio'.

no children. Nothing could be more secular and theatrical than the Handmaid's Air in act I, scene I:

> *How joyful the Triumph, how sweet the Content*
> *O'er Rivals in Love to prevail,*
> *When you fully revenge, what you greatly resent,*
> *Till Pride her Preferment bewail;*
> *When you bid her each Day and each Night to despair,*
> *And urge that Reproach, which no Temper can bear.*

In *Abimelech* (1768), which was set to music by Samuel Arnold, devotional fervour is joined to the 'earthy' motive of sexual jealousy, and even more violently than in *Hannah*. A note of adoration is heard in Abraham's recitative in part I ('*O great and glorious! at whose footstool falls/The seraph adoration*'), but he is in fact praying about Abimelech's passion for Sarah ('*curb his passions,/Lest beauty tempt his ruin*'). Abraham is praying at the same time about his own desire to keep Sarah:

> And, Oh, thy special blessings send,
> On all that Abraham calls his own,
> But chief, my fair domestic friend,
> Still to be mine, and mine alone.

The Chorus joins in to support Abraham's prayer:

> *Attend to Abraham's prayer attend,*
> *And aid his vows as they ascend,*
> *Ye cherub hosts who keep your posts,*
> *Where love and rapture have no end.*

But the eighteenth-century oratorio was a hybrid form, and just as it would be wrong to minimize the 'earthy' element in the plots of *Hannah* and *Abimelech*, it would also be mistaken to deny the genuine devotional feeling implicit in the genre. Benjamin Stillingfleet, for example, expressed his devotional purpose with his own brand of excessive humility, in the Dedication of *Paradise Lost* (1760) to Mrs. Montagu: 'Our country is much indebted to the late Mr. Handel for introducing a new kind of entertainment, where one of the finest arts is made subservient to the noblest and most exalted affection belonging to human nature, and which alone could furnish subjects adequate to his wonderful conceptions. You will easily see that i mean devotion. Music in all ages has been looked upon as a proper accompanyment to religious acts, and if we can make religious thoughts accompany our diversions, it should seem that we have obtained no small improvement of them. I shall therefore think that i have not misemployed my time in endeavouring to contribute, as far as lay in my power, towards carrying on an entertainment, which the best and wisest of both sexes judge not unworthy of their encouragement.' Thomas Morell, who wrote the libretti for several of Handel's oratorios, also expressed the need for music 'as a proper accompanyment to religious acts'. In his sermon, *The Use and Importance of Music in the Sacrifice of Thanksgiving* (1747), he speaks of the human voice's needing the accompaniment of musical instruments if it is 'to express the strong Sentiments of the Soul, when in its devotional Ascent to Heaven it has something astonishingly great in view. . . . The Soul still labours after higher Transports; still panteth to magnify God, and his Goodness, in a more exalted Strain, and *make his Praise glorious*; and not only desireth to bless God with greater Fervency and Elevation, but also in more grateful Terms to speak her own Felicity and Joy.' In this sermon, Morell is preaching specifically about church music, but he would certainly have supported Stillingfleet's antithesis, and agreed that religious thoughts should be encouraged at musical entertainments in the theatre. The desire to bless God with 'Fervency and Elevation' is therefore expressed in his oratorios. In *Judas Macchabeus* [1746], for instance, Judas maintains that 'The Lord of Hosts, who, still the same,/We trust, will give attentive Ear/To the Sincerity of Pray'r.' The Chorus then sings a prayer, 'O Father, whose Almighty Pow'r/The Heav'ns, and Earth, and Seas, adore!' Another example from the same oratorio is Judas's triumphant gratitude to God after his defeat of the Egyptians:

> FAther of Heav'n! from thy eternal Throne,
> Look with an Eye of Blessing down,
> While we prepare with holy Rites,
> To solemnize the Feast of *Lights*,
>   And thus in thy Praise
>   This Altar raise
> With Carols of triumphant Joy.

Or, to take an example from another of his libretti, Morell
shows in *Nabal* (1764) a characteristic devotional attitude of
mind. In part II, scene II, where David sends Asaph to beg
food from the rich Nabal, in order to feed the hungry people in
the wilderness of Paran, David prays:

> Meanwhile
> Let us address with Pray'r the God of Heav'n,
> Whose bounteous Providence o'er all his Works,
> Oft chears the sad, and bids the famish'd Soul
> Luxuriant feast, till Nature craves no more.

> AIR.
> *Great Creator, who kindly feedest*
> *With thine Hand the Brute-Creation,*
>   *Blest with nutrimental Store,*
>   *Favour'd with peculiar Care,*
>   *Let not Man,*
>   *Pine with Hunger, and deep Despair.*

Our studies of the religious poetry of Christopher Smart lead us
to expect a strong devotional attitude of praise and thanksgiving in his oratorios. But the point to be made here is that
when Smart praised and adored God in his oratorios, he was
writing in a conventional style of the genre. Hence, Hannah's
resignation ('upon her bended Knees,/With Heav'n-directed
Eyes'), her prayers for deliverance, and her gratitude when God
hears her prayers, and the choral '*Glory, Glory is thy Due*' at the
close of Act I, and the final Grand Chorus:

> *To Thee stupendous in thy Ways,*
> *To Jacob's God the Blessed Uncreate*
> *Be all Dominion, Pow'r and Praise,*
> *And Laud and Adoration in the Height.*

In *Hannah* this note of adoration almost transfigures the 'earthy'
plot, but in *Abimelech*, as has already been suggested, the
juxtaposition of devotion and human relationships is uneasy,
not to say ridiculous. In one breath, Abraham is gloriously
pious, in the next he turns his mind to his treaty with
Abimelech:

> *I will ascribe the glory with the gifts*
> *To great Melchizedeck, the prince of peace,*
> *Whose glorious face I saw, and unto whom*
> *I gave the tithe for ever—in his name*
> *I make a league with thee and thine most faithful,*
> *And Phicol too shall ratify the deed.*

From Melchizedech to Abimelech to Sarah: Abraham's exalted thoughts finally turn to 'what tender soft emotions,/ Lovers reconcil'd receive!'

One knows from Morell's *Nabal* that a librettist felt at liberty to impose a stricter pattern on his story than the Biblical text warrants. The Biblical account does not unduly emphasize the hunger of David and his people in Paran, but Morell wanted to make a dramatic antithesis between Nabal's wealth and David's want, and secondly between the feeding of the Children of Israel in the wilderness and the hunger of David's people in Paran:

> Have Mercy on us, Lord; our Fathers cried
> When press'd with Hunger in this dreary Waste
> The Lord in Mercy heard their Pray'r,
> And fed them with the Bread of Heav'n

> AIR.
> *Food they ask'd, and all around*
> *Quails, and Manna sweet of Taste,*
> *Wing'd the Air, and spread the Ground;*
> *Blessing all with kind Repast.*

But in answer to this plea for mercy, Nabal asks churlishly, 'dost thou envy the vast Store of Wealth,/With which our new-shorn Flocks have heap'd our Barns?', and Nabal eventually falls into a 'drunken song', for which there is no Biblical precedent.

Throughout the texts of *Hannah* and *Abimelech* we find that Smart arranges and embroiders the Biblical stories for theatrical effect. In the 'Argument' prefixed to *Hannah*, Smart gives the reader a synopsis of I Samuel 1, and a reference to the 'Song of Hannah' which begins I Samuel 2. This is followed by the statement, 'The only Liberty Mr. *Smart* has taken with the sacred Story is that he has introduced the Song of *Hannah* as a

Thanksgiving immediate upon her Acceptance in *Shilo*, whereas it was not composed till after the Birth of *Samuel*. This Liberty he humbly hopes is more pardonable than the total Omission of so pious and beautiful a Piece.' It is an understatement to say that the *only* liberty taken with the sacred text is the rearrangement of episodes. The need for dramatizing the Biblical story means that Peninnah's vindictive jealousy or Elkanah's benevolence to Hannah has to be expressed imaginatively, and the simple statements of the Bible are therefore exaggerated and complicated almost beyond recognition.

Although no one would be prepared to take *Hannah* very seriously as poetry, there is no doubt that Smart was bent on transfiguring the Biblical story with his poetic imagination. For Smart subordinates speech, action, and characterization to a 'poetic' theme of fertility versus barrenness, expressed through symbolic imagery. This theme is stated at the beginning of the oratorio, in the songs of Peninnah, her Handmaid, and Hannah herself. Peninnah is the mother of many sons and daughters, and she is the first to state the theme of fertility by means of references to the genealogy of Abraham, 'whose un-number'd Progeny/Are known to him who calculates the Stars', and by the symbolism of the turtles, '*Still returning Love for Love,/Dove proceeding still from Dove,/How your beauteous Race endures?*' Peninnah's delight in her own fertility is expressed in an ecstatic desire for music, 'O for Musick,/And every Form of Joy to bless and Praise'. The rather odd link between music and fertility in *Hannah* makes one wonder whether the jubilant creatures invoked in *Jubilate Agno* are evidence of the teeming fertility, as well as the more obvious variety and beauty, of the creation.

The Handmaid replies to Peninnah, and opposes fecundity to barrenness. She says of Hannah's honour, that it 'Is not hereafter in the sweet Idea/Of Self continued in a genuine Race.' She then states the theatrical as opposed to thematic conflict of the oratorio, by setting Peninnah and Hannah, the wives of Elkanah, against each other as rivals for his love. In one sense, these women are the rivals of heroic drama; in another sense they are symbols of a poetic conflict between destructive infertility and creative fecundity.

Hannah's opening song is likewise a poetic definition of the theme. She sees her own miserable situation reflected in barren Nature (she 'costs such Care, and yields no Fruit'), and she seeks thorns for a wreath, and joins in *'the bleak Winds as they blow,/And howl o'er the desolate Heath.'* And whereas Peninnah desired music, Hannah bids *'Adieu to the Timbrel and Lute,/Adieu to the Strains of the Lyre'*. But Smart is always conscious of his dramatic theme, and later Hannah gives a more down-to-earth description of her situation when she complains to Elkanah that the cruel taunts and triumphs of her rival are too much to bear. Elkanah begs her to cease lamenting, and a Levite advises her to trust in God's great goodness as it was shown to Sarah and Rebecca. The parallel between these barren women and Hannah is obvious, and we recall Smart's own statement of the theme in *Jubilate Agno* B1.16, 'Let Sarah rejoice with the Red-wing, whose harvest is in the frost and snow. For the hour of my felicity, like the womb of Sarah, shall come at the latter end.' The theme of Hannah, the misery of her infertility, is one of Smart's reiterated themes throughout his religious poetry. For some cryptic reason he was able to identify himself with these Old Testament women. We can only guess why he found their situation like his own. Perhaps enforced chastity during con-finement for madness had made him frustrated and conscious of the fact that he had fathered two daughters but no sons. Perhaps he was thinking of creative barrenness, and his hopes that as he grew older he would write finer poetry. We just do not know. But perhaps we should remember that in *Hannah*, Smart is making an indirect psychological statement about himself, as well as a poetic and dramatic version of a Biblical story.

In Act II, Peninnah's cruel taunts are expressed through a more complex poetic symbolism. For Hannah's infertility becomes not merely despicable but actually criminal. She is 'As barren as the Wilderness of Sin.' The nature of her sin-fulness is flung at her in the accusation, 'base, Ingrate!' Smart had written in *Jubilate Agno* B2.324 that ingratitude is the sin against the Holy Ghost. He is trying to show that Peninnah's accusation is terrible because it is to a certain extent true. Hannah *is* sinful in being disconsolate and ungrateful towards a provident God:

> *Every Bird that pipes a Note,*
> *Every Shrub that bears a Bloom,*
> *Thine Unkindnesses upbraid;*
> *Grateful is the Linnet's Throat,*
> *Grateful is the Bay's Perfume,*
> *And to God their Tribute's paid.*

This a lyrical statement of one of Smart's most deeply-felt convictions. But it is nevertheless spoken in wicked spite and directed against Hannah who has little to be grateful for, whereas the 'Shrub that bears a Bloom', like Peninnah, has everything to be grateful for. Smart is obviously feeling his way towards one of the greatest riddles of the religious faith to which he clung so dramatically: God is provident and man must be grateful, but what has the deprived and maimed man to be grateful for? But he never articulated the question, and he preferred to avoid the issue, and to describe how a divine miracle made Hannah's gratitude possible. Throughout Act II, Smart does not allow the theme to flag. Once again Hannah sees her condition as inherently unnatural, 'where is Peace?/ She dwells not but with Plenty—where is Plenty?/She lives with pregnant Nature, loaded Vines,/And Fields that laugh again with Corn and Olives.' This can be compared with Hymn XXIII in the *Hymns for the Amusement of Children*, entitled 'Peace', illustrated with the horn of plenty, and concluding with a stanza that would not be out of place in *Hannah* itself:

> Sustain the pillars of the state,
> Be health and wealth conjoin'd;
> And in each house thy turtles mate,
> To multiply mankind.

The poetic theme can be traced through Act III of *Hannah*. The parallel between fruition and music is reiterated in Eli's air:

> All Things are Void of Worth and Fruit
> Till God his Blessing send,
> Whose Voice can harmonize the Mute,
> And make the Deaf attend.

This recalls a more bizarre statement of the same idea in *Jubilate Agno* B1.24, 'For the praise of God can give to a mute fish the notes of a nightingale.' The 'Song of Hannah' continues the theme, but here, Smart's authority is the Biblical text itself, and he makes only a slight variation to suit his own theme, as when he transcribes I Samuel 2.5, 'the barren hath born seven; and she that hath many children is waxed feeble' as '*The fruitful Womb must fail,/The Barren shall prevail,/And reckon to the seventh Son.*' Smart had always admired the 'Song of Hannah'. He had associated Hannah and music in *Jubilate Agno* B2.458, 'For the Old Greeks and the Italians are one people, which are blessed in the gift of Musick by reason of the song of Hannah and the care of Samuel with regard to divine melody.' In the *Hymns and Spiritual Songs for the Fasts and Festivals of the Church of England*, published a year after *Hannah*, Smart makes one or two references to the 'Song of Hannah'. In Hymn I, 'New Year', Smart associates Hannah with his hero, David,

> Sing like David, or like Hannah,
> As the spirit first began,
> To the God of heights hosanna!
> Peace and charity to man.
> (*Collected Poems*, ii. 790)

And in Hymn IX, 'The Annunciation of the Blessed Virgin', the 'Song of Hannah' is seen as a forerunner of the 'Magnificat', 'Praise Hannah, of the three,/That sang in Mary's key'.

In Act III scene II, one of Hannah's Attendants draws the various threads together:

> *O may thy Gratitude prepare*
> *Thy Heart for Zeal's transcendent Blaze,*
> *And may the happy* Hannah *bear*
> *The fruit of everlasting Praise.*

Instead of Peninnah's command to Hannah to be grateful for her barrenness, the Attendant's command to Hannah is to be grateful for her new fruitfulness. During the course of the action of the oratorio, Hannah has been given a rational foundation for her duty to give gratitude to God. The ecstatic desire for music expressed by the fruitful Peninnah at the beginning of the oratorio is replaced by the finale, the universal desire for music:

> Ye *Levites*, blow the Trumpets in the East,
> Ye Damsels, smite the Timbrels and rejoice
> In these my Words prophetic of Salvation.

And the stupendous God is then lauded to the heights by the Grand Chorus.

The story of *Abimelech* is found in Genesis 20. While Abraham sojourns in Gerar, he pretends that his wife, Sarah, is his sister. She is subsequently abducted by Abimelech, King of Gerar. But God reveals to Abimelech in a dream that Sarah is a married woman, and Abimelech swears that he has not yet touched her, and that he has acted in innocence because he was assured that Sarah was Abraham's sister, not his wife. God agrees that Abimelech is innocent, but Sarah must be restored to her husband. Abimelech is reassured by the fact that Abraham is a prophet and will therefore pray for Abimelech and make his soul live. Abimelech nevertheless demands why Abraham has brought such great sin upon Gerar. Abraham answers, 'Because I thought, Surely the fear of God is not in this place: and they will slay me for my wife's sake.' He justifies the lie by pointing out that Sarah *is* his half-sister as well as his wife. Abimelech then restores Sarah to her husband with gifts, and permits Abraham to settle in Gerar. The story is obscure and not a little comical. But the eighteenth century had unshakeable confidence in the solemnity of the Bible, and the quotion from Virgil on the title-page of *Abimelech*, 'ET SOROR ET CONJUX', was not intended as a joke.

As we have seen, Smart imposed his own themes of barrenness and fertility upon the Biblical story of Hannah. In *Abimelech*, his theme is lust—despite the fact that the whole point of the Biblical story is that Abimelech abducts but does not seduce Sarah. When Sarah informs Abraham that Abimelech has declared his love for her, Smart's premise is that the Gentiles are more brutal than the Faithful:

> *Lo, her ears*
> *Have suffer'd profanation from the lips*
> *Of an enamour'd Gentile—Couldst think,*
> *That men remoter from the truth of God,*
> *And more of brutal nature, should controul*
> *Their appetite from such a form as Sarah's?*

In Part III, the Queen of Gerar seems to agree that the Gentiles
are morally inferior:

> He to whom God indulges light,
> Shou'd in proportion make it shine.
> Can heathen minds, involv'd in night,
> Like thee discern, like thee divine?

Smart seems to be rejecting the Deist view that God indulges
'light' to all men alike, regardless of their creed. The Deists
held that this light of nature is synonymous with conscience,
that knows what is right even if ethical instruction is lacking.
Presumably, Smart would have rejected as blasphemous and
infidel the Deist view as expounded, for instance, by Matthew
Tindal: 'let me ask you, Whether there's not a clear and
distinct Light, that enlightens all Men; and which, the Moment
they attend to it, makes them perceive those eternal Truths,
which are the Foundation of all our Knowledge. And is it not
God himself, who immediately illuminates them?'[4] In Abraham's
song in part I, Smart does for a moment suggest that even
brutes have conscience:

> The brute that in lust would rebel,
> Has conscience coercive within,
> At once to restrain and to quell,
> And to terrify passion from sin.

But the Chorus immediately takes the opposite view that lust
can completely overwhelm 'conscience coercive within'. In fact,
Smart has now got to the point where he states the lawless lust
of all mankind, not simply of the heathens alone:

> When love controuls the human heart,
> Or mad'ning passion fires the brain,
> Nature then shines exempt from art,
> And prince and peasant are the same.

Smart is still categorically opposed to the Deist interpretation of
nature as synonymous with the light of conscience. For Smart,
in this context, nature means the old-fashioned lawlessness
which is the antithesis of art, the civilizing and refining power

---

[4] *Christianity as Old as the Creation*, 1730, 11.

of civilization. For the Deist, Nature was good, for Abraham in *Abimelech* nature is barbarous and lustful.

Smart's ideas about instinct and nature, light and conscience, are expressed in a very confused way in *Abimelech*, but the prevailing, garbled, anti-Deist position held in the oratorio is probably Smart's attempt to rationalize his emotional condemnation of 'brutal nature'. For the theme of chastity versus lust in *Abimelech* would not be remarkable if it were not for its association in Smart's mind with a God revolted by sex: *'God is love./To lust and filth his hatred is so mighty,/That every check is given to stop their rage.'* It is the poet who is revolted, not God. It is the kind of revulsion that prompts the theme of Hymn II in *Hymns and Spiritual Songs for the Fasts and Festivals of the Church of England* on 'Circumcision', where Abraham's role is to chastise from carnal sin, his house and all his kin, and where Christ's role is to fulfil the law 'Which checks the fleshly-will'd,/And o'er the passion gives controul.' It is kind of revulsion that prompts also the essay on 'horns' in *Jubilate Agno* C.118–162. It is irrelevant here to ask whether Smart's revulsion sprang from bitter experience, real or deluded ('the false and disgusting hints against her fidelity' writes Father Devlin, gallantly, of Anna-Maria's innocence, and Smart's obsession with cuckoldry).[5] But what does matter, is that Smart's obsessions, deluded or otherwise, did affect his poetic creativity. The consciousness of his own infertility—carnal or literary we do not know—influenced the symbolism of *Hannah*, and his own sexual problems seem to have affected the way in which he elaborated the Biblical story of Abimelech, and made the abduction of Sarah an occasion for his own ideological discussion of lust and divine displeasure.

[5] *Poor Kit Smart*, 112.

[X]

A Translation of the Psalms of David

— i —

'all expressions, that seem contrary to Christ, are omitted'

WE KNOW from our study of *A Song to David* that Smart idolized King David as a religious poet, as a sinless man, and as a progenitor of Jesus Christ. Smart's enthusiasm for David's poetry was so great that eventually he versified the whole Book of Psalms, and brought it out in 1765 as *A Translation of the Psalms of David, Attempted in the Spirit of Christianity, and Adapted to the Divine Service.* We also know from our study of Smart's religious poetry that he liked to interpret the Old Testament in the light of the New. In the *Translation of the Psalms* he takes this view of the Old Testament to its logical extreme, and states in the brief preface. 'IN this translation, all expressions, that seem contrary to Christ, are omitted, and evangelical matter put in their room;—and as it was written with an especial view to the divine service, the reader will find sundry allusions to the rites and ceremonies of the Church of England, which are intended to render the work in general more useful and acceptable to congregations.' In the first part of this chapter we shall see that Smart was not alone in his wish to introduce Christian allusions into the Psalms. But he was alone in his single-minded, deliberately non-violent interpretation of David's poetry.

Quite a number of the scores of versions of the Psalms that appeared in the eighteenth century included a certain amount of Christian material. In his *Psalms, Hymns, and Spiritual Songs* (1714), for instance, the non-conformist Rev. Daniel Burgess set out to accommodate the devotional part of scripture to vulgar use in a most affectionate manner. At least, that was the opinion of John Billingsley, who wrote a 'Prefatory Epistle' to Burgess's book, which had '*met with great Acceptance, and been of singular Use in that Congregation to which this good Man ministered in holy Things*'. Burgess made a Christianized version of Psalm 45, for instance, and the first verse in the Book of Common Prayer, 'MY heart is inditing of a good matter: I speak of the things which I have made unto the King', becomes:

> MY boiling Heart doth over-flow
> With a transcendent thing;
> A Verse by Inspiration made
> Of and to CHRIST the King.

This may be compared with Smart's similar version:

> EXALTED by a blessed thought
> My soul is on the wing;
> I speak, as in the spirit taught,
> The praise of Christ my king.
> (*Collected Poems*, ii. 492)

A more well-known dissenting minister, the Rev. Dr. Isaac Watts, stated on the title-page of his version of the Psalms the bold changes that he planned to make in the Biblical text: *The Psalms of David, Imitated in the Language of the New Testament, and Applied to the Christian State and Worship* (1719). Throughout his book, therefore. Watts made changes similar to Burgess's, so that the Biblical 'King' in Psalm 45.1 automatically became 'my Saviour-King,/JESUS the LORD'. But in his *Hymns and Spiritual Songs* (1720) Simon Browne had certain reservations to make about Watts's evangelical method: '*Some* [Psalms] *are plainly evangelical in their sublimest sense, and direct reference. It is easy to give many more an evangelical turn. Mr.* Watts *has given many excellent* specimens *in his* Psalms *of* David imitated in the language of the *New Testament. The only exception I have against that admirable per-formance, wherein I think he has out-done himself, is, lest he should have carried too much of the Gospel into the* sweet singer *of* Israel, *and should lead some (who will not remember that this is only an imitation) to mistake his sense for the proper meaning of the inspir'd Writer.*' Despite this qualification, however, Browne gave an evangelical 'turn' to his own version of the Psalms, as, for instance, in

R

Book I, Hymn CXCVII, when he rendered Psalm 1.6 in the Book of Common Prayer, 'Therefore the ungodly shall not be able to stand in the judgement: neither the sinners in the congregation of the righteous', as follows:

> Among the just they shall not stand,
> When Christ to judge the world shall come,
> Divided to a different hand,
> They'll then receive their dreadful doom,
> And be adjudg'd to fire and pain,
> When saints shall with their Saviour reign.

Smart, too, gave a Christian version of this verse, though he did not give such a precise allusion to the Last Judgement:

> The sinners therefore shall be far
> From confidence, when at the bar
>   Of God's tribunal tried;
> Nor can the folk, with hearts unsound,
> Assemble to maintain their ground
>   With men to Christ allied.
>   (*Collected Poems*, ii. 386)

Thomas Coney's *The Devout Soul: Or, an Entertainment for a Penitent* (1722) was divided into eleven books, each consisting of a prose meditation, a poem, two prose hymns, and two prayers. The subject of the meditation is always linked to the hymn that follows. Hence a meditation 'Of the Ascension of Christ' is followed by a poem which is in fact a Christian version of Psalm 47 in which the Messiah and incarnate God is introduced into verse 4, and the Ascension into verse 5. Hence, 'God is gone up with a merry noise: and the Lord with the sound of the trump' in the Book of Common Prayer becomes in Coney's version,

> But now from *Sion's* Hill our King ascends;
> The Clouds are parted, and the Heaven bends.
> The shouting Angels line the glitt'ring Way,
> And sprightly Trumpets sound the pompous Joy.

Smart likewise paraphrases this verse as an account of the Ascension:

> Christ is gone up, the king of kings,
> And joyful acclamation rings,
> As thankless earth he spurns;
> The marshall'd cherubs stand in rows,
> From inmost heav'n the trumpet blows
> While God from death returns.
> (*Collected Poems*, ii. 497)

In *A Paraphrase on some Select Psalms* (1722) Richard Daniel stated '*that keeping too close to the Text, must of necessity sink the Poetry into Rhime and Doggerel*'. He decided therefore to make a periphrastic version: '*Since then the Psalms will by no Means bear with a close Translation, this being the Rock on which some of our best Poets have unfortunately split, I was resolved to try what sort of Figure they would make in Paraphrase*'. It is in keeping with the extreme elaboration of the Biblical text in his version, that when he introduces evangelical material, his Christian interpolations are more long-winded than anything encountered so far. Psalm 16.11 in the Book of Common Prayer, for instance, 'For why? thou shalt not leave my soul in hell: neither shalt thou suffer thy Holy One to see corruption' becomes in Daniel's version:

> So when the great *Messiah* shall arise,
> And GOD shall stand confess'd to mortal Eyes;
> Ah! what return shall the Redeemer find
> For proffer'd Pardon, and for Life design'd?
> A sinful World its Saviour shall disown,
> And with curs'd Thorns his bleeding Temples crown;
> Sharp is the Fate he must expect to meet,
> Sharp as those Nails which pierc'd his sacred Feet.
> Unthinking Crowds shall stand deridding by,
> Can they deride, for whom he came to dye?
> But oh! when Earth and Hell shall be at strife,
> And struggle which shall hold the Lord of Life;
> Thou shalt his Body from Corruption save,
> And raise the King of Glory from the Grave.

Smart's Christian version of the same verse is modest in comparison with Daniel's:

> Thou shalt not leave my soul in hell,
> Nor with the wretched fiends that fell
> Thy holy one to stay:

> The third day, and he shall arise,
> Nor shall be like to him that dies,
> And turns corrupted clay.
>
> (*Collected Poems*, ii. 412)

In *A Paraphrase on a Select Number of the Psalms of David: Done from the Latin of Buchanan* (1764), James Fanch distinguishes between a 'Psalm' and a 'hymn'. He gives, for instance, a straightforward versification of Psalm 122, but then goes on to give an alternative rendering which he calls 'An IMITATION. Being a New-Year's HYMN'. It is only in the latter that he introduces Christian terms, and it is obviously this factor that determines for Fanch whether a version will be called a 'Psalm' or a 'hymn'. 'Come kneel before JEHOVAH's Throne' in the Psalm version therefore becomes 'Come, kneel before your SAVIOUR's Throne' in the hymn. '*David*'s race' becomes '*David*'s Son'. 'O *Salem*! royal Patroness/To younger Cities seated round' becomes 'O heavenly *Salem*! royal Nurse/To thy young Coverts seated round'. Smart too introduces Christian allusions into his version of Psalm 122. He bids 'On Jesus let us wait,/ And to his temple speed', and 'For Christ, and for the brethren's sake' he will ever wish Salem well. But there is no suggestion that Smart ever agreed with Fanch's particular distinction between a Psalm and a hymn. Smart's Psalms correspond to Fanch's hymns in that they are Christian versions intended for congregational use. As for the *Hymns and Spiritual Songs for the Fasts and Festivals of the Church of England*, Smart never gives any indication that they were meant for congregational use. Like the *Song to David*, they seem much more like the poetic offering of the individual to God.

The indiscriminate evangelical expressions to be found in the Psalms of Burgess, Watts, Browne, Coney, Daniel, Fanch, and Smart himself must be distinguished from the more precise method used in *The Psalms of David, Translated into Heroic Verse* (1754) by Stephen Wheatland and Tipping Silvester. To each 'heroic' rendering of the Psalms, Wheatland and Silvester add a cautious academic documentation of the literal, figurative, and prophetic meanings. This cumbrous critical apparatus allows them to make a Christian interpretation of David's poetry, as in their 'Argument' to Psalm 45: '*Most interpreters conclude it to have been compos'd on the Marriage of* Solomon *with* Pharaoh's *Daughter, who it is probable was a* Proselyte *to the* Jewish *Religion; tho' at the same Time it carries its View to the* Lord Christ. *Accordingly the* Chaldee Paraphrase, Abenezra, *and* Solomon Jarchi, *affirm, that it was a Prophecy of the* Messias. *And then it is of the same Nature with the Book of* Canticles, *describing the Union with* Christ, *under the Figure of a* Nuptial Solemnity.' But Wheatland and Silvester do not allow this scholarly interpretation to appear in the actual versification of Psalm 45. Verses 14 and 15 in the Book of Common Prayer, 'The King's daughter is all glorious within: her clothing is of wrought gold. She shall be brought unto the King in raiment of needle-work: the virgins that be her fellows shall bear her company, and shall be brought unto thee', become therefore in Wheatland and Silvester's version:

> Within the fair is grac'd with charms untold,
> Her clothing is of purled works of gold:
> In garments by the flowering needle wrought,
> She'll to her monarch's longing arms be brought:
> Attended by her virgin choirs of state,
> She shall be brought to her majestic mate:

Characteristically, Smart incorporates the kind of interpretation that Wheatland and Silvester reserve for their notes, into the poetry itself:

> The bride of Jesus Christ is great
>   In glories of the soul,
> Of regal gold a precious weight
>   Adorns her flowing stole.
>
> Before her Saviour shall she stand
>   In needle-work array'd,
> And those wise virgins of her band
>   With blazing lamps display'd.
>   (*Collected Poems*, ii. 494)

Perhaps we should note that Smart's evangelical method differs also from that used in John and Charles Wesley's *Collection of Psalms and Hymns* (3rd edition, 1744). For the Christian variations that the Wesleys introduce into their

Psalms are intended to teach their congregations the Methodist emphasis on repentance, grace, and spiritual rebirth—a cycle of religious experience which occurs in Smart's *Hymn to the Supreme Being*, bur scarcely at all in the rest of his poetry. Psalm 2.7 in the Book of Common Prayer, 'I will preach the law, whereof the Lord hath said unto me: Thou art my Son, this day have I begotten thee', is therefore rendered by the Wesleys as follows:

> I publish the Divine Decree,
> That all shall live who trust in me:
> Look unto me ye Ransom'd Race
> Believe, and ye are sav'd by Grace.

Smart too makes a Christian version of the same verse, but without Methodist emphasis:

> This is my gospel and my lot,
> That God himself should say—
> 'Thou art my Son whom I begot,
> And magnify this day.'
> *(Collected Poems, ii. 387)*

If we have undertaken the formidable task of reading through Smart's *Translation of the Psalms*, we find that the casual sprinkling of references to Christ and the Christian church is not the most striking feature of Smart's evangelical method. We become much more intrigued with his wholesale revision of the Old Testament ethos of the Psalms and his refusal to accept David's violent hatred of his enemies. As was pointed out in another chapter, the eulogistic portrait of David in *A Song to David* presents him as being perfect in every detail. Only in the *Translation of the Psalms* is there any suggestion that Smart found some aspects of David's character—his aggressiveness and desire for revenge—less than perfect. This wholehearted change of ethos in Smart's version of the Psalms was by no means characteristic of those we have just looked at. Daniel Burgess, for example, wrote that his boiling heart overflowed with a transcendent thing. But in his version of Psalm 35.8, he nevertheless retained David's malevolence, which appeared in the Book of Common Prayer as 'Let a sudden destruction come upon him unawares, and his net, that he had laid privily, catch himself: that he may fall into his own mischief':

> Let swift Destruction these befal,
> And what they meant for me,
> O make the very self same Snare
> Their own Destruction be.

Smart, however, was determined that David should show Christian charity to his enemies, and his version of the same verse was as follows:

> Let no violent perdition
> Come upon them unaware;
> Let them scape by true contrition
> Every terror, every snare.
> (*Collected Poems*, ii. 466)

In *The Psalter in its Original Form: Or the Book of Psalms Reduced to Lines* (1759), George Fenwick was perfectly aware that David's violence is inconsistent with a Christian version of the Psalms. But he is much more cautious than Smart, and dares not turn the meaning of the Psalms inside out. Instead, he compromises by using sophistry, as his notes on his version of Psalm 109.5 reveal. In the Book of Common Prayer, the verse appears as 'Set thou an ungodly man to be ruler over him: and let Satan stand at his right hand.' Fenwick transcribes this as 'Him to The Wicked-One Thou wilt commit:/And, on his Right-Hand, *Satan* will appear.' Fenwick is trying his best to soften the impact of the original text, and he justifies himself by the following argument, which is anything but convincing: 'In the Hebr. indeed, we now read *Commit thou* which possibly may be an Idiom of the Hebrew, meaning the same as *Thou wilt commit;* or else the Mistake of some Transcriber, from the near Resemblance of the Letters which make the Difference. However it be, as all the following Verbs are plainly future, and the Speaker here is, manifestly, that meek and Poor-One, the Man *Christ Jesus*, who, on the very Cross, prayed for his Murderers; it seems most reasonable to take the whole as a Prophecy, and so a gracious Warning, not only to *Judas*, but to the whole Nation of Apostate *Jews* (to whom *St. Austin* applies it) or rather, to *all his Enemies*'. Smart's revision of the Psalms is comical but at least it is free from Fenwick's foolish sophistry:

> Set thou a man of virtuous fame
> My foe to rule and to reclaim,
> And let thy holy angel stand
> To guide the motions of his hand.
> (*Collected Poems*, ii. 675)

In *The Book of Psalms in Metre* (1751), Samuel Pike had also been worried about the malevolent Psalms, but he did not even attempt Fenwick's mild form of revision. Instead, he tried justifying David's violence. He admits that there have been objections made against the vengeful spirit of the Psalms—'as if', he says in horror, 'the spirit in the inspired Psalmist then, like the evil spirit in men now, lusted to envy. Horrid insinuation!' David was the king of God's visible church and people and it was in this public capacity that he prayed earnestly for the disappointment, the confusion, and destruction of the church's and God's implacable enemies. In all those Psalms where such curses are written, says Pike, the holy Psalmist is to be considered either as an inspired prophet, foretelling the judgements of God on the wicked, or as a type of Christ, and personating him, denouncing, or imprecating the vengeance of God on his impenitent and implacable enemies.

Smart would have none of this. David loathed the ungodly and wicked doers. 'Reward them according to their deeds: and according to the wickedness of their own inventions. Recompense them after the work of their hands: pay them that they have deserved. For they regard not in their mind the works of the Lord, nor the operation of his hands: therefore shall he break them down, and not build them up.' When one remembers that at this period of his life, Smart felt that he was being persecuted by vindictive literary critics, the charity that he expresses in his version of Psalm 28.4–6 in the Book of Common Prayer is pathetic but rather valiant. Obviously he was trying to follow the law that he had laid down in *A Song to David*, 'The slander and its bearer spurn,/And propagating praise sojourn', and 'The generous soul her saviour aids,/But peevish obloquy degrades;/The Lord is great and glad':

Yet do not thou, O Lord, requite
My foes acording to their spite,
   But bless them to repent;
Nor give the sinners like for like,
The measure they for others strike,
   And frauds that they invent.

Retaliate not their mighty wrongs,
Nor recompense them as belongs
   To these their works malign;
The wages of their sin remit,
And keep their souls from out the pit,
   Which they for others mine.

Tho' they regard not in their mind,
The works omniscient love design'd,
   And hands almighty skill'd,
Yet may they for their crimes atone,
And all on Christ the corner stone
   In clemency rebuild.
            (*Collected Poems*, ii. 446–47)

—ii—

'our Bards at this Time are confoundedly tedious' ('On the Merit of Brevity')

Smart's *Translation of the Psalms* is certainly interesting from the 'psychological' point of view, in that it reveals another facet of his obsession with King David. And it shows also how far the religious mania which had made Smart kneel in the streets to pray, now expressed itself in a fanatical revision of David's malevolence in the Psalms. But if we try to evaluate the *Translation of the Psalms* from the purely literary point of view, we have to admit that we are faced with a huge body of uninspired and tedious versification. The language of the Authorized Version, or even Coverdale's version in the Book of Common Prayer cannot be surpassed for beauty and harmony. Although numerous eighteenth-century versifiers tried rewriting the Psalms according to the literary standards of the age, the results were almost inevitably unsuccessful—tedious and banal.

James Gibbs, for instance, was influenced by the prevalent taste for refined simplicity and elegance, in reaction to the more ornamental style of the age of Cowley. He therefore proposed that his *First Fifteen Psalms of David, Translated into Lyric Verse* (1701) should be an essay in perspicuity and coherence, and he specifically rejects the '*Disadvantageous Paraphrase*' of Apolinaris, Duport, Beza, Eobanus Hessus, Ford, Patrick, Milbourn, and the '*Paraphrastical Additions*' of George Buchanan. Sir John Denham would have agreed with Gibbs, for in his *Version of the Psalms of David, Fitted to the Tunes used in Churches* (1714), he claims that 'this Work of mine is but a mere Translation; and being so, I durst not add any new Ornamentals of my own to so rare and accomplish'd a Piece.' He has now 'recover'd from the youthful itch of quaint Expressions', and he is determined to confine himself to such a proper plainness as might not be condemned by the learned, yet understood by the vulgar. In fact he has followed that learned judge, Horace, and has tried not to be too short for fear of obscurity, nor too prolix 'lest my Nerves and Spirits shou'd fail.' At the other extreme from Gibbs and Denham, Richard Daniel favoured what he called a 'paraphrase'—we have already seen how he felt that a close translation of the Psalms had been the rock on which some of our best poets had unfortunately split. Sir Richard Blackmore took a liberal position somewhere between the two extremes. In *A Paraphrase on some Select Psalms* (1722), he states that the many translations of the Psalms into English verse may be ranged under two heads, those which have kept strictly to the original text, and those which have taken poetical liberty and not confined themselves to the letter of the text. '*The first sort are generally dry, cramp'd, obscure, prosaick and unmusical; the last are too loose, paraphrastical, and full of figurative Beauties and Turns, of a* modern Fashion. *If my Endeavours have succeeded, I have avoided both Extreams; I have attempted to give a* Version *close without Obscurity, full without Redundancy, and clear without Diffusion.*' We wonder how far they practised what they preached, and how far did these various principles continue to affect versions made in the middle of the eighteenth century, Smart's included.

The following versions of Psalm 1.3, 4, 'And he shall be

like a tree planted by the water-side: that will bring forth his fruit in due season. His leaf also shall not wither: and look, whatsoever he doeth, it shall prosper', in the Book of Common Prayer, illustrate how the literary theories were put into practice:

(1) For as a Tree, whose spreading Root
   By some prolific Stream is fed,
Produces fair and timely Fruit,
   And num'rous Boughs adorn its Head:

Whose very Leaves, tho' Storms descend,
   In lively Verdure still appear;
Such Blessings always shall attend
   The Man that does the *LORD* revere.   (Gibbs)

(2) As Trees, when set in even Ranks,
   Where living Streams inrich their Banks;

Their Branches swell'd with quickening Juice,
   In season joyful Fruits produce;
No Blasts the Bud, or Leaf impair:
   So all his Actions prop'rous are.   (Denham)

(3)   As a fair spreading Tree which long has stood,
   The verdant Honour of some peaceful Flood;
Thick with *Autumnal* Fruit is richly crown'd,
And with its loaded Branches sweeps the Ground,
No ruffling Winds its well spread Trunk can move,
But fix'd, it smiles, the Beauty of the *Grove*.
   'Tis thus the righteous Man shall still be seen
Gay in his Fruitage, and a lively green,
No furious Passions in his Bosom roll,
Calm is the even Motion of his Soul,
His easy Mind shall all the Bliss receive
Which ruddy Health and Innocence can give;
In a soft Stream of Life he journeys on,
And fair Success shall all his Actions crown.   (Daniel)

(4) He'll, like a Tree by Waters fed,
   His Fruit in Season give;
He his unfading Leaf shall spread,
   And always prosp'rous live.   (Blackmore)

There is an obvious disparity between Blackmore's spare
version (4) and Daniel's periphrastic exploitation of the
Biblical simile between the tree and the righteous man (3).
Although we should expect Gibbs and Denham to give the
plainest versions of the four, their method of versification in
fact is more elaborate than Blackmore's, though infinitely less
so than Daniel's. Although Gibbs criticized Buchanan's paraphrastical additions, he inserts a 'spreading Root', a 'prolific'
stream, 'fair' fruit, numerous boughs adorning the head of the
tree, and lively verdure still appearing, into the original text.
Denham claimed that he had recovered from the youthful itch
for quaint expressions, but the trees of the Biblical version are
not set in even ranks, neither do their branches swell with
quickening juice, nor do they bear buds. In other words,
periphrasis was more prevalent in the practice of the Psalm-
writing of the early eighteenth century than would seem likely
from a glance at the poetic theory.

Yet even in the middle of the eighteenth century, there were
still some versifiers who wrote in the convention of Richard
Blackmore. Samuel Pike felt that 'Closeness to the TEXT, and
Smoothness of the VERSE, are prefer'd to RHYME.' He therefore transcribed Psalm 1.3, 4, as

> He shall be like a planted tree
> Beside the water streams;
> That in due season yields his fruit,
> Whose leaf shall never fade.

George Fenwick had similar ideas, for he wrote that 'The Stile
also, and Manner of rendring, tho' often literal, it is to be
hoped will be found so very plain and easy to be understood,
that the Sense . . . may easily be perceived, without consulting
voluminous Commentators, or Paraphrasts.' He translated
Psalm 1.3, 4, in a spare way,

> As is a Tree planted near running Streams,
> Fruit in its Season sure to yield;

> A Tree whose Leaf is ever fresh and firm:
> So all he does shall prosper well.

But there were also some literary descendants of Richard

Daniel writing Psalm versions in the middle of the eighteenth century. Wheatland and Silvester *said* that they had determined 'in Favour of a close Translation', but their qualification was a large one: *'we do not therein mean to exclude a sparing Use of the* Periphrasis *or Circumlocation. For tho'* Sir John Denham *censures Mr.* Barton *upon this Account, yet we may venture to affirm, that if it is a Fault, 'tis the most excusable of any, which one, engag'd in such a Work, can be guilty of. For it relates only to the* Diction, *and may be us'd without any Addition to, or Diminution of the* divinely inspir'd Matter.' They argue that some alteration must be made in the transfusion from one language to another, and this indulgence should be granted to the diction, so that it may serve the end of perspicuity, to gain scope for the rhyme to turn in, and for framing the measures. Wheatland and Silvester therefore translate:

> This blessed man shall future seasons see
> His honours spreading, as a verdant tree;
> Which riv'lets, that divide the winding mead,
> With fertile stores from plenteous currents feed:
> He shall with timely fruit unfading stand,
> And all shall prosper which he takes in hand.

With characteristic sophistry, they need to justify the periphrasis of 'riv'lets, that divide the winding mead' by pointing out in a note that in Hebrew, 'rivulets' are called 'plagim' which means 'divisions' or 'partitions'. 'In hot countries they used to plant gardens near springs of water, from whence the husbandman deriv'd many little backs, or riverets, to run in the roots of trees, set in a row, whereby they were moistened and made fruitful.'

When we look at Smart's version of Psalm 1.3, 4, we find that he too was fond of periphrasis, and therefore belongs with the literary heirs of Richard Daniel—though no one imitated the extreme elaboration of the text achieved by the latter:

> He like the tree, that bow'ring wide
> Upon the river's sunny side
>   Has timely fasten'd root;
> Shall duly each succeeding year,
> In beauty and abundance rear
>   His bud, his bloom, and fruit.

His leaf shall spread a lasting shade,
Of ever-green that may not fade,
  Or wear a languid hue;
And look ye forward to his end,
Success shall every work attend,
  He takes in hand to do.
                              (*Collected Poems*, ii. 385)

It comes as something of a surprise that Smart has to be placed among the tedious paraphrasts. There is marked contrast between the characteristic brevity and pithiness of *Jubilate Agno* and *A Song to David* on the one hand, and the phlegmatic long-windedness of his version of the Psalms on the other. Not even the most partisan of Smart's admirers could find the slightest literary merit in his *Translation of the Psalms*. The interminable periphrasis, as each verse of the Coverdale version is laboriously expanded into a stanza of English verse, make the *Translation of the Psalms* almost impossible to read with the least spark of interest. We are therefore forced to agree with the opinion of the contemporary reviewer, who damned the *Translation of the Psalms* without mercy.

The review that appeared in the *Critical Review* for September 1765 attacked Smart by comparing him, unfavourably, with James Merrick. The comparison is an interesting one because there is just a possibility that Smart was in fact aware that Merrick was making a translation at a time when Smart was writing or planning his own, for he wrote in *Jubilate Agno* D.203, 'Let Merrick, house of Merrick rejoice with Lageus a kind of Grape. God all-sufficient bless & forward the Psalmist in the Lord Jesus.' The respective versions by Smart and Merrick do indeed differ from each other on every score. Merrick's explicit aim is 'a mixture of Translation and Paraphrase', but 'little more of the latter kind than what may be useful either in opening the sense, or in pointing out the connexion, of the Original.' Merrick's 'original' was in fact the Hebrew Bible, and *The Psalms, Translated or Paraphrased in English Verse* (Reading, 1765) is therefore presented to the public as a learned work, with acknowledgements to Robert Lowth and John Loveday, and the Rev. Dr. Bolton, Dean of Carlisle, who has lent him expositions of the Psalms by Geierus,

Michaelis, Houbigant, as well as Celsius's *Hierbotanicon*, Hillerus's *Hierophyticon*, and several new versions of the Psalms in different languages. This is in marked contrast to Smart's version, which makes no mention of a single learned authority. Smart was, of course, a very intelligent man. His Cambridge career, the casual but learned references in his periodical publications, his translations of Horace and Phaedrus, all combine to make us wonder for a moment why he too did not provide the scholarly references so admired by other eighteenth-century versifiers of the Psalms. Perhaps the answer lies in the fact that although he saw David as the 'scholar of the Lord', he saw him first and foremost as the poet of the Lord, and that textual problems would have seemed to him irrelevant to a version of David's Psalms made in the finest poetry of the eighteenth century. Smart avoided scholarship, but unfortunately failed to write good poetry. But at least we are grateful that he did not share James Merrick's attitude: 'As those annotations which have been put into my hands are . . . such as will not be understood by any persons who have not applied themselves to the study of the learned languages, I have rather chosen to reserve them for a separate volume than to subjoin them to the Version or Paraphrase which is here presented to the reader.' The *Annotations on the Psalms* were duly published in Reading, three years later, and reveal the pedantic nature of his version and the contrast it offers to Smart's cavalier version. Merrick felt the need to justify the slightest 'poetical' variation on the original—in that, he is rather like Wheatland and Silvester—and this can be illustrated by his version of Psalm 2.12, 'Kiss the Son, lest he be angry, and so ye perish from the right way' in the Book of Common Prayer:

> O, lest Ye perish from the way
> That leads to realms of endless day,
> With awful love, and holy fear,
> His Son, the World's great Hope, revere:

The apparently superfluous 'realms of endless day' is explained learnedly in the *Annotations on the Psalms*. He quotes Dr. Lowth, who feels that the Hebrew signifies 'the right way' rather than simply 'way', and is comparable with the 'via vitae' in

Lucretius. Since 'the way of life' is thus implicit in the Hebrew, Merrick feels justified in describing heaven with its realms of endless day. Merrick's scrupulosity is in contrast to Smart's casual omissions, and his complete change in the sense, which he never troubles himself to defend:

> Embrace the doctrine and the priest,
> In which ye shall not die
> (*Collected Poems*, ii. 388)

The respective versions of Smart and Merrick can be contrasted also in relation to the way they introduce Christian allusions. Like Wheatland and Silvester, Merrick provides an elaborate framework of annotation for his version of the Psalms, which allows him to make some cautious Christian interpretations, as in his notes to Psalm 2: 'That this Psalm has a relation to the Messiah was allowed by the antient Jewish Writers themselves. See Bp. Pearson, Exp. of the Creed. Art.2.p.136. Note ed.1723. Agreeably to which supposition, part of the Psalm is expressly applied to Christ in the New Testament. See Acts iv.25, 26, 27. Acts xiii.33. Heb.i.5. And as I can discover no one circumstance in the whole Psalm but what is applicable to Christ, I see no necessity of supposing that any part of it relates to David, or to any other person besides Christ.' But like Wheatland and Silvester, Merrick confines his Christian interpretation to his *Annotations on the Psalms*, and gives no hint of it in his version of Psalm 2, as can be illustrated by his translation of verses 4 and 5:

> God from on high their threats shall hear,
> Laugh, as the tumult meets his ear,
> And, arm'd with vengeance, thus aloud
> Superior quell the frantic Croud:

Characteristically, Smart has no such scruples, and his version of the same verses, 'He that dwelleth in heaven shall laugh them to scorn: the Lord shall have them in derision. Then shall he speak unto them in his wrath: and vex them in his sore displeasure' in the Book of Common Prayer, is as follows:

> He that in heav'n supports his reign,
>   Of spotless virgin born,
> Shall give them blessing for disdain,
>   And charity for scorn.

> Then shall he make his day-spring shine
>   In evangelic peace;
> And sinners from the wrath divine,
>   Thro' faith in him release.
>   (*Collected Poems*, ii. 387)

The *Critical Review* did not compare Smart and Merrick from the scholarly or the evangelical point of view. He chose first of all to criticize both writers for an 'attempt to raise their numbers by an affected pomp of words.' The reviewer quotes Psalm 42.1 in the Book of Common Prayer, 'LIKE as the hart desireth the water-brooks: so longeth my soul after thee, O God' as being 'remarkably plain and simple'. But, he goes on, the various poetical versions of this Psalm have encumbered it with additional ornaments and fictions of the imagination. He quotes Tate and Brady, and Wheatland and Silvester, to make his point, and then compares them with the respective versions by Christopher Smart and James Merrick:

> 'Like as the hart desires the brook,
>   *In summer's heat extreme degree,*
> *With panting breast and wishful look,*
>   So longs my soul for thee.'   Smart.

> 'As pants the heart for *cooling* springs,
>   So longs my soul, *O king of kings,*
> *Thy face in near approach to see;*
>   So thirsts, *great source of life*, for thee.'   Merrick.

In these quotations, the reviewer shows by his italics where Smart and Merrick have indulged in 'an affected pomp of words', and he comments, 'this instance will shew us, that the *genuine* graces of the Hebrew muse are not to be expected in any translation which is embarrassed by the fetters of rhyme.'

But having said so much, the reviewer goes on to compare Merrick's version with Smart's, to the decided disadvantage of

s

the latter. Although he disapproves of indiscriminate periphrasis, the reviewer concedes that it is 'impossible to compose
a poetical version without the help of adscititious embellish-
ments'. But 'it requires the utmost skill and address to preserve
that venerable air of simplicity, which is one of the character-
istical marks of that poet, without sinking the expression or the
sentiment into contempt.' It is on this score that Smart is
severely criticized. His version of Psalm 84.3, 'Yea, the sparrow
hath found her an house, and the swallow a nest where she may
lay her young: even thy altars, O Lord of hosts, my King and
my God', is accused of having a ludicrous appearance:

> 'Yea, there the sparrow takes her *perch*,
>   And builds her house on high,
> And swallows in their Maker's *church*,
>   Their craving wants supply.'

The italics show that the reviewer objected to the contemptible
rhyme on 'perch' and 'church', while the italics in Merrick's
lines point to a certain pomposity. Yet on balance, Merrick's
version 'represents the same idea in a more poetic stile':

> 'Eternal king, within thy dome,
> The sparrow finds her peaceful home;
> With her the dove, a licens'd guest,
> Assiduous tends her infant nest,
> And to thy altar's sure defence
> Commits th'*unfeather'd innocence.*'

The reviewer then goes on to discuss the ways in which
various versifiers have dealt with the 'sublime' style of the
Psalms, and once again, Merrick is commended—while Smart
is completely ignored: 'The Psalms contain many descriptions
of the Supreme Being which are inimitably grand and beautiful;
but which of our translators has caught the least spark of that
celestial fire which glowed in the bosom of the sacred author?
The ordinary followers of Hopkins and Sternhold have miser-
ably deformed those tremendous images which the Hebrew poet
has exhibited in the 18th Psalm. Mr. Merrick is the only one
who has represented them to the reader's imagination with any
solemnity and magnificence.' In the final paragraph, the
reviewer gives the laurels to Merrick, without any further

reference to Smart: 'The reader will undoubtedly be glad to find that the Psalmist is at last delivered from a crowd of wretched poets, who had overwhelmed his native grace and dignity under the rubbish of their despicable rhimes: the admirers of these beautiful compositions may read them with pleasure in Mr. Merrick's translation.' I have not quoted extensively from Merrick's version, but enough, probably, to show that his version is in fact quite undistinguished—and even more tedious than Smart's in being more pompous and more pedantic. No one is going to make any literary claims for Smart's *Translation of the Psalms*. But Merrick, as well as Smart, helped to bury the native grace and dignity of the Psalms under the rubbish dump of bad poetry.

[XI]

Hymns and Spiritual Songs for the Fasts and Festivals of the Church of England

THE *Hymns and Spiritual Songs for the Fasts and Festivals of the Church of England* were published in 1765, bound up with the *Translation of the Psalms*, and the second edition of *A Song to David*. Robert Brittain suggests that although it is impossible to determine the exact order of composition of these three works, 'they were all done during the last years of Smart's confinement and the first few months after his release.' Brittain quotes *Jubilate Agno* D.148 and D.199 in support of his argument:

> Let Fig, house of Fig rejoice with Fleawort. The Lord magnify the idea of Smart singing hymns on this day in the eyes of the whole University of Cambridge. Nov.ʳ 5 1762ᵗʰ N.S.
> Let Audley, house of Audley rejoice with The Green Crown Bird. The Lord help on with the hymns.

He comments, 'The first of these entries prompts the conjecture that when he made it Smart had just written his "Hymn xxix. The Fifth of November," and makes one wonder whether, with some notion of propriety, he had set himself the task of writing the hymn for a certain fast or feast on the day of its celebration. If so, this would mean that they were all composed during 1762, which would account for their being ready for the press in April, 1763, when they were announced. It would also mean that the second reference would correspond roughly to the time of composition of "Hymn xxxiii. St. Stephen" (December 26), and that with only two more to be written Smart saw the end of his labors in sight.'[1] Arthur Sherbo agrees with Brittain,

[1] *Poems by Christopher Smart*, ed. Brittain, 277.

up to a point: 'Brittain's conjecture may seem to be confirmed by other lines in D. Thus, Smart mentions "St. Luke's day 1762" (October 18) in line 132, written on October 20, and "All Saints. N.S. 1762" (November 1) in line 144 (written November 1). Line 44, written on July 25, has a reference to Glover the martyr; July 25 is St. James' day, and St. James was martyred. And Stead sees in line 110, written on the Eve of St. Michael and All Angels, a reference to this holy day in Smart's "there be millions of them in the air" (p. 265). All these holidays are subjects of poems in the *Hymns and Spiritual Songs*. There is nothing, however, in the two references to "hymns" in *Jubilate Agno*, nor in the coincidence of saints' names with their appropriate dates in the poem, to exclude the possibility that the *Hymns and Spiritual Songs* were largely composed before the writing of D (June 12, 1762, to January 30, 1763).' Sherbo's qualification, and the implication that the *Hymns and Spiritual Songs* were in fact composed before Smart wrote Fragment D of *Jubilate Agno*, are essential points in Sherbo's argument, for he devotes the whole of his article to proving that the *Song to David*, the *Psalms*, and the *Hymns and Spiritual Songs* were composed during the period between March 1759 (the probable date of the beginning of Fragment A) and the 26th August 1760 (the almost certain date of the last line of Fragment B2). Sherbo 'cannot reconcile the theory that Smart wrote the magnificent *Song*, and the almost equally magnificent poetry of many of the *Psalms* and *Hymns and Spiritual Songs*, during the last years of his confinement with the ineluctable fact that [in the later fragments of *Jubilate Agno*] he was doggedly composing one thoroughly pedestrian line (or pair of lines, *Let* and *For*) each day for the last year and a half of his confinement.' Sherbo argues that Smart was probably composing the *Song to David*, the *Psalms*, and the *Hymns and Spiritual Songs* while he was writing the beautiful poetry of Fragments A, B1, and B2 of *Jubilate Agno*.[2] We agree that the earlier parts of *Jubilate Agno* do contain some beautiful passages, but we also remember that Fragment B2 contains Smart's mad exercises

[2] 'The Probable Time of Composition of Christopher Smart's *Song to David*, *Psalms*, and *Hymns and Spiritual Songs*', *Journal of English and Germanic Philology*, lv, 1956, 41–57.

on the Greek cat, the Latin mouse, and the English bulldog. It is difficult to believe, with Sherbo, that Smart could have been writing the mad visions of *Jubilate Agno*, the prosaic version of the Psalms, and the controlled *Song to David* and the *Hymns and Spiritual Songs*, at one and the same period. It is a paradoxical fact about *Jubilate Agno*, that the aesthetic organization of the poem points directly to the deranged mind of the poet. On the other hand, the careful organization of the *Hymns and Spiritual Songs* is artificial but entirely sane. In the thirty-five hymns in the collection, the fasts and festivals are dealt with in chronological order, beginning with the New Year and ending with the Holy Innocents. In addition, the hymns are composed within a rigid rhetorical framework, based on the device of anadiplosis or epanastrophe. This means that the last line of one hymn is always linked to the first line of the next. Sometimes, Smart merely repeats a word, as in the last line of Hymn XXXIII, 'Hosanna! halelujah! and amen', and the first line of Hymn XXXIV, 'HOSANNA! yet again'. But more often, the connection is more subtle, as where 'The sons of unbelief' in Hymn XXX is followed by 'AH! Thomas, wherefore would'st thou doubt' in Hymn XXXI, or where, 'All in heav'n receiv'd and seal'd' in Hymn XXVIII is followed by 'WHAT impression God and reason . . .' in Hymn XXIX, where the connection is based on the image of making an impression upon sealing wax with a signet ring. The care with which Smart makes his connections is clearly illustrated by the fact that even the last line of the last hymn is linked with the first line of the first hymn— 'In the worship of the WORD' connecting with 'WORD of endless adoration'.

— i —

'Albeit there are appointed times/For men to worship and to fast' (Hymn VII)

It was not entirely novel to make a collection of hymns for the church calendar. In 1655, Jeremy Taylor had appended to his *Golden Grove*, a collection of *Festival Hymns, According to the Manner of the Antient Church*. He included hymns for Advent, Christmas Day, St. John's Day, the Holy Innocents, Epiphany, Lent, the Conversion of St. Paul, the Purification of the

Blessed Virgin Mary, Good Friday, the Annunciation, Easter Day, Ascension, and Pentecost. In his *Festival Hymns*, Taylor used a variety of poetic rhythms, in contrast to the sing-song metres of hymns intended for congregational use. His theme was a simple but effective parallel between the 'inward' and the 'outward' event—in his hymn 'Of Christ's Birth in an Inne', for instance, the action moves from the stable to the human heart, 'O make our hearts, blest God, thy lodging place'. The literary background to Smart's *Hymns and Spiritual Songs* contains at least one example of true poetry, but in this particular case, the seventeenth-century texture of Taylor's poems seems remote from Smart's idiosyncratic, eighteenth-century hymns, and little can be gained from comparing the two works.

A volume of *Hymns for the Festivals, and on other Solemn Occasions* was published in Portsmouth in 1748. It contained hymns for Christmas Day, Easter Day, Whit Sunday, New Year's Day, Epiphany, Ash Wednesday, St. Cecilia's Day, Good Friday, Ascension Day, Holy Communion, and for Funeral Services. But it is in fact a collection of hymns by a number of authors, including an 'Ode for Christmas' taken from Pope's *Messiah*, and several hymns by Tate and Brady, John Cosin, Dryden, Austin, and Samuel Wesley. Once again, therefore, one cannot make any useful comparisons between these *Hymns for the Festivals*, of assorted authorship, and Smart's unified collection of *Hymns and Spiritual Songs*.

Indeed, if any single work on the church calendar influenced Smart's *Hymns and Spiritual Songs* more than any other, it was probably Robert Nelson's prose work, *Companion for the Festivals and Fasts of the Church of England* (1704). There is no direct evidence that Smart ever read Nelson's work, and I have not come across any reference to it in Smart's poetry, or for that matter, in his prose writings. But from internal evidence in the *Hymns and Spiritual Songs* it does seem likely that while he was composing his hymns, Smart occasionally referred to Nelson's *Companion* as a dictionary of Church of England saints and martyrs. This conjecture is made more likely by the fact that the *Companion for the Festivals and Fasts* was very widely read. The account of Nelson in the *Dictionary of National Biography* states that the work achieved unrivalled popularity as a popular manual of Anglican theology, that ten thousand copies were printed in less than five years, and that it reached a thirty-sixth edition in 1826. For the quotations in the present chapter I use an edition of 1843. As we shall see, Smart did not apparently use Nelson's work for composing his hymns for the Crucifixion, the Ascension, and so on. And four of Smart's hymns were written for occasions which Nelson did not include in his *Companion*: Hymn V, 'King Charles the Martyr' (a Fast enjoined by the Act of Uniformity in 1662), Hymn XVII, 'The King's Restoration' (likewise introduced by the Act of Uniformity), Hymn XXVI, 'The Ascension of King George III' (it was out of the question in 1704 for the non-juring Nelson to celebrate the ascension of Queen Anne), and Hymn XXIX, 'The Fifth of November' (introduced as a Festival of the Church by Royal Proclamation in 1605). But I think it is fair to say, that in quite a number of his hymns, Smart seems to have been helped by Nelson's *Companion for the Festivals and Fasts of the Church of England*.

The first two hymns in Smart's *Hymns and Spiritual Songs*, on the New Year and the Feast of Circumcision, are covered by Nelson's chapter, 'The Circumcision of Our Lord Jesus Christ, or New Year's Day—January 1.' There are remarkable parallels between the theological statements made by Nelson and Smart respectively. Nelson points out the historical significance of the Festival, and its meaning for the modern church: '*Q. What rite of admission into the Christian Church answers to that of circumcision under the Law?* A. The sacrament of baptism, called by St. Paul the circumcision of Christ, whereby the children of Christian parents are made members of Christ'. To substantiate this parallel between Baptism and Circumcision, Nelson cites Colossians 3. 11, 12, 'Where there is neither Greek nor Jew, circumcision nor uncircumcision, Barbarian, Scythian, bond nor free: but Christ is all, and in all. Put on therefore, as the elect of God, holy and beloved, bowels of mercies, kindness, humbleness of mind, meekness, longsuffering'. Verse 10 of the same chapter refers to 'the new man, which is renewed in knowledge after the image of him that created him', but there is, after all, no direct reference to Baptism. Nelson's esoteric point is nevertheless taken up by Smart. Nelson's point that circumcision 'was first enjoined to Abraham, as a token of the covenant of God made with him and his posterity', is expressed in Smart's hymn:

> WHEN Abraham was bless'd,
> And on his face profess'd
>   The Saviour Christ hereafter born,
> 'Thou pilgrim and estrang'd,
> Thy name, said God, is chang'd,
>   Thy lot secur'd from want and scorn.
>
> 'O Abraham, my friend,
> My covenant attend,
>   Which Shilo's self shall not repeal,
> Chastise from carnal sin
> Thy house and all thy kin,
>   Thy faith by circumcision seal.'
>   (*Collected Poems*, ii. 790)

Then, following Nelson, he parallels God's covenant with Abraham and Baptism—but where Nelson refers to Infant Baptism, Smart prefers to allude to the Baptism of Christ, 'Ye swans that sail and lave/In Jordan's hallow'd wave,/Ah sweet! ah pensive! ah serene!' And he creates a characteristic image of God's ring, set with a pearl, Christ's eternal worth, and inscribed with a 'posy', based on the Biblical words on the Baptism of Christ, ' "This is my HEIR of GRACE,/In whose perfections I rejoice." ' One recalls the strange lines in *Jubilate Agno* B1.31, 'Let Machir rejoice with Convolvulus, from him to the ring of Saturn, which is the girth of Job; to the signet of God from Job & his daughters BLESSED BE JESUS. For there is a blessing from the STONE of Jesus which is founded upon hell to the precious jewell on the right hand of God.' We may also remember that in *Abimelech*, Abraham is full of sexual anxieties. In this hymn, where Smart sees Abraham as chastising his house from carnal sin and Christ is seen as checking the fleshly-willed, there is some support from Nelson: 'Q. *What does circumcision figuratively represent to us?* A. That as our birth is impure by reason of original sin, so we ought to *lay apart all filthiness, and superfluity of naughtiness,* putting off the body of the sins of the flesh by the circumcision of Christ; mortifying the pleasures of the body, which bewitch the mind, and make us captives to sin and death. Q. *What may we learn from the observation of this Festival?* A. The necessity of spiritual circumcision, or the change of the heart and life, which our Lord hath made the condition of salvation; in order to which, the mortifying of our corrupt affections and sinful lusts is necessary.' Nelson's vocabulary, 'filthiness', 'corrupt', and 'lusts', is similar to Smart's:

> Come every purer thought,
> By which the mind is wrought
>   From man's corruption, nature's dust;
> Away each vain desire,
> And all the fiends that fire
>   The soul to base and filthy lust.
>   (*Collected Poems*, ii. 791)

Smart's Hymn III corresponds to Nelson's 'The Epiphany.— January 6.' Both writers take the Star as an image of Grace. Nelson asks, why did God manifest his Son to the Gentiles, and answers, 'That his grace might appear to all men. For as the Jews had notice of our Saviour's birth by the appearance of angels to the shepherds, so the Gentiles received it now by the appearance of a star'. Smart writes,

> GRACE, thou source of each perfection,
>   Favour from the height thy ray;
> Thou the star of all direction,
>   Child of endless truth and day.
>   (*Collected Poems*, ii. 792)

And both writers find in the story of the Epiphany a similar lesson for the individual Christian. What may we learn from the observation of this Festival, asks Nelson, and answers, 'To make the outward acts of our adoration, and the doing homage to the Deity, real expressions of the sense of our minds and inward affections. To offer him the treasure of our hearts, which is the chief sacrifice he requires.' In the same spirit, Smart exclaims, 'Fill my heart with genuine treasures,/Pour them out before his feet'. And he then characteristically calls upon the creatures to thank their Creator 'with all your modes of praising'. Nelson too asks how we ought to commemorate the manifestation of our

Saviour to the Gentiles, and answers, 'With great thankfulness of mind'.

There seem to be few parallels in Smart's Hymn IV and Nelson's chapter, 'The Conversion of St. Paul.—January 25.' If Smart referred to Nelson at all, he ignored the sweeping survey of St. Paul's life and works, and concentrated on Nelson's comment on St. Paul's conversion, 'it was wonderful in itself, and a miraculous effect of the powerful grace of God'. In Smart's hymn, the Lord consented 'there, where pity had no place,/To fill the measure of his grace', and the whole of the hymn is devoted to a series of Old Testament miracles. There is perhaps an echo of Nelson's 'An Apostle in an extraordinary manner set apart to be a preacher of that Gospel which he had persecuted', in Smart's final line,' "Go, persecutor, preach and praise." '

Smart's Hymn VI, 'The Presentation of Christ in the Temple' corresponds to Nelson's chapter, 'The Purification of the Blessed Virgin. February 2.' Both writers refer to the substitution of the Temple at Jerusalem by the Church, the symbolic temple of Christ's body, the doctrine based on St. John 2.19–21. Nelson writes of the old law, under which mothers were obliged to present their first-born in the temple and pay a ransom to the priest. He asks what the redeeming of the first-born should signify for us. 'The redemption of God's people, called the Church of the first-born, which are written in heaven, and not redeemed with corruptible things, as silver and gold, but with the precious blood of Christ.' Smart adopts this doctrine, but expresses it through the imagery of his poem, rather than by direct statement. The temple at Jerusalem, 'a house of godlike style' was finished in Solomon's reign, which 'O'erlaid with gold the glorious pile'. But this rich and godlike temple was not grand enough to contain the godhead, and another building arose, the 'fabrick of the poor', meaning not the church in the physical sense, but the church as the body of Christ, 'That God should in the world appear/Incarnate—as a child'. This theme of poverty is essential to Nelson's chapter as well as to Smart's hymn. We may learn from this Festival, says Nelson, 'Not to despise, but to respect the poor, who, in their outward circumstances, bear so great a resemblance to the blessed Jesus, and his holy family. . . . Above all, to clothe ourselves with humility, to be meek and lowly in heart, that we may find rest for our souls.' Nelson ends with a prayer, 'ALMIGHTY and everlasting God, I humbly beseech thy majesty, that, as thy only-begotten Son was this day presented in the temple in substance of our flesh, so I may be presented unto thee with a pure and clean heart, by the same thy Son Jesus Christ our Lord. *Amen.*' In the same spirit, Smart prays,

> Present ye therefore, on your knees,
>   Hearts, hands resign'd and clean;
> Ye poor and mean of all degrees,
> If he will condescend and please
>   To take at least what orphans glean.
>   (*Collected Poems*, ii. 797)

Smart's Hymn VII corresponds to Nelson's chapter 'Ash Wednesday, or the First Day of Lent.' Both Nelson and Smart make repentance the theme of the Fast. Nelson writes that 'to repent of our sins, is to be convinced that we have done amiss; which follows hearty sorrow for our past follies, and a firm and effectual purpose and resolution of mind to forsake them for the time to come.' And Smart writes,

> Albeit there are appointed times
>   For men to worship and to fast;
> Then purge your conscience of its crimes
>   At least while those shall last.
>   (*Collected Poems*, ii. 799–800)

Both writers disapprove of death-bed repentance. Nelson writes that 'delaying it for the present, and deferring it to some future opportunity; either till the heat of youth is over, or till sickness, old age, or death overtakes them . . . is highly wicked, in that we abuse God's patience, who gives us time and opportunity for it at present'. And Smart laments that we 'leave repentance to the gasp/Of hope-retarded death'.

Smart's Hymn VIII corresponds to Nelson's chapter, 'Saint Matthias the Apostle.—February 24.' There is one notable verbal parallel between the two works. Having described the election of St. Matthias in place of Judas Iscariot, Nelson writes that we may learn from this Festival 'To use our best diligence, if we are patrons of churches, in providing persons duly qualified for the great trust we commit to them; and not to suffer any worldly consideration to bias us in a choice'. Smart is not concerned with the patronage of churches, but he does seem to retain an echo of Nelson, repeating 'bias' and echoing 'worldly consideration' with 'worldly reasons':

> If we celebrate Matthias,
>   Let us do it heart and soul;
> Nor let worldly reasons bias
>   Our conceptions from their goal.
>   (*Collected Poems*, ii. 800)

Watchfulness is a major theme in Nelson's chapter. We may learn from this Festival 'to be watchful and upon our guard, because, if an Apostle fell, who had all the advantages of our Saviour's conversation, what security can we promise ourselves?' Perhaps the theme of watchfulness influenced Smart's opening image of the cockerel proclaiming the morning. And perhaps Nelson's warning that we must watch against the pleasures of the senses prompted Smart's command, 'Ward from wine, and from the shambles,/Sight and appetite, and taste.'

There are no obvious parallels between Smart's Hymn IX and Nelson's 'The Annunciation of the Blessed Virgin Mary. March 25', nor between Smart's Hymns X and XI and the corresponding chapters in Nelson's book, 'Good Friday' and 'Easter Sunday'. There may be some connection, however, between Smart's Hymn XII and Nelson's 'St. Mark the Evangelist.—April 25.' In his historical account of St. Mark, Nelson writes; 'He was converted by some of the Apostles, probably by St. Peter, to whom he was a constant companion in all his travels; supplying the place of an amanuensis and interpreter.' The particular proof of St. Mark's impartiality is 'that he is so far from concealing the shameful fall and denial of St. Peter, who was his dear tutor and master, that he relates it with some particular circumstances and aggravations, which the other Evangelists take no notice of.' Nelson refers to St. Mark 14.66 ff., the account of Peter's denial of Christ, and Smart too alludes to this passage, and, like Nelson, refers to St. Mark as Peter's amanuensis and particular biographer:

And tho', as Peter's scribe and son,
Thou mightst a charity have done
   To cover his disgrace;
Yet strictly charg'd thou wouldst not spare
At large the treason to declare,
   And in its order place.

                  (*Collected Poems*, ii. 813)

Smart's Hymn XIII corresponds to Nelson's chapter 'St. Philip and St. James the Less.—May 1.' Both writers characterize these saints in similar ways. Nelson describes St. Philip as a man with 'Forwardness of mind to direct others in the same way of happiness with himself', while Smart describes him as cheerful and a man of 'quick compliance'. Nelson describes St. James as an honourable, pious and virtuous man, while Smart describes him as 'JUST'. Nelson discusses whether St. James was in fact the brother of Christ, pointing out that in the language of the Jews, 'brother' denotes consanguity as well as fraternity. This discussion may account for the hesitant note in Smart's lines, 'James, of title most illustrious,/Brother of the Lord, allow'd'. Smart states that both St. Philip and St. James died 'in imitation |Of their Saviour's final hour.' Nelson records that St. Philip was hanged up by the neck against a pillar, or, as some say, was crucified. He describes St. James's death: 'they loaded him with a shower of stones, till one, with a fuller's club beat out his brains'. Nelson reads into the lives of these saints a practical lesson on self-denial which is echoed, perhaps, in Smart's description of the saints as 'Both of love and self-denial'.

    There appears to be little connection between Smart's Hymn XIV and Nelson's 'The Ascension of our Lord Jesus Christ', or between Smart's Hymn XV and Nelson's chapter on 'Whitsuntide', except that in the latter, both writers are concerned with missionary work. Nelson asks to what end were the Apostles endowed with all languages, and answers, 'To enable them to spread and diffuse the knowledge of Christianity over the world, the Gospel thereby making a greater progress in a few years, than it could have done in human probability without it, in many ages.' Smart maintains that 'This great miracle was wrought,/That the millions might be taught'.

Smart's Hymn XVI corresponds to Nelson's chapter 'Trinity Sunday'. Nelson warns that we should learn from this Festival that we ought 'To contain ourselves within the bounds of sobriety, without wading too far into abstruse, curious, and useless speculations.' Smart agreed with him and wrote,

> Ye books, that load the shelves,
> To lead us from ourselves,
> Where things, in doubt involv'd,
> Are rather made than solv'd;
>   Render to the dust and worm
>   All ye question or affirm.
>   (*Collected Poems*, ii. 820–21)

Smart's Hymn XVIII corresponds to Nelson's chapter, 'St. Barnabas the Apostle.—June 11.' There is no striking parallel here. The story of Barnabas selling his lands and bringing the money to the Lord in Acts 4. 36, 37, means that both writers inevitably conclude that we should 'be ready to contribute to the relief of our fellow Christians', or as Smart puts it, 'To the Lord your wealth resign,/Distribution is divine,/Misers have no hope.' But this is by no means a principal theme in Nelson's chapter—he is far more interested in the dispute between Barnabas and St. Paul and how to maintain a Christian spirit when circumstances oblige us to go to law. Smart is evidently not interested in this aspect of St. Barnabas's story.

Smart's Hymn XIX corresponds to Nelson's chapter, 'The Nativity of St. John the Baptist.' Both writers are concerned, predictably, with the idea of St. John as the forerunner of Christ, and both emphasize the asceticism of his life, which was, according to Nelson, 'more than ordinarily rigorous and austere', while Smart observed that he 'led a life of rigour,/And th'abstemious vow obey'd'.

Smart's Hymn XX corresponds to Nelson's chapter, 'St. Peter.—June 29.' They both make this an occasion for a bout of anti-Catholic propaganda. '*Does it appear*,' asks Nelson, '*that our Saviour gave any personal prerogative to St. Peter, as universal pastor and head of the Church?*' Nelson feels that our Saviour most definitely did not. 'Though he is placed first among the Apostles . . . it does not appear that he enjoyed any other particular privilege; because, in confessing Christ, he spoke not only his own, but the sense of his fellow Apostles, and which Nathanael professed as well as he; if he is styled the rock, all the Apostles are equally styled foundations, upon which the wall of the new Jerusalem is erected; and the power of the keys is promised to the rest of the Apostles as well as to St. Peter.' Smart's antagonism to the Roman Church is even more bluntly expressed. St. Peter might have risen from repentance 'To the magnitude requir'd' (Smart's phraseology is occasionally very obscure),

> But he is a stranger still
>   To the Roman frauds and fees;
> He nor sold to vice her will,
>   Nor to Mammon left his keys.
>
> (*Collected Poems*, ii. 829)

Smart's Hymn XXI corresponds to Nelson's 'St. James.—July 25.' Both Nelson and Smart emphasize the lowly estate from which St. James was called by the Master. Nelson writes 'that we ought not to contemn men of the meanest employment, that are honest and industrious', and he prays for contentment in a mean condition. Smart writes that 'a seaman's lot is bless'd', and makes his point by an allusion to contemporary affairs:

> Yea, from fishers on the coast,
>   Poor, and by the nations scorn'd,
> With our navy's gallant host
>   Seas are crouded and adorn'd,
> Whereso'er the billows toss,
> Bearing Christ's triumphant cross.
>
> (*Collected Poems*, ii. 831)

The Gospel fishermen were employed with 'low concerns and cares', but were released by the call of Christ. Smart bids St. James, 'Go, and preach the Spaniard peace', referring to the legend which Nelson recounts rather sceptically: 'The Spanish writers contend, that after he had preached the Gospel in Judæa and Samaria, he planted Christianity in Spain. But of this there is no account earlier than the middle ages of the Church; therefore it is safest to confine his ministry to Judæa and the parts thereabouts.'

Smart's Hymn XXII corresponds to Nelson's 'St. Bartholo-
mew.—August 24.' Both writers draw the same inference from
the saint's character. Nelson writes of him that he was a man of
true simplicity and integrity, an Israelite indeed in whom was
no guile, no art of hypocrisy or deceit. He goes on to discuss the
nature of sincerity—how it respects God, and man—and he
prays for 'SINCERITY TOWARDS MAN.' Smart makes a similar antithesis between hypocrisy and sincerity. 'SINCERITY, belov'd of
Christ' had always been associated in Smart's mind with
precious stones. In this hymn, sincerity 'wears the precious ring
that holds/Each jewel of the tribes.' Sincerity is the standard by
which the purity of all things must be tested:

> Gold is not very gold, nor myrrh
> True myrrh, nor rubies glow,
> If first not try'd and prov'd by her
> That they indeed are so.
> (*Collected Poems*, ii. 833)

Set against sincerity, 'Hypocrisy shall gnash its tooth'. The
theme of sincerity in *Jubilate Agno* B1.40 was similarly associated
with images of precious stones, 'Let Hamul rejoice with the
Crystal, who is pure and translucent. For sincerity is a jewel
which is pure & transparent, eternal & inestimable.'

Smart's Hymn XXIII corresponds to Nelson's chapter, 'St.
Matthew.—September 21.' Both writers stress the Hebrew
element in St. Matthew's writings. Nelson calls him 'a Hebrew
of Hebrews; both his names discover him to be of Jewish
origin', and therefore, he wrote his Gospel, designed for the use
of his countrymen, in the Hebrew language. Smart too wrote
that 'Matthew for an obvious praise,/His in Hebrew chose to
raise,/That easterns might adore.'

Smart's Hymn XXIV corresponds to Nelson's chapter, 'St.
Michael and All Angels.—September 29.' They both refer to a
series of Biblical episodes concerning angels, but they do not
make the same selection of incidents. They coincide in several
instances, as where Smart refers to the Apocryphal tale of
Moses and the Angel:

> If Satan's malice was withstood
> Where Moses cold and breathless lay,

T

> Give Michael, patient, meek, and good,
> Through Christ, the glory of the day.
> (*Collected Poems*, ii. 835)

Nelson makes much of the same story, taken from the Book of Jude, and he explains the dispute between Satan and St. Michael over Moses's body in literal and figurative terms. Nelson devotes some time to the belief in guardian angels, 'There was a common opinion among the heathens, and a constant tradition among the Jews, that every man, at least every good man, had a guardian angel appointed him by God, to take a special care of him and his concerns, both spiritual and temporal'. Smart refers to the same idea in the final stanza of his hymn:

> These, one for every man, are sent
> God in the spirit to reveal,
> To forward every good event,
> And each internal grief to heal.
> (*Collected Poems*, ii. 836)

Smart's Hymn XXV corresponds to Nelson's 'St. Luke the Evangelist.— October 18.' Both writers make metaphorical use of St. Luke's profession. Nelson prays for the health of our minds, 'ALMIGHTY God, who calledst Luke the physician, whose praise is in the Gospel, to be an evangelist and physician of souls; may it please thee, that by the wholesome medicines of the doctrine delivered by him, all the diseases of my soul may be healed, through the merits of thy Son Jesus Christ our Lord.' For Smart, too, St. Luke is the 'physician of the wounds,/ Where the troubl'd conscience stings', and is begged, 'Med'cines of the soul disperse/To the wicked and perverse/Thou wert wont to join.'

Smart's Hymn XXVII corresponds to Nelson's 'St. Simon and St. Jude.—October 28.' Both writers tell how St. Simon is said to have come to England. Nelson writes that 'He is said also to have passed into Britain, where, after having converted many to the faith, and suffered many persecutions, he was crucified by the infidels, and there buried.' Smart writes:

> He his pilgrimage perform'd
> Far as the Britannic coast,

> And the ready converts swarm'd
>   To receive the Holy Ghost.
>   (*Collected Poems*, ii. 839)

There are few parallels between Smart's Hymn XXVIII and Nelson's chapter, 'All Saints.—November 1.' But Hymn XXX is remarkably similar to Nelson's chapter, 'Saint Andrew, November 30.' Having recounted the conversion of the Apostle as it is told in the Gospel, Nelson goes on to write of his mission to Patrea in Achaia, and his martyrdom there:

> . . . that his death might be more lingering, he was fastened to the cross, not with nails, but with cords. . . . as he was led to execution, he shewed a cheerful and composed mind, and that being come within the sight of the cross, he saluted it with this kind address: 'That he had long expected and desired that happy hour; that the cross had been consecrated by bearing the body of Christ; that he came joyful and triumphant to it, that it might receive him as a disciple and follower of Him who once hung upon it, and be the means to carry him safe unto his Master, having been the instrument upon which his Master did redeem him.' Having prayed and exhorted the people to constancy and perseverence in their religion, he was fastened to the cross, whereon he hung two days, teaching and instructing the people all that time . . .

The body of the martyr was later removed to Constantinople, by Constantine the Great, and buried in the great church that he had built there to the honour of the Apostles. Smart versified the story as follows:

> At length the words prevail
>   Which Christ prophetic spake,
> And to the cross the saint they hale
>   That ruffian traitors make.
>
> Tormented, tried, and bound
>   Two well-supported days,
> His life his dying accents crown'd,
>   E'en to their last essays.
>
> His body was remov'd
>   From Patræ to the Turk,
> Where it, through Christ, shall be improv'd
>   To do a glorious work.
>   (*Collected Poems*, ii. 844)

Smart's Hymn XXXI corresponds to Nelson's chapter, 'Saint Thomas, December 21.' The idea of Doubting Thomas leads logically to the idea of Christian faith, and both writers therefore refer to I Corinthians 13.13, 'And now abideth faith, hope, charity, these three; but the greatest of these is charity.' Nelson prays, 'ALMIGHTY and everlasting God, give unto me the increase of faith, hope, and charity; and that I may obtain that which thou dost promise, make me heartily to believe what thou hast revealed, and to love that which thou dost command, through Jesus Christ our Lord. *Amen*.' Smart prays likewise that 'Our faith and hope increase,/Our charities extend.'

Smart's Hymn XXXII and Nelson's 'The Nativity of Our Lord, Or the Birth Day of Christ, Commonly Called Christmas Day, December 25' cannot be compared on any grounds except for their common sense of exhilaration and use of the adjective 'stupendous'. According to Nelson, the angels 'give glory and praise to God for his wonderful works towards the children of men. . . . it is our constant duty to acknowledge his majesty and greatness, those peerless prerogatives of power, wisdom, and goodness, which appeared with the greatest lustre in the stupendous incarnation of the Son of God.' Smart asks the swains of Solyma to lead him to 'this stupendous stranger'.

There appear to be few significant parallels between Smart's Hymn XXXIII and Nelson's 'Saint Stephen, December 26', except for the fact that both writers note that he was the first martyr, and that both emphasize grace in association with martyrdom. Nelson writes 'That when malice and cruelty combine to deter men from the profession of the truth, by inflicting the most barbarous torments, the good providence of God often makes them ineffectual by assisting his faithful servants with an extraordinary communication of his grace.' Smart writes, 'O GRACE, thou never rais'd a sweeter flow'r./ Which sprang, and gemm'd, and blossom'd in an hour.'

Smart's Hymn XXXIV corresponds to Nelson's chapter, 'Saint John the Evangelist, December 27.' Both writers try to show that Christ's especial love for one disciple did not exclude great love for the rest. 'Our Saviour', writes Nelson, 'hath by his example and authority sanctified the relation of friendship, and those closer bonds of amity, which natural affection or special inclination may form between particular persons, without any prejudice to a general charity.' Smart too writes of St. John:

> O dear to Christ supreme,
>   His bosom friend declar'd,
>   And yet for all he car'd
> With tenderness extreme.
> *(Collected Poems*, ii. 849)

Smart's final Hymn XXXV corresponds to Nelson's chapter, 'The Holy Innocents.—December 28', but there are no significant parallels between the two works.

Obviously, the internal evidence in the *Hymns and Spiritual Songs* is not strong enough to make us absolutely certain that Smart referred to Nelson's *Companion* for information about the saints and martyrs of the Church of England. But the detailed comparison between the two works shows us that even if Smart's direct source was not after all Nelson's *Companion*, at least we realize that many of the images, descriptive details and theological interpretation in the *Hymns and Spiritual Songs* derived from the commonplace traditions associated with the church calendar in the eighteenth century. Smart had no need to do much research to find the details of the mission of St. Simon to Britain, or the martyrdom of St. Andrew in Patrea in Achaia—the stories were part of the mythology of the eighteenth-century church. The connection between Abraham's circumcision and Christ's Baptism, or the connection between the presentation of Christ in the temple and the theme of poverty, may not be immediately obvious to the twentieth-century reader, but were commonplace associations to the eighteenth-century reader of the *Hymns and Spiritual Songs*. As usual, a careful reading of Smart's poetry shows that the conventional elements are strong, although the general tone may be eccentric and highly individual. The comparison between the *Hymns and Spiritual Songs* and Nelson's *Companion* suggests the more conventional aspects of Smart's work. A study of the four hymns written for occasions which Nelson ignored in his work, suggests the more idiosyncratic emphasis of some of Smart's poems.

In the eighteenth century, the church prescribed an annual

Fast to commemorate the martyrdom of Charles I, and a corresponding Festival to celebrate the restoration of Charles II. Yet the loyal subjects of the Hanoverian monarchs usually shunned the embarrassing presence of the Stuart family, who threatened the peace of mind of the grand tourist to Rome. This contradiction is mirrored in Smart's work. He lets slip the occasional burst of loyalty for the Stuart cause, 'Let Anathoth bless with Saurix, who is a bird of melancholy. For I pray God be gracious to the house of Stuart and consider their afflictions' in *Jubilate Agno* B1.71, and 'Let Stedman, house of Stedman rejoice with Jacobæa St James's Wort. God be merciful to the house of Stuart' in D.206. But these subversive sentiments are more than offset by his indiscriminate enthusiasm for George II and his hated son, Frederick, Prince of Wales, and for George III and his small son, the Bishop of Osnabrug, future Duke of York, 'and all the royal family'. *A Solemn Dirge, Sacred to the Memory of His Royal Highness Frederic Prince of Wales* (1751) had been humbly inscribed by the author to His Royal Highness Prince George, on the much lamented death of his father. In that poem, Smart had been sure that Prince George would revive his father's fame, that honour, glory and wisdom would bless him, and that he would put into practice the advice given by George I to his grandson, Frederick, ' "Be honest and be brave." ' (Smart was almost certainly referring to Frederick's 'Instructions for my son George, drawn by my-self, for his good, that of my family, and for that of his people, according to the ideas of my grandfather, and best friend, George I', written in 1748, and including statements like 'never give up your honour nor that of the nation. A wise and brave prince may oftentimes, without armies put a stop to confusion, which the ambitious neighbours endeavour to create.' And he advised George to test the trueness of his friends by encouraging them to tell the truth, even if it sometimes ran contrary to his prejudices.[3] Prince George, Albion's Consolation, came to the throne in 1760, and Smart was as loyal as ever, pointing out in Hymn XXVI that monarchs and just princes rule under the auspices of Wisdom. The king began his reign in the middle of the Seven Years' War, and Smart depicts George's greatness by

[3] J. C. Long, *George III A Biography*, 1960, 37.

referring to the victories won by our gallant fleet. The young king has fatigued his righteous spirit to bring peace to the nation 'Yet more and more the Papists leagu'd/To mar the world's increase'—Smart's perennial concern with adoring the great, and fulminating against Roman Catholics, are clearly expressed in his hymn on 'The Accession of King George III'.

The hymns written in commemoration of the Stuarts also gave Smart scope for expressing his anti-papist sentiments. On the 30th January 1748, while he was still at Cambridge, Smart had been appointed by the Vice-Chancellor of the University to deliver the annual speech in memory of the martyrdom of King Charles I. There is no extant record of what Smart actually said on that occasion, which presumably took place in St. Mary's Church, Cambridge, 'at two of the clock'.[4] Perhaps some of the points made in his speech were later incorporated into his hymn on 'King Charles the Martyr', where he laments the heresies and sectarian controversies of the seventeenth century, as well as deploring the king's unfortunate marriage. The emphasis was a personal one, for Smart must have seen his own unhappy marriage to the Roman Catholic Anna-Maria Carnan reflected in King Charles's marriage to Queen Henrietta-Maria:

> Ah great unfortunate, the chief
> Of monarchs in the tale of grief,
> By marriage ill-advis'd, akin
> To Moab and the man of sin!
> (*Collected Poems*, ii. 796)

The feeling in the hymn on 'The Fifth of November' is much more violently anti-papist. Smart shows that England was 'dissolv'd in slumber,/Toil and emulation ceas'd', and how this spiritual torpor of the nation encouraged the machinations of the Roman Catholics:

> This was deem'd a fit occasion
> For the Papists to be bold,
> For the children of evasion
> To come sneaking from their hold.
> (*Collected Poems*, ii. 842)

[4] Arthur Sherbo, 'Christopher Smart and the Problem of Ordination in the Eighteenth Century', *Church Quarterly Review*, 1966, 45.

There is no greater perdition in the history of mankind, says Smart, and then changes without warning to rejoicing in God:

> God, in a stupendous manner,
>   Bade the spendthrift nation home—
> Let us therefore fix the banner
>   On the high cathedral's dome.
>
> Play the musick—call the singers—
>   Open wide the prison door—
> Make a banquet for the ringers—
>   Give to poverty the store.
>
> Fire away the joyful volley,
>   Deck your houses, bless your wine;
> Triumph o'er the Papists folly,
>   Who their God would undermine.
>   (*Collected Poems*, ii. 843)

Hymn XVII on 'The King's Restoration' is much more complex and much more obscure. Smart makes the Restoration of 1660 the occasion for a triumphant review of the splendours of English history, narrated with the spiritual fervour of one who was able to hail the Almighty Jesus as the sole original and cause of all heroic actions, the God of patriot deeds and gracious laws, who founded this western empire on the power of the seas. As will be seen, the obscurity of Smart's allusions and phraseology make it difficult to unravel all the historical references in this hymn. Smart thanks God that although we were despised as barbarians, we have now excelled the rest of the world in all things: 'The progeny, that God's free woman bare,/In all their leagues and dealings faithful, just and fair'. Smart goes on to describe the splendid occasion when the army, exalted by 'George's gallant horse', embarked where 'the dome of CHRIST supreme' stands over 'the spacious stream,/Thrice rolling thro' the sounding arch', ready to fight 'Against the fraud and pride of Moab's spurious seed'—another burst of hostility against the Roman Catholics. Smart cares little for the orderly sequence of historical events. He goes on to thank God for our naval sway over subject seas, and for the homage paid to the great Britannic fame by submissive nations.

He thanks God for Queen Elizabeth's reign, and for the seamanship of Charles Howard, first Earl of Nottingham, Sir Martin Frobisher, and Sir Francis Drake. Smart was full of admiration for their 'triumphs on the main', their campaigns against the Spanish Armada and Drake's voyage round the world, for in the 'Ode to Admiral Sir George Pocock', he again mentions the three heroes:

> Nor HOWARD, FROBISHER, or DRAKE,
>   Or VERNON's fam'd *Herculean* deed;
> Nor all the miracles of BLAKE,
>   Can the great Chart of thine exploits exceed.
>   (*Collected Poems*, i. 15)

Smart then veers from the Elizabethan to contemporary seamen, giving thanks to God for the feats in the West Indies performed by Forrest, Suckling, and Langdon. Smart then retreats into the Middle Ages, but the enemy is still the French, as Edward the Black Prince and Edward III do battle 'At Poictier's and Cressey's field/Against vain Moab must'ring ten to one'. There follows an obscure reference to Cam, 'Immortal from the hour he bled', who dammed the torrent rushing on his leader's head. In the same stanza, Smart gives glory to God's name for Henry's gifted sword, and Edward's noble stall.

The next three stanzas all begin with the same line, 'The glory to thy name for Ann'. Smart remembers the queen 'for the houses that she built'. This could indicate a reference to the poet's unsuspected enthusiasm for Queen Anne domestic architecture—supported by a line in *Jubilate Agno*, 'Let Stapleton, house of Stapleton rejoice with Scythis a precious stone the Lord rebuild the old houses of England.' (This prayer in *Jubilate Agno* D.49 could of course refer to the continuity of ancient families, but *Jubilate Agno* D.31 also shows Smart's concern for old buildings: 'Let Oldcastle, house of Oldcastle rejoice with Leucopthalmos. God put it in heart of king to repair & beautify Dover Castle.') Yet it seems more likely that in his hymn Smart was referring to the provision in the nineth year of the reign of Queen Anne, for a tax on coal to pay for the building of fifty new churches in or near the

Cities of London and Westminster. Smart goes on to praise the hero of the reign, the Duke of Marlborough, 'that great victorious man,/Who ran profane oppression to the hilt'. He then remembers the queen's 'charitable plan,/By which the poor may preach, and have his food', a reference to Queen Anne's Bounty, a grant to the Church made in 1704, from the crown revenues from tenths and first fruits. (Smart's concern for the poor clergy here reminds us of his indignant support for Dr. Webster in his poem on anger and forgiveness.) Smart then recalls other heroes of Queen Anne's reign—John Richmond Webb, Edward Russell, Sir Cloudesley Shovell, Sir George Rooke, and John Benbow. But at the end of this list of heroes comes a curious anachronism—the name of Admiral John Byng. His story is of course a familiar one: In 1756, Byng was sent to the defence of Minorca against the French. He knew that the squadron was undermanned, and he left England prepared for defeat. He mishandled the ships, returned to Gibraltar, and was sent to England for court-martial. The trial and the sentence of execution aroused great controversy, for it was felt by many that Byng was in fact the scapegoat for an incompetent war ministry. Smart makes his own position quite clear, when he includes Byng's name, rather oddly, among the Queen Anne heroes.

Perhaps the various triumphs against the French recorded in his hymn reminded Smart of the ousting of Roman Catholicism at the Reformation. In the next stanza, Smart gives thanks for the means by which the Reformation rose, 'Thy grace to stop the bloody scenes/Of pride and cruelty, thy deadly foes'. The triumph of the Church of England leads Smart to give gratitude for 'The church her seemly course of practic pray'r and laud.' And this in turn leads to one of the most obscure stanzas in the hymn:

> We give the glory for the eyes
>   Of science, and the realm around;
> The two great rivals for the prize,
>   Ingenuous to a blessing on the sound.
> Well may their schools and num'rous chapels teach,
> 'The word is very Christ, that we adore and preach.'
>   (*Collected Poems*, ii. 824)

Some light may be thrown on this stanza by *Jubilate Agno* B2.616-619:

> For all Foundation is from God depending.
> For the two Universities are the Eyes of England.
> For Cambridge is the right and brightest.
> For Pembroke Hall was founded more in the Lord than any College in Cambridge.

The hymn stanza seems to mean, then, that the two Universities, like the Church of England, teach that ' "The word is very Christ, that we adore and preach" '—though what Smart means by 'Ingenuous to a blessing on the sound' is beyond me.

In the first fourteen stanzas of his hymn, Smart has outlined the grandeur of England—its triumphs in war, in religion, in education. But, he warns, these fair possessions and spiritual wealth were nearly laid and lost on King Charles's block 'What time the constitution's health/Was broke, and ruin'd by the general shock'. But God was implored by loyal prayers, and 'THIS DAY saw the heir acknowledg'd and restor'd.' The Restoration must therefore be celebrated by remembering Christ's love, and by wearing the royal oak—for the 29th May, Oak Apple Day, celebrated Charles's escape from the Parliamentarians by hiding in the oak at Boscabel, as well as the Restoration. 'And to the skies, the caps of freedom hurl'd,/ Should thus proclaim the queen of islands and the world.' He begs 'Ye soldiers reverend with scars' to remember that Chelsea Hospital for the old and disabled soldier was founded by Charles II, and no doubt his exhortation of 'ye students of the stars,/Remov'd from seaman's toils to fair alcoves' refers to the king's other charitable foundation, Greenwich Hospital. It was, of course, conventional to admire these two buildings in one and the same breath—Samuel Rogers wrote 'Chelsea and Greenwich Hospitals'

> Go, with old Thames, view Chelsea's glorious pile;
> And ask the shatter'd hero, whence his smile?
> Go, with the splendid domes of Greenwich;—go,
> And own what raptures from Reflection flow.

The final stanza of the hymn seems to have very little connection with what has gone before. Smart bids the reader 'Remember all ye may of good'. We must select the nosegay from the sod but leave the brambles in the wood. We must seek out the beautiful just as the sun of charity brings virtue into the light; we must reject the ugly just as the sun leaves 'slips and crimes' in the shadow.

Enough has been said to show that Hymn XVII illustrates some of Smart's perennial themes—his unflagging enthusiasm for the martial character of illustrious Englishmen, for the adulation of heroes, and his inveterate hatred for the Roman Catholic nations, France in particular. It should have become clear, also, that although Smart's major theme, the triumphs of the Englishman on sea and land, is clear enough, the scheme is muddled by a strange chronology which jerks from the Elizabethan age to the Middle Ages, to the age of Queen Anne, to the Restoration of Charles II. The muddled scheme is complicated by obscure historical references, and 'dark' phrases like 'Ingenuous to a blessing on the sound', and irrelevant stanzas like the final one on nosegays and charity. The general scheme of the *Hymns and Spiritual Songs* is perfectly clear, as Smart moves through the Fasts and Festivals of the Church of England in strict chronological order. As we shall see in the next part of this chapter, the ordering mind of the poet was at work in the creation of a seasonal cycle of imagery throughout the hymns, and the result was some exquisite lyrical poetry. But it would be misleading to imply that the *Hymns and Spiritual Songs* are invariably beautiful, well-ordered, and sane. Hymn XVII shows clearly what when he composed his hymns, Smart was still partially disorientated in his intellect.

— ii —

'Muse, accordant to the season,/Give the numbers life and air' (Hymn XIII)

In the *Hymns and Spiritual Songs*, the Biblical and historical events of the church calendar interact with the cycle of events as spring passes into summer, summer into autumn, and autumn into winter. I have not yet discovered any other eighteenth-century poet who composed a consistent, poetical church calendar comparable with the *Hymns and Spiritual Songs*, but the theme of God's manifestation in the circling year is certainly a motif of individual hymns of the age. The most remarkable example that I have come across is Philip Doddridge's version of Psalm 65.11, 'For New-Year's Day' in his *Hymns Founded on Various Texts in the Holy Scriptures* (1755):

> 1 ETERNAL Source of ev'ry Joy!
> Well may thy Praise our Lips employ,
> While in thy Temple we appear,
> Whose Goodness crowns the circling Year.
>
> 2 Wide as the Wheels of Nature roll
> Thy Hand supports the steady Pole:
> The Sun is taught by thee to rise,
> And Darkness when to veil the Skies.
>
> 3 The flow'ry Spring at thy Command
> Embalms the Air, and paints the Land;
> The Summer Rays with Vigour shine
> To raise the Corn, and chear the Vine.
>
> 4 Thy Hand in Autumn richly pours
> Thro' all our Coasts redundant Stores;
> And Winters, soft'ned by thy Care,
> No more a Face of Horror wear.
>
> 5 Seasons, and Months, and Weeks, and Days
> Demand successive Songs of Praise;
> Still be the chearful Homage paid
> With opening Light, and evening Shade.
>
> 6 Here in thy House shall Incense rise,
> As circling Sabbaths bless our Eyes;
> Still will we make thy Mercies known,
> Around thy Board, and round our own.
>
> 7 O may our more harmonious Tongues
> In Worlds unknown persue the Songs;
> And in those brighter Courts adore,
> Where Days and Years revolve no more.

Doddridge's hymn is almost a synopsis of the theme of James Thomson's *Seasons*, and its sentiment is very much like Thom-

son's in 'A Hymn on the Seasons',[5] which begins with the
statement, 'THESE, as they change, Almighty Father! these/Are
but the varied God. The rolling year/Is full of thee.' Thomson
then proceeds through the seasons, spring, summer, autumn,
and winter, and demands that God should be praised:

> Nature, attend! join, every living soul
> Beneath the spacious temple of the sky,
> In adoration join; and ardent raise
> One general song!

Then, men are exhorted to join their voices to the deep organ
and 'Still sing the God of Seasons as they roll.' Both Doddridge
and Thomson move from the temporal to the eternal. Doddridge turns from the seasons of this earth to 'those brighter
Courts . . . Where Days and Years revolve no more.' Similarly,
Thomson writes that

> When even at last the solemn hour shall come,
> And wing my mystic flight to future worlds,
> I cheerful will obey; there, with new powers,
> Will rising wonders sing

The themes in these individual hymns—the seasonal imagery,
the adoration of the God of the Seasons, the temporal-eternal
dichotomy—are implicit also in the *Hymns and Spiritual Songs*.
Smart has taken a contemporary 'motif' and woven it elaborately into the structure of a closely-knit series of thirty-five
hymns.

We already know from *A Song to David* that Smart was aware
of the beauty of the passing seasons. 'For ADORATION seasons
change,/And order, truth, and beauty range,/Adjust, attract,
and fill', he wrote in stanza LII, and then went on to describe,
briefly but evocatively, the progression of spring, summer,
autumn, and winter. In *Jubilate Agno* B2.340 and 576, he had
paraphrased Acts 1.7, 'And he said unto them, It is not for you
to know the times or the seasons, which the Father hath put in
his own power':

For TIMES and SEASONS are the Lord's—Man is no CHRONOLOGER.
For there is no knowing of times & seasons, in submitting them
to God stands the Christian's Chronology.

[5] *The Poems of James Thomson*, 245–49.

It is a theological statement which is as difficult in the original
as it is in Smart's variant reading in *Jubilate Agno*. Obviously, it
had special significance for him, for he refers again to the way
the 'Christian's Chronology' works, in Hymn XII. It is by 'the
dress and airs/Of nature' that 'the man of pray'r computes/His
year, and estimates the fruits/Of every time and tide.' And in
the following poem, Hymn XIII, Smart seems to make a clear
statement of his artistic purpose in the *Hymns and Spiritual Songs*:

> Muse, accordant to the season,
>   Give the numbers life and air;
> When the sounds and objects reason
>   In behalf of praise and pray'r.
>   (*Collected Poems*, ii. 814)

In the imagery of the *Hymns and Spiritual Songs*, there is an
essential balance between the supernatural vitality of a winter
redeemed by the advent of Christ, and the natural fruition of
God's world in spring and summer. In Hymn XXXII, 'The
Nativity of Our Lord and Saviour Jesus Christ', Michael is
called upon to celebrate Christ's birth with a tune on the
shepherd's reed, to be played in heaven 'Where the scenes are
ever vernal'. Immediately, this everlasting spring of Paradise is
paralleled by a supernatural spring on earth:

> Boreas now no longer winters
>   On the desolated coast;
> Oaks no more are riv'n in splinters
>   By the whirlwind and his host.
>   (*Collected Poems*, ii. 847)

As Smart had written in *Jubilate Agno* B2.305, 'For before the
NATIVITY is the dead of winter and after it the quick.' Hymn
XXXIII, 'St. Stephen', makes it clear that the manifestation
of God in human flesh meant also God's manifestation in the
works of creation. But Smart emphasizes the fact that even
redeemed nature is inferior to heaven:

> God! great and manifest around,
> In earth, and air, and depth profound.
> In every movement, animals that breathe,
> And all the beauties visible beneath.

> But nobler works about his throne,
> And brighter glories are his own,
> Where high o'er heav'n the loves his Spirit mates,
> And virtues, graces, mercies he creates.
> (*Collected Poems*, ii. 848)

The sexual connotations are of course suited to the idea of the rebirth of spring. To emphasize the idea that spring in winter is a supernatural event, Smart describes St. Stephen as a 'flow'r', although his Festival is celebrated in the depths of winter, on December 26th: 'o GRACE, thou never rais'd a sweeter flow'r./ Which sprang, and gemm'd, and blossom'd in an hour.' There are similar paradoxes in Hymn I, 'New Year'. The angels sally from 'everlasting bow'rs', but they play symphonies for periods of earthly time, 'Years, and months, and days, and hours.' Likewise the 'budding rods' in heaven symbolize the redemption of now 'guiltless nature' on earth, although it is but January 1st and still winter. Smart is thus interweaving the heavenly and earthly worlds in an eternal spring. A similar idea is found in another hymn 'For New Year's Day' in Doddridge's *Hymns Founded on Various Texts in the Holy Scriptures*. Doddridge first addresses heaven, where the bright seraphim sound the Honours of God on ever-blooming hills. He then addresses the earth, enlightened by the rays divine, and pregnant with grass and corn and oil and wine. Eventually he links both heaven and earth:

> Burst into Praise, my Soul; all Nature join;
> Angels and Men in Harmony combine:
> While human Years are measur'd by the Sun,
> And while Eternity its Course shall run,
> His Goodness, in perpetual Show'rs descending,
> Exalt in Songs, and Raptures never-ending.

In Smart's hymn on 'Circumcision', the Feast is celebrated on January 1st with an out-of-season 'rose of maiden flush', but perhaps the 'herb of ever-grateful green' is a reminder that it is still winter, even though a winter full of green life. Likewise in Hymn III, 'Epiphany', the Feast is celebrated by kids, lambkins, and colts, but they are visualized in a winter landscape, 'Bounding through the leafless grove.' The Conversion of St.

Paul represents another advent of the spiritual into the material world, and the miraculous fruition on January 25th is expressed in the image of the sower, 'To make the fruitless soil to hold/Ten thousand times ten thousand fold.'

In Hymn VI, 'The Presentation of Christ in the Temple', Smart is perfectly aware that the list of creatures called upon to praise God is unseasonal. It is only February 2nd, and on earth the trees are still bare:

> Praise him ye doves, and ye that pipe
> Ere buds begin to stir;
> Ev'n every finch of every stripe;
> And thou of filial love the type,
> O stork! that sit'st upon the fir.
> (*Collected Poems*, ii. 798)

We scarcely expect the imagery of flowers and bees in a February poem, but Smart is probably making an elaborate simile to express a religious concept:

> Praise him ye flow'rs that serve the swarm
> With honey for their cells;
> Ere yet the vernal day is warm,
> To call out millions to perform
> Their gambols on your cups and bells.

> *   *   *

> Praise him ye cherubs of his breast,
> The mercies of his love,
> Ere yet from guile and hate profest,
> The phenix makes his fragrant nest
> In his own paradise above.
> (*Collected Poems*, ii. 798, 799)

The phoenix was of course a traditional emblem of Christ. The details of the legend vary, but in broad terms, the story goes that when the phoenix is five hundred years old, it stands on a cedar of Lebanon, dips its wings in incense and is consumed on the altar of the sun. Three days after, it rises from the fragrant ashes and flies away. Inevitably the myth became a symbol for the death and resurrection of Christ. What Smart seems to be saying in his hymn is that the vernal day on earth has not yet come, and neither has the vernal day arrived when Christ will enjoy everlasting spring in Paradise. But just as the sun will bring spring to earth, and the bees in their millions to the flowers, so will the sun of the phoenix legend consume Christ and bring him into 'paradise above'.

In Hymn IX, 'The Annunciation of the Blessed Virgin', God is seen as the source of all natural and supernatural events:

> Hail mystery! thou source
> Of nature's plainest course,
> How much this work transcends
> Thine usual means and ends
> (*Collected Poems*, ii. 803)

The images of newness and freshness refer not only to the new life to be born in Christ, but also to the seasonal renewal of nature, for Smart goes on to praise the Creator:

> To praise the mighty hand
> By which the world was mann'd,
> Which dealt to great and small
> Their talents clear of all;
>   Kind to kind by likeness linkt,
>   Various all, and all distinct.
> (*Collected Poems*, ii. 803)

We are led to expect the natural rebirth of spring, as opposed to the spiritual rebirth of nature at the Advent of Christ. But in Hymn X comes the Crucifixion, and this represents a setback in the steady progression of the fruition of the season, for 'THE world is but a sorry scene,/Untrue, unhallow'd, and unclean'. The desolation of the world at the death of Christ is in contrast to the invigoration of the earth at the Nativity. But, as we should expect, the earth flowers on Easter Day, in Hymn XI,

> The flow'rs from every bed collect,
>   And on the altar lift;
> And let each silver vase be deckt
>   With nature's graceful gift.
> (*Collected Poems*, ii. 811)

Then come the hymns of spring. Hymns XII and XIII, celebrating the Feast of St. Mark and the Feast of St. Philip and

St. James, are among the most vivid of the *Hymns and Spiritual Songs*. 'PULL up the bell-flow'rs of the spring', cries Smart in Hymn XII, 'And let the budding greenwood ring/With many a chearful song'. The second stanza of the hymn is a mesh of interwoven themes and images that recur throughout Smart's religious poetry:

> To whom belong the tribe that vie
> In what is musick to the eye,
>   Whose voice is 'stoop to pray'—
> While many colour'd tints attire
> His fav'rites, like the golden wire,
>   The beams on wind flow'rs play.
>   (*Collected Poems*, ii. 812)

Smart had written in *Jubilate Agno* B2.508 that 'flowers are musical in ocular harmony', and in this hymn, he is expressing the same idea through imagery. He is making an implicit equation which could be written out as: the sun plays on flowers as the wind plays on harpstrings. The wind flowers are like the golden wires of a harp, and the visual beauty of the sunlit flowers is as the aural beauty of music when the wind plays over the harp strings. The allusion to the harp is indirect, but we detect it because it is a frequent theme in Smart's poetry. He is referring to an Aeolian harp, and we are reminded of 'Inscriptions on an Æolian Harp' (first printed in the *Student* in August 1750) with the Latin tag, 'PARTEM aliquam, O venti, divûm referatis ad aures!' and a Latin poem translated as follows:

> Hail, heav'nly harp, where Memnon's skill is shown,
> That charm'st the ear with music all thine own!
> Which, though untouch'd, can'st rapt'rous strains impart,
> O rich of genuine nature, free from art!
> Such the wild warblings of the sylvan throng,
> So simply sweet the untaught virgin's song.
>   (*Collected Poems*, i. 27)

The association of flowers with prayer is a characteristic theme of Smart's religious poetry. For instance, in *Jubilate Agno* B2.499, 'For the flower glorifies God and the root parries the adversary', and in the *Song to David*, it is for Adoration that the bell-flowers bow their stems (stanza LIII). Hymn XIII should not really be quoted in part—it is so exquisitely complete that it is spoiled by being broken up. But since it is composed of nineteen quatrains, we shall have to be contented here with a summary of the poem. The Festival of St. Philip and St. James falls on May 1st, when the earth is coming fully to life, 'All the scenes of nature quicken', and 'Earth her vigour repossessing'. Smart directs all his poetic genius towards reproducing in imagery the abundant fertility of spring, the tansy, calaminth, and daisies thriving on the river bank, and the trees and flowers of the following stanzas:

> Beeches, without order seemly,
>   Shade the flow'rs of annual birth,
> And the lily smiles supremely
>   Mention'd by the Lord on earth.
>
> Couslips seize upon the fallow,
>   And the cardamine in white,
> Where the corn-flow'rs join the mallow,
>   Joy and health, and thrift unite.
>   (*Collected Poems*, ii. 814)

But in the midst of this exultant catalogue of the beauties of the earth, Smart appears to be dissatisfied, perhaps because it is after all the eternal spring in supernatural winter that he awaits, rather than the spring on this earth, however beautiful it may be:

> Pray'r and praise be mine employment,
>   Without grudging or regret,
> Lasting life, and long enjoyment,
>   Are not here, and are not yet.
>   (*Collected Poems*, ii. 815)

Immediately, this craving for eternity is put aside, and the hymn is filled once more with spring imagery—the blackbird and the goldfinch, the hornet, bluecap and coney. But the slight hint of melancholia adds pathos to the interaction of time and eternity in the *Hymns and Spiritual Songs*. Smart has implied, however briefly, that there is something unsatisfactory even in the vigorous, youthful beauty of spring. Spring must be redeemed as surely as barren winter has to be changed by the Advent of Christ. Hymn XIV, celebrating the Ascension, is

concerned with this theme of the salvation of space and time,
the salvation by grace of the human, animal, and vegetable
kingdoms:

> For not a particle of space
>   Where'er his glory beam'd,
> With all the modes of site and place,
> But were the better for his grace,
>   And up to higher lot redeem'd
>   (*Collected Poems*, ii. 816)

The motley tribes who pair and skim to cover, the raven urgent
in prayer, and the birds singing their woodland hymns, became
the immediate care of the ascended Lord. The creatures who
roamed the howling wastes and lived upon the blood they
spilled received their fill from his own hands, and 'The beast of
sleek or shaggy fur,/And found their natures to recur/To what
they were in Eden's field.' Those who dwelt in the deep ocean
confessed his mighty power to save when he gave peace to the
floods—creatures that are mean ('the worm/Probationer to
fly'), and the vast flocks of fish that have no mouths to bleat
(Smart was strangely obsessed by the muteness of fish), all
'were bless'd beneath his feet'. And man himself was redeemed
likewise:

> 'Twas his the pow'rs of hell to curb,
>   And men possess'd to free;
> And all the blasting fiends disturb
> From seed to bread, from flow'r and herb,
>   From fragrant shrub and stately tree.
>   (*Collected Poems*, ii. 818)

But the redemption of the flowering shrub was nearly as important to Smart as the redemption of man.

As we pass into summer, we find that the sunshine and growing plants are present even in the metaphorical account of the
derivation of languages from Hebrew, given in Hymn XV on
Whitsuntide:

> Every speech beneath the sun,
>   Which from Babel first begun;
> Branch or leaf, or flow'r or fruit
> Of the Hebrews ancient root.
>   (*Collected Poems*, ii. 819)

In Hymn XVIII, 'St. Barnabas', the seasonal imagery is used for metaphorical effect. The theme of this hymn is the sacrifice of earthly wealth for 'everlasting store'. The first stanza ostensibly reflects upon the nature of Christian treasure, but it also contributes to the chronology of the *Hymns and Spiritual Songs* by introducing the imagery of high summer:

> DARING as the noon-tide ray
> On the summer's longest day,
> Is the truth of Christ supreme;
> Proving at its sacred touch,
> Whether Ophir's gold be such,
> Or a shift to seem.
> (*Collected Poems*, ii. 825)

In Hymn XIX, 'The Nativity of St. John the Baptist', the imagery of summer accords with the seasonal backcloth to the theology of the hymns:

> Lo the swelling fruits of summer,
> With inviting colours dy'd,
> Hang, for ev'ry casual comer,
> O'er the fence projecting wide.
>
> See the corn for plenty waving,
> Where the lark secur'd her eggs—
> In the spirit then be saving,
> Give the poor that sings and begs.
> (*Collecting Poems*, ii. 827)

Gentle nature seems to love us, says Smart, for all is beauteous blue above us and all beneath is cheerful green. He is in fact creating a metaphor of fruition, to symbolize the fruition of Elizabeth's barren womb. We know from *Hannah* what an important theme this was for Smart, and we can guess at the exultation with which he wrote of the warmer days ripening from their prime, and 'She that was as barren reckon'd,/Had her course completely run', and brought forth John, the child of Zacharias.

We have traced winter, spring, and summer through the *Hymns and Spiritual Songs*. We have to admit that after the vivid seasonal imagery of these hymns, autumn gets short shrift. We

can ferret out one or two suitable images if we have a mind to
do so—the Papists leaguing to mar the world's increase and the
prayer that George III should be blessed with the fruit of his
loins in Hymn XXVI, or the metaphor in Hymn XXVII:

> Fair sincerity's the ground
>   For the Lord to sow his seed,
> That will flourish and abound
>   With a goodly crop indeed.
> *(Collected Poems,* ii. 839)

But this, of course, is just not comparable with the rich autumn
imagery of the relevant 'Adoration' stanzas in *A Song to David.*
As usual, we seem to find in Smart's poetry strong evidence of
creative order, only to discover that sooner or later the organization appears to break down for no particular reason. But at
least we can say of the *Hymns and Spiritual Songs,* that they reveal
Smart's awareness of the contemporary poetic link between
God and the Seasons, and the related theme of the interaction
of time and eternity. And we have found, that far from sounding like another Thomson or another Doddridge, he imposes
upon the conventional motifs his own individual poetic signature, contained in characteristic image clusters and his own
particular mode of adoring God.

[XII]

The Parables *and the* Hymns for the Amusement of Children

IN THE LAST YEARS of his life, Smart brought out two religious works for children—*The Parables of our Lord and Saviour Jesus Christ. Done into Familiar Verse, with Occasional Applications, for the Use and Improvement of Younger Minds* in 1768, and the *Hymns for the Amusement of Children* in 1770. The *Parables* were dedicated to Master Bonnell George Thornton, of Orchard Street, Westminster, son of Bonnell Thornton, who had been the sole editor of the *Student* when it first came out in 1750, and Sylvia Thornton, youngest daughter of Colonel John Brathwaite, governor of Cape Coast Castle. The reviewers sneered at the idea of dedicating a work to a three-year-old child, but in actual fact the Dedication is rather charming—and entirely characteristic of Smart's wish to please those who had been kind to him:

> THERE are sundry Instances of our Blessed SAVIOUR's Fondness for Children, as a Man; and He has assured us, we can have no Part in Him without imitating their Innocence and Simplicity. This is so evident, that though you are yet scarce three Years of Age, you will soon be able to read and understand it: and in a Season will reflect, I trust, with Pleasure, that you have been the Patron of a well-intended Work, almost as soon as you could go alone. It is very natural to suppose, that you will one Day make no small Progress in Science, and rise with great Ease from one Degree of Eminence to another under the Eye, Example, and Blessing of such Parents, and be enabled to thank GOD, amongst other good Scholars, that there is nothing so pleasant as Wisdom, and nothing so useful as Learning.
> I am with the greatest Sincerity and the most inevitable

Affection to the Eldest Son of BONNELL and SYLVIA THORNTON,
Your most hearty Friend,
CHRISTOPHER SMART.

Westminster,
Febr. 24, 1768.

The Dedication of the *Hymns for the Amusement of Children* was a much grander affair: 'TO HIS ROYAL HIGHNESS PRINCE FREDERICK, BISHOP OF OSNABRUG, THESE HYMNS, COMPOSED FOR HIS AMUSEMENT, ARE, With all due Submission and Respect, HUMBLY INSCRIBED TO HIM, AS THE BEST OF BISHOPS, BY HIS ROYAL HIGHNESS's Most Obedient and Devoted Servant, Christopher Smart.' The little volume of hymns was graced with an engraved portrait of the second son of George III, the seven-year old Prince Frederick Augustus, who had been elected to the bishopric of Osnabrug when he was six months old (and retained it until its dissolution in 1803).[1] We do not know how Smart obtained permission to use the Bishop's name. Hawkesworth mentioned that Smart 'was going to dine with an old friend of my own, Mr. Richard Dalton, who has an appointment in the King's library',[2] and in a letter to Panton, Smart himself referred to his benefactor, the Rev. William Mason, as 'the King's Chaplain'[3]—perhaps Dalton or Mason obtained permission for Smart to dedicate the book to Prince Frederick Augustus.

The text of the *Parables* is not nearly so pleasant as the Dedication, and it would be tedious to attempt a lengthy appreciation of all seventy-three parables and the ten extra poems which Smart justified by writing that 'Though the following Passages of the New Testament be not Parables, yet

---

[1] Mr. Oliver Millar, Deputy Surveyor of the Queen's Pictures, has kindly informed me that the portrait of the Duke of York, engraved for Smart's *Hymns for the Amusement of Children*, is by Benjamin West, and that the original is at Buckingham Palace. Mr. David Piper, former Keeper of the National Portrait Gallery, has referred me to a clipped impression of an engraving of the Duke of York in the National Portrait Gallery. It varies in several minor details from the frontispiece of the *Hymns for the Amusement of Children* and includes two mottoes, 'TRIA JUNCTA IN UNO' and 'HONI SOIT QUI MAL Y PENSE'. Benjamin West was, of course, Historical Painter to George III.

[2] *Poems of the Late Christopher Smart*, 1791, I. xxv.

[3] Cecil Price, 'Six Letters by Christopher Smart', *Review of English Studies*, n.s. vol. viii, 1957, 145.

as they are altogether pertinent to our present Design, we have not scrupled to insert them.' Smart's transcription of the rhythms of the King James prose into undistinguished rhyming couplets seems merely destructive—we have already seen how the eighteenth-century versifiers had no scruples about chopping up the Coverdale text, for instance, although they had no true poetry to offer in exchange. Smart's Parable VII illustrates the pedestrian nature of his versification:

> Again, the kingdom of heaven is like unto a net, that was cast into the sea, and gathered of every kind:
> Which, when it was full, they drew to shore, and sat down, and gathered the good into vessels, but cast the bad away.
> So shall it be at the end of the world: the angels shall come forth, and sever the wicked from among the just,
> And shall cast them into the furnace of fire: there shall be wailing and gnashing of teeth.   (St. Matthew 13.47–50)

> AGAIN—the kingdom's like a draught
> Of fishes in the ocean caught;
> With which of every kind well stor'd,
> The net they on the strand explor'd,
> When some in vessels they collect,
> And some they sever and reject.
>   So shall it happen in the end,
> The Lord th'angelic host shall send
> To sever from amongst the just
> Those, that attentive to their lust,
> Were dead to Jesus preaching truth,
> Now doom'd to wail and gnash the tooth.
>   (*Collected Poems*, ii. 858)

Not only is this boring, but it also fails to make any appeal to the 'Innocence and Simplicity' of childish minds. Smart makes no attempt to alter the Biblical vocabulary, and in fact he makes the syntax more rather than less difficult: the Biblical 'the angels shall come forth' is more straightforward than Smart's 'The Lord th'angelic host shall send'.

But the 'Occasional Applications' are generally rather more interesting, and take the form of italicized commentaries appended to some of the parables. Smart admired the homely, concrete imagery of the Parables, and he was prepared to adopt and develop that imagery in his commentaries. In Parable XXXVII, Smart says that Christ consecrated the name of every object that he spoke of:

> *He therefore oft his proverb brings*
> *From lowly life and common things,*
> *That they (whom high-flow'n thoughts offend)*
> *The vulgar might attention lend:*
> *And, while their sov'reign source they seek,*
> *Wit, learning, genius, might be meek.*
> (*Collected Poems*, ii. 901–2)

Smart accepted the consecrated pictures of the Gospel, and added a few details of his own. Where he found the mustard-seed growing into a tree in Parable III, he made the tree into a symbol of Christ growing in humility—by way of an allusion to Isaiah 11.1, 'AND there shall come forth a rod out of the stem of Jesse, and a Branch shall grow out of his roots'. The birds that nested in the mustard-tree in the Biblical version become singing saints in Smart's commentary—a development that recalls Hymn VI in the *Hymns and Spiritual Songs* where Christ is seen as the phoenix, making 'his fragrant nest/In his own paradise above.' Another example of Smart's method of extending the Biblical metaphor is found in Parable VIII, which tells how murder, fornication, fraud, and blasphemy defile a man: 'Such things all purity defeat,/Not with unwashen hands to eat.' In the commentary, Smart develops the image to include running water—we remember that Smart liked to pray in the rain, and that in the *Song to David* he wrote, 'For ADORATION, all the paths/ Of grace are open, all the baths,/Of purity refresh':

> *The blessed men our Saviour chose*
> *To hear his doctrine, share his woes,*
> *Still as they waited by his side*
> *Were by his glory purified.*
> *No limpid rill, no polish'd vase,*
> *But were unclean before his face.*
> *Where'er he travell'd, or remain'd,*
> *Inevitable sweetness reign'd;*
> *And by his very word applied,*
> *He cleans'd, he bless'd, and sanctified.*
> (*Collected Poems*, ii. 860)

These 'Applications' have just a spark of originality in that they are not simply a word-for-word transcription of the Biblical text—but that is as much as can be said for them. It is possible to see in some of the commentaries some of Smart's perennial themes and obsessions, especially his hatred of the Roman Catholic Church. In Parable XV, for instance, the five unwise Virgins are Catholics:

> *Wretches like these would all to* Rome,
> *And go to them that sell perfume,*
> *And to the* man of sin *apply,*
> *There pardons and indulgence buy:*
> *But Christ against the fools, that put*
> *Their trust in man, his door has shut.*
>
> *(Collected Poems,* ii. 871)

In Parable LVIII, when Christ foretells his death and resurrection, and Peter cries 'God forbid!', Christ turns on him—'Satan recede, and get thee hence!' Peter's temptation of Christ comes directly after he has been called 'the rock' and promised the keys of heaven and hell, and Smart therefore interprets Christ's rebuke as a timely warning that Peter must not become too proud of his new honour. Smart uses the occasion for anti-Catholic propaganda:

> *When Peter found that he was prais'd*
> *By Christ, and o'er his brethren rais'd*
> *In his esteem, he in that hour*
> *Began to dream of wealth and pow'r:*
> *For satan, at his elbow, said,*
> *Thou of the church art sov'reign head;*
> *And all mankind, as thou think'st fit,*
> *Thou shalt condemn, or shalt acquit;*
> *In costly garbs thou shalt be drest,*
> *And feast on viands of the best;*
> *Thou shalt from kings exact renown,*
> *And make thyself a triple crown—*
> *But Jesus bade the dev'l recede,*
> *Or Peter had been Pope indeed.*
>
> *(Collected Poems,* ii. 923)

In 'The fiery Disciples', one of the ten additional poems which

are not strictly parables, James and John wish to call down fire
from heaven to consume the Samaritan village that refused to
give Christ a lodging. They are rebuked: 'For Christ his
mission's not design'd/To sacrifice, but save mankind.' This
gives Smart the opportunity to suggest that Christ, like Smart,
was a Protestant:

> *All bold opposers to consume*
> *In the true stile of modern Rome,*
> *These zealots were for fire and sword,*
> *To make Christ's holy name ador'd.*
> *But he against such zeal* PROTESTS,
> *His peaceful sway no wrath infests;*
> *But all his reign, and all his race,*
> *Are truth and mercy, love and grace.*
> (*Collected Poems*, ii. 955)

To many eighteenth-century readers, the occasional blast of
hostility against the Roman Catholic church was obviously
welcome enough—we may remember that the *Monthly Review*
had praised the *Ode to the Earl of Northumberland* because Smart
had fought against the Whore of Babylon with a truly British
spirit. To twentieth-century readers, it seems deplorable that
Smart should have taught Master Bonnell George Thornton
and the rest of his infant readers the principles of sectarian
hatred. It was fortunate for the Bishop of Osnabrug and his
fellow-readers that Smart included a hymn on 'Moderation'
in the *Hymns for the Amusement of Children*. Smart states that he
has long chosen his own party:

> Blessed be God, that at the font
>   My sponsors bound me to the call
> Of Christ, in England, to confront
>   The world, the flesh, the fiend and all.

But despite his allegiance to the Church of England, Smart will
not be subject to pique, prejudice, or pride, and he is determined to keep his tongue free from censure, 'The Jew, the
Turk, the Heathen bless,/And hold the plough and persevere.'
The Roman Catholic is not included among the Jews, Turks,
and Heathens, but at least the prevailing sentiment is healthier
than that of the *Parables*:

There's God in ev'ry man most sure,
  And ev'ry soul's to Christ allied:
If fears deject, if hopes allure,
  If Jesus wept, and pray'd and died.

There is only one parable that really helps us to understand
the nature of Smart's religious experience, and the expression
of that experience in his poetry. This is Parable VI, a version of
St. Matthew 13.45, 46, with the addition of an 'Application' of
six lines:

> Again, the kingdom of heaven is like unto a merchant man,
> seeking goodly pearls:
> Who, when he had found one pearl of great price, went and sold
> all that he had, and bought it.   (St. Matthew 13.45, 46)

> AGAIN—'tis like a man that made
> The search of precious stones his trade,
> Who when he found a *pearl indeed*,
> Of price all others to exceed,
> He chose from all his wealth to part,
> And bought the jewel of his heart.

> *All parts must center in the whole.*
> *This pearl's salvation of the soul,*
> *And he that stedfastly denies*
> *To deal in pomp and vanities,*
> *Shall gain by tenure not to cease,*
> *His Saviour and eternal peace.*
>   (*Collected Poems*, ii. 857–58)

This parable brings to mind the enigmatic line on pearls in
Jubilate Agno:

> Let Hushim rejoice with the King's Fisher, who is of royal beauty,
> tho' plebeian size.
> For in my nature I quested for beauty, but God, God hath sent
> me to sea for pearls.

When I first juxtaposed Parable VI and *Jubilate Agno* B1.30,
I realized that they could be interpreted tentatively with the
help of Jungian psychology. Smart seems to be saying that he
has failed to find 'beauty' in his own nature, and that he has
been forced to look elsewhere, to the person of Christ who is

symbolized as the pearl in the ocean. The poet's soul is now centred not 'in my nature' but 'in the whole'—his soul has become God-centred instead of self-centred. In Jungian terms, Smart has turned away from the ego (self), centre of consciousness, towards the Self, centre of the totality of consciousness and unconsciousness. For Smart, this totality was Christ's nature, and the experience of this totality was salvation. Jung himself has pointed out that the experience of the Self can be specifically Christian—Christ and Buddha being the two most highly differentiated expressions of the archetype of Self yet reached by mankind—and also that the symbol of the Self is often a jewel, especially a diamond or a pearl.

This seemed to me a valid way of approaching Smart's religious experience—by using modern psychology for understanding his behaviour and interpreting his poetry. But at that time I had not read William Law's *The Spirit of Prayer* (1749). When I did so, it was remarkable to find that the interpretation of Smart via Jung was even further illuminated by Law, who wrote, 'there is a *Root*, or *Depth* in Thee, from whence all these Faculties of thine come forth, as Lines from a *Centre*, or as Branches from the Body of the Tree. This Depth is called the *Centre*, the *Fund* or *Bottom* of the Soul.'[4] When Adam sinned, this depth or centre of his soul lost its God, but with the advent of Christ, Adam was saved: 'from that Moment all the Riches and Treasures of the Divine Nature came again into Man, as a *Seed* of Salvation sown into the *Centre* of the Soul'.[5] Law bids man seek in the depths of his soul for the riches and treasures of the divine nature: 'Begin to search and dig in thine own Field for this *Pearl of Eternity*, that lies hidden in it; it cannot cost Thee too much, nor canst thou buy it too dear, for it is *All*'.[6] I have found no evidence that Smart had read *The Spirit of Prayer*, but it nevertheless seems valid enough to interpret certain lines in his poetry, which seem at first to be very obscure, in the light of Law's theology.

Parable VI may help to illuminate other parts of Smart's religious poetry, but taken by itself, it is no more remarkable than the rest of Smart's undistinguished parables. The *Hymns*

[4] *The Works of the Reverend William Law*, ed. G. Moreton, 1893, vii. 28.
[5] *Ibid.*, vii.29.   [6] *Ibid.*

for the Amusement of Children, published only two years after the *Parables* is an altogether superior production, and it is only just to make a more serious and searching analysis of Smart's last published work.

Smart's father-in-law, John Newbery, is now remembered as the first publisher to bring out books for children on a large scale. The books were published under fanciful pseudonyms, and it is quite likely that Smart is hidden under one or two of them: *The History of Jack the Giant Killer* by Master Billy Pentweazle, for instance, which was advertised in *The Horatian Canons of Friendship* in 1750. After his mental breakdown, Smart felt bitterly resentful towards his father-in-law, and his later work was no longer printed for Newbery. Smart preferred to send his work to the Tonsons, the Dodsleys, Flexney or Owen. But two years after the death of John Newbery in 1767, there was some sort of reconciliation between Smart and his wife's family. Thomas Carnan decided to do something for his brother-in-law, who was getting deeper and deeper into debt, and Smart was his usual grateful self. 'Dear Sir', he wrote from Spring Gardens on the 16th April 1769, 'Being informed first by Mr Leach & afterwards by Messrs Mason and Stonhewer that you have determined very benevolently in my favour, I think it incumbent on me to be thankful. Indeed if mercy be not shewn to me somewhere or other I do not see how I can possibly escape a prison. I congratulate you therefore upon your kind resolution, as you may depend upon it, that it will not only be finally a great thing for yourself, but people even now will applaud your generosity and goodnature. I desire my duty to Mrs Newbery & will wait on you or give you the meeting when & where you will please to name. Yours most sincerely and affectionately Christopher Smart.'[7] Smart did not escape a prison, but Carnan at least provided him with work. A year later, the *Hymns for the Amusement of Children* was entered at Stationers' Hall.

By making his children's books 'amusing' or 'entertaining', Newbery had tried to sugar the pill of instruction. This is clearly expressed, for instance, in the Preface to *Fables in Verse*,

[7] Ms. Montagu, d.1, fol. 223, 224, in the Bodleian Library.

for the Improvement of the Young and Old by Abraham Aesop, Esq. (5th edition, 1765): 'LITTLE need be said to recommend any thing that bears the character of utility about it. Those who but open this book will see that the author has, under agreeable allegories, given the children such lessons in prudence and morality, as may be of service to them in their riper years, and help to conduct them through the world with peace and tranquility; and has made choice of this method of conveying his sentiments, as the most entertaining, and the most likely to make a lasting impression on the mind.' Most eighteenth-century poets and hymnists were willing to educate through pleasure—a surprisingly modern concept of teaching. John Vowler went so far as to publish *An Essay for Instructing Children on Various useful and Uncommon Subjects* (Exon., 1743), in which school exercises, History, Geography, Astronomy alike, are turned into religious verse. The Geometry lesson, XLIV, for instance, begins with the pious declaration,

> I'LL sing my MAKER's wondrous Name,
> Who built and rules this glorious *Frame*.
> Wisdom's display'd in every Line:
> His Power and Goodness brightly shine.

Vowler's book is recommended by Philip Doddridge in an introductory Preface. Doddridge feels that Vowler's work is fitted 'to *entertain* and to *instruct* Children'. Unfortunately, Doddridge's own efforts to write poetry for children were not very successful, and were not in the same class as his hymns for adults, already referred to in the chapter on the *Hymns and Spiritual Songs*.

Smart would have approved of Vowler's views on education, for in Hymn XVI, 'Learning', he wrote:

> Humanity's a charming thing,
> And every science of the ring,
>   Good is the classic lore;
> And these are helps along the road,
> That leads to Zion's blest abode,
>   And heav'nly muse's store.

If Smart was in fact the editor of the *Lilliputian Magazine*, as is

W

generally supposed,[8] the following pronouncement, made in
1752, gives some idea of the importance he attached to education: 'As education, therefore is a matter of such vast importance, that our happiness and misery (and in some measure)
the welfare of the kingdom and government must rest upon it,
what care ought not to be taken, to unloose the minds of
children, from the fetters of habit and custom, to enlarge their
ideas, enoble their sentiments, and fix them firmly in the
principles of virtue and good manners', and he quoted a
couplet by Pope:

> 'Tis *education* forms the tender mind;
> Just as the *twig* is bent, the *tree*'s inclin'd.

When the stress on the importance of education was harnessed
to the Newbery ideal of teaching through pleasure, Smart was
able to produce one of his best volumes of poetry, the *Hymns for
the Amusement of Children*.

The typical eighteenth-century attitude to children contrasted strongly with that of such seventeenth-century writers
as Abraham Chear, James Janeway, and Benjamin Keach.
Chear undoubtedly had great tenderness for children. In *A
Looking-Glass for Children* (1672), that servant of the Lord,
Mr. Abraham Chear, expressed his well-wishes to the souls of
divers poor children, to whom he then stood nearly related and
dearly affected. He addressed them individually as '*Sweet
Child*' or '*SWeet John*' or '*DEar Cousin Sam*', just as Smart
addresses his readers as 'ye little prattlers' in Hymn XXV. But
the harsh religious doctrine of the age meant that Chear's
children were blackened with original sin. A young virgin is
sent a Bible, and is reminded,

> There you may read what guilt of sin,
>   into the world of sin you brought;
> And since what filthiness hath bin,
>   in Word, in Deed, in Thought:

Smart does suggest in Hymn VIII that Fortitude is necessary
in 'dang'rous giddy youth', but he implies that the war must be

[8] See William J. Thoms, *Notes and Queries*, ser. ii, vol. iii, 30th May 1857, and
Roland B. Botting, 'Christopher Smart and the *Lilliputian Magazine*', *Journal of
English Literary History*, ix, 1942, 286–87.

waged against external corruption. He never ever suggests that children are inherently corrupt. His view of the child's nature is optimistic, as in Hymn XIII:

> 'Tis in the body, that sweet mien,
> > Ingenuous Christians all possess,
> Grace, easy motions, smiles serene,
> > Clean hands and seemliness of dress.

With a black view of human nature goes the desire to reform it. It is inevitable therefore, that Chear commands his children to kiss the rod, while Smart seems quite unaware that children may need to be physically punished:

> Oh! with what grief upon their wayes,
> > Should Parents then reflect;
> Whose fawning in our infant dayes,
> > doth Word and Rod neglect!

It was fitting that some of Chear's hymns should be included in James Janeway's *A Token for Youth*, published in the 1670s. This was a work written mainly in prose, with blood-curdling subjects described on the title-page as the lives and glorious martyrdoms of several young persons who suffered death with the most cruel tortures for the profession of the true religion. To which Janeway adds an account of God's gracious dealings with some young persons and children, and of their conversion, holy and exemplary lives, pious discourses and expressions, in the time of their sickness and at their death. Although children brought filthiness into the world, they were thus capable of glorious martyrdom. Benjamin Keach, writing for youths, dwelt on the sin rather than the glory. In *War with the Devil: Or the Young Man's Conflict with the Powers of Darkness* (1676), the young man is inherently vile, and has to be badgered and insulted and cajoled by Truth, and has to go through two forms of conversion, Legal Reformation and the Second Birth, before he sheds his hypocrisy and sinfulness and is accepted by Jesus.

John Bunyan was writing during the same period as Chear, Janeway, and Keach. But his *Book for Boys and Girls: Or, Country Rhimes for Children* (1686), known after the ninth edition (1724) as *Divine Emblems, or Temporal Things Spiritualized*, is in quite a different sphere. It is the work of a true poet, and he had the poet's flair for expressing ideas through concrete imagery. By making a visual appeal to the child, Bunyan was the direct ancestor of the religious poetry for children that Smart and his contemporaries were writing a century later. The didactic emblem, in which a brief but vivid verbal picture was followed by a moral tag, was calculated to appeal to the child. Bunyan's verses are full of such verbal pictures—a fish in the water, the swallow, the bee, the mole in the ground, the horse in the mill, a penny loaf, a lanthorn, a pair of spectacles, a boy on his hobby-horse. Smart too knew how to make his poetry charming with imagery of children's playthings. In Hymn XVII, 'Praise', he shows that when they try hard to please, children should be frequently praised and rewarded: ' "Good child, thou soon shalt go abroad,/Or have such things as these.–'

> 'This silver coin'd by sweet queen Anne,
>   'This nosegay and these toys,
> 'Thou this gilt Testament shalt scan,
> 'This pictur'd Hymn-book on a plan,
>   'To make good girls and boys.'

Smart was offering the good child his own *Hymns for the Amusement of Children*, just as Isaac Watts had suggested that duty should be turned into reward: 'by giving them the privilege of learning one of these songs every week, if they fulfil the business of the week well, and promising them the book itself, when they have learnt ten or twenty songs out of it.' Smart inherited, then, some of Bunyan's talent for writing pictorial verse for children. But there is an essential difference between their religious attitudes to the child. Bunyan may give a vigorous picture of a child chasing a butterfly, but the infant reader is not allowed to enjoy himself for very long:

> He hollo's, runs, and cries out here Boys, here,
> Nor doth the Brambles or the Nettles fear:
> He stumbles at the Mole-Hills, up he gets,
> And runs again, as one bereft of wits;
> And all this labour and this large Out-cry,
> Is only for a silly Butter-fly.

The butterfly turns out to be an emblem of the 'painted Nothings and false Joys' of this world. Smart did not dream of making the child's play a symbol of adult sinfulness. He allows his children to play on. Hymn XXXIII, 'For Saturday', is illustrated by a woodcut of four children playing with dolls and a rocking-horse:

> NOW's the time for mirth and play,
> Saturday's an holiday;
> Praise to heav'n unceasing yield,
> I've found a lark's nest in the field.
>
> A lark's nest, then your play-mate begs
> You'd spare herself and speckled eggs;
> Soon she shall ascend and sing
> Your praises to th'eternal King.

In Chapter X we found that Isaac Watts's evangelical method may well have influenced Smart's decision to interpret the Psalms from a Christian standpoint. We wonder, therefore, whether Watts's *Divine Songs Attempted in Easy Language for the Use of Children* (1715), which went through a hundred editions before the middle of the nineteenth century, had any influence on the *Hymns for the Amusement of Children*. Watts did not undertake his task lightly. The Preface to the *Divine Songs* is addressed to all who are concerned in the education of children, and he warns them that 'IT is an awful and important charge that is committed to you.' But he realizes the important truth that a child learns better through pleasure than through fear: 'There is something so amusing and entertaining in rhymes and metre, that will incline children to make this part of their business a diversion.' And he means to join this entertaining rhyme to a simplicity of language: 'I have endeavoured to sink the language to the level of a child's understanding, and yet to keep it, if possible, above contempt'.[9] Smart would have agreed entirely with these principles. We know that he set out to be amusing as well as instructive, and he too made a conscious effort to simplify his language, as is shown in his prayer for 'plainness' in Hymn XV on 'Taste':

> O Guide my judgment and my taste,
> Sweet SPIRIT, author of the book

[9] In Chalmers's *English Poets*, xiii, 86.

> Of wonders, told in language chaste
> And plainness, not to be mistook.

But both writers were faced with the impossible task of expressing Christian doctrine in plain language, and predictably, neither managed to express the idea of redemption at the level of a child's understanding. In 'Praise to God for our Redemption', Watts made no attempt to unravel the doctrine:

> He honour'd all his Father's laws,
>   Which we have disobey'd;
> And bore our sins upon the cross,
>   And our full ransom paid.

Smart repeats the same doctrine, parrot-fashion, in Hymn XXI, 'Generosity':

> The Lord shed on the Holy Rood
> His infinitely gen'rous blood,
>   Not for himself, but all;
> Yea e'en for them that pierc'd his side,
> In patient agony he died,
>   To remedy the fall.

When Watts and Smart write on the same topic, we are given the opportunity to compare their attitudes to their child readers. In Watts's hymn, 'A Morning Song', for instance, the child greets the morning sun, and like the sun wants to fulfil the business of the day. In Smart's Hymn XXXV 'At Dressing in the Morning', the child likewise rises from bed 'empow'r'd by Thee,/The glorious Sun to face'. Both children pray for grace. There is a slightly ominous note in Watts's prayer:

> Give me, O Lord, thy early grace,
>   Nor let my soul complain
> That the young morning of my days
>   Has all been spent in vain.

This note is absent from Smart's prayer, 'O clothe me with humility,/Adorn me with thy grace.' But it would be misguided to suggest that the *Hymns for the Amusement of Children* are all sweetness and light. Smart could not bring himself to believe that small children were cursed with original sin, but the brevity and charm of childhood filled him with melancholic reflections on the transience of living things. His melancholy is expressed rather alarmingly in Hymn XXXVI, 'At Undressing in the Evening', where the child feels that cordial sleep is akin to death, and begs the Lord for help 'if much agonizing pain/ My dying hour await'. In 'An Evening Song', Watts emphasizes not only the transience of life, but also the sinfulness of the mortal child. Both writers share, therefore, one of the pre-occupations of the century. Frank Baker notes a similar obsession with death in Charles Wesley's hymns for children: 'many of the poems would certainly not be recommended by modern educationists for the use of children, and in particular there is a frequent preoccupation with death, due partly to the high child mortality of the time and the lack of any strong contemporary desire to shield children from contact with death, but also to the sometimes morbid strain in Charles Wesley himself.'[10] So Watts pronounces in 'Solemn Thoughts of God and Death' that 'A thousand children young as I,/Are call'd by Death to hear their doom.' And 'The Danger of Delay' points out that 'A flower may fade before 'tis noon,/And I this day may lose my breath.' And Smart writes in Hymn XXIV on 'Melancholy':

> As soon as born the infant cries,
>   For well his spirit knows,
> A little while, and then he dies,
> A little while, and down he lies,
>   To take a stern repose.

But if Smart shares some of Watts's melancholia, Watts never shares Smart's contrasting, high-spirited delight in the day-to-day life of children, the joy that characterizes the best of the *Hymns for the Amusement of Children*. Watts suggests that on the morning of the Lord's Day 'I would go with cheerful feet/To learn thy will, O Lord', but how could he share Smart's pleasure in seeing the rustics adorning themselves in roses and children in their best apparel, when he had already written 'Against Pride in Clothes'? Watts feels that it is a mark of pride to call clothes rich and new when 'the poor sheep and silk-

---

[10] *Representative Verse of Charles Wesley*, 140.

worm wore/That very clothing long before.' In his more melancholic moments, Smart would probably have agreed with Watts, for he had written in *Jubilate Agno* A.91, 'Let Huldah bless with the Silkworm—the ornaments of the Proud are from the bowells of their Betters.' But in Hymn XXI, Smart was simply prepared to be grateful that 'the fleecy care,/'Not for themselves are shorn'. Their mutual concern for the sheep is rather absurd, but it sums up how the cast of Watts's mind differed from Smart's. The man who could tell his readers to cast a glance at the sports of children from five to fifteen years of age and see what toys and fooleries are these—would a race of wise and holy beings waste so many years of early life on such wretched trifles[11]—was obviously very different from the usually tolerant and benevolent Smart.

The seventeenth-century distinction between the harsh didacticism of Chear, Janeway, and Keach on the one hand, and the more colourful and cheerful didacticism of John Bunyan on the other, continued into the eighteenth century. John Wright's *Spiritual Songs for Children: Or, Poems on Several Subjects and Occasions* (1727) is harsh and glowering and there is nothing but the title-page to suggest that the heavy, dull, melancholic hymns were intended for children. The only poem that seems to be written even *about* a child is 'The Dying Infant', which asserts gloomily that 'Infants are Drops of *Adam*'s filthy Blood'—but he offers the consolation that 'Grace acts on Passives'. At the other extreme, Thomas Foxton followed in the footsteps of John Bunyan with his *Moral Songs Composed for the Use of Children* (1728), which was recommended to the reader by Isaac Watts himself. Foxton's aim was a sensible one: '*the Subjects handled in this little Book, are not taken from imaginary Conferences of Birds, Beasts, &c. but from those real Occurences which Children daily meet with, and in which they themselves are the principal Actors.*' But unfortunately, Foxton's pictures of children at play are subjected to severe moral interpretations, very much in Bunyan's fashion. The picture of the child with her doll in Song XXIV, 'Upon a little Girl's playing with a painted Baby', seems at first the epitome of childish innocence:

[11] C. J. Abbey and J. H. Overton, *The English Church in the Eighteenth Century*, 1878, ii. 275, citing Watts's *Ruin and Recovery of Mankind*.

> With Ribbons she adorns its Hair,
> To make her Beauty look more fair,
>   And decks the Head with Lace;
> Sometimes she lays it on a Bed,
> Where Crimson Curtains round it spread,
>   And guard the quiet Place.

But the doll is a symbol of evil, a tempting idol which delusion makes bright. Similarly, the picture of boys skating on ice prompts the reflection that the ice may crack, or the boys may trip or jostle one another, and this in turn prompts the warning that where wild companions join in dangerous scenes of mirth and wine, a thousand accidents may arise. We know already that Smart never destroyed innocent pleasure in this mournful way.

Both Bunyan and Foxton owed something to the emblem convention. Their use of a verbal picture followed by a didactic message is very similar to the orthodox emblem which consisted of a drawing, a verbal description, and a moral tag. It is likely that Smart was at least aware of the emblem convention. There is a typical example in the *Lilliputian Magazine*, where a woodcut of a peacock surmounts the following brief poem:

> THE Peacock, of his gaudy train
> And tread majestic idly vain,
> Each simple gazer views with joy,
> And dotes upon the feather'd toy;
> And when he screams with hideous cry.
> The ear is plagu'd to please the eye.
>   MORAL.
> By this allusion justly stung,
> Each tinsel'd fop should hold his tongue.

The technique is comparable with that used in *Riley's Emblems* (1772), the most well-known of the eighteenth-century emblem books. Emblem XL consists of a picture of a peacock and a short poem which illustrates the title, 'Of Vain Glory':

> BEHOLD that silly bird, how proudly vain,
> Of the bright colours of his gaudy train!
> Ev'n to a proverb grown his idle pride
> By outward shew alone in worth supply'd,

For no harmonious sound, no chearful note,
Must ever issue from that hideous throat,
Nor of the hundred eyes that grace his tail,
Can one for sight, or real use avail.

O son of vanity be wise in time!
Apply the moral of this homely rhyme,
To *real worth* alone should praise be giv'n,
And *real worth* inherits it from Heav'n.

Likewise in *Emblems, for the Entertainment and Improvement of Youth* [1750?], XVIII, no. 8, is 'A Peacock displaying his Tail. *Sibi pulcherrimæ merces.* He is fine in his own Conceit.' The *Hymns for the Amusement of Children* have the immediate visual appeal of the emblem books, with all but three of the hymns surmounted by a woodcut. In some cases, the picture is a symbol rather than a simple illustration of the hymn, though Smart does not make use of moral tags. In Hymn V, for instance, 'Justice' is symbolized by a female figure with sword and balances; in Hymn VII on 'Temperance', the illustration shows a woman holding a cup and serpent; Hymn XXIII on 'Peace' is illustrated by a woman bearing the horn of plenty. But in most cases, the woodcut is simply a straightforward illustration of the text of the poem. Hymn XI on 'Beauty. For a Damsel' is therefore illustrated by a young girl melodramatically rejecting her dressing-table. Hymn XVI on 'Learning' by a gentleman in his library, Hymn XVIII on 'Prayer' by a small child kneeling by a chair. Sometimes, however, there seems to be little connection between poem and picture. This fault hints at a general deterioration of standards in book production; John Ashton points out that after 1800, 'The type and wood blocks were getting worn out, and never seem to have been renewed; publishers got less scrupulous, and used any wood blocks without reference to the letter-press, until, after Grub Street authors worked their wicked will upon them, Catnach buried them in a dishonoured grave.'[12] One wonders whether even before the turn of the century, wood blocks were sometimes used without reference to the letter-press. In Hymn XIII, for instance, 'Elegance' is described by Smart as a quality of the intellectual

[12] *Chap-Books of the Eighteenth Century,* 1882, p. vii.

robes that invest the saints in heaven, and of the robes given
to the Prodigal Son when he returned to his father. But the
hymn is illustrated by a woodcut of a formal garden. Perhaps
Smart meant to explore two meanings of the idea of elegance,
one pictorially and the other verbally, but we cannot be sure
about it. Similarly, Hymn XV on 'Taste', is about taste in
literature. Take the Bible from the shelf, says Smart, and read
it on your knees:

> Respect, adore it heart and mind.
>   How greatly sweet, how sweetly grand,
> Who reads the most, is most refin'd,
>   And polish'd by the Master's hand.

Yet the hymn is illustrated by a picture of St. Paul's Cathedral.
It could be that Smart meant to show that artistic taste can be
expressed through architecture as well as through literature.
But it looks more as if the printer used a convenient cut which
is in fact quite irrelevant to the text of the poem. Although,
then, the *Hymns for the Amusement of Children* looks superficially
like a familiar book of emblems, and certainly seems to owe
something to that convention as far as lay-out is concerned, the
relationship of pictures and poems in Smart's book was erratic
in comparison with the close interaction of cut and verse in the
emblems. But in the last resort, we recognize that, as usual,
Smart's poetry is individual, and bears the characteristic
traces of his peculiar themes and obsessions.

In Hymn II on 'Hope', for instance, we find Smart's characteristic obsession with Hannah's barrenness, 'Till strong in hope
she now conceives.' In Hymn X we find the physico-theological
statement of the stars, firmament, and sun being the glorious
work and great design of God, and we find a reference to the
greatest of physico-theological poets, King David:

> Hence David unto heav'n appeals,
>   'Ye heav'ns his righteousness declare;'
> His signet their duration seals,
>   And bids them be as firm as fair.

(King David is not only truthful, but elegant too, for he appears
in Hymn XIII on 'Elegance': 'Whoever has thy charming

pow'rs,/Is amiable as Kidron's swan'.) In Hymn XI on 'Beauty. For a Damsel', we find Smart the gardener, 'Then will I thy carnations nurse,/And cherish every rose'. In Hymn XVIII on 'Prayer' we remember that Smart had once taken the injunction to pray without ceasing to its logical extreme:

> PRAY without ceasing (says the Saint)
> Nor ever in the spirit faint;
> With grace the bloom, and faith the root,
> The pray'r shall bring eternal fruit.

In Hymn XXII on 'Gratitude' we hear the poet who, all his life, was obsessively grateful: 'Christ our gratitude shall win you,/Wean'd from earth, and led to God.' Gratitude is also the theme of the penultimate poem in the book, 'Plenteous Redemption':

> DAVID has said, and sung it sweet,
> That God with mercy is replete:
> And thus I'll say, and thus I'll sing,
> In rapture unto Christ my King.
>
> King of my heart and my desires,
> Which all my gratitude inspires,
> Bids me be great and glorious still,
> And so I must, and so I will.

Most casual readers associate Smart's work with a peculiarly jubilant state of mind, and two or three of the poems in the *Hymns for the Amusement of Children* are among the best of his elated poetry. We have seen how Hymn XXXIII, 'For Saturday' catches the joy of the children at play. In Hymn XXXIV, Sunday is as cheerful as Saturday, as the rustics adorn themselves with roses and the little girls and boys, arrayed in their best apparel, pray better than the preacher 'For heav'n's eternal joys.' Hymn XXV on 'Mirth' begs the children in the church galleries to sing away if they feel merry, because tomorrow it will be May and we shall run in the fields, decking ourselves with 'the blooming thorn' ever before daybreak. The flowers are in full bloom—in the gardens ('My pinks already shew;/And my streak'd roses fully blown'), and in the fields ('cowslips in the mead'), and the sky is streaked like the roses:

With white and crimson laughs the sky,
  With birds the hedge-rows ring;
To give the praise to God most high,
And all the sulky fiends defy,
  Is a most joyful thing.

I feel, however, that it would be more fitting to end this book by quoting one of the more pathetic poems in the *Hymns for the Amusement of Children*. In Hymn XXIX, 'Long-Suffering of God', the four stanzas form a single simile by which the slow growth of a man's soul to heaven is compared with the 'noble Aloe' which grows for a hundred years before making 'all this glorious show'. It restates Smart's certainty that the long-suffering God will eventually bestow his grace upon the barren human soul—'For the hour of my felicity, like the womb of Sarah, shall come at the latter end', he had written in *Jubilate Agno* B1.16. But the manic exultation of the final stanza shows only too clearly that for Smart, presentiments of the grace and mercy of God were inseparable from madness:

ONE hundred feet from off the ground
  That noble Aloe blows;
But mark ye by what skill profound
  His charming grandeur rose.

One hundred years of patient care
  The gardners did bestow
Toil and hereditary pray'r
  Made all this glorious show.

Thus man goes on from year to year,
  And bears no fruit at all;
But gracious God, still unsevere,
  Bids show'rs of blessings fall.

The beams of mercy, dews of grace,
  Our Saviour still supplies—
Ha! ha! the soul regains her place,
  And sweetens all the skies.

APPENDIX I

(*see* above, p. 67)

The following poem appeared in the *Midwife*, ii, 1751, 56–57, and has been attributed to Smart by Cross in the *History of Henry Fielding*:

VERSES *written in a* London Church-yard.

MARIA now I'll cease to sing,
And all the op'ning Sweets of Spring:
The *Chop-house* in my Verse shall ring,
    Where lives my lovely *Jenny*.

Where antient Cooks exert their Art;
No youthful Damsel bears a Part:
Yet one has broil'd my very Heart,
    And that was lovely *Jenny*.

Brown as the Wallnut is her Hair,
Her skin is like the Napkin fair,
More blooming than red Cabbage are
    The Cheeks of lovely *Jenny*.

Each sav'ry Dish to Cit and Fop
She bears, herself a nicer Chop;
How far more elegant to sop,
    And feast on lovely *Jenny*.

More tempting than the smoaking Stake,
Or sweetest Tart her Fingers make!
I'd lose my Dinner for the Sake,
    Of tasting lovely *Jenny*.

But when I pay for Stake or Tart,
I act the very Miser's part,
At once the Money and my Heart
    I give to lovely *Jenny*.

Let *Jove* his fam'd Ambrosia eat,
And youthful *Hebe* ever wait;
I envy not his Joy or State,
    While serv'd by lovely *Jenny.*

While *British* Herrings *Britons* love,
Or City Throats with Custard move,
While Nectar pleases mighty *Jove,*
    So long shall I love *Jenny.*

And when at length the Beauty dies,
Oh! cut her into little Pies!
Like Jelly-stars she'll grace the Skies,
    So bright is lovely *Jenny.*

St. *Clement's Church-yard, May* 1, 1751.

A poem written in the same form appeared in the *Covent-Garden Journal* on Tuesday, the 23rd June 1752. Arthur Sherbo agrees with Cross that it is probably Smart's work. In the *Covent-Garden Journal*, ed. Jensen, ii. 35–37, the poem appears as follows:

—*Versus inopes rerum, nugæqve canoræ.* HOR.

—*Verses of Matter void, and trifling Rhimes.*

TO

Sir *Alexander Drawcansir,* Knt.

Sir Alexander,

I AM one of the constant Readers of your Paper, and am greatly offended, that you seldom or ever entertain us with any Thing but Prose. 'Prithee Knight hast thou no harmony in thy Soul? For my part, I've always had such a strange Disposition to Rhiming, that I may say with a great Poet,

I lisp'd in Numbers, for the Numbers came,

You'll tell me perhaps, that a Poet and a Rhimer are two different Things, and that the coming of Numbers signifies Nothing, unless Genius, Fire, Fancy, &c. comes along with them. You will confess however, that we often see the silliest Things applauded only because they're tagg'd with Rhyme? And did not the finest Poem in our

Language, lie for Years neglected, for no other Reason (that I know)
but its wanting that Advantage? Without further Apology, I
present you a Song which I have lately made on my Mistress.

> Tho' Polly's and tho' Peggy's Charms,
> Each Youthful Poet's Bosom warms;
> None gives the Heart such fierce Alarms,
>   As Lovely Jenny Weston.
>
> No Violet, Jessamin, or Rose,
> Or spicy Gale that afric blows,
> Does half such fragrant Sweets disclose,
>   As waft round Jenny Weston.
>
> Let other Swains to Courts repair,
> And view each glitt'ring Beauty there,
> 'Tis Art alone makes them so fair,
>   But Nature Jenny Weston.
>
> What Paint with her Complexion vies?
> What Jewels sparkle like her Eyes?
> What Hills of Snow so white, as rise
>   The Breasts of Jenny Weston?
>
> Give others Titles, Honours, Pow'r,
> The Riches of Potosi's Shore,
> I ask not Bawbles; I implore
>   The Heart of Jenny Weston.
>
> Possest of this alone,
> Of India's Monarch I'd look down,
> A Cot my Palace, and my Throne
>   The Lap of Jenny Weston.

And now, Sir, if you will not allow me to be inspired with the
Raptures of Poetry, you will at least allow me the Inspiration of a
Lover; and as such I doubt not your Favour to,
Your very humble Servant,
GEOFFRY JINGLE.

APPENDIX II

(*see* above, pp. 86-87)

The following poem appeared in the *Covent-Garden Journal* on Tuesday, the 7th April 1752, and has been attributed to Smart by Jensen and Cross. In the *Covent-Garden Journal*, ed. Jensen, i. 298–300, the poem is printed as follows:

At Frederick's Shrine, near Thame's imperial Strand,
Their Vigils all the sacred Choir shall keep;
Mute o'er his Urn a mournful Train shall stand,
And ev'ry Muse, and ev'ry Virtue weep.
To dress the Spot where rests his princely Shade,
Fresh Garlands from the Plains each Swain shall bring;
From deep'ning Vale, and Woodland high, each Maid
Shall strip the flow'ry Bosom of the Spring,
There too the graver Patriot, good and old,
Shall come, and stoop to Earth his streaming Cheek;
And, as he kneels to kiss, the hallow'd Mold
Shall mourn, in 'Words that weep, and Tears that speak'!
Mean Time the Clouds shall drop their wat'ry Head,
The South and Western Breeze shall jointly blow;
And wide, upon their spicy Pinions spread
The Sweets that issue from his Tomb below.

Ah me! the Swans that sail'd in stately Pride,
And whilom stopt by Kew's lov'd Vale to sing;
How slow and sad they row along the Tide!
How droop their Necks beneath their faded Wing!
But now, since Fate the cruel Arrow sped,
Sad Change befalls the Scenes that charm'd before;
The parting Genius of the Plains is fled,
The Fauns, and Dryad Train are seen no more:
The Nereids sigh beneath their coral Cave,
Their Sea-green Wreathes in rude Disorder torn;
The Bird of Calm forsakes the trouble'd Wave,
The Groves and Springs, and all their Echoe's mourn.

From this sad Hour to many a future Day,
As led by Love to drop a pious Tear;
The Stranger takes his solitary Way,
Thro' these blest Haunts to old Remembrance dear:
The village Hind that wont to tread the Place,
Long Tales of his departed Lord shall tell;
With sorrowing Steps his custom'd Walks shall trace,
And point the Bow'r where most he lov'd to dwell.
'Beneath this Beech, beside that hallow'd Stream,
'Oft with his Lyre he hail'd the op'ning Year;
'And still th'harmonious Strains, and pleasing Theme,
'Hang musical on ev'ry Shepherd's Ear.
'Oft fir'd to nobler Views, with godlike Mind,
'He sought yon poplar Shade in pensive Mood;
'For Britain's Weal some Patriot Plan design'd,
'Best, firmest, Architect of public Good.'

O! How we hail'd him in his mid Career!
How dawn'd his Morn! Meridian blaz'd how bright!
'Till envious Death deform'd the rising Year,
In Winter's Solstice like the sudden Night!
So thron'd in Amber Car the radiant Sun,
All glorious mounts the purple Road of Day;
Before his Steeds, *Life*, *Warmth*, and *Vigour* run,
As round he pours in Tides his golden Ray:
But see!—as down he slopes his hasty Flight,
Dark, sudden Clouds obscure his Ev'ning-Eye;
In dewy Mists he shrouds his shorten'd Light,
And sets in Tears beneath the western Sky.

But you, ye Guardians of the sacred Shears
That wheel the adamantine Spindle round;
Long, long extend Imperial Caesar's Years,
And spare the Thread with which his Life is wound.
Place to the Sire's Account the just Arrear,
Due to his Annals whose fresh Loss we mourn;
Late may we shed for George a second Tear,
Late may his Ashes fill their fated Urn.
So Peace shall spread her graceful olive Shade,
Pale Faction hang her Head and shun the Light;
Fair Freedom bid her tow'ring Spires invade
The Clouds, and rival Heav'n's unmeasur'd Height.

Mean Time rich Commerce wide from Pole to Pole,
Shall stretch her Sails, remotest Climes explore;
And, wafted back by prosp'rous Breezes, roll
The Wealth of either World to Albion's Shore.

CANTABRIGIENSIS

APPENDIX III[1]

(*see* above, p. 207)

'Let Ash, house of Ash rejoice with Callaica, a green gem. God be gracious to Miss Leroche my fellow traveller from Calais' (*Jubilate Agno* D.42).

W. F. Stead, W. H. Bond, and Father Devlin, are all intrigued by this reference to Smart's visit to the continent. Stead refers to the *Gentleman's Magazine* which recorded the death of Ezekiel le Roche on the 8th June 1768 at Newington Butts,[2] but he does not identify Smart's Miss Leroche. I have not been able to find out anything about Smart's trip abroad, but I do think that I can identify Miss Leroche. There seems little doubt that in this line, Smart is referring to the notorious Elizabeth Roach, ex-mistress of Sir Francis Blake Delaval. It is necessary to give some details of her early life in order to explain how she became acquainted with Delaval—and Smart.

Deodata and Elizabeth Roach made history while they were still children. They were born in Madras, Deodata on the 3rd November 1729, and Elizabeth on the 18th March 1730/31, the offspring of Major John Roach of Fort St. George, and his bigamously married wife, Mary Anne Raworth. While they were still infants, the Roach sisters were brought to England by their mother, and when their father followed them home two years later, he found that they had been boarded out with the family of Mr. Richard Quane. Quane was on the verge of going bankrupt, and when he retired to Paris with his wife and son, Tom, then fourteen years old, the Roaches and their daughters went with them. Roach gave Quane £800 to board the children at the convent of English nuns in Paris, and then returned to England. The Roach children were looked after by

[1] Most of the information about the Roach sisters in this Appendix is derived from Frances Askham, *The Gay Delavals*, 1955, with some additional details from Philip Journeaulx, *Proceedings in a Cause lately depending before the Parliament of Paris*, trans. Parker, 1743.

[2] *Rejoice in the Lamb*, 259.

the nuns of the Convent of Cherche Midi. For some reason that does not appear, the children went under the name of Macmahon.[3] Six months later, on the 22nd February 1738, Major Roach died. Apart from legacies to Quane and a Mrs. Macnamara who also lived in Paris, the Major's fortune was to be shared between the two children, when they came of age, or on their marriage if they wed before the age of twenty-one. Quane contrived to keep the children in Paris, despite numerous petitions in the Court of Chancery that they should be brought back to England. In 1741, Quane married off Deodata Roach, aged eleven years, to his son Tom, aged seventeen, who was now entitled to share half of Roach's fortune. The scandal was brought to the public eye by Philip Journeaulx, but in France, the marriage was recognized as being legal.

The next stage in the history of the Roach sisters is an interesting one from our own point of view, the dating of Smart's channel crossing:

> There is no indication why, in 1748, when the heiresses were eighteen and nineteen respectively, the Quane party allowed itself to be bought out for the amount of the long-delayed legacies. Two years would have seen Deodata reach her majority; three, and they could have had Betty as well.
> Fourteen hundred pounds change hands, and the little Roaches at last cross the Channel to make a great stir in the business of Chancery where for so long their names have been familiar, and to find themselves in the end given into the charge of that 'artful and violent' woman their mother.[4]

Apart from the voyage to England when the Roach sisters were still babies, this is the only channel crossing mentioned by Mrs. Askham in *The Gay Delavals*. At least one date can be suggested, therefore, for Smart's trip abroad—1748. (It may be worth recalling that on the 7th January 1747/48, Smart wrote to Dodsley from Pembroke Hall about a projected 'Collection of Odes', that on the 30th January he delivered a speech at St. Mary's Church, Cambridge, on the Martyrdom of Charles I,

---

[3] The name turns up twenty years later in quite another context, when Mrs. Smart goes to sell Dr. James's Fever Powder in Mr. McMahon's shop in Caple Street, Dublin.

[4] *The Gay Delavals*, 43.

but that 'we have no information concerning Smart's activities for the rest of the academic year'.)[5]

In November 1748, the problem of the guardianship of the Roach sisters came to court again, and the girls were placed under the protection of the Under-Secretary of State for Ireland, John Potter. Deodata absconded almost immediately, but Elizabeth remained in his house until he died, only six months later. He left a widow, Susanna, who was to marry her first cousin, John Delaval, in April 1750. As Lady Susanna Hussey Delaval, she was to be the recipient of Smart's 'Female Dignity', printed in his *Poems on Several Occasions* in 1763.

But in the summer of 1749, immediately after the death of her first husband, Mrs. Susanna Potter went north to Seaton Delaval, and took with her Miss Elizabeth Roach. Francis Delaval arrived later in the summer, and in a very short time, seduced the young heiress. By Christmas 1749 she had followed him to London, and calling herself Elizabeth La Roche, became openly his mistress. This liaison did not however prevent Francis Delaval from marrying an ageing widow, Lady Isabella Nassau Pawlet, whose first husband had been a younger brother of the Duke of Bolton. (It is probably no coincidence that the 'houses' of Pawlet and Bolton are juxtaposed in *Jubilate Agno* D.47, 48: 'Let Bolton, house of Bolton rejoice with Polygrammos, a kind of Jasper with white streaks. Let Paulet, house of Paulet rejoice with Chalcites, a precious stone of the colour of Brass.') The wedding took place at St. George's Church, Hanover Square, on the 8th March 1750. On the 7th March 1751, Francis Delaval brought a private performance of *Othello* to the Drury-Lane Theatre, with his mistress and her sister taking the female roles. Mrs. Askham quotes the report that appeared in the *Daily Advertiser* the next day:

> 'On Thursday night, their Royal Highnesses the Prince and Princess of Wales, the Duke of Cumberland, Princess Amelia, Prince George and Princess Augusta with the greatest number of the nobility, foreign ministers and gentry of both sexes went to the Theatre Royal in Drury Lane to see the play *Othello* acted by several ladies and gentlemen for their diversion. The company

[5] *Poems by Christopher Smart*, ed. Brittain, 19.

was the most brilliant ever seen in a Playhouse in this Kingdom, the streets and avenues were so filled with coaches and chairs that the greatest company of the ladies and gentlemen were obliged to wade through dirt and filth to get to the house which afforded good diversion and benefit for the pickpockets and other gentlemen of that trade.

'We hear Francis Delaval Esq. played *Othello*; John Delaval Esq., *Iago*; Thomas Delaval Esq., *Cassio*; Mr. Sim Pine, *Brabantio* and *Ludovico*; Capt. Stevens, *Roderigo*; Mrs. Quane played the part of *Desdemona* and Miss La Roche, *Emilia*.'[6]

Smart, of course, provided the Prologue and Epilogue for Mrs. Deodata Quane, and he was presumably present at the performance to see Miss Roach, or Miss La Roche, play Emilia 'With strong French accent and stomacher ablaze with magnificent diamonds'.[7] Smart basked in the glory of being connected with such a brilliant, not to say disreputable company, and published the poems written for the occasion, dedicating the work 'TO *FRANCIS* AND *JOHN DELAVAL*, Esqrs. THIS PROLOGUE and EPILOGUE, WRITTEN By their DESIRE, AND For their ENTERTAINMENT, *Are humbly inscribed By their obliged Friend*, Christopher Smart.'

By 1754, Elizabeth Roach had borne Francis Delaval two children, and Lady Isabella had instituted divorce proceedings against her husband on the grounds of adultery. According to Mrs. Askham, Delaval suborned her witnesses and produced dubious evidence of Lady Isabella's own adultery, and the case was dismissed. A pamphlet of the proceedings published some time later is interesting from our point of view because it prints Elizabeth Roach's name in a form most nearly resembling the 'Miss Leroche' of *Jubilate Agno*: *The Trial of Sir Francis Blake Delaval, Knight of the Bath, at the Consistory Court of Doctors Commons for committing Adultery with Miss Roach, alias Miss La Roche, alias Miss Le Roche* [1782?].

In 1758, the ten-year liaison between Francis Delaval and Elizabeth Roach came to an end. She tried her hand at acting at the York Theatre. She tried to persuade Francis's younger brother, John Delaval, to settle her debts of £2,000. And she

---

[6] *The Gay Delavals*, 56.
[7] *Ibid.*, 55.

managed to marry, in September 1758, 'a stripling Irish Baronet', Sir Henry Echlin, who was eighteen years old. Because this marriage in Edinburgh was probably legally suspect, she married Echlin again, in Dublin, in January 1762, as soon as her husband reached his majority. The marriage was announced in the *Gentleman's Magazine*. Six months later, Smart was begging God to be gracious to Miss Leroche in *Jubilate Agno* D.42.

The later history of Elizabeth Roach can be told briefly enough. She seems to have left her husband soon after their second marriage, and then passed from hand to hand in Dublin. Delaval provided her with fifty pounds a year, but she ended her days in Seymour Street, Portman Square, shunned by everyone, sick, querulous, and destitute.

Index

Y